POPULAR EDUCATION
AND SOCIAL CHANGE IN
LATIN AMERICA
LIAM KANE

Chapter 4 is based on an earlier article published in *Studies in the Education of Adults* (Kane, 2000e).

The right of Liam Kane to be identified as the author of this work has been asserted by him in accordance with the Copyright, Designs and Patents Act 1988.

First published in the UK by the Latin America Bureau
Latin America Bureau
1 Amwell Street
London EC1R 1UL

The Latin America Bureau is an independent research and publishing organisation. It works to broaden public understanding of issues of human rights and social and economic justice in Latin America and the Caribbean.

A CIP catalogue record for this book is available from the British Library.

Translations from the Spanish and Portuguese by the author.
Editing: Marcela López Levy
Design: Liz Morrell
Cover design: Andy Dark
Cover image: Detail of painting 'Grito de los Excluidos' by Pavel Eguez, 1999
Oil and granite on canvas.
Cartoons: conceived by the author, adapted and drawn by Elisaberta Torino.

Printed by Russell Press, Nottingham

Contents

Chapter 6
Popular Education and Ideology 143

Chapter 7
Assessing the Impact of Popular
Education at Micro Level 170

Chapter 8
Assessing the Impact of Popular
Education at Macro Level 192

Acknowledgements

This book could not have been written without inconveniencing the lives of several people. I particularly thank
- Anne, who bore the real brunt (though the pay-back beckons)
- Duncan, Kevin and Catherine, who bore a lesser brunt (but at least learned the meaning of 'epistemology')
- Kenneth Milligan and Agnes Mackenzie, who bore a different brunt (but clearly enjoyed the peace nevertheless)

A special thanks also to
- Jean Barr, for her prompt, detailed, helpful, sometimes brutal but always encouraging feedback
- Elisabetta Torino, for her wonderful cartoon drawings
- Mike Gonzalez, a terrific popular educator, who first inspired my interest in Latin America
- Those people in DACE – you know who you are – whose constant, merciless insults meant I couldn't give up
- Marci López Levy, Kate Moriarty and Liz Morrell of LAB, for their support and friendliness throughout
- The reviewers from Latin America: Roberto Antillón, Elda Marleny Blanco, Maria Clara Bueno Fischer, Moacir Gadotti, Gelsa Knijnic, María del Carmen Mendoza Rangel, Paddy Welsh, Carlos Zarco
- Action Aid, the Carnegie Institute and the University of Glasgow for funding my research.

Among many others to have helped were:
- Brazil: Marcos Arruda, Carlos Bellé, Roseli Caldart, Dirilete Dellazeri, Clara Fischer, Sergio Haddad, Jorge Muñoz, Miguel Stédile, Jeannette and teachers in MST, Viamão; the staff of the Paulo Freire Institute and UNISINOS Education Dept
- Dominican Republic: the Diaz family, Cañadabonita
- El Salvador: Ana Bickel, Morena Barraza, Luís Orellano, Vladimir Reyes, Marta Vega, the people of San Luís & Las Vegas and the staff of Prodecosal and Angélica of CIAZO
- Haiti: the popular educators of Dupetit
- Mexico: Roberto Antillón, Yolanda Castro, Cuauc López, Carlos Núñez, Efrén Orozco, Rosa Luz Pérez, Mike Pickard, Daniel Ponce, Acela Vásquez, Rocío & Alejandro at COPEVI
- Nicaragua: Gustavo Pérez Casaron, Iouri Langlet, Emir López, Rita Muckenhirn, María Verónica Ruíz, Sergio Sáenz, Patricio Welsh
- Spain: Manolo Collado, Concha Macías, María del Mar Herrera Menchén

- UK: David Archer, Lalage Bown, Chris Dolan, Mike Gonzalez, Morven Gregor, Alison Norris, Maria Slowey, Tom Steele

Last, and certainly least, Denis Ferrie and Danny McClure, the oldest adolescents in Scotland.

Introduction

'Popular Education in Latin America' has something to teach everyone, everywhere, who engages in educational, cultural or political work or who has an academic interest in the social sciences. It is particularly relevant to three areas of study or activity.

Firstly, to understand the politics, society and culture of contemporary Latin America, some familiarity with the topic is important, given its massive impact on and beyond the region over the last thirty years. It is an appropriate moment to examine its significance since, after the heyday of the 1970s and 1980s, in the 1990s popular education has undergone a fundamental review of its practice and new developments have started to take shape. It is now possible to evaluate its recent past and speculate on future directions.

Secondly, in the field of adult education, in large part due to the Latin American influence, the term 'popular education' has gained increasing currency over the last ten years in the UK and Europe (an example being the emergence of the Popular Education Forum in Scotland). With names like Freire and Boal gaining world-wide recognition, it is commonly believed that exciting things happen in Latin America from which others can learn. However, given a lack of available information in English, for British educators, at least, there is a danger that a superficial understanding of the Latin American experience could lead to distorted perceptions of what these lessons might be: an awareness of the interplay between popular education and the Latin American social context is important. In light of recent developments, in which popular education addresses its relationship to the formal sector, the topic becomes relevant to progressive schoolteachers as well.

Thirdly, in all types of bodies seeking social change in the UK and Europe – whether NGOs or voluntary organisations, campaigning groups, 'New Social Movements' or even political parties – supporters, campaigners and activists are *de facto* involved in 'informal education' in some shape or form. Since popular education in Latin America is intimately linked to collective, organised action for change, it is a potential source of inspiration and practical assistance for European organisations attempting to address the educational dimension of their work in a more systematic fashion.

This book aims to provide a comprehensive introduction to Latin American popular education relevant to people approaching the subject from these different perspectives. It was written primarily with a European audience in mind, highlighting differences in context and making comparisons where appropriate. It addresses both theoretical considerations (from discussions on the nature of knowledge to an examination of the relationship between popular education and the state) and practical applications (from the number of staff working in a 'centre' to the activities used in an educational 'workshop'). While generally supportive of the popular education 'movement', it draws attention to problems, weaknesses and areas of debate. It is written in the belief that intrinsic interest aside, the Latin American experience of popular education also offers insight and inspiration to educators and activists working for radical social change in the UK, albeit in widely different contexts.

A Personal Journey

After the formative experience of living and travelling in Latin America, I worked for Oxfam in Glasgow as a development education worker in the mid 1980s. In further research visits to Latin America, I was impressed by the activities of ordinary people organising for change. In the shanty towns of Mexico City, in contrast to the corruption of conventional politics, I saw inspirational levels of participation and democracy. In Acapulco, grassroots organisations imaginatively resisted being uprooted by the development of tourism: bell-ringing networks warned of visiting oppressors, mystified police searched for activists while old women hid them under their skirts, animals were renamed 'Figueiroa pigs' in honour of the governor who tried to have impoverished people moved out of sight. By the late 1980s, grassroots organisations all over Mexico had formed umbrella groups strong enough to pose a serious threat to the machinations of the ruling party.

From reading reports, visiting projects and talking to Oxfam partners in Latin America, it was clear that this kind of grassroots, popular organising was happening all over the region and inspiring a new kind of hope. For Oxfam (and other progressive Non Governmental Organisations), 'social organisation' became a key goal of any development project. Strength came from the active and democratic participation of as many people as possible in collective action for change: 'participatory democracy' was now a key ingredient of social organisation.

Inevitably, attempts to develop successful grassroots organisations involved activists and participants in an educational process. Organisations and supporting NGOs started to pay close attention to this process – the ideas of Paulo Freire were gaining widespread recognition – and when the educational aspect of the work took on a life of its own it was known by the term 'Popular Education'. In Mexico, in 1989, for all its staff in Latin America, Oxfam held a week-long training event on popular education, such was its growing importance to grassroots development. I participated as a British representative and since then have been interested in what the Latin American experience can teach radical educators elsewhere.

About the Book

On Ideological Perspectives

I have attempted to be professional, scientific and objective throughout the book. In the end, however, it is not possible to write about popular education – or anything else, for that matter – from some imagined, politically neutral perspective. Consciously or otherwise, the values and beliefs of authors inevitably influence the research questions they pose, the evidence they select and the analyses they develop.

The best way to be scientific (and non-manipulative), I believe, is to ensure that an author's values and beliefs are openly available for inspection, not just subtly embedded in a text. Readers can then take these into account in working towards their own, independent conclusions. My own beliefs are explained in chapter 5 as part of the discussion on popular education and ideology.

Linkages between Chapters

While each chapter examines a different aspect of popular education, all chapters...

- take historical developments into account, from the 1960s to the present day
- overlap and inter-relate. It is difficult to discuss methodology without reference to Freire and ideology, for example, or to examine a case-study without also considering methodology and impact assessment. The constituent elements of popular education have to be looked at together – in their 'dialectical relationship', as popular educators are (rather mysteriously) wont to declare – so while each chapter has its particular focus, the connections between them are important and signalled where appropriate.

Terminology

Some of the terms used in Latin American popular education are complex, with no obvious English equivalent. These – and more general Latin American concepts – are italicised in the text and explained in the Glossary of Abbreviations and Terminology.

The Response from Latin America

There is value in an outsider attempting to write an introduction to popular education in Latin America. To communicate the experience beyond Latin America, cultural as well as linguistic translation is required, a task in which people from the target audience must be involved. And what is mundane, obvious or routine to Latin Americans may be curious or novel from the outside; moreover, in making observations or asking questions of a basic nature, or from a different perspective, visitors often challenge 'insiders' to rethink what they have long taken for granted. In writing this book, then, I make no apology for not being Latin American: I am even hopeful that Latin Americans themselves will find it relevant.

But the exercise has limitations too. Outsiders might misinterpret what they see and arrive at mistaken conclusions; the analysis is not based on years of accumulated, practical experience *in situ*; the subject area is vast and any introduction is necessarily selective in its choice of illustrations (though this would also apply to a Latin American author). To compensate, I arranged for each chapter to be reviewed in Latin America – by different people involved in popular education – for inclusion in the book. This had three main purposes: firstly, to offer Latin Americans the opportunity to legitimise, correct, add to or disagree with what was being said – a 'right to reply'. Secondly, to engage, in a small way, in a 'dialogue of knowledges' which would be of greater benefit to readers than the views of the author alone. Thirdly, in the process, to have a range of Latin American voices heard (as opposed to that of one single reviewer).

Reviewers were a priori sympathetic towards LAB's project but had complete freedom to speak openly and honestly. Their remit was to:
- emphasise anything they considered valuable in the chapter
- correct what they thought was mistaken
- add anything they thought was missing
- discuss and evaluate the author's arguments
- say anything else of importance which occurred to them

Reviewers had access to the whole book though due to heavy workloads and problems of translation, each chapter was normally reviewed in isolation from the rest (so sometimes points were raised which may have been covered in other chapters). Mostly reviewers read the original text in English (though chapters 5 and 6 were firstly translated into Spanish) and wrote the reviews in Spanish or Portuguese for translation; the review of chapter 7 was written in English.

And Finally... A Word on 'Social Movements'

Both internationally and in Latin America, there is now a burgeoning, sociological literature describing and theorising what are commonly known as '(New) Social Movements'. The grassroots organisations previously mentioned – the 'schools' in which popular education takes place – usually come into this category.

This book considers social movement theories as and when they relate to the examples of popular education being examined. However, a few general observations are relevant beforehand:

- A movement implies large groups of people consciously and willingly engaged in a form of collective action for change which has taken on a momentum of its own (rather than a tight-knit organisation run by an all powerful leadership)
- There is no clear-cut definition of what constitutes a social movement, though they are generally seen as: autonomous from the state and political parties; more loosely-structured, democratic and participatory than traditional political organisations (such as trade unions); advancing particular interests and ideas within the context of 'civil society' rather than in the workplace or political institutions. It would be easy to find social movements where one or more of these characteristics do not apply, however.
- They come in many shapes and sizes. Some are categorised as 'strategic' or 'instrumentalist', pursuing concrete gains (urban movements campaigning for social services, for example); some as 'expressive', concerned with asserting the collective identity of their members and changing society's cultural values (such as movements based on ethnicity). However, 'instrumentalist' and 'expressive' characteristics are not mutually exclusive and frequently overlap.
- Though it is common to contrast 'new' social movements (such as environmental and indigenous peoples' movements) with the 'old' (trade unions and left-wing parties), this can be misleading. Some 'new' movements have been around for a long time, a high percentage of activists belong to both types of movement and in many instances 'new' and 'old' movements work hand in hand for common goals.
- While social movements are normally considered progressive, they can also be conservative or reactionary.
- In the Europe of wealthy economies and welfare states, social movements are generally considered to be more middle-class and less concerned with basic, material needs than their Latin American counterparts. Again, nothing is absolute.
- Social movements come and go with various degrees of longevity. Some see this as a weakness; others consider that even when movements disappear,

their influence is sustained through those who, having learned how to be politically active, go on to create and participate in other movements.

- Attracted by their emphasis on independent action and participatory democracy, some theorists have a romantic view of the ability of social movements to effect large-scale social change (though this has taken a dent in recent years); others see them as too fragmented and localised to mount a serious, sustained challenge to the existing social and political order.

- Finally, an important consideration is the extent to which social movements are theorised in terms of the cultural politics of 'identity and difference', on the one hand, or political economy and social class, on the other. Theorists of the former (often referred to as 'social movement theorists', 'post-structuralists' or 'postmodernists') see social movements as a reflection of a pluralist society, of groups engaged primarily in a struggle over cultural meaning (what it is, or should be, to be black, a woman and so on) which, in an extreme version, is unrelated to the economic organisation of society. Theorists of the latter, usually Marxists, look more towards the structural level of society – to political and economic developments and their impact on class struggle – for an underlying explanation as to why social movements emerge and take the form which they do. In reality, some see merit in both these theories and there are a range of positions between their two polar extremes.

Further reading

Foweraker (1995) compares different theories of social movements between the United States, Europe and Latin America. Radcliffe (1999), Hellman (1995) and Jelin (1997) provide useful introductions to social movements in Latin America. Escobar & Alvarez (1992) and Alvarez et al (1998) are two inter-related, seminal publications offering case-studies in a wide range of Latin American movements; additional case-studies appear in the journal *Latin American Perspectives* (1994). For a discussion of the politics of 'class' versus 'identity' see Smith (1994), Hellman (1995), Veltmeyer et al (1997) and Allen & Eade (2000).

Chapter 1
Popular Education in Latin America:
An Overview

'I used to be desperately poor and couldn't even write my name. Now I'm just desperately poor'.
Latin American cartoon.

'Some kinds of education are worse than no education at all'
Amada, community council member, Guarjila, El Salvador

'But I would go as far as to say that in my experience, the worst educated people in Latin America generally know how to read and write and have university PhDs'.
Eduardo Galeano (1991:62)

For almost forty years, 'popular education' in Latin America has played a major role in the struggle of grassroots organisations to bring about social change. Its theoretical and practical contribution to radical education has been acclaimed throughout the world. It has relevance for people involved in a wide range of social practices – from teachers, social workers and lawyers to community activists, campaigners and leaders of progressive organisations. It has produced at least one of the major educationalists of the twentieth century and its challenge to conventional education can no longer be ignored.

Nevertheless, the concept of popular education is notoriously difficult to define. It has changed over the years, it overlaps with other areas of political and cultural activity, it is interpreted in many different ways and there have been deliberate attempts to fudge and confuse its meaning. Given the variety of political contexts in Latin America, moreover, and the range of social movements to which popular education relates, its practice comes in many shapes and sizes.

This chapter outlines the main characteristics of popular education in Latin America. It highlights the areas of contention and provides an introductory overview of the themes to be examined in subsequent chapters.

The Characteristics of 'Popular Education'

The Meaning of 'Popular'

'Popular education' is the standard English equivalent of the Spanish 'educación popular' or Portuguese 'educação popular'. However, important connotations are lost in translation. The Spanish 'barrio popular', for example, means 'poor' (or 'working class') neighbourhood'. It would be completely wrong to translate this as 'popular' neighbourhood since most inhabitants of a 'barrio popular' would much rather live somewhere else. A 'barrio *popular*', in fact, could be a very *un*popular neighbourhood!

In Spanish or Portuguese, 'popular' means 'of the people', 'the people' being the working class, the unemployed, 'peasants' the 'poor' and sometimes even the lower middle-class: it excludes and stands in contradistinction to the well-off middle class and the rich. The 'people' are often referred to as 'the popular classes' or 'the popular sector'. Trade unions, neighbourhood associations, peasant associations, women's groups, co-operatives, human rights groups, for example – would all be considered 'popular' organisations (it is even common to talk of the 'popular' as opposed to the 'established' church). Sometimes 'popular' communicates the idea of 'working in the interests of' rather than 'composed of' the popular classes: thus, for example, a human rights group campaigning on behalf of landless peasants would also be considered a popular organisation, even though its main activists were sympathetic, middle-class lawyers. A 'popular movement' refers to a single organisation, such as the 'Landless People's Movement' in Brazil; *the* 'popular movement' is a way of speaking collectively of the popular organisations existing within a particular region or country, as in the sentence 'the popular movement in Mexico is very strong'. While sociologists increasingly talk of '(New) Social' Movements' to describe actors operating outwith[1] conventional politics, 'social' says little of the class-based

---

[1] Outwith is a word commonly used in Scotland. It combines the notions of 'excluding' with 'outside of'. The dictionary gives 'outside' or 'beyond' as alternatives in English.

nature of 'popular' organisations and, for clarification, sometimes both adjectives are used: the Landless People's Movement in Brazil is often referred to as a 'popular social movement', for example. However, like most linguistic terminology, 'popular' can be imbued with different interpretations and Wanderley (1994) argues that a lack of precision in the meaning of 'people' and 'popular' (in Spanish and Portuguese) is a problem.

A class analysis, then, is at the heart of 'educación/educação popular', the task of which, essentially, is to pursue an educational practice which will best serve the interests of the 'popular classes'. The nearest UK equivalent – but with a very different history (see Crowther, 1999) – has generally been known as 'radical (adult) education' though partly due to the Latin American influence the term 'popular education' is currently much in vogue: it is important not to lose sight of its original meaning.

Political Commitment and 'Utopia'

What distinguishes popular education from 'adult', 'non-formal', 'distance' or 'permanent' education, for example, is the belief that in the context of social injustice, education can never be politically neutral: if it does not side with the poorest and marginalised sectors – the 'oppressed' – in an attempt to transform society, then it necessarily sides with the 'oppressors' in maintaining the existing structures of oppression, even if by default. Fundamental to the concept of popular education, then, is an a priori *political* commitment in favour of 'the popular classes' in which the role of education is to help people in the struggle to overcome oppression and injustice: 'popular education is always a political and political-pedagogical position; it is a commitment to 'the people' with regard to the whole of their education' (Puiggrós, 1990:13); 'for us, the essential characteristic of popular education ...is that it is defined by its conception of class, class commitment and its organic link with the popular movement' (Núñez, 1993:55).

Not all education done within the popular sector qualifies as 'popular education'. Governments, private companies and other institutions may be involved in educational programmes in poorer areas, including the teaching of literacy, health education and vocational training. Sometimes, these programmes deliberately set out to promote a politically conservative message (Carr, 1990); sometimes, they are simply 'assistentialist' in that while their objectives are concerned with helping the poor, in the absence of an underlying political analysis of poverty they do nothing to challenge existing social relations. In that they target the popular sector, both types of programme may *claim* to practise popular education but the lack of political analysis and engagement means they clearly lie outside the popular education movement in Latin America.

Whatever the differences within this movement, it is at least clear that an explicitly political engagement is an essential prerequisite of membership.

A 'commitment to the oppressed', however, is itself open to a variety of interpretations and popular educators have been motivated variously by religious, revolutionary, nationalist, social-democratic or even liberal ideals. While popular education has clearly been to the left of centre politically, its precise relationship to different political-philosophical ideologies is under-researched. In times of dictatorship, ideological differences within popular education remained beneath the surface but in the current, diverse political climate they are becoming more evident. This theme will be developed in chapter six.

It would be a mistake, however, to think of popular education as an ideological battleground between left and right, where the aim is to supplant, in the mind of the learner, one set of (albeit progressive) ideas for another. Treating learners as passive recipients of information – if not propaganda – would be the antithesis of popular education, a process which places high value on the knowledge already possessed by the 'popular classes' and on the active process of learning and the development of capacity for critical thought.

Underpinning the political commitment of popular education is a radical vision, or dream, of a much better world. In Spanish and Portuguese this is often referred to by the word '*utopía*' (with different people having different '*utopías*'). Unlike its English equivalent, the Latin American usage generally implies a future which is possible, rather than unattainable. From the 1960s onwards, socialism and revolutionary change were the *utopía* of many movements. Since the early 1990s, however, with the failure of the Sandinista revolution and the apparent triumph of 'neo-liberal' capitalism, the question of what constitutes a feasible '*utopía*' is sometimes hotly debated (Betto et al,1993).

Education and Action – Subjects and Objects

As the aim of popular education is to help the popular classes liberate themselves from oppression, it is inextricably linked to political action for change. While it necessarily helps people analyse their own social reality – hopefully provoking a deeper understanding of oppression – organised action is always encouraged and becomes the constant focus of critical evaluation. Indeed action or 'social practice' is the primary concern of popular education; people are encouraged to step back, metaphorically, from their practice, examine it objectively and then, strengthened by this reflective process, re-engage in action. In its turn, the new form of action is subject to the same critical appraisal, in a constant spiral of action-reflection-action, what Freire, borrowing from Marx, referred to as 'praxis'. In educational terms, this emphasis on helping people explore the

BOX 1:1
Popular Educators in Guarjila, El Salvador

Photographer: Anne Kane

'Guarjila is a highly organised community with an active community council and regular popular assemblies to promote local participation. One of the Basic Rights which people are denied is education. The government said it would provide them with one teacher but there would be conditions attached to the curriculum. But what the government wanted to teach about history, for example, was very different from what had been experienced by the community so they rejected the government's offer and set up their own popular educators instead. Amada, a member of the community council, told us 'some kinds of education are worse than no education at all'. While I was there I came across the teachers, all aged about 19, sitting in the community dining area, the only place with a light, preparing their classes in English, History, Economics and Politics at eight o'clock on a Saturday night'.
Kane, A (1996)

dialectical relationship between reflection and action (or 'theory' and 'practice') has been referred to variously as the 'Pedagogy of Praxis' or the 'Conception of a Dialectical Methodology' (Jara, 1989).

Brandão highlights two important consequences of the concern with action: 'In the first place it means that popular education is neither based exclusively on (explicitly) educational events nor gives priority to any particular educational mode. It is part of a wider process and while it may often appear informal and arbitrary, it is done very deliberately' (Brandão, 1989:73). 'In the second place it implies that popular education turns both reality and the process of transformation themselves into educational events' (ibid). It is this premeditated, deliberate intention to treat social practice as an area of educational enquiry which differentiates popular education from other types of political action.

But popular education is also concerned with the authors of transformatory action. Just as Marx saw socialism as the self-emancipation of the working class, Freire argued that the 'oppressed' themselves must be the 'subjects' of their own liberation, not passive 'objects' led blindly by either populist politicians or vanguard revolutionaries. Popular education's concern with political action, then, is not confined to the objective success or failure of a particular course of action (it would be quite possible for a community campaign for better services to be successful, say, but if this were due to the charisma of one particular leader or a 'favour' granted by an opportunist politician, its net result could be to reinforce passivity in the wider community). Rather, it attempts to widen participation, to make people less dependent on leaders – though leaders still have a crucial role to play – and to promote democratic practice throughout the struggle for change. 'By popular education we mean a collective process through which the popular sectors manage to become historical subjects, directors and protagonists of a liberatory project in their own class interests' (Peresson, 1983:116).

The Importance of the Popular Movement

Since the 1970s, the most important feature of popular education – and perhaps the least understood outside Latin America – has been its organic link to the 'popular movement'. If the purpose of popular education was to help the oppressed take action, collectively, and become 'subjects' of change, then the most effective way to do so was to work with the plethora of grassroots organisations emerging all over the region and already taking action for change. Throughout the 1980s, the main focus of popular education was to make a contribution, educationally, to the greater effectiveness of these organisations in their struggle for change: 'the practice of popular education has as its objective the strengthening and consolidation of class-based organisations' (Jara, 1989:56); 'we understand that popular education loses its original characteristic as an emerging educational movement and redefines itself as intermediary, political work to service popular projects, "subjects", movements and their likes' (Graciani, 1997:63). 'Their likes' would also include so-called 'new social movements' emerging in the late 70s and early 80s around issues of gender, ethnicity and race.

These popular and social movements have had an important role to play in Latin America and, for some (Cubitt, 1995), have contributed much to the demise of dictatorship and the 'transition to democracy'. Generally speaking, these are quite different from social movements in the UK and Europe. While both have certain elements in common – they operate outside conventional politics, they are more participatory and less authoritarian than conventional institutions – it is commonly argued that compared to Latin America, in Western Europe 'the state's penetration of civil society has been far greater and [...] the welfare functions of the state have been much more effectively established' (Slater, 1985:8). The concerns of European social movements are often seen to respond to a post-industrial society and project post-material values; they attempt to 'democratise democracy' (ibid:9) and 'extend the 'political space' available to citizens, bringing into the public realm the concerns of 'everyday life' and of the 'personal' (Hellman, 1992:53). If they have a defined social base, 'it is among the educated middle classes who have the time and income to organise and agitate' (Foweraker, 1995:31). However, 'the basic issue for most communities and associations in Latin America remains how to consume enough to survive, and material demands remain paramount for the great majority of social movements. It is mainly the lower or 'popular' classes which mobilise for reasons of work, wages, services and housing' (ibid:31).

In Latin America, popular organisations and movements have been, in effect, the principal 'schools' in which popular education has taken place (it is, in fact, common to talk of 'the movement' as the school'). Their struggles and actions, their forms of organisation, their 'culture', in the broadest sense, constitute the starting point of popular education and its ongoing field of enquiry. Much of the discourse of popular education – 'starting/theorising from practice', 'pedagogy of praxis', 'dialectical methodology', for example – only makes sense within this conception of an educational process submerged in a social movement.

Knowledge, Culture and Ideology

A concern with epistemology – the theory of knowledge – is central to the practice of popular education. Popular education has generally been underpinned by a 'dialectical theory of knowledge', the belief that knowledge is not acquired merely through abstract, rational thought ('idealism') but by experiencing, interacting with and reflecting on the material world in which we live. Since they experience the world in different ways, different people (and social groups) possess different kinds of knowledge: 'the way in which the popular classes (the dominated class) "live" or "experience" social reality is different from the way in which other social classes "live" or "experience" this same reality. Consequently, the way in which each social class theorises – i.e. learns about and explains social events – is also different' (Costa, 1987:14). Popular education is concerned with the ways in which these different, socially-produced types of knowledge interact and how this affects the ability of the 'oppressed' to work for social change.

BOX 1:2
From Rhyme to Poetry

Shortly after the triumph of the Revolution in Nicaragua, the ministry of culture organised a poetry competition for *campesinos*. We sent in eighty-seven poems from the '*campesino* cultural movement'. A jury including Ernesto Cardenal (one of Latin America's most famous poets) was to select the best five for publication. Off we went, enthusiastically, to our first poetry competition, full of the joys of revolutionary Nicaragua.

Wearing his black beret, Cardenal comes into the hall, sits down, turns off the television and asks

'Are all the participants here?'

'Yes, we're here'

'Well, we've come to tell you that none of the poems is worth reading. They're all rubbish. We're not going to publish any'

We were stunned. Eventually someone asked

'So how come they're so bad?'

'Too much rhyme', he explained. 'Poetry should be free. If you spend all your time worrying about rhyme you end up forgetting what you're supposed to be saying in the first place'

Then one *compañero*, Secundino, gets up and says

'Look, you might know a lot about poetry but our poems aren't rubbish, it's just that we've never heard this before. We'd never met you till today and we just thought that was how you were supposed to do it. But if that's how poetry should be, all loose and free, how about this then? Listen:

I'm a fisherman
I leave my house
grab my net
throw it over my shoulder
and set off.
When I reach the river
I drop the net
open it
throw it into the water.
When I take it out
it's full of fish
The big ones I keep for myself, to eat;
the small ones, back to the water'

'That's a lovely poem. What's your name?'

'Secundino Ríos Canales'

'I'm going to put you down as the best *campesino*-poet we have in Nicaragua. That's what I call a poem'.

'Are you kidding?', said Secundino 'I could recite poems like that all night! You know, I thought it was supposed to be much more difficult than that'.

And everyone began to write poetry. Cardenal was brutal, at first, but when we saw his reaction to Secundino, we were all motivated to write. And now there's a lot more poetry in Nicaragua.'

From *The People Know Best...Anecdotes and testimonies from Latin American popular educators* (Núñez, 1990: 13)

At one level, there is a need to challenge the prevalence of the ideas championed by the dominant classes. In part this is due to their power to influence public opinion through control of mass media and other forms of cultural and ideological persuasion, including formal education. In part, since they have been the most successful in structuring society according to their interests, the ensuing social order is the reality from which everyone draws their knowledge of the world. Since there is no alternative to which it can be compared, this social order appears 'natural'. In this way the dominant classes achieve what Gramsci calls 'hegemony' – domination by consent – over other classes, a concept much discussed in popular education today. (In a modernised version of Gramsci's 'hegemony', Chomsky (Herman & Chomsky, 1994) talks of 'manufacturing consent'). In trying to counter the pervasiveness of the dominant world-view, popular education is often described as an attempt to create an 'anti-hegemonic' culture.

The dominant idea of what constitutes 'knowledge' – normally scientific, academic and technical knowledge – is seen as corresponding to the particular interests of the dominant (or 'hegemonic') classes. In placing little or no value on knowledge acquired through the experience of belonging to a different class or cultural reality – indeed this is usually referred to as 'ignorance' – the dominant class has no conception of the cultural world of other classes. Even when genuine attempts are made to use 'dominant' knowledge to improve the situation of the poorest – albeit without upsetting the balance of power – the knowledge and cultural gap between classes can lead to disaster. The entire 'third world', for example, is littered with failed, inappropriate and expensive development projects (dams, agricultural production, tourism and so on) implemented by 'experts' with no understanding of the cultural world into which they tried to intervene. When the Dominican Republic passed apparently progressive 'green' legislation against deforestation, the poorest peasants were the first to be imprisoned (Kane, 1988); from their perspective, however, cutting down trees for fuel was a matter of immediate survival. It is a fundamental component of popular education, then, to subject the dominant ideology to critical analysis and deconstruction.

At another level, in its attempt to help enable the 'popular classes' bring about change, popular education is concerned with exploring, understanding and systematising what is described as 'popular' knowledge and culture. The first task is to treat popular culture with respect and help people value what they may have been taught to see as ignorance. Martinic (1994:83) discusses this in relation to the systematic devaluation of indigenous culture from the time of the conquest: 'the sacred becomes profane, important bodies of knowledge are considered superstitious, equal exchange and the common ownership of land are seen as an archaic tradition against the expansion of the market and individual property', while Costa argues that 'popular knowledge about medicine, engineering, agriculture, or economics is not valued or legitimised as real or useful knowledge. Why not? Because it is not acquired in school but through direct contact with plants and their medicinal effects, with machines and tools, with the land and with different forms of exploitation of labour. Popular knowledge is not recognised as having any value for solving society's problems (or even the problems of the popular classes) because, if it were, the solution to the problems would be different' (Costa, 1987:17). There is much to be respected in popular culture and an important aim of popular education is to challenge negative perceptions and promote a greater sense of self-worth among those who constitute the 'popular classes' – in the educational work of the Landless People's Movement in Brazil, for example, people learn, deliberately, to stop looking down at the ground and to look middle-class people straight in the eye (Caldart, 1998).

From within popular education itself, however, criticism has been directed at a tendency to take this to extremes, to see all 'bourgeois' culture as bad and all 'popular' culture as good. This is known as 'basismo', loosely translated as 'basism' or 'grassrootsism': 'We must reiterate that we distance ourselves from any position based on 'spontaneity' or 'basism', where everything the popular classes do – no matter what – is valid and true' (Nuñez, 1993:56). A more mature position recognises the impossibility of a 'pure' popular culture: 'It is a politically ambiguous culture in which conservative and progressive positions exist simultaneously, where elements of the dominant ideology intermingle with the remnants of ancient cultures which are recycled by the popular classes, but uncritically, and often in a way which is functional to the established power. This ambiguity comes out in the conceptions shared between classes: the inferiority of women, the need for authority, ethnic rivalries [...] the normality of the existence of different classes' (ibid:116). Importantly, it is recognised that educators too absorb the dominant culture and their biases and prejudices 'can manifest themselves in our own behaviour and practice' (Pérez, 1993:47).

While respecting popular knowledge and culture, then, and trying to understand their complexity, a process of popular education will also subject them to critical examination and attempt to disengage what can be considered 'popular' from what has been absorbed from the dominant culture. Equally, there are large elements of the dominant culture which the 'popular classes' ought to appropriate. There should be no 'basist' ejection of the baby with the bathwater but, instead, what Ghiso (1993) calls a 'dialogue of knowledges' in which the best of 'popular' and 'scientific' knowledge comes together to produce a new popular knowledge which will better equip popular organisations to take forward their struggle.

Educational Methodology and the Role of the Educator

Independently of the issues under investigation, a concern with the way in which the educational process is organised – the 'methodology' employed by the educator – is a fundamental feature of popular education. Indeed the methodological approach has often been seen, mistakenly, as its trademark. The main characteristics of this methodology are, firstly, that consistent with its principles and as a precursor to deeper understanding, the starting point of any educational endeavour should be an attempt to understand the 'social reality', in all its complexity and contradictions, of those (organisations) seeking to bring about change. Secondly, in recognition of the existence of different 'knowledges' and the need for the educational process to 'enable large sections of the popular masses to acquire the capacity to think for themselves' (Jara, 1994:103), the role of the educator is not to pass on expertise or deliver answers to problems but to promote a 'dialogue of knowledges' in which collectively, everyone participates in discussion, analyses problems and considers options for action. If people are to be 'subjects' of change, it is important they learn to act independently of 'teachers' or 'experts' though depending on the situation, 'expert' knowledge may make an important contribution.

The educators' role thus differs from that of traditional teachers. Instead of being the experts and sole arbiters of right and wrong, they are aware of their limited understanding and of the need to inspire people to articulate their own view of the world. They need to have the ability to engage people in dialogue, ask challenging questions, provoke analysis, summarise and synthesise discussions, throw this back at participants for verification and further analysis – all backed up by a variety of appropriate pedagogical techniques (for which popular education has rightly become famous). It would be a mistake, however, to see the 'popular educator' as a mere 'facilitator', given the implied neutrality of this latter term. While they do fulfil some of the roles of a facilitator, popular educators are clearly more interventionist: though there is no predisposition to transmit a particular set of ideas, they start with an a priori political commitment to the organisation, have a clear idea of its main aims and objectives and in bearing the major responsibility for the eventual shape of the learning process, have a major influence over what is likely to be learned. As participants in a collective process, they also have a right to contribute their thoughts on the issues under discussion.

Changing Contexts, Changing Practice

All educational initiatives are affected by the political, social and economic context in which they are embedded, especially where, as with popular education, the context itself is the focus of enquiry. Both geographically, across the region, and historically, over the last forty years, Latin America has seen an enormous variety of contexts, each giving rise to different expressions of popular education practice.

After a colonial history which encompassed slavery, mass exploitation and genocide, Latin America today is a kaleidoscope of ethnicities and cultures in which the dominance of European, African, indigenous American or 'mestizo' ('mixed' ethnicity) influence varies from place to place. At one extreme, while maintaining aspects of a nationalist culture, wealthy elites will characteristically have much in common with their counterparts in the United States, many being graduates of their universities or military academies. At another extreme – with many variations in between – indigenous people, worse off than before the arrival of the first conquistadors, determinedly defend their culture against local and global capitalism. The interplay between local (sometimes rival) elites, foreign states or investors and the economically and culturally 'oppressed' is the background against which the struggle for change is played out and which gives rise to myriad regional and national contexts.

At times only the use of severe repression has enabled the dominant classes to keep control. In this context popular education has operated under two different scenarios. In one, it has been forced to work within the ideological constraints imposed by the oppressors, in which case it has usually been driven underground and disguised as something else. While people will always find a way to struggle against ideological oppression and there are many examples of this (c, 1990) there is no doubt that the potential for popular education is limited. By contrast, in the other scenario, such as in El Salvador in the 1980s, where guerrilla opposition created 'liberated zones' in the midst of a radicalised population, popular education is let loose and totally unobstructed (Pearce, 1986; López Vigil, 1995). Similarly, it had the same free hand in self-regulated refugee 'camps' in Honduras.

Most often, popular education has operated in a political context in which, though considered subversive, it has been tolerated, albeit to varying degrees and with periodic clamp-downs. At one extreme, it may be on a permanent state of alert, liable to be on the receiving end of repression if it goes too far, as happened in Argentina in the 1970s (Puiggrós, 1994b). In the middle ground, where governments claim more liberal credentials, there has been a 'dialectical relationship' between popular education and the state: the state allows popular education to operate, but will try to limit its effect, while popular education's critique of the state can bring about reform. Currently, Brazil and Ecuador show how both quantitative and qualitative changes in state-run adult education have come about in response to a popular education critique: Freire's own work as minister for education in São Paulo from 1990-91 would be a specific example.

Front and back of a T-shirt produced by Grupo Maíz in El Salvador, a centre specialising in 'communication' within popular education and which takes advantage of El Salvador's vibrant T-shirt culture. The front says 'What would men do without women? Wash. Cook. Run the house. Clean bottoms. Look after the sick' and the back 'and demand, together with women, that housework should be recognised, shared and well paid.' Photographer: Liam Kane

In this liberal context, as well as effecting change at local level, popular education can fulfil a nation-wide role, taking advantage of the inadequacies of formal adult education. Further to the left, 'populist' governments have claimed to be on the side of 'the people' but still maintain a top-down, pro-capitalist perspective. While this continues to impose constraints, it constitutes a 'window of opportunity' in which the tone of public debate is receptive to a popular education discourse. It was under just such a populist government – that of João Goulart (1963-64) – that Freire was able to carry out his earlier work.

In Nicaragua in particular (as well as Cuba and Grenada), Latin America also provides an example of a revolutionary society which saw nation-wide popular education as a crucial part of its development. The image of 40,000 enthusiastic urban volunteers going out to teach literacy to *campesinos* and to encourage participation in the making of a new society is a tremendous inspiration to anyone interested in education for change (Arnove, 1986).

Areas of Specialisation

Many aspects of popular education have developed into areas of semi-specialisation. While some of these relate to the type of group being supported or to specific social issues, others relate to particular methodological concerns.

One such area is 'systematisation'. Popular educators 'confront situations which are fluid, unstable, changing and uncertain; everything seems messy and confused, a collection of interacting problems' (Barnechea et al, 1994). 'Systematisation', usually taking the form of a written document, is the attempt to bring order to, reflect on, interpret, and make sense of a practice which intervenes in this constantly changing reality. Palma (1992) and Magendzo (1994) point to a diversity of motives behind the drive to systematise. One is to enable communication between organisations and educators so that each may learn from the other's experiences, successes, problems and failures; another is to help a group of educators analyse and evaluate their own work; a third is a deliberate attempt to use systematisation as part of the educative process, where writing down and interpreting developments is part of a conscious effort to help a group reach new levels of understanding. Crucially, however, the concept of systematisation is not of dispassionate, detached, 'neutral' report-writing: those who collectively engage in systematisation are also, unashamedly, part of the focus of enquiry, both 'subjects' and 'objects' at the same time. Jara emphasises that systematisation should not simply be about narrating, describing and classifying events but should pay attention to 'the interpretation which "subjects" give to these events so that a space is created in which these interpretations are discussed, shared and challenged' (Jara, 1994b:24).

Another area is research. Torres argues that popular education's commitment to action has been made at the expense of proper research into its own activities, partly due to 'a certain mistrust of academia and institutionalised research, identifying these as reproductive centres of the current system' (Torres, AC, 1994:117). While this mistrust is rooted in reality, such wholesale, 'basist', rejection of dominant epistemologies has been equally discredited. In recent years there has been increasing recognition of the need for proper, rigorous research, albeit in a manner consistent with the principles of popular education. Closely associated with popular education is the concept of 'Participatory Research' (or 'Participatory Action Research'), where attempts are made to engage whole communities – as opposed to individual specialists – in collective research into their own social reality. This has now developed into a world-wide movement in which Latin Americans such as Orlando Fals Borda, Jorge Osorio and Francisco Vio Grossi are particularly prominent. Participatory Research has certainly proved an effective technique in popular education activities – encouraging people both to think and take action – but its record in actually producing new knowledge is questionable. Exponents of Participatory Research are aware of its shortcomings – Pedro Demo makes a harsh critique of its claim to be serious research, concluding that it 'has leaned much more towards participation than towards research' (Demo, 1994:114) – but feel, nevertheless, that it is an area which still has important contributions to make to the struggle for social change.

In a study carried out by the Latin American Council of Adult Education (CEAAL, 1992: 55-56), the theme of 'communication' – or, more specifically, 'popular communication' – emerged as a major concern of popular educators. Though definitions of communication were imprecise, it was seen to cover a number of important areas. It was considered an integral part of all education work and given the complexities of relating to different cultural worlds, educators firstly felt the need to develop appropriate communication skills for themselves. The forms of communication taking place within any popular organisation were also seen to affect the whole educational process: there was a concern to democratise these forms of communication, ensuring that everyone had a voice – not just the leadership or the most articulate – and to promote dialogue and critical thinking. More normally, communication was understood as that which related to a mass audience, taking the message of the popular struggle from a micro to a macro level. This concern covered many areas which themselves were further specialisations: one was the production and dissemination of education materials to help educators in their practice. These could be anything from board games to slide-tape shows, the best known examples being the two tomes on 'participative techniques' by Bustillos and Vargas (1993) which have sold over 100,000 copies all over Latin America. Another was how to make inroads into the mass media, given its control by the dominant class. As a counterweight to this approach, there was a also a concern to develop an 'alternative' media, where videotapes excluded or banned by the mainstream press could be distributed independently and shown to the public through popular communication networks (this has been commonplace in Mexico with videotapes made by the Zapatistas). Community radio stations have also played an important role in developing alternative media and new technology has opened up different possibilities, with various networks of educators researching the possibilities of the Internet. In Quito, Ecuador, the community radio station *Pulsar* combines both types of technology, e-mailing an excellent, alternative digest of Latin American news on a daily basis, all free of charge and downloadable in text and audio (see *Pulsar* under web sites). The subject of communication has also produced some important figures in popular education, such as Mario Kaplun or Francisco Gutiérrez, who in turn have inspired a broader interest in this particular specialism.

Other fields of interest include the training of popular educators: some of the gaps between rhetoric and actual practice in popular education have been explained by insufficient training and CEAAL (1993) has set up various initiatives to address this problem. Given the closeness of popular education to matters of organisation, another focus is the process of 'self-management' and, by association, the role of 'popular leadership', important issues to be addressed if popular education is concerned with empowerment, participatory democracy and strengthening the ability of popular organisations to effect change. The fashion for particular areas of specialisation may vary, either in response to changing priorities within popular education or due to changes in the external world. Currently, the relationship between popular education and 'technology', particularly the Internet, is attracting a lot of attention.

Popular Education: Who Does It, Where, When And How?
Confusing Conceptions
Though popular education is a discipline in its own right, in practice it may be difficult to tell it apart from the many other aspects of political-cultural action with which it overlaps: anyone visiting Latin America in search of pure, explicit, popular education could well end up disappointed. Three points are worth making to address any possible confusion.

Firstly, I think it is helpful to conceptualise popular education as a *generic* educational approach which relates to multiple, *specific* areas of activity. In effect, it divides into sub-categories: 'popular education and human rights', for example, 'popular education and community development' or 'popular education and gender'. The list is long and constantly changing: 'popular education' and (or 'with') 'workers'; 'peasants'; 'basic education'; 'indigenous peoples'; 'interculturalism'; 'popular economics'; 'co-operativism'; 'self-management'; 'health education'. Recent additions would be 'democracy'; 'citizenship'; 'justice and peace'; 'school education'; 'street-children' and 'local government'.

Confusion appears when, depending on perceptions, what some might consider 'popular education' is seen by others as 'gender education' or 'education for citizenship', for example. Though it is perfectly possible to adopt a popular education approach towards the theme of 'citizenship', say, it would be equally possible to reject it: 'education for citizenship', then, may or may not constitute, simultaneously, popular education. The multi-dimensional nature of popular education is confirmed by a glance at the names of many organisations which, being affiliated to the Latin American Council of Adult Education (CEAAL), are consciously engaged in popular education but whose public identity emphasises something different: 'Women's Network' in Brazil, for example; 'Integral Corporation for Social and Cultural Development', Colombia; 'Uruguayan Institute of Socio-Economic Promotion'(Núñez et al, 1992:133-134).

Secondly, as a consequence of these overlaps, many who work with popular organisations may not perceive themselves, primarily, if at all, as 'popular educators' even though their work presupposes an educational role. When I visited a local NGO project in Santo Domingo, for example, it included a group of committed architects who were helping shanty-town dwellers design plans to improve their neighbourhood. Their work embraced all the principles of popular education, encouraging a political analysis of problems and promoting organised action for change. However, the personnel involved described themselves to me as 'architects' rather than educators. Similarly, other professional activists may call themselves agronomists, lawyers, researchers, trainers, ecologists or nurses and so on (see McDonald, 1998). But in the course of lending support through their particular expertise, many workers become aware of the importance of their educational role and seek out some sort of training in popular education. The extent to which these specialists consciously articulate and emphasise the educational element of their work will depend on themselves, their experience and the particular project in which they are engaged: some may consider themselves subject specialists who need to learn a bit about education while others may come to see themselves as popular educators, primarily, who happen to work in a particular, specialist area.

Thirdly, all educational practice – whether 'popular' or otherwise – implies 'intentionality': that is to say, a deliberate attempt is made to bring about learning. There will be many examples of popular organisations engaging in action for change and, in the process, of members learning new skills and new ways of thinking. If this is left to chance, though it might be considered popular education by default, it would be more accurately classified as 'informal' education. In looking at the actions of different popular organisations, though they may superficially engage in similar activities, properly speaking, only those which consciously and deliberately reflect on the educational dimension, planning and preparing for learning, are involved in 'popular education'. To the casual observer, then, it may not be possible to tell at a glance the extent to which any organisation – or individual activist – is consciously engaged in this process.

The Organisation of Popular Education

I find it helpful to think in terms of three different levels of practice. First and foremost, at the grassroots, there is the popular education which takes place within popular organisations themselves. As these organisations engage in the struggle for change, the advantage taken of educational opportunities will depend on the abilities of the members themselves, their key leaders and activists plus any support given by outside bodies.

Also at the grassroots are the thousands of small-scale 'development projects' funded by Non Governmental Organisations to improve the economic status of poorer communities. While some NGOs never emerge from an assistentialist position, others understand the political nature of poverty and the importance of concurrently promoting community organisation. In this context, with its experience of starting from immediate concerns (such as water, health, housing, income generation and so on) and relating these to wider issues of politics, power and organisation, popular education has an important role to play.

Crucially, at an intermediate level, independent of the state and funded by NGOs, there is a vast array of 'support centres' which exist to offer different kinds of assistance to different types of popular organisation. Staffed by professionals with educational responsibilities, these centres come under a variety of names and guises, though some would simply be known as 'popular education centres'. They may vary in size, from two to up to thirty full-time staff, and specialise in selected areas of expertise; some work with many different organisations and some may even only work with one, operating, in effect, as the educational wing of that particular organisation.

The specific support provided by these centres varies but a key element is the training of activists in the principles and methodology of popular education. The Mexican Institute of Community Development, for example, runs a 'School of Methodology' attended by activists from popular organisations throughout the country. Four times a year they participate in a week-long workshop, going back to their organisations in between to test out the methodology in practice. Not only does this enable key activists (and their organisations) to become more effective, the act of bringing together different organisations itself contributes to the strengthening of a wider popular movement.

Though structurally separate from the centres, another group operating at intermediate level are the radical priests, nuns, and religious who, through the liberation theology 'option for the poor', involve themselves in popular education within the specific context of Christian Base Communities.

At a higher level still are the popular education networks where educators and centres come together to share resources and expertise. Again, a by-product of such collaboration is the strengthening of links between organisations. This networking takes place at both national and regional levels; one example is

María Verónica Torres Ruíz and Gustavo Pérez Casaron, popular educators working for CANTERA, prepare for a meeting with the community of Mateare, on the outskirts of Managua, Nicaragua. Photographer: Liam Kane

Alforja, a network of seven popular education centres covering Mexico and Central America. At the highest level, practitioners, centres and networks from all over Latin America come together through the Latin American Centre for Adult Education (CEAAL). CEAAL organises working parties on different aspects of popular education (the training of educators, 'popular communication' and so on), encourages research and co-ordinates debate on educational issues through a regular newsletter, *La Carta* and a weightier, termly journal on education and politics, *La Piragua*.

Who Are the Popular Educators?

Roughly speaking, these divide into two groups, the 'professionals' and those who emerge 'organically' from the popular movement.

Rivero (1993:174) concurs with CEAAL that in Latin America 'the majority of popular educators have their roots in left-wing politics, the Church or the social sciences. Few directly live out the reality of the 'popular' world and its organisations' (Núñez et al, 1992:31). These are the professionals, those of middle-class origin, normally university graduates, who have acquired particular skills and opted, politically, to put these at the service of the 'oppressed'. An issue frequently raised – and not only in Latin America – is the extent to which the professional's middle-class culture interferes in his or her ability to work effectively: quasi-religiously, some notable projects in radical education require educators to give up their worldly goods and become one with the poor (Duke, 1990). But the very nature of popular education recognises, a priori, the different world-views of different class relationships. Normally, as Vio Grossi (1994) points out, the key issues are not the class of origin but the quality of the educators' contribution and whether or not they show commitment and loyalty to the popular movement: if a peasant organisation has friendly lawyers at their disposal (apparently some do exist), normally it would not want to see them waste time cultivating land in a gesture of solidarity.

The other group are those members of popular organisations who in the course of struggle have emerged as key leaders, motivators or activists. It has been argued that 'the most important popular educator of all isn't the field-worker or an educator based in a centre or a support institution. The most important popular educator should be the leader of an organisation' (IMDEC, 1994: 60). In their particular role, these key activists have an impact on the educational experience of their whole organisation and as such they are important targets for those centres providing training in popular education philosophy and practice. This is the ideal situation, where organisations produce not only 'organic intellectuals', in the Gramscian sense, but 'organic popular educators' as well.

Historical Developments in Popular Education

Quoting Jiménez, Soethe (1994) traces the origins of popular education to revolutionary France, in 1789, from where the ideals of universal, free and compulsory education made their way to Latin America. According to Puiggrós (1994a), by the start of the twentieth century the principal critique of mainstream education was made by those associated with anarchism, socialism, radical liberalism or popular nationalism. Gómez and Puiggrós (1986) present several case studies of early radical education, including the 1890-1920 Workers' Education Movement in Chile, the 1920 'Plan of the 5,000 million' in Argentina, under President Yrigoyen, and the popular universities set up in El Salvador and Peru in the mid 1920s. Along with Núñez (1992), they attach considerable importance to Sandino's educational practice during the 1920 anti-imperialist struggle in Nicaragua in which his guerrilla army developed its own education sector. Núñez goes on to argue that with his particularly Latin American interpretation of Marxism, his respect for indigenous culture and his encouragement of organised action, it was the Peruvian thinker José Carlos Mariátegui who was the main ideological founder of the practice which would later develop into popular education. Oscar Jara (1994a) finds the origins in the emergence of an industrial working class at the start of the twentieth century, where collective organisation, whether in trade unions or political parties, led to numerous alternative cultural and educational opportunities.

Given the historical moment, it is not surprising that many of these earlier attempts at radical education pursued a traditional methodology in which 'teachers' instructed learners on what to think. While some showed early signs of an embryonic, learner-centred approach to educational matters, others leaned more towards crude propaganda. In its contemporary sense, however, popular education in Latin America is generally understood as having three stages of development.

BOX 1:3
Movimento de Educação de Base (MEB)
(Grassroots Education Movement)
One of the earliest and better-known projects in popular education was the MEB in Brazil. Making extensive use of radio and with financial help from the government, the Catholic Church set up the MEB in 1961 to bring literacy, basic education and 'self-improvement' to the rural poor. But educators quickly became radicalised, adopted the educational methodology of Paulo Freire and encouraged peasants to think about the structural causes of poverty and take action for change. In one year alone, the MEB trained as many as 3870 educators and had 111,066 graduate learners (Costa et al, 1986: 125). The military coup of 1964 killed off its growing radicalism though it surfaced elsewhere in the more independent Comunidades Eclesiásticas de Base (Christian Base Communities).

The first began in Brazil, in the late 1950s and early 1960s, with large scale attempts to bring basic education to the urban and rural poor: it continued till the end of the decade. In its attempt to survive the crisis of 'import substitution industrialisation', the government of João Goulart courted the popular vote and provided funding for literacy programmes throughout the country, a significant political gesture in a country where illiterate people were denied the vote until 1983. Concurrently, within the context of an emerging liberation theology, the radical church organised the Grassroots Education Movement (see Box 1:3) which saw education as a means of promoting political awareness and community organisation. At this time political radicalism was thriving due to increasing economic hardship, the relative freedom offered by a populist government and the inspiration of the 1959 Cuban revolution. The pioneering educational work of Paulo Freire emerged from this context. After the Brazilian military coup of 1964, Freire went into exile and continued his work in Chile. He began to have an enormous impact all over Latin America, especially as the radicalisation of the Church intensified, embodied in the bishops' conference of Medellín, in 1968, where it officially adopted the 'option for the poor'. While the term popular education started to be used in the sixties, it was seen as an educational initiative, first and foremost, which happened to have political ramifications, rather than the other way round.

The second period embraces the 1970s to the mid-1980s when the expansion and modernisation of capitalism caused rapid urbanisation and increasing economic hardship, often accompanied by repression and dictatorship. The lack of conventional channels to work for political change led to a spectacular growth in the number of popular organisations and movements and these proved to be fertile ground for popular education (CEAAL, 1994). Significantly, popular education was seen as subservient to these movements: whereas in the sixties it was hoped that education and 'conscientisation' would lead to action, now it was action which led to the demand for education. This was the boom period in popular education, a time when popular education networks, including CEAAL and Alforja, were set up all over the region. Many writers (Gutiérrez Pérez & Castillo, 1994; Núñez, 1992) comment on the strong ideological influence of Marxism on popular education during this period. From 1979 onwards, the Sandinista revolution in Nicaragua also provided an opportunity to put the ideas of popular education into practice on a large-scale. It was a time when those involved in popular education felt that real, radical change was just around the corner.

The third period covers the late 1980s to the end of the century, in which many practitioners (Mejía,1995, for example) have talked of a crisis in popular education and a need to rethink the basics. External events and internal weaknesses have both contributed to this crisis. Externally, it is argued, the world has changed considerably since the early 1980s in that in general, there has been a demise in authoritarian, dictatorial governments, more space has opened up for the participation of civil society and popular education therefore no longer needs to be subversive: it is time to reconsider its relationship to state education (indeed many popular educators have started working in the state sector) and much is currently being done to develop 'popular' state schools for children (Gadotti, 1994; Do Vale, 1992).There is also a crisis of ideas: it is argued that since 1989, with the fall of the Berlin wall and the defeat of the Sandinistas in Nicaragua, the idea of large-scale, revolutionary change has died ('utopia unarmed', in the words of Castañeda, 1994) and popular education needs to adapt to this new reality; in this context, Marxism is considered a spent force and the influence of post-modernism is increasingly evident. From within, critics such as Gutiérrez Pérez & Castillo (1994) argue that popular education has been so involved with political action and ideology that it is difficult to isolate the uniquely 'educational' and that the quality of education has always been difficult to assess: they claim that many activist-educators have only superficial notions of education, equating this with participatory techniques or games. They argue the need to take the specifically pedagogical more seriously, paying close attention to research into how adults learn. CEAAL (1995) now recognises that the question of quality – and how it can be measured – has become central to all popular education practice.

On the surface, then, the popular education of the 1990s seems to have lost some of the radical edge of earlier years, even though neo-liberal economics have exacerbated social inequality. However, there are different interpretations of its place within society and these themselves are open to change. Despite the uncertainties, Núñez argues that since popular educators have always promoted a political practice 'from and with the people... this has been our insurance against disaster' (Núñez, 1993: 49).

Conclusion

Though it is difficult to define with precision, popular education in Latin America has generally been understood as a process of non-formal, adult education committed to helping grassroots organisations work for social change. A generic term which covers a variety of specific practices, it has developed an inspiring, participatory methodology and stimulated much thought on the various roles of educators, learners and popular knowledge and culture. In recent times, with political and ideological change in the wider world and accusations of weakness in aspects of its practice, it is in the process of reinventing itself for the twenty-first century. It is an appropriate moment to learn from its past and speculate on the future.

Review of Chapter 1

A graduate in psychology and sociology, from his early youth onwards Carlos Zarco Mera has been involved in education in the 'popular' neighbourhoods of Mexico City, particularly in the context of popular Christian communities and urban movements. He has been an adviser and trainer for a range of social organisations throughout Mexico; in an academic capacity he has worked for NGOs and a number of universities. In 1997 he was elected general secretary of CEAAL, a post he still holds and from which he has acquired a Latin American perspective on popular education. He is married to Laura Fuentes, with whom he shares the search for a more just and humane society, and they have a beautiful, intelligent, five year-old daughter and an energetic, smiling, one year-old son.

In this chapter the author addresses and attempts to define the phenomenon of popular education, highlighting its constituent elements (its characteristics) and deciphering their various connections. In both the bibliography reviewed and the way in which each element is explored, we are offered a text which is both exhaustive and instructive. The author successfully explains what popular educators have written about their own practice and where there were gaps in information he has been successful in inferring and offering his own formulations. In short, what we have is a serious intellectual exercise which offers us, through its analysis and synthesis, a preliminary, panoramic view of the nature of popular education in Latin America.

Briefly, I would say that popular education is the (political and pedagogical) conceptual expression of a movement of educators throughout Latin America who opted to join and work alongside the organisations which were being created by poor people to defend their rights and advance their interests and aspirations. The management of knowledge has been central to this process, a process of self-reflection, a key for opening up and making sense of reality and its contradictions, for recognising strengths and opportunities. It is through this combination of the personal, the collective and the social that we discover the subjective and political (and therefore educational) potential of the struggle for change.

In that sense, more than trying to define popular education, we have to interpret what it means and take responsibility for the consequences of our understanding. I consider that, in the end, the author successfully deciphers the principal coordinates of that cultural and political movement with its corresponding mode of thinking, popular education. And I would particularly emphasise these two expressions of the phenomenon: on the one hand it is a broad and open movement, with a degree of articulation and organisation (such as CEAAL, Alforja and other national networks) while, on the other, it is a particular branch of critical thinking (with its conceptual formulations, its 'systematisation' of experiences, its dialogue with the social sciences, its publications and so on). To approach popular education, then, implies reading the bibliography but also reading the movement as it really exists.

This chapter successfully clarifies the meaning of 'popular', its pedagogical implications (that the poor should become subjects of their own history, that their knowledge is recognised and valued, that participatory processes should be promoted) and its political implications (identification with subaltern classes, a push for popular organisation, the building of utopic visions, commitment to social transformation). However, I believe that it misses what lies at the root of these implications, the *raison d'être* or the ethical and philosophical basis of popular education. Allow me, then, to offer some ideas I think would complement what the author has written in his overview.

Popular education is above all an ethical commitment in favour of humanisation and opts, therefore, to work firstly with those people whose objective living conditions most militate against this. But, at heart, it is about the full humanisation of everyone. The humanisation of both the educator and learner, the oppressor and the oppressed is the final goal of this educational and political movement (in political terms, this humanisation could be classified as liberation or emancipation). Seen from this perspective, popular education has a more universal appeal: the proposals emerging from popular sectors relate to the whole of society, in all its diversity, so it should be possible to engage in a political and pedagogical dialogue with other sectors (universities, political parties, public policy makers, international organisations etc) and search for common ground. For me, this implies a cultural change in favour of dialogue, consensus building, tolerance (other sectors, too, have contributions to offer) and cooperation: this has not been easy for popular educators. Highlighting humanisation, then, radicalises the compromise with poor people and offers the possibility of building bridges to other sectors in society; highlighting only the concept of social class can isolate popular education and make it appear too radical.

But we have to intervene, socially and politically, in the process of humanisation; we have to consider what institutions might contribute to the strengthening of social movements and the promotion of our proposals. This is the political dimension of popular education. What lessons from history, what type of organisation best serve our promotion of an equal and just society? When we face military dictatorships or authoritarian regimes, the options for opposition may be clear. But with the advance of democratisation, with its broadening of pluralism and citizens' rights, the question of political options is more complex: it demands greater discernment as well as respect for different viewpoints. By that I mean that today, in its ideological or party-political preferences, the popular education movement cannot only have one voice, not even at national level. In that sense, it is even more important to highlight its ethical commitment and pedagogical components rather than particular political options.

Finally, the diversity of social movements in Latin America has been considerably enriched. To depict them as 'popular' no longer reflects the multiple expressions of struggle in favour of respect for human rights, equity, justice and democracy (unless we seek to emphasise the particular dimension of poverty and social exclusion). Thus, movements of women, indigenous peoples, young people, groups reclaiming sexual diversity, disabled people, the struggle for the recognition of children's rights and so on – all ask questions of popular education and its potential contribution to their particular struggle for dignity and respect and against subordination and social exclusion.

From the organic link which popular education has with these movements, new demands have arisen with regard to what can be considered political or pedagogical. So when we talk of gender, interculturality, environment, generational dialogue, the building of citizenship, of a culture of peace and human rights – we not only address new themes and areas of activity in their own right but issues which relate to the core of popular education itself; they also question the essence of social science which, until now, has been carried out within the hegemony of patriarchy, ethnocentrism and adult-centrism.

In light of these new challenges, popular education, in my view, needs to renew itself not only adjectively but also substantively. It should renew its 'popular' option (making it more consequential, radical and effective) as well as its educational contribution. Being a generic educational approach – as the author rightly points out – it should reconsider its educational consistency, engage with contemporary educational and pedagogical debate, be open to discussion with (educational) policy-makers and improve the training offered to popular educators. With its particular version of critical thinking, it ought to participate in the general cultural life of society, not restrict itself to narrow educational concerns.

If its pedagogical aim is to help create subjects of change (or to promote their 'self-creation'), popular education should draw attention to itself, argue for the importance of its educational contribution, bring its accumulated experience into the public arena and be willing to have its ideas and methodologies adapted for other areas and social sectors. In this way, even if it loses identity, its influence may spread far and wide: like a pinch of salt which, to provide flavour, has to dissolve in the soup.

Carlos Zarco, general secretary of the Latin American Council of Adult Education (CEAAL).

Author's note: chapter 2 discusses 'humanisation'; chapter 9 examines recent developments in popular education and its relevance to newer social movements and the whole of civil society.

Chapter 2
The Work of Paulo Freire

"I WISH THIS BLOKE FREIRE WOULD STOP MOANING ABOUT 'BANKING EDUCATION' IT'S ABOUT TIME SOMEONE PAID US TO GO TO SCHOOL"

Background to Freire's Thinking

A familiarity with the work of Paulo Freire is central to an understanding of popular education in Latin America. Freire's importance extends beyond this, however, as he has had an enormous impact on both formal and non-formal education throughout the world, including the industrialised 'north', particularly through his seminal work, *Pedagogy of the Oppressed*. For some (Allman & Wallis, 1997), he is the pre-eminent educationalist of the twentieth century. He has been criticised from a variety of political perspectives, however, and, in practice, educators have chosen to interpret his work in different ways. This chapter gives a brief overview of Freire's work and thought, examines the views of his critics and considers his relevance to popular education at the start of the twenty-first century.

A Brief Biography

Freire was born into a middle-class family in Recife, Brazil, in 1921. The economic depression of the early 1930s brought severe, if temporary, hardship and the experience of hunger, with its detrimental effect on his own ability to learn, made a profound impression on Freire as a boy. Eventually, with the aid of family connections and an upturn in economic fortunes, he was enrolled in a well-run school and completed his secondary education. He went on to Recife university to study law and philosophy.

Feeling powerless to help people in any real way, Freire was unhappy as a lawyer and had barely begun to practice when he abandoned the idea altogether and returned to his old school to teach Portuguese. In 1947 he joined an adult learning project which brought him into contact with industrial workers, peasants and fishermen – all of whom were in the process of organising political struggles. This rekindled his childhood awareness of the links between social class and education, taught him to respect the wisdom contained in popular culture and made him see the connections between education and action. A practising Catholic, he was also involved in the Catholic Action Movement and the Christian Base Communities, both of which were questioning how religion could better serve the needs of the poor.

He completed a doctoral thesis on education in 1959 and started working in Recife University. In 1961 a progressive Mayor invited him to organise a literacy programme for the city of Recife and it was here that the famous Paulo Freire Method was developed. The success of the programme brought Freire to national prominence and he was asked to organise a national literacy campaign under the populist government of João Goulart. This was a period of growing radicalism in Brazil but a right-wing military coup in April 1964 cut it short and removed Goulart from office. Freire was considered a threat by the new regime: illiterate people were not allowed to vote and if Freire's national campaign were successful, it would enfranchise millions whose sympathy would naturally lie with more progressive politicians. Freire was briefly jailed and went into exile in Bolivia, then Chile, on his release.

In Chile Freire published his Brazilian experience in 'Education As The Practice of Freedom' (Freire, 1974a). In what was a period of political radicalism in Chile, in the years prior to the election of Salvador Allende, Freire worked in the government's programme for adult literacy and agrarian reform. Stimulated by this new work, it was in Chile that he wrote *Pedagogy of the Oppressed*, and due to Brazilian censorship, the first publication actually appeared in English, rather than Portuguese, in 1970. This work deals more with the wider, political aspects of education than 'Education As The Practice of Freedom', which examines individual, psychological processes of change. After a brief spell at

Paulo Freire
Courtesy of Instituto Paulo Friere

Harvard University, Freire went to Geneva to work for the World Council of Churches. From there he was able to travel the world, collaborating on educational programmes in many countries. His thinking was further radicalised while working with the revolutionary government of Guinea Bissau, in Africa, in 1975-76; his reflections on this experience were captured in his correspondence with officials, subsequently published in *Pedagogy in Process* (Freire, 1978).

Freire was able to return to Brazil in 1980 where he became professor of education at the Pontifícia Universidade Católica in São Paulo and a founding member of the new Partido dos Trabalhadores (PT) (Workers' Party). In the 1980s he co-published a series of 'talking books', where discussions between himself and other prominent educators were taped, transcribed and edited into a coherent publication. The most significant of these was *We Make The Road By Walking* (Horton & Freire, 19990), co-produced with Myles Horton of the Highlander Centre (Tennessee, USA), an independent centre of international repute for radical adult education.

When the Workers' Party surprisingly won control of São Paulo in the local elections of 1989, Freire was made minister for education. It was a chance to see what his ideas – those of popular education – could achieve within the formal sector when there was political will to support them. He stayed in post for almost two and a half years, reflecting on the experience in *Education in the City* (Freire, 1991).

Pedagogy of Hope (Freire, 1993) relates his thoughts on *Pedagogy of the Oppressed* twenty years on, responding to some of his critics and optimistically reflecting on the role of radical education in a time of ideological uncertainty. He continued to write on formal education, directly addressing classroom teachers in *Teachers As Cultural Workers* (Freire, 1995) and *Pedagogy of Autonomy* (Freire, 1996), until his death in May 1997.

Philosophy and Theory of Knowledge

Freire was a philosopher of education, a thinker who drew his ideas from a wide variety of intellectual sources and whose educational practice was an extension of his philosophical beliefs. As a Christian humanist influenced by Mounier's philosophy of Personalism, Freire believed in the intrinsic worth of human beings and that they had a natural instinct – an 'ontological vocation' – to make the most of themselves, to become fully human, not as selfish individuals but in 'communion' with others. Where people do not progress towards full 'humanisation', he saw this as a distortion of their vocation, that they had been 'thwarted by injustice, exploitation, oppression and the violence of the oppressors' (Freire, 1972: 20). From Marxism he acquired tools of social analysis, an understanding of the role of the dominant ideology and a strengthening of his belief in dialectical thinking, though he rejected mechanistic interpretations of Marxism and crude notions of economic determinism. While he accepted that human beings are conditioned by their environment, he also believed in subjectivity, that it was possible to change this environment. Along with existentialist thinkers like Sartre and Jaspers, he was concerned with 'authentic' states of existence, that people should not merely exist in a state of passivity but be free to act on the world as 'subjects'. Writers like Fanon, Marcuse and Fromm gave him insights into the psychological consequences of oppression: how oppressed people can become dependent on their oppressors, internalise their values, aspire to become oppressors themselves and believe the myths spread about their own ignorance. He was interested in phenomenology, the philosophical attempt to describe how individuals experience the world – rather than how they explain and understand it – as part of an investigation into consciousness; this would be reflected in his educational work when his first recommended step was to encourage learners to describe, not analyse, their perceptions of the world. Taylor (1993: 45-48) traces much of Freire's thought to Aristotle, particularly his debate with Pythagoras on theory and practice: while Pythagoras argued that true freedom came from objective understanding, from being a spectator on the world, Aristotle countered that absolute freedom could only emanate from active participation in the world. Freire was also influenced by those he considered authentic, revolutionary leaders, including

Amílcar Cabral, of Guinea Bissau, and the Argentine-Cuban, Ernesto 'Che' Guevara. Guevara, indeed, is one of the most quoted figures in Freire's work.

With so many influences, some more explicit than others, Freire has often been described as an eclectic thinker who discovered nothing new but whose genius lies in having synthesised great ideas into an identifiable educational practice. An important part of this practice, related to his philosophy, is his understanding of epistemology, the theory of how we acquire knowledge.

Freire had a dialectical theory of knowledge (see also Chapter 3). People are firstly conscious of their world phenomenologically, through their senses and feelings, but knowledge is then acquired through interaction with the social reality in which they find themselves, i.e. both the physical, material world and the people with whom they communicate. It is in this sense of interaction that Freire talks of knowledge as an 'act of knowing'. As people inhabit different social realities, so too, will the knowledge they acquire be different.

But people develop variable levels of consciousness. It can be what Freire calls 'magical' or 'naïve' consciousness, accepting and uncritical of what is being experienced. This, argues Freire, is typically the case among the oppressed who have internalised the dominant ideology. What differentiates humans from animals, however, is their ability to step back from and reflect on experience: when people are able to do this it becomes, for Freire, 'critical consciousness' though this is never fully achieved but is, rather, an on-going process of 'becoming'. It follows that for those interested in social change, the best way to acquire knowledge is to take action for change and then reflect critically on the experience: this is the oft-cited dialectical relationship between theory and practice (or reflection and action), what Freire calls 'praxis'. Genuine class or revolutionary consciousness comes not from abstract theorising but from involvement in a struggle to bring about change.

Finally, knowledge is produced socially in that it is acquired by individuals through social interaction with other people. Even here, though, the process of knowing is dialectical, not a one-way transmission of packaged knowledge from one person to another. For this knowledge to be authentic, the recipients have to engage actively, as 'subjects', in a critical appreciation of this knowledge, inventing and re-inventing for themselves the knowledge which is passed on: 'knowing is the task of Subjects, not objects. It is as a subject, and only as such, that a man or woman can really know' (Freire, 1974b: 101).

Educational Philosophy and Practice

The foundation of Freire's *educational* philosphy developed from a combination of his general philosophical beliefs and his work in basic education with fishermen, peasants and workers in the 1950s, a period when workers and peasant organisations were increasingly active in organising for change. He developed a critique of traditional education which, he argued, attempted to 'domesticate' learners into accepting oppression and he began to formulate his own ideas on education for 'liberation'.

Education for Domestication

In his analysis of society, Freire distinguished between a dominant and dominated class, between oppressors and oppressed, though he declined to explain these terms with any precision. In the context of Brazil, the oppressors could be the former colonial power (the Portuguese), the contemporary neo-colonialists of the industrialised north (particularly the USA) or the elites indigenous to Brazil. The system of oppression 'dehumanises', he argues, and has a negative effect, culturally and educationally, on its victims. In order to preserve their privileges, the oppressors propagate a mythical view of reality: that people live in a free society, 'that the street vendor is as much an entrepreneur as the owner of a large factory... that if they don't like their boss they can leave him and look for another job... the myth of the industriousness of the oppressors and the laziness and dishonesty of the oppressed' (Freire, 1972: 109-110). People become socially alienated, partially internalise these myths and develop a dual relationship with the oppressor. While they do want to break free from oppression, they have also been socialised into emotional dependency and the 'fear of freedom': 'the oppressed are insecure in their duality as beings which "house" the oppressor. On the one hand, they resist him; on the other hand, at a certain stage in their relationship, they are attracted by him' (ibid: 114). In a context of extreme oppression, this can lead to what Freire (1974a: 8) calls a 'massified society of adjusted and domesticated people', where, through manipulation, the majority become uncritical and easily-controlled. In this scenario, lacking the means and opportunity to articulate their own view of the world, the oppressed are alienated and immersed in what Freire (1985: 60) called 'the culture of silence'.

Freire argues that whether in schools or in adult literacy classes, in the hands of the oppressors the traditional form of education is used as a tool to 'domesticate' the oppressed. He coined the term 'banking education' to describe an approach in which educators are seen as supposed bearers of truth whose job is to 'deposit' their knowledge into the empty vessel of the learner's mind, like money in a bank. This deposit, however, is only the 'truth' of the oppressors; no value is placed on the knowledge of others; people become victims of 'cultural invasion', having been denied the chance to examine and articulate their own view of the world; they are encouraged into passivity while the oppressors become 'subjects' of history.

Given this scenario, Freire argues that, politically, 'education can never be neutral' (1974b: 149) for 'washing one's hands of the conflict between the powerful and the powerless means to side with the powerful, not to be neutral'

(1985: 122). For those educators choosing to side with the powerless, the question then becomes how to engage in an educational practice which works towards 'liberation' as opposed to 'domestication'.

Pedagogy of the Oppressed

For Freire, education for 'liberation' or 'cultural action for freedom', as he often called it, cannot be simply a question of banking education with a different, liberatory message to deposit. In essence, even if carried out by revolutionary leaders working to free the oppressed, banking education de-humanises: it has no respect for the learners' existing knowledge, it would suffer from the same elitism as before – only this time with revolutionaries as the assumed bearers of truth – and would continue to encourage dependency, placing the oppressed in a passive role, as objects rather than subjects of change.

There are several elements to Freire's 'pedagogy of the oppressed'. Firstly, consistent with his philosophy on the human 'ontological' vocation, he argues the importance of trusting people and having faith in their ability to become 'subjects' of history: 'if the people cannot be trusted, there is no reason for liberation' (Freire, 1972: 99-100). In many ways, this remains a revolutionary concept: that ordinary people, not just talented leaders, can and should be the agents of change. While this harks back to Marx's (and even Trotsky's) view of socialism as the *self*-emancipation of the working class, it is something which is arguably completely ignored or forgotten by much of the organised left throughout the world. Secondly, Freire defends the role of human subjectivity in the shaping of history and argues that people can and do bring about change, that they are not merely prisoners of their objective social environment. In his dialectical understanding of objectivity and subjectivity, he rejects the notion that material forces are all-powerful and that history is predetermined: again, this is reminiscent of Marx's comment that 'men make their own history but they do not make it just as they please; they do not make it under circumstances chosen by themselves' (Marx, quoted in Elster, 1989: 277). This means that even when objective conditions are bad, we should always be hopeful that people can bring about change. To re-emphasise this point, in the early 1990s when increasing social problems, the 'triumph' of neo-liberalism and the perceived demise of radical ideology were responsible for a climate of despair in much of Latin America, as Freire reflected on the impact of *Pedagogy of the Oppressed* twenty years after its publication, he named his new book *Pedagogy of Hope*. Social and political change was possible and though education, on its own, would not change the world, it had an important contribution to make.

A pedagogy which aims to help the oppressed become 'subjects' of change has to enable people to see through the myths of the oppressors without engaging in a 'cultural invasion' of its own; it should help people move from a 'magical' or 'naïve' to a 'critical' state of consciousness, able to see the causes of oppression and consider possibilities of action for change, a process Freire called 'conscientisation' (though the term was not his own invention). Since authentic knowledge is acquired through a dialectic of acting and reflecting on the world, and interacting with others, then this is what learners should be encouraged to do; as the knowledge which individuals acquire reflects their own particular experience, and 'there are neither utter ignoramuses nor perfect sages' (Freire, 1972: 63), the progressive educator cannot be the authoritarian figure of old.

In lieu of 'banking education', then, Freire argues for a pedagogy of the oppressed to be based on 'problem-posing' education and on 'dialogue' between learners and teachers, as well as amongst learners themselves. A class (or, less formally, a 'culture circle') is where different people should meet to share their different 'knowledges' in a common, collective search for understanding in order to change the world.

In this conception of education, the teacher has a different role: 'the practice of problem-posing education first of all demands a resolution of the teacher-student contradiction' (ibid: 53). Instead of simply transferring knowledge, the educator for liberation recognises the importance of reciprocity, of finding out what the students know and being prepared to be taught as well as to teach, a view summed up in Freire's famous quotation 'no one teaches another, nor is anyone self-taught. People teach each other, mediated by the world' (ibid: 53).

Whereas traditional educators start from what they think people should learn, an educator for liberation should start by finding out as much as possible about the learners' view of the world. For Freire, in his earlier work in Brazil, this meant a 'thematic investigation' of the learners' existential reality. Like anthropologists, teams of researchers would study communities of potential learners to find out which themes or concerns 'generated' most discussion. Educators would work to prepare concrete visual representations (photographs, slides or drawings) of these 'generative themes' which could serve as a focal point for discussion and analysis with a group of learners. (In Freirian terminology these visual representations are known as 'codifications'). A good visual captures a situation which, though clearly familiar to the learners, contains a degree of ambiguity or vagueness of meaning. If the meaning is either too explicit or too obscure, it will stifle the need for analytical discussion. Ideally, while it will focus on one particular theme, it will also suggest links to others, to a wider, integrated reality.

The purpose of such visual representations – or 'codifications' – is to objectify reality, to enable learners to step back from the immediacy of daily life and observe it from a distance, to reflect on their social situation and their own place within it. A codification is presented to learners as a visual image in need of interpretation, a problem to be analysed. Encouraged by the educator's questions, learners go through a process in which they firstly describe in detail what they think they see, thus revealing the unanalysed, spontaneous perceptions and interpretations of the reality presented before them; the idea is to bring to the surface, to make explicit, for everyone to see, the learners' consciousness of the world. More open-ended questioning then encourages a deeper analysis, pursues an explanation of the representation, of the 'codified' reality – searching for cause and effect – and, in the light of ensuing discussions (in which the educator may also contribute his or her understanding), challenges learners to reconsider their previous understanding. In Freirian terminology, this process of description and analysis is called 'decoding' or 'decodification'. 'By stimulating 'perception of the previous perception' and 'knowledge of the previous knowledge', de-coding stimulates the appearance of a new perception and the development of new knowledge' (ibid: 87).

Freire gives an example of how the process of de-codification can reveal important understandings about the learners' view of the world which are unlikely to emerge in banking education.

'In one of the thematic investigations carried out in Santiago, a group of tenement residents discussed a scene showing a drunken man walking on the street and three young men conversing on the corner. The group participants commented that "the only one there who is productive and useful to his country is the souse who is returning home after working all day for low wages and who is worried about his family because he can't take care of their needs. He is the only worker. He is a decent worker and a souse like us".

The investigator had intended to study aspects of alcoholism. He probably would not have elicited the above responses if he had presented the participants with a questionnaire he had elaborated himself. If asked directly, they might even have denied ever having taken a drink themselves. But in their comments on the codification of an existential situation they could recognise, and in which they could recognise themselves, they said what they really felt.

There are two important aspects to these declarations. On the one hand, they verbalise the connection between earning low wages, feeling exploited and getting drunk – getting drunk as a flight from reality, as an attempt to overcome the frustration of inaction, as an ultimately self-destructive solution. On the other hand, they manifest the need to rate the drunkard highly... After praising the drunkard, the participants then identify themselves with him, as workers who also drink – "decent workers".

In contrast, imagine the failure of a moralistic educator, sermonising against alcoholism and presenting as an example of virtue something which for these men is not an example of virtue' (ibid: 89-90).

In this process of 'decodification', the discussion normally oscillates between the abstract and the concrete, between the visual representation and the learners' real, everyday lives. As different themes are analysed through different codifications, learners are encouraged to consider links between themes and to develop an understanding of social reality in its totality. 'Experts' may be invited to dialogue with the group but as co-investigators of truth, rather than its bearers. In moving from a condition of 'naïve' to 'critical' consciousness, learners are encouraged to identify specific elements in the structures of oppression which limit their ability to develop their full human potential. The attempt to overcome these 'limit situations' then becomes the focus of 'praxis', of action and reflection for change.

But for Freire the concept of the educator is a wide one and chapter four of *Pedagogy of the Oppressed* addresses itself to those who see themselves as part of a revolutionary leadership. Freire quite clearly supports revolution (in the sense of the radical transformation of society, rather than guerrilla warfare) but he warns that authentic revolution must be a communal act based on dialogue between 'leaders' and 'people' and that there can be no place for manipulative, cultural invasion and anti-dialogical action in any authentic revolution:

> 'Manipulation, sloganizing, "depositing", regimentation and prescription cannot be components of revolutionary praxis...It is absolutely essential that the oppressed participate in the revolutionary process with an increasingly critical awareness of their role as Subjects of the transformation...Sooner or later, a true revolution must initiate a courageous dialogue with the people. Its very legitimacy lies in that dialogue. It cannot fear the people, their expression, their effective participation in power. It must be accountable to them, must speak frankly to them of its achievements, its mistakes, its miscalculations and its difficulties' (ibid: 97-99).

Freire is not denying the crucial role of leadership nor the importance of a leader's experience, knowledge and skills. Equally, he does not suggest that 'the people' have all the answers: he recognises that many of their ideas are problematic as they still 'house' the oppressor inside. However, a 'cultural synthesis' between leaders and people, realised in constant dialogue, is the only way forward for authentic revolution:

'Revolutionary leaders commit many errors and miscalculations by not taking into account something as real as the people's view of the world: a view which explicitly and implicitly contains their concerns, their doubts, their hopes, their way of seeing the leaders, their perceptions of themselves and of the oppressors, their religious beliefs (almost always syncretic), their fatalism, their rebellious reactions. None of these elements can be seen separately, for in interaction all of them compose a totality... For the revolutionary leaders, the knowledge of this totality is indispensable to their action as cultural synthesis' (ibid: 149).

Throughout his life, even though he may have agreed with their political analysis, Freire was always a hard critic of left-wing activists and organisations who sought to impose their views on people rather than engage in dialogue as part of a process of conscientisation.

Finally, Freire talked frequently of the importance of love. Love for humanity, he argued, was fundamental to any 'act of revolution' and he was want to quote Che Guevara in support: 'Let me say, with the risk of appearing ridiculous, that the true revolutionary is guided by strong feelings of love. It is impossible to think of an authentic revolutionary without this quality' (Guevara, quoted in Freire, 1972: 62).

Teaching Literacy and the 'Método Paulo Freire'

World-wide, Freire is probably best known for his method of teaching literacy. Though this is sometimes seen in purely technical terms, as a means to an end in enabling people to read and write, it is essentially only one manifestation – in this case, within the field of basic adult education – of the educational philosophy already discussed. As part of an education for liberation, Freire argued that in itself literacy was of little use unless it helped people understand the world better, what he called 'reading the world', in order to be able to change it, a point neatly captured in a Latin American cartoon where a newly-literate peasant declares 'I used to be desperately poor and couldn't even write my name – now I'm just desperately poor'.

For Freire, then, even the teaching of literacy had to be problem-posing. It had to start from the learners' perceptions of reality, be based on dialogue between learners and teachers and work towards the 'conscientisation' of the oppressed. Freire's successful experience of working in the culture circles of northern Brazil, where he had found that people responded well to the process of analysing 'generative themes', led him to consider how this process might be adapted to the teaching of literacy. In the end, it was by grafting-on literacy to his existing educational approach which gave rise to his dynamic, new methodology.

As before, educators would conduct a 'thematic investigation' of the learners' social world. This time, however, instead of only finding 'generative' themes, the task was to search, more specifically, for 'generative words'. These would be generative in two, completely different senses. In the first, the word would represent a generative theme, a topic known to galvanise discussion. In the second sense, co-incidentally, the word would also generate a range of letters and sounds useful to the acquisition of literacy skills. In an urban context, for example, the word '*FAVELA*' (meaning 'slum' in English) often fulfilled this role. Thematically, it was generative in that the *favela* itself was a constant talking point of its inhabitants; linguistically, it generated important syllables – 'FA', 'VE' and 'LA' – which could serve as building blocks to literacy. Freire found that in Spanish or Portuguese all the sounds could be covered with around fifteen to eighteen key words. When a list of generative words was drawn up, the final task in the preparatory phase was to produce a visual 'codification' for each word-theme. As before, while these visual representations would be familiar to the learners, their meaning would be somewhat open-ended.

A literacy class would begin in the same way as the 'culture circles' described in the previous section: learners would be taken through the process of describing, analysing and 'de-codifying' the visual representation in front of them. At an appropriate stage in the discussions, learners are shown the written word which corresponds to the codification, and are then introduced to vowels. Freire (1974a: 82) describes the sequence:

> a)   First a slide appears showing only the word:
> FAVELA
> b)   Immediately afterward, another slide appears with the word separated into syllables:
> FA-VE-LA
> c)   Afterwards, the phonemic family:
> FA-FE-FI-FO-FU
> d)   On another slide:
> VA-VE-VI-VO-VU
> e)   Then:
> LA-LE-LI-LO-LU
> f)   Now, the three families together:
> FA-FE-FI-FO-FU
> VA-VE-VI-VO-VU *Discovery Card*
> LA-LE-LI-LO-LU
> The group then begins to create words with the various combinations.

The learners are encouraged to 'cut-and-paste' the different syllables to try and make new words. The word *favela* 'generates' a number of possibilities: 'FALO' or 'FALA' meaning 'I talk' or 'He/she talks', 'LE' meaning 'he/she reads', 'LULA', the name of the current leader of the Workers' Party, for example. When a few more generative words are added and treated in the same way, countless combinations start to open up and learners are encouraged to begin writing complete sentences.

In the Freirian method, then, instead of starting with the alphabet and dealing with isolated letters and sounds, the teaching of literacy focuses from the beginning on whole words (or even phrases) which have important meanings for the learners. There should be no literacy 'primer' to domesticate the learners' thinking: instead, from the start, literacy should be built into an ongoing educational process leading towards conscientisation, another tool enabling the oppressed to 'read the world' and, through writing, to communicate their own experience to others. As a practical method of teaching (basic) literacy quickly, it has proven fairly successful, though some would argue it has several weaknesses: citing the work of Otto and Stallard (1976), Taylor (1993) argues that Freire's choice of nouns for generative words, rather than verbs, detracts from the attempt to encourage action for change (though Freire's own examples show how learners quickly start to use verbs) while Action Aid's highly acclaimed REFLECT project (see Box 2:1) argues the need to include more visual stimulae in the literacy process (Archer & Cottingham, 1996a). Furthermore, many groups have even sought to co-opt Freire's method to their own ends, ignoring the political and philosophical principles on which it was based (Carr, 1990).

BOX 2:1
REFLECT (REgenerated Freirian Literacy through Empowering Community Techniques)

REFLECT is an increasingly influential, world-wide educational project in basic, community, popular education. It has been inspired by Freirian principles but recognises problems in putting them into practice: a 'generative-word' approach can lapse into traditional teaching, still allows educators to dictate the agenda and often fails to provoke meaningful dialogue, for example; also, in the context of the poorer countries of the South, most literacy teachers are volunteers with little formal education and few opportunities to study and train properly in the intellectually challenging Freirian approach to education.

REFLECT attempts to make Freirian principles more practical by
- abandoning the idea of a 'literacy primer' or of educators choosing generative words
- working within a process of community development where, collectively, groups are encouraged to discuss, analyse and produce a range of visual representations of their communities. These take the form of maps, charts, calendars, graphs

---

and diagrams which visually illustrate a community's perception of its economic situation, its social and political relationships, its links to formal institutions and so on. The visuals can even be drawn on the ground with a stick (though they would be later copied onto paper). These techniques have been developed from the practice of Participatory Rural Appraisal (see Box 3:1) and can be learned quickly in training sessions.

• the production of visuals stimulates a need and demand for literacy and numeracy, skills which are then introduced as and when appropriate.

One facilitator argues that REFLECT helps popular education 'keep its feet on the ground'; chapter 7 examines an evaluation of the project in El Salvador. REFLECT involves a great variety of NGOs world-wide and is co-ordinated by Action Aid.
    See Phnuyal et al (1998)

Maria Paula Sánchez, a literacy 'facilitator' elected by the community of San Luís, near San Salvador, in a REFLECT project run by the Salvadorean agency PRODECOSAL. Formerly Maria saw no need for literacy but when the community was encouraged to organise, have meetings and prepare project proposals, it stimulated a need and demand for literacy. Now Maria is proud to be able to help others.
Photographer: Liam Kane

A Critique of Freire

Criticism has always accompanied the work of Freire, some of it hostile, some ambiguous, some ill-informed and some constructive, the latter from those sympathetic to Freire but experiencing difficulties in applying – or 're-inventing' – his ideas to their different areas of educational practice. In keeping with his own 'dialogical' principles of education, Freire accepted criticism as an essential part of his educational development, constantly engaged in his own auto-critique and was prepared to modify his views publicly in light of illuminating, critical analysis. This section outlines the different types of criticism directed at Freire and, where appropriate, Freire's reactions.

From the right, not surprisingly, he has been accused of being too overtly political. In the aftermath of the 1964 coup in Brazil he was considered a 'traitor to Christ and the Brazilian people' (Torres, RM, 1988a: 28) and on being imprisoned was asked 'Do you deny that your method is similar to Stalin's, Hitler's, Perón's and Mussolini's? Do you deny that with your supposed method what you are trying to do is turn the country into a nation of Bolsheviks?' (ibid). Outwith the context of violent repression, politically hostile comment from conservatives was of little relevance to Freire: 'I don't address myself to right-wing parties. Obviously, I have nothing to say to them' (Freire et al, 1988: 56).

From the left, on the other hand, he has been accused of being insufficiently political, of being immersed in 'idealism' by implying that merely through a process of conscientisation people would be able to change the world. His concern with humanism, culturalism and 'psychologism' (Torres, RM, 1988a: 22) and his focus on individual freedom and autonomy, rather than socio-economic structures, was seen as politically naive. Freire accepted this criticism with regard to *Cultural Action for Freedom* but claimed that he was different from *Pedagogy of the Oppressed* onwards. 'I criticised myself ... when I saw that it seemed as if I thought the critical perception of reality necessarily implied its transformation. That is idealism. I overcame that phase, those moments, those wanderings through the streets of history when I was fooled by psychologism or subjectivism' (ibid: 35). As early as 1972, in fact, Freire stopped using the word 'conscientisation' as he felt it was being abused by 'idealists' and talked about as if it were a magical pill: 'A thousand pills for a reactionary boss. Ten for an authoritarian union leader. Fifty for an intellectual who doesn't practice what he preaches' (Freire, 1991: 114). From a Marxist perspective, while he acknowledges Freire's shift away from idealism, particularly in Guinea Bissau (cf *Pedagogy in Process*) where his work was more firmly related to the mode of production, Youngman (1986) concludes that on balance, Freire over-emphasises the importance of cultural factors at the expense of political and economic structures. In his later work, Freire makes it clear that in his view neither human subjectivity nor objective, material reality negates the other but that both interact dialectically.

He has been accused of vagueness and obfuscation, especially in his use of the terms 'oppressors' and 'oppressed'. Who are they, exactly? Taylor (1993) condemns such a stark, bifocal division as simplistic, Schugurensky (1998) says it is possible to be both 'oppressor' and 'oppressed' at the same time and Weiler (1996) asserts that the categories are too universal, lack specific location (though she believes Freire is really talking about social class) and should openly include issues of gender, race and difference. Schugurensky (1998) sees little clarity from Freire regarding programmes of action for change while Youngman (1986) believes Freire causes endless confusion by talking of revolution in isolation from any revolutionary theory, which, for Youngman, would be Marxism. Taylor (1993) claims Freire fails to elaborate on what an educator should 'see' in order to work with the oppressed. It has been argued that given such lack of clarity, it is hardly surprising that many ideologically disparate groups can claim Freire as their own though particularly as Freire sought to clear up any misunderstandings in his later works, Allman blames the reader, rather than Freire, concluding that 'I agree that Freire's ideas have been and can be used in ways which are anything but radical. However, this is a problem which lies at the point of reception and not with the ideas themselves. I also seriously doubt that further clarification or depth of analysis, on Freire's part, would make any difference to the way in which readers who are unaware of the sources and structure of oppression interpret his writings' (Allman, 1988: 94-95).

There have been complaints about the inaccessibility of Freire's language: 'They tell us we have to apply the reflexive-critical method which they say comes from Paulo Freire, but it's as if they were teaching us in English. There are loads of words you can't understand', says an Ecuadorean literacy teacher (Torres, RM, 1988a: 22), echoing the sentiments of many throughout the world. While Freire tried to be more accessible in his later work, in general he still defends his original writings, saying that complex ideas cannot always be accessed without effort. He suggests that part of the problem, at least in the English-speaking world, is not so much his language as the reader's lack of familiarity with dialectical thinking (Freire, 1993: 70-74), an argument supported by Carlos Torres (in Gadotti, 1996: 119). Accordingly, while intellectuals engage in academic debate, at the grassroots it is often the case 'that the adoption or rejection of Freire's thought does not derive from a direct reading of his work ... It is more the result of an oral or pamphleteering culture, where ideas are transmitted by word of mouth, from seminar to seminar, workshop to workshop, becoming ever more blurred in the process' (Torres, RM, 1988a: 21-22). The sexism in Freire's language also receives constant attention, mainly on account of the exclusive use of 'man' instead of 'human beings' in his earlier work. While a feminist critique also rebukes his failure to address, specifically, the oppression of women, some feminists still acknowledge the contribution Freire has made to their pedagogy of liberation (Weiler, 1996; hooks, 1994). Again,

Marta Vega (second from right), a popular educator working for PRODECOSAL in San Salvador, stimulates discussion in the community of San Luís. From her own experience Marta feels that popular educators have generally received too little training to make the principles of popular education work in real-life situations. But she feels the approach used in the REFLECT programme helps popular education 'keep its feet on the ground'.
Photographer: Liam Kane

this is an example of Freire being accused of a failure he later corrected. He accepted that he had been unaware of this issue in his earlier years, thanked his critics for enlightening him, stopped using sexist language himself and was happy for people to change the sexist nature of his language in citations (Taylor, 1993), as I have done in this chapter.

Aside from his political and philosophical positions, various problems have been experienced in attempts to put Freirian principles into practice. Firstly, there are the many examples of 'pseudo-Freirian' education where the idea of political liberation has been abandoned or rejected. Archer & Costello (1990: chapter six) document one example in a governmental project in Mexico City, Carr (1990) shows a multinational company doing the same in Honduras while in the UK, Gibson (1994) sequesters Freire for 'business education' (though Carmen (1995) justly takes him to task). Even where co-option is not an issue, the results may not be spectacular. Archer & Cottingham (1996a: 12-19) claim that the magic of 'codifications' rarely works, that teachers are just ordinary people (not the ideal envisaged by Freire) who often struggle to promote dialogue in groups and that Freirian efforts usually end up either concentrating on literacy skills or conscientisation but seldom achieve a balance of the two. In most cases, they oppose encouraging action against the real oppressors as this can lead to depression and an increased sense of powerlessness, if it is not successful, or, indeed, repression, if the action is taken at a tactically inopportune moment: they argue instead for groups to start with small actions, based on meeting immediate needs, to build up confidence and strengthen grassroots organisation before attempting anything more ambitious. Taylor (1993: chapter five) analyses the examples of codifications Freire presents in 'Education As the Practice of Freedom' and argues powerfully that these are much more directive, manipulative and imbued with the educator's values than Freire ever imagined. Freire has been accused of paying no attention to the differences between individual learners and in the context of formal education outwith Latin America, some have found that with the presence of different oppressions within a single classroom, mainly around issues of race, gender and institutional power, where some may perceive others in the class as oppressors, dialogue and discussion of generative themes is potentially destructive (Weiler, 1996; Ellsworth, 1994).

Freire has been accused of having an over dichotomised view of the world, that absolute divisions between oppressors and oppressed, domestication and liberation, banking and problem-posing education, for example, do not reflect the complexity of reality. While acknowledging Freire's methodological contributions, Youngman (1986) finds it hard to see how any educational endeavour can avoid some element of 'banking' education; Lovett (1983) thinks Freire over-emphasises the importance of methodology and that what counts is the political purpose of liberatory education, even if this involves a degree of 'banking' education in the transfer of essential knowledge and skills; in his championing of democracy in the classroom, Freire has been accused of naively portraying learners and educators as equals (something he denied) or of seeing education as 'non-directive' (which, again, he disputed, repeatedly saying that while all education was directive to an extent, it could avoid being authoritarian and manipulative); he has been seen as patronising towards ordinary people, on the one hand, with his notions of 'naïve consciousness' and the 'culture of silence' (because, it is argued, ordinary people are much more critical than Freire would have us believe) and, on the other, of having a naïve faith in their ability to bring about change.

The amount of critical review Freire attracted was essentially a measure of his stature, it took place, mostly, within a framework of general support and though the list of criticisms is lengthy – and illuminating – it does not detract from the significance of his contribution. Freire's main complaint was that his critics often harped back to his earlier works and refused to recognise evolution in his thinking.

Paulo Freire and Popular Education

Though he spent many years in exile, throughout his life Freire had an umbilical link with popular education in Latin America. He was there at the start, the main protagonist in a new movement set to spread throughout the continent. Brandão describes how 'already learning with Paulo Freire, in the years 1960-61, when we in Brazil were working with a different concept of education, we were searching for a name to give to this new entity. The name chosen was *popular education* though in a sense it came a bit late on the scene: the first had been *liberatory education*, which even Freire himself used' (CEAAL, 1985: 8 quoted in Torres, RM, 1988a:94). By 1970, the year of *Pedagogy of the Oppressed*, Freire's ideas were already influential and had even made a significant impact on the Catholic Church's declared 'Option for the Poor' at the bishop's conference in Medellín, Colombia, in 1968. Torres (in Gadotti, 1996: 121) argues that 'probably one of the main reasons for the success of Freire was the close relationship between his initial educational philosophy and catholic thinking'.

Freire left Latin America for Europe as popular education was set to enter a new phase (see chapter 1). Now, rather than an explicitly educational project pushing for action for change, increasingly, popular education lent its support to the struggles of the emerging popular movements. In a climate of political radicalisation, with capitalist states seriously under threat, popular education became more conspicuously political than before. For many, it had now transcended the initial, Freire-centred phase, had evolved and diversified its practice, broadened its theoretical, political and ideological understanding and surpassed Freire 'in the field of its political option, compromise and struggle' (Torres, RM, 1988a:43). Despite the exciting developments taking place in Freire's absence, popular education remained thoroughly imbued with his thought. His influence over the principles described in chapter 1 is obvious and few contemporary publications on popular education will have failed to acknowledge his importance. Furthermore, while the understanding of Freire among popular educators was often second-hand and based on his earlier publications, those in a position to follow his evolving educational philosophy saw that the linking of popular education to popular movements was something he fully supported.

There is no doubt that the educational principles elaborated in *Pedagogy of the Oppressed* remain central to discussions on popular education today. In *Pedagogy of Hope*, Freire himself clearly stands by their continuing relevance. While much of his later writing is about clarifying and updating some of his earlier arguments, or addressing some of his critics, in other respects Freire has also made an important contribution to the theorising of popular education in its current phase, where issues of ideological (dis)orientation and the relationship to formal education are being re-considered. Firstly, he argues powerfully that popular education must maintain its politically radical vision (or '*utopía*') and should not succumb to propaganda about the end of history and the irreversible domination of neo-liberal, capitalist economics: 'I am convinced that we have never had a greater need for radical politics ...than we have today' (Freire, 1993: 48). Ironically, in a rare moment óf personal bitterness, he rails against former Marxists who once criticised his lack of reference to 'social classes' but who would now claim that these no longer exist (ibid: 86). When he returned to Brazil, Freire worked in the formal sector and much of his writing addresses the contribution popular education might make within this context. His last book, *Pedagogy of Autonomy*, written in a highly accessible style, is directed at classroom teachers, for example. His work as Secretary of Education in São Paulo from 1989-1991 is an important case-study in the relationship between popular education and the state; it may also give us clues about the potential of popular education to effect social change on a large-scale. These issues are examined in more detail in chapter 8.

Conclusion

Paulo Freire is the most prominent name associated with popular education in Latin America. His principal ideas, published most famously in 1970 in *Pedagogy of the Oppressed*, remain challenging and relevant to a wide range of 'cultural workers' (as Freire called them), including adult educators, professional trainers, political activists, social workers and school-teachers; they address both the 'first' and 'third' worlds (Costigan, 1983), having inspired educationalists and activists in a variety of political, social and economic contexts throughout the globe (Kirkwood, 1989; Arnold et al, 1983 & 1994); they are not restricted to political education but cross all aspects of an educational curriculum, from mathematics to modern languages (Kane, L, 2000), from geology to flower-arranging.

But there is also substance to the many thoughtful critiques of Freire's work, though familiarity with his later writings lays some of them to rest. In many cases, it is possible, dialectically, to be in agreement both with what Freire says and with the criticisms levelled against him. His vagueness on the identity of 'oppressors' and 'oppressed' may weaken his political impact, but it has allowed him to relate to an extremely wide audience; the process of 'decodification' may not guarantee magical results but it remains an important pedagogical tool in the bag of a competent educator; the oppositional nature of 'banking' and 'problem-posing' education may not be as stark as Freire made out but they are important concepts to consider when planning any educational activity;

achieving a balance between teaching a particular skill (such as literacy) and promoting 'conscientisation' may be demanding, but it can inspire some wonderful teaching.

The real danger with Freire is that due to the eclecticism of his educational philosophy – his humanism, Christianity, Marxism, methodological concerns – and the undoubted need to re-invent his ideas for different social contexts, it has proven easy for educators, intentionally or otherwise, to home in on particular aspects of his philosophy at the expense of others. Often this translates into a dilution of his radical political agenda and an over-emphasis on psychological concerns: this is what is happening, I believe, when I hear it said that the problem in the 'first world' is not oppression but 'alienation'; in the worst of scenarios it leads to the deliberate co-option of his methodology for politically conservative ends. Given the variety of interpretations accorded to Freire's work, then, including many which bewildered Freire himself, it has become almost meaningless to talk, in the abstract, of a 'Freirian' approach to education. Claims to be engaged in such an approach require close examination, particularly in relation to their underlying, political philosophy: are they inspired by a radical, liberal or conservative reading of Freire? Equally, unless content to ignore or fudge the issue, practitioners of a 'Freirian approach' need to make their own political understanding of Freire explicit.

While it would appear that Freire can mean all things to all people, a related problem, in counter-weight to his critics, is his regular elevation to guru or cult-like status. As a prominent intellectual widely renowned for his humility, warmth and passion for life, Freire seemed to make an impact on everyone he met. As his fame grew, his modesty, respect for others and constant exhortation to engage critically with his ideas seemed to add even more to his stature. Much of the literature on Freire is of a personal nature, extols his virtues and leaves its critical faculties behind; he has been treated as a popstar (Hall, 1998) and at times would seem to have been idolised by a quasi-religious following (Coben, 1998); perhaps understandably, in the aftermath of his death in 1997, recent writing on Freire has leaned towards the hagiographic. Given the originality and large-scale impact of his contribution to the world of education, Freire does indeed command enormous respect: in view of the variety of groups who claim to follow his teachings, however, and the many problems experienced in putting his ideas into practice, 'cult-status' is something to be avoided.

I believe that a critical engagement with Freire's ideas is of enormous benefit to radical educators and activists throughout the world. Despite his occasional, over-emphasis on the importance of abstract, idealised, humanist values – making it possible for some readers to de-emphasise the political aspect of his work – to his dying day, Freire made it perfectly obvious that he was a man of the left, a socialist who wanted to see revolutionary change and an end to the rule of the market: 'I am hopeful, convinced that the time will arrive when, having overcome its stupefaction at the fall of the Berlin wall, the world will compose itself and attack once again the dictatorship of the market, founded, as it is, on the perverse morality of profit ' (Freire, 1996: 144); he felt that an education which encouraged critical reflection and action – without being manipulative – could make a contribution towards this. In discussing the differing, sometimes distorted interpretations of Freire's ideas, in the final analysis Allman (1998) rightly puts the blame on the point of reception rather than on Freire himself. A political battle is being – needs to be – fought over the true nature of Freire's ideas. I believe it is important to defend the radicalism of Freire's vision against those who seek, wittingly or otherwise, to disguise his revolutionary potential.

Review of Chapter 2

Moacir Gadotti is a professor in the University of São Paulo and Director General of the Paulo Freire Institute of the same city. He was a close friend of Freire. He has written several books which have been translated into many languages, including 'Reading Paulo Freire: His Life and Work' (Gadotti, 1994b) and 'Pedagogy of Praxis: a Dialectical Philosophy of Education' (Gadotti, 1996b), with a preface by Paulo Freire. As yet untranslated into English, his work includes Paulo Freire: uma biobibliografia (Gadotti, 1996) which, with more than 780 pages, is the most complete work available anywhere on Freire.

I have been familiar with Liam Kane's work since we met at the First International Encounter of the Paulo Freire Forum in São Paulo in April, 1998, in commemoration of the first anniversary of Freire's death. I have carefully read the chapter he has written for the Latin America Bureau's book on popular education in Latin America and it gives me great pleasure to engage with him in this 'literary dialogue'. I think it is very opportune that there should be a book written in English about Popular Education, a concept which emerged in Latin America in the second half of the twentieth century and which constitutes, in my view, the region's major contribution to universal thinking on education.

It is absolutely essential that any book about Popular Education includes a section on Freire. Some of the foundations of this paradigm of education are inspired by the original intuitions of this educator. Among those I would highlight are: education as the production, not merely the transmission of knowledge; the defence of an education for freedom, a pre-condition for a democratic society; the rejection of the authoritarianism, manipulation and ideologisation which necessarily emerges when rigid hierarchies are established between the teacher who knows (and who therefore teaches) and the pupil who has to learn (and who therefore studies); the defence of education as a process of dialogue in the rigorous but imaginative search to discover the fundamental *raison d'être* of things; the idea that science should openly address the needs of the popular sector and that public planning should involve community participation.

Liam Kane's chapter captures these intuitions in his account of the philosophy, the method and the practice of Freire. He quite properly opened with a brief biography, inseparable from Freire's work, showing that his thought is profoundly existential. He was true to the facts, even when speaking of the method. I would only add a brief comment on a point which is still seldom mentioned when the 'Paulo Freire Method' is discussed.

Freire did not consider himself the inventor of a method or a system of teaching. He considered himself an educator who was proud to be a teacher. With regard to what nevertheless became known as the 'Paulo Freire Method', he undoubtedly made an enormous contribution, as early as the 40s and 50s. When many adult educators were using the same methods as those applied to children, he developed a method specifically for use in the education of adults. This was a new contribution which the so-called 'Paulo Freire Method' made to pedagogy in general, the beginnings of what later was referred to as 'andragogy'. For that reason, some of its interpreters called it the 'psycho-social method of adult education'.

Later on Paulo Freire debated the subject with various popular educators in Latin America. Among these were Carlos Rodrigues Brandão, Carlos Alberto Torres, Celso de Rui Beisiegel, Rosa Maria Torres and Osmar Fávero, who all wrote on the same theme. When he was leader of the Secretariat of Education in the Municipality of São Paulo (1989-1991), in discussion with the leaders of MOVA-SP (the Literacy Movement for Young People and Adults in the City of São Paulo) he made reference to this method, affirming that his principles remained valid but that new techniques had arisen in the field of literacy teaching and that these had rendered obsolete the 'syllabilisation' which he had used in the 60s. Some members of the MOVA-SP team still maintained that constructivism did not make the technique of syllablisation obsolete and that it was perfectly possible, in practice, to successfully combine it with other techniques. However, it is important to recognise that new research in the field of the psychogenesis of language (and writing) points towards the need to work with the learner with whole concepts, in context, not with fragments of words as in syllablisation. When children learn to speak they learn the whole word, not part of it. At the very least, the syllabalisation used in the 60s was limited. The whole text and the context has to be considered, not just isolated words.

Even at that, the 'generative word' and 'generative theme' can still be used as a motto, a starting point for discussion. Adult literacy today deals more with what we in the Paulo Freire Institute call the 'generative context'. Paulo Freire can be considered a constructivist. But a critical constructivist.

I agree both with the critique of Freire's thought which Liam Kane elaborates in his text as well as his conclusion that 'Paulo Freire is the most prominent name associated with Popular Education in Latin America'. On that I would add that the future of Freire's thought is intimately linked to the future of Popular Education in general.

It is more than 30 years since *Pedagogy of the Oppressed* was written. Heavily influenced by this work, Popular Education continues to be a great point of reference for Latin American education. It is a theoretical framework which continues to inspire a number of experiences, no longer only in Latin America but also in the world; not only in the countries of the Third World but also in technologically advanced countries and in very different social contexts.

Popular education is a movement to which Paulo Freire belonged and to which he made an enormous contribution. Popular education has passed through various stages. It is a dynamic movement nourished by an immense mosaic of innumerable visions. Not all these visions identify themselves with the thought of Paulo Freire but from the warrior-like optimism of the literacy campaign in Nicaragua, to non-formal community schools and to state education itself, all make allusion to the theoretical paradigm he developed. There is no doubt that Freire's work has to continue developing in many – and perhaps sometimes irreconcilable – directions. He will be unable to control this and cannot be held responsible for what happens, just as Marx is not responsible for the different Marxisms or for all that is done in his name. And the critiques, positive and negative, must also continue.

I would conclude by thanking the Latin America Bureau for its invitation to contribute this review and by saying that for me the strength of Freire's work lies not so much in his theory of knowledge as in his having insisted on the idea that it is possible, necessary and urgent to change the direction of things. He did not convince so many people in so many parts of the world through his theories and practice alone but also because he stirred in them the capacity to dream of a reality which would be much more human, less ugly and more just. He was a sort of guardian of utopias. That was his legacy, not only for a few institutions or 'followers' but for all those who remain hopeful of a better world.

São Paulo, May 2nd 2000
Third year from the death of Freire.
Moacir Gadotti

Chapter 3
The Methodology of Popular Education

Popular education in Latin America is commonly identified with a particular way of 'doing' education, where instead of passively listening to lectures or speeches (Freire's concept of 'banking' education), learners take part in a range of activities designed to make learning 'dialogical', engaging in collective discussion, debate and analysis of their own particular reality. For the educator, the practical teaching ideas and activities enabling this process to take place are commonly known as 'participative techniques'. Developed in the seventies and eighties, they were an important contribution to the practice of popular education, flesh on the bones of the methodological principles outlined by Freire. Aside from their educational value, these technique-activities can be fun to do and have inspired many educators throughout the world in their attempts to make education a more interesting experience for learners (see also Arnold & Burke, 1983). It sometimes appears, in fact – though mistakenly – as if 'popular education' and 'participative techniques' are synonymous.

Two preliminary cautions are helpful in any discussion of popular education methodology. Firstly, though the two are often confused, 'methodology' and 'techniques' are different concepts. A methodology is a set of principles on how to organise an educational experience; a technique is an exercise used at a particular moment in time to put these principles into practice. Secondly, popular education cannot be reduced to a collection of techniques: the purpose to which they are put, not the techniques themselves, indicates whether or not popular education is being practised.

This chapter explains some of the better-known techniques and considers their importance to popular education; it examines the concept of methodology promoted by the Central American network Alforja and describes the content of a 'school of methodology' for popular educators in Mexico; it makes reference to a range of popular education materials (slide-tapes, board-games and so on) and discusses the role of the educator. Where appropriate, the relevance of the methodology to the UK is also considered.

Participative Techniques

Participative techniques are used by popular educators in a 'workshop' situation to encourage people to think, speak and take action for change. They include discussion activities, problem-posing exercises, role-plays, drama, board and simulation games, artwork and allegorical analysis. In their two-volume classic *Participatory Techniques for Popular Education*, Bustillos and Vargas (1993) classify their examples under the headings of (a) warm-up activities (b) techniques of general analysis (c) exercises in abstraction (d) communication exercises (e) organisational and planning activities (f) techniques for structural analysis (g) techniques for economic analysis (h) techniques for political analysis and (i) techniques for ideological analysis. However, many techniques are flexible and can be used at different stages, and for different purposes, in the educational process. Here is a sample:

Warm-up Activities
Lifeboats
- Participants are standing. The co-ordinator explains that all are on a boat which, having just hit an iceberg, is rapidly sinking.
- To save themselves, they must get into a lifeboat: however, the ship's lifeboats only hold 4-6 people (the co-ordinator keeps changing the number).
- Participants have a few seconds to run around, grab people and form a group of the appropriate number. Those who are left out 'drown'; the game can be played until there is only one group of survivors.
  Variation:
- The co-ordinator tells people to organise themselves into lifeboats of four people according to the kind of music they like, work they do, hobbies they have, place they live, organisation they belong to etc.
- Participants run around asking each other questions, trying to find a kindred group to occupy a boat.

- If appropriate, those who end up without a lifeboat can argue that they, rather than someone else, have a better case for entry into a particular boat.
- Each group discusses their common interest for a few minutes.
- This is repeated three or four times.

The Mail

- Chairs are arranged in a circle. There is one chair less than the number of participants.
- Everyone sits down and the person who has no chair (in the first instance, the co-ordinator) becomes the post(wo)man and stands in the middle.
- The post(wo)man says 'I have a letter for all those who have a moustache, are wearing black shoes, have drunk coffee today, came here by bus etc'.
- Those who come into these categories get up and change seats (as does the post(wo)man). Because there is one seat short, a scramble ensues.
- The person failing to find a chair becomes the new post(wo)man and chooses the next category to call.
Variation:
- There is the same number of seats as participants.
- The co-ordinator chooses all the categories according to what he or she thinks might be useful to learn about members of the group e.g. 'I have a letter for all those who had to walk here today, come from villages which don't have water, have been in the organisation less than three months etc'
- As before, people coming into the various categories change seats. This time, however, they spend a minute or two discussing with a partner various aspects of the issue just raised: why doesn't your village have water, has it always been like that, do you think it might change etc?
- This is repeated using different categories.

Comment: these would probably be called 'ice-breakers' in the UK though it is a term I personally avoid in the west of Scotland as they are regarded by many with distrust, seen variously as a complete waste of time, emotionally manipulative or too 'touchy-feely' for our traditional, calvinistic culture. They do perform an important function, I believe, in enabling people to relax and talk to each other, but they work better here when they serve an educational purpose at the same time. This appears less of a problem in Latin America, where the fun element is seen as an important counterweight to the hard work of serious education. It is not uncommon in the middle of a serious workshop to take a ten-minute break and 'dance salsa', for example, just to recharge the batteries. A stunt like that in Glasgow could seriously damage your health!

In their varied formats, however, these activities do serve a practical purpose in addition to providing fun. The anarchy of 'Lifeboats' works well with large groups gathering for the first time – I have used it with over eighty participants – and everyone makes several new acquaintances in record time. When the co-ordinator asks each group to explain their common interest, it provides a quick, visual way of finding out something about almost everyone in the room. 'The Mail' also provides useful preliminary information about any group: in different contexts I have used it to find out who has been to Latin America, read class handouts on popular education or taken part in a political demonstration, for example. 'Eavesdropping' on the paired discussions takes this a step further and means that educators have something to relate to when they begin to speak.

Statues (or 'Sculpting')

The technique of building human statues allows a group to analyse, visually, their collective understanding of abstract themes like democracy, justice, trade unionism, bureaucracy, education and so on. It can be used at the beginning of an educational process, to find out people's initial perception of a particular issue; in the middle, to explore a particular aspect in depth; or at the end, to clarify what has been understood after a period of study. It can also be used to envisage how, ideally, people would like things to be and the changes they would like to see being made.

- Once the theme has been selected, the co-ordinator asks for a volunteer 'sculptor'.
- Using the other people present (and improvising with props such as chairs, tables, cardboard and anything else to hand), the sculptor builds a statue which represents his/her understanding of the theme being explored.
- The sculptor is in charge and the others are obedient, malleable material. They have to sit, stand, pose and change facial expressions according to the sculptor's instructions.
- When the statue is completed, the sculptor explains (or 'decodes', in Freirian terminology) what it stands for.
- The co-ordinator then asks if everyone agrees with the sculptor's representation. Does anyone else want to be the sculptor and make any changes, add something or knock the statue down and build a new one from scratch?
- People take turns at being the sculptor, changing the statue and explaining its new meaning. The co-ordinator ensures that the discussion stays focused on the statue, and does not wander into abstract theorising and speech making.

- An attempt is made to work towards a statue which captures an agreed, collective understanding of the theme under discussion (though it does not matter if this is achieved).
- The length of the exercise depends on the importance of the discussion taking place (but better too short than too long): participants should be advised as to when there are only five minutes left.
- It can be useful to photograph the statue(s) for further discussion at a later date.

Comment: This is a wonderful exercise. It is easy to organise, requires little preparation and often produces spectacular results. As they comment on a specific, concrete action – rather than giving an abstract speech – less confident speakers can find it easier to express their views in public. Sometimes, even, it humbles the eloquent who normally like to hold court! The physical movement keeps learners awake (an important consideration, after a hard day's work); it provides a common focus for discussion and discourages irrelevant rambling; by requiring people to think visually, it can stimulate new, creative thinking. The visual aspect is an aid to memory: people remember the shape of statues when speeches are long forgotten. Last but not least, it can be great fun to do, providing many laughs between discussions, as the sculptor forces people into a variety of different, unusual poses.

I have used it extensively in Scotland, in a variety of settings, from a public meeting, analysing the poll-tax, to a post-graduate class in education, summarising the main ideas of Freire's *Pedagogy of the Oppressed*. Though ideally it is better for someone in the group to start off – so that the starting point is the learners', not the educator's knowledge – if the exercise is not familiar I think it is easier for the co-ordinator to begin with a demonstration.

Poster Exercise

The objective is for small groups to produce a graphic, symbolic representation of their views on a particular theme and present this to a larger group for discussion and analysis. It can deal with a wide range of themes, abstract and concrete, from politics and religion to propaganda and soap opera. In the training of popular educators, it is commonly used to analyse the political-social context in which popular organisations are working.

- In small groups, participants 'brainstorm' and discuss their understanding of the theme being explored. Someone notes the main ideas on paper.
- They then discuss how to represent their ideas symbolically, in a drawing. Rough sketches are made to accompany the discussion. When a final graphic is agreed, this is made into a poster.

Maria Cruz Cortés explains the significance of the 'social tree' produced by the inhabitants of San Luís, near San Salvador, as they analysed their economic situation. The tree represents the community, the roots the crops which feed them, the animals below are even more important and the cards around the branches give details of community income and expenditure. It is part of a REFLECT project carried out by the Salvadorean agency PRODECOSAL in which literacy skills are taught side by side with social analysis. Photographer: Liam Kane

- The small groups come together, presenting their poster in turns to the larger group.
- The group presenting the poster keeps quiet while the co-ordinator invites everyone else to (a) describe (b) interpret what they see in the poster.
- The group who produced the poster then give their own explanation to the larger group.

Comment: another wonderful exercise. The task of producing a symbolic representation gives focus to the discussion and helps clarify ideas. I always enjoy the moment when the large group describes and interprets the different posters. They often see things not intended by the original artists, thus making explicit the large group's own ideas, some of which may not have surfaced without this external stimulus. As well as the serious element, it can provide moments of hilarity, especially if the standard of drawing is poor (something which in no way detracts from the exercise) and interpretations are far off the mark. Like 'statues', the posters are visually memorable; they can be brought out at a later date and usefully copied onto A4 paper, with an accompanying, explanatory paragraph, if the event is being documented. The exchange of interpretations between small and large groups provoke deeper discussions: it is an imaginative, entertaining way to provoke meaningful, group discussion.

Sociodramas

Sociodramas are short drama sketches which problematise unresolved conflicts taken from the concrete, real-life experience of the learners. They allow people to reconstruct this experience, analyse it from a distance and consider options for change. Again, it can deal with a wide range of themes or topics, from the abstract to the specific, such as the conditions of health, housing or poverty in a particular community.

- Participants divide into groups (4-8 people) to discuss the problems they have experienced (or witnessed) relating to the theme being explored.
- They then select one or more of these which they think are (a) generally representative of the group's experience (b) suitable to re-enact in front of others (albeit artistic license is permitted).
- They decide on (a) the brief story-line (b) the physical layout of the room so that it resembles the appropriate location (c) who will play what character in the sketch (c) the kind of dialogue in which the characters engage.
- After some rehearsals, they act out the sociodrama in front of the larger group.
- As before, the co-ordinator stimulates wider discussion in two stages, firstly inviting people to *describe* what they see happening in the sociodrama and then to *interpret* what it is meant to reveal.
- Having heard the audience's views, the 'actors' then explain what it was all about and the whole group engages in further discussion and analysis.

Variation:
- Groups are instructed to ensure that sociodramas present problems for which they have found no easy solution.
- Once a sociodrama has been performed and analysed, it is acted out once more, only this time the audience can stop it at any point, replace the characters, improvise changes to the dialogue/storyline and try and push the sociodrama towards a different conclusion, forcing everyone to consider possible actions for change.

Comment: the way people interpret different characters (doctors, workers, peasants or even educators) can sometimes reveal, non-verbally, points of view not normally expressed in discussion. They can make people see everyday events in a different light, as participants can be oblivious to issues which are obvious to an observer (when a group of community activists in Easterhouse, Glasgow,

Theatre of the Third Age perform their play about discrimination facing older people. In this scene a teenager refuses to give up the reserved seat for an elderly gent.
Photographer: Morven Gregor

performed a sociodrama to illustrate their practice, it became clear, for the first time, that their organisational procedures were a mess). Like 'statues' and 'posters', they can be fun to do, are visually memorable and can allow people to express themselves in a different way. The danger with sociodrama is that if not done properly, its content can be trivial or it can be so funny (as people laugh at their friends' acting) that it detracts from the serious business in hand. Practise makes perfect, however, and it can be well worth the effort.

The Work of Augusto Boal

Sociodramas are an off-shoot of the work of Augusto Boal, a Brazilian dramatist who was strongly influenced by Paulo Freire and invented a new and exciting approach to theatre and drama. His theories and case studies of their application are described in his first book, *Theatre of the Oppressed*. His subsequent *Games for Actors and Non-Actors* provides a host of examples and tips for popular educators on how to put his ideas into practice: it is impossible to read it and not be inspired!

Boal began as an activist who sought to use theatre as a form of political struggle. He then toured Latin America, writing and performing plays which explained the political causes of poverty to grassroots communities and suggested what they should do about it. When groups attempted to follow his suggestions, achieving nothing and sometimes putting themselves in danger, he learned that he had no right to instruct others in what to do as he himself was not part of, and could not fully comprehend, their particular social reality. Instead, he developed the idea of using theatre as a forum for helping others explore issues and consider for themselves potential actions for change.

A la Freire, Boal and his team of actors would try and discover the 'generative themes' prevalent in any particular community and then write short plays which would end, not with suggested solutions, but by posing problems to be solved. The actors would perform a play in public and a co-ordinator/popular educator (whom Boal calls the 'joker') would explain to the audience that the play would be enacted again only this time spectators could stop it at any point, dispute its realism or validity, come on as actors themselves and try to push the play in a different direction. For Boal, the theatre is a mirror in which the audience see the reflection of their own reality, spectators become *spect-actors* and the play provides a forum for discussion – indeed Boal calls it *Forum Theatre* – and an opportunity to 'rehearse' different forms of struggle. In the everyday practice of popular education, sociodramas constitute an amateurish form of Boal's 'forum theatre'.

He also developed the notion of 'invisible theatre', where, in real life (on a train, in a shop, on the street, for example), as opposed to on a stage, a group of actors perform a scene deliberately designed to provoke public debate. Boal (1992: 14-17) describes an example of invisible theatre he tried out in Europe, with a group campaigning for safer streets in Stockholm, Sweden. Four actors set up a table in the middle of a busy street, preventing cars from passing, and sat down to breakfast. The first cars to arrive were 'plants' and the driver-actors got out to ask what was going on; when the campaigner-actors explained that they had as much right to the streets as cars, the driver-actors started to debate this, some sympathising with the campaigners and some shouting at them to get out of the way. Meanwhile 'real' drivers started to arrive. They too left their cars and on hearing the debate (which they believed to be genuine) started to join in. Lookouts whisked campaigners away before the arrival of police; the 'real' people had taken part in an event-cum-debate likely to keep them thinking for some time. In invisible theatre, real life and theatre become interchangeable.

Boal went on to work with mental health patients, an experience recorded in *Rainbow of Desire*. In 1992, in the local legislative elections in Rio de Janeiro, he and his team offered to run forum theatre to support the Workers' Party's campaign. For publicity – and against his will – it was decided to put Boal forward as a candidate. To his amazement he was elected into office and his drama group became his cabinet. Working within and pushing against all the constraints of local government, he attempted to use forum theatre to engage deprived communities in the design of local laws. This experience is documented in his latest book, *Legislative Theatre*.

Under the guidance of Augusto Boal's Centre of the Theatre of the Oppressed, a group of young people perform their play about police harassment. In this scene, the woman, a member of the audience, tries to convince the police of her rights.
Photographer: Morven Gregor

A Critical Look at Techniques and Methodology

Participative techniques have been a central feature of popular education in Latin America but they should not be confused *per se* with popular education.

Firstly, not unlike the co-option of Freire's methods, participative techniques can be used for a variety of different purposes. The United States Central Intelligence Agency (CIA), no less, once tried to order up two thousand copies of Bustillos and Vargas (1993) *Participatory Techniques for Popular Education* (Kane, 1995). To find out whether popular education, or something entirely different, is being practised, we have to look to the aims and objectives of the wider educational programme in which the techniques are being used, a point made emphatically by the authors in the warning they give to readers at the start of their book:

'On its own, the use of Participatory Techniques for Popular Education gives no guarantee whatsoever that popular education is actually being practised.

Generally, techniques are for enabling people to participate, getting them in the mood, helping them lose inhibitions or organising them into a group; or for simplifying or making more comprehensible the content or themes being examined etc.

The techniques in this book also serve these purposes (depending on their form and content) but above all they should be used as TOOLS WITHIN A PROCESS WHICH HELPS TO STRENGTHEN POPULAR CONSCIENTISATION AND ORGANISATION. Lacking a clear understanding of this point, many groups and institutions use the techniques without contributing towards this objective. More seriously, there are some groups who use them precisely to go against this objective, disguising their intentions with pseudoparticipation.

What about you? How do you intend to use these techniques and for what purpose?'

(Bustillos and Vargas, 1993: 1)

Secondly, even within a genuine programme of popular education, techniques are simply a set of 'pedagogical tools' in the bag of the popular educator. If the wrong tool is selected for the wrong job, or at the wrong time, then the learning experience will suffer. If a particular technique proves enjoyable to enact, for example, but fails to stimulate serious learning, it can trivialise the whole concept of popular education (unless, at a particular moment, 'enjoyment' is seen as the principle, legitimate aim, such as to help people unwind or to develop group dynamics). Gutiérrez Pérez & Castillo (1994) clearly believe that popular education has often been little more than the indiscriminate application of these techniques by poorly trained educators. As tools of the trade, then, participatory techniques are only as good as the people doing the job and they should not be invested with a power they do not possess. Thirdly, it would be a caricature to portray popular education as a permanent process of animated dialogue, physical movement and exciting, drama-related activities. Within a dialogical approach to education, at a particular moment in time it could be entirely appropriate to study and discuss a passage from a book, for example, or invite someone to explain, without interruption, their understanding of a particular theme. Even something as traditional as a 'lecture', could still have its place, the difference being that a speaker is not considered the bearer of undisputed truth but a stimulus for deeper discussion and reflection. The methodology of popular education should not be rigid or formulaic but something requiring constant reinvention in practice.

The problem is that though the two are often confused, 'methodology' and 'techniques' are conceptually quite distinct. A methodology is a set of principles which guide educational practice; techniques are tools which (may) help implement these principles in a particular context. Concerned by the confusion, a number of popular education centres work hard to promote a deeper understanding of methodology among educators and activists.

BOX 3:1
Participatory Rural Appraisal (PRA)

Among many branches of participatory methodology, PRA is fast gaining popularity in development work throughout the globe. It encourages groups to analyse their economic and social world while simultaneously creating visual representations of their collective discussions. It developed as a method for helping illiterate rural communities communicate their needs and concerns to (and challenge the perceptions of) development officials. Robert Chambers (1993), the key figure in PRA, acknowledges its debt to Freire and there are clear overlaps with the methodology discussed in this chapter. These visuals might include:

- 'maps showing who lives where and the location of important local features and resources such as water, forests, schools and other services
- flow diagrams to indicate linkages, sequences, causes, effects, problems and solutions
- seasonal calendars showing how food availability, workloads, family health, prices, wages and other factors vary during the year
- matrices or grids, scored with seeds, pebbles or other counters, to compare things – such as the merits of different crop varieties or tree species, or how conditions have changed over time' (IDS, 1996:1).

But they are subject to the same limitations and abuse as other 'participatory techniques'. In fact, much of the discourse of PRA is directed at official policy makers – including institutions like the World Bank (ibid) – and it generally lacks an overt political analysis. On the other hand, its techniques can also be used towards more radical ends; imaginatively, the REFLECT programme (Box 2:1) finds them a useful springboard for teaching skills of literacy and numeracy within a popular education framework.

Case Study: Alforja and 'Schools of Methodology' in Central America and Mexico

(In this section, some of the terminology of popular education is translated literally and may sound strange. See glossary – and the conclusion to the section – for further discussion)

Alforja is a well-known popular education network in Latin America and brings together seven centres, one each from Mexico, Nicaragua, Costa Rica, Honduras, El Salvador, Guatemala and Panama in a joint attempt to share and learn from each other's experience. An important collaboration has been the running of 'schools of methodology' throughout the region, offering training in popular education to the activists of grassroots organisations. From this experience they developed a theoretical-methodological construct known as the 'Conception of a Dialectical Methodology' (the CDM). The CDM is, essentially, a philosophy-cum-modus-operandi for understanding reality and acting to change it, an attempt to put a name on a particular way of approaching all aspects of transformatory practice, of which popular education is one. It grew out of the need to overcome what Alforja experienced as 'the reductionism, to the merely pedagogical, which existed with regard to the question of methodology' (Antillón & Orozco, 1992: 57). This section firstly considers what is meant by 'dialectical thinking', examines what Antillón (1994) calls 'the essential elements of the CDM' and goes on to look at the general content of Alforja's programme for training popular educators in Central America.

Dialectical Thinking

The word 'dialectical' appears frequently in the jargon of popular education in Latin America (see Gadotti, 1997). It has been suggested by no lesser figures than Carlos Alberto Torres (Torres, 1996: 119), an Argentinian academic working in California, and Paulo Freire himself (Freire, 1993: 70-74), that 'dialectical thinking' is a concept alien to English-speaking cultures which are dominated by positivistic explanations of society. Though it is a sweeping generalisation, I suspect it contains some truth: it would be useful, then, to consider the meaning of 'dialectics' (or 'the dialectic') before going on to examine the 'Conception of a Dialectical Methodology'.

In the time of the early Greeks, 'dialectic' referred to a form of Socratic argument used to pursue philosophical truth. Advocates of competing views would debate and defend their respective understanding of a particular proposition. Debate and discussion was meant to eliminate intellectual weakness so that the best arguments on both sides of the proposition would prevail, progressively approximating participants (and observers) towards the truth.

In the early nineteenth century, the German philosopher Freidrich Hegel took up this notion of the dialectic and in an attempt to explain the historical evolution of ideas turned it into a major philosophical system. He argued that any particular philosophy or set of ideas (a *thesis*) automatically provokes a contradictory set of ideas (an *anti-thesis*). When thesis and antithesis confront each other, the strongest arguments of both sides prevail, coming together to form a new set of ideas (a *synthesis*): an example would be the belief that when the ideas of Christianity encountered those of Marxism they synthesised into Liberation Theology. This synthesis (in this case Liberation Theology) then becomes, in its own right, a new thesis. It produces its own antithesis and synthesis which, in turn, becomes another new thesis: the process is constant and seen as the driving force behind the development of ideas throughout history.

With the assistance of Engels, Marx is credited with having taken Hegel's concept of the dialectic and stood it on its head, arguing that while the resolution of conflict was indeed at the heart of historical development, the principle contradictions were to be found in the real, material world rather than at the level of ideas. In this concept of 'historical materialism', these contradictions are most important in the economic sphere where the clashes between different modes of production (feudalism versus capitalism, for example) and the interests of different social classes (such as capitalists versus workers) constitute the 'history of all hitherto existing society' (Marx & Engels, 1996: 3).

In a different sense, the word 'dialectic' is also used to describe a general philosophical position within Marxism. Whereas for Hegel, the 'idealist', ideas were responsible for shaping the world, Marx saw it the other way round, that real experience and the material conditions of existence, as opposed to abstract philosophising, were the generator of ideas. Ideas change in accordance with the developing economic, political and social reality from which they first spring: feudalism, the various stages of capitalism, revolutionary upheavals, for example, all stimulate different ways of thinking (thus, to explain the emergence of Liberation Theology, instead of seeing it as the product of purely intellectual debate, Marxists would look more to developments in the material world: that Christianity spread through Latin America through a military-political conquest, that economic crises in the 1950s and 60s sparked a search for new ideas, that the Cuban revolution of 1959 inspired a radicalism to which the Church had to respond, that political repression meant the Church was sometimes the safest place to organise resistance and so on). Equally, within any one social system, different material realities give rise to different sets of ideas: while the prevailing ideas correspond to the interests of the dominant classes, the different ways in which, for example, peasants, workers or capitalists experience the world affects how and what they think of it. At its crudest, the primacy of 'materialism' over 'idealism' means that unlike those who are comfortably off, peasants or workers constantly engaged in a struggle for survival have no time to read, write and consciously develop their thinking. Marx did not see the relationship between the material world and ideas as deterministic (unlike some of his followers) but dialectically inter-related, albeit with the material world as the dominant partner. Ideas spring from the material world, then, but they also come back, in their turn, to re-shape it. This philosophical understanding of the interplay, the 'dialectical' relationship, between ideas and the material world is what later Marxists came to call 'dialectical materialism' (Bottomore, 1988: 120-121).

Rees (1998: 3-10) argues that there are four fundamental principles involved in dialectical understanding (though the focus here is social reality, it is also possible to think dialectically about an organisation, the natural world, personal development, the human body and so on). The first is 'totality': nothing happens in isolation from anything else. A mud-slide which kills people in Colombia, for example, is connected to the wider world in a million different ways. Poverty forces people to live in vulnerable areas; local and international exploitation perpetuates poverty; exploitation is institutionalised through legal systems, political and cultural domination, the sale of weapons and the international division of labour; relief efforts use machines which, constructed from raw materials extracted from the earth by labour, have been researched, designed and built by people who firstly had to be taught a particular set of skills. The second is 'mediation'. This means that not only is everything in society inter-connected, each constituent part has an effect on, or mediates, every other. In the former Yugoslavia, for example, economic changes (IMF-induced debt) led to political changes (politicians were encouraged to seek regional autonomy); together these exacerbated cultural tensions which, in turn, had political consequences (to develop their power base, people like Slobodan Milosovic promoted inter-ethnic rivalries); this then affected military decisions (leading to ethnic cleansing) which had further economic and cultural repercussions (making things more difficult for the many organisations campaigning for a multi-ethnic society) not to mention the military consequences of NATO bombings and refugee crises. So political, economic, cultural, military, personal factors and so on – not only are they inter-connected, they each transform or 'mediate', each of the others. Illustrating this point, a common analogy in popular education is to think of reality as a piece of music played over a hi-fi system, with the dialectical relationship of its component parts captured in the image of a 'graphics equaliser': one dial might represent the influence of politics, while another represents economic, historical or cultural influences or the strength of the popular movement. Discussion of the synthesised 'music' revolves around how high each dial is turned up and which dials need to be 'tuned', in which direction, to improve the final symphony (Nuñez, 1993:55-56).

The third is 'change': never static, society exists in a constant process of evolution. The past has a 'mediating' effect on the present; the present struggles to become something else. Everything changes so quickly, claimed Heraclitus, an early Greek dialectician, that it is impossible to bathe twice in the same river: the second time the river will be different and we too will have changed (Gadotti, 1997: 16). As soon as we analyse the dynamics of society, then, things are already changing, and each change is having a mediating effect on the others. The fourth, the driving force behind change, is the principle of 'contradiction', already discussed with reference to Hegel and Marx. The constant struggle or tension between opposite and contradictory forces, whether within the material world (such as different economic classes), the world of 'ideas' (different political ideologies) or between the 'ideal' and 'material' worlds themselves (theory and practice, reflection and action) pushes everything forward.

Dialectical thinking, then, is both a theory of how knowledge is acquired (an epistemology) and a philosophical-research method for understanding the world. It differs most obviously from other philosophical interpretations – whether rationalist, empiricist or mystical – in that contradiction is not considered an aberration but an essential ingredient of development.

The Conception of a Dialectical Methodology (the CDM)

Based on the principles of 'dialectical thinking', the 'Conception of a Dialectical Methodology' (CDM) is a theoretical-methodological construct for approaching all aspect of grassroots work for change, though in the case of Alforja its main application has been to the area of popular education: 'participatory techniques' make their contribution only within this broader framework.

Broken into its constituent parts, the *conception* refers to the appropriation by educator-activists of the philosophy and principles of popular education described in the previous chapters. This requires a political commitment and an organic link with the popular movement.

Educator-activists are encouraged to think *dialectically*, to reflect on the interplay between different – and, indeed, conflicting – social forces at any moment in time. This is considered helpful to educators in at least three important areas. The first is the relationship between theory and practice, since it is argued that 'social practice is the source, test and ultimate end of the process of knowing, the principle which renders invalid all action emanating from preconceived, abstract theories: the application of such theories to reality merely becomes mechanical and laboured' (Antillón, 1994: 226). In other words, when working with popular organisations, activist-educators should not set out with pre-planned programmes of what groups ought to do. They should find out what is already being done and start their analysis from there. This is a dialectic between action and reflection. The second area is to see social change as a dynamic process in which the actions and practice of social subjects interact with the context – the history, time and place – of which they are part. Groups are thus encouraged to analyse their context closely, including its historical development, for a better understanding of what type of action to take. The third is to see reality as a single, total entity, albeit with multiple, complex and contradictory dimensions. Human relationships take place in many contexts (at work, home, church, in struggle and so on) and it is possible to be, for example, a progressive in one context (a popular organisation, say) and an authoritarian figure in another (a *macho* husband at home). In practice, for a better understanding of social reality, educators should encourage groups to bring to the surface, not conceal, its complexities and contradictions.

A dialectical '*methodology*' seeks to enable educator-activists to operate in a manner consistent with these principles in all aspects of their work with popular organisations. Firstly, this means 'theorising from practice'. The 'project of liberation' should be developed from the particular social practice of the organisation, something which is expressed through its routine, political, economic, ideological and cultural activities as well as the inter-personal relationships of its members. This requires an on-going examination of the interplay between the three different elements of (a) what the organisation thinks it is doing (its *conception* of its practice) (b) what the organisation actually does do (its *practice*) and (c) the circumstances in which it is operating (the *context* of its practice). Secondly, in aspiring to an 'internal consistency' with these principles, educators need to conduct themselves in a manner which promotes democracy and participation: a project cannot work for liberation if key activists reinforce values produced by the system of oppression. Accordingly, workers should develop appropriate, non-authoritarian styles of leadership and know how to encourage and enable people to participate and share responsibility in the organisation's activities; for occasions given over to deeper reflection and analysis ('workshops'), they should become competent in the use of a wide range of pedagogical tools including 'participatory techniques'. Thirdly, unlike the functionalist practice of those who parcel up reality into professional specialisms, whatever the thematic focus of a particular organisation, activist-educators should encourage people to explore all its aspects – cultural, political, economic – and consider how their own particular concerns link with those of other 'oppressed' people in a wider, integrated reality.

In summary, the CDM 'gives life to the organisational process, generating a style of working, a vision of the world and the appropriation of new values and theoretical knowledge which are then expressed in a new way of being. The CDM applies globally to all processes of social transformation and is not restricted to strictly educational events' (Jara,1989:58).

A Training Course for Popular Educators:
IMDEC's 'School of Methodology' in Mexico

But how does this 'conception of a dialectical methodology' work out in practice? The school of methodology in Mexico run by the Mexican Institute of Community Development (IMDEC), one of the centres affiliated to Alforja, brings together a group of 30-40 activists from a variety of popular organisations around the country. In the course of a year, at three-month intervals, these activists participate in four training workshops, each workshop lasting a week. The design of the programme emphasises the dialectical relationship between theory and practice. The first workshop concentrates on 'Practice'; the second on 'Theory'; the third on 'In-depth Analysis'; and the fourth on 'Back-to-Practice'. The training aims to provide experiential learning for activist-educators; having themselves experienced the CDM in action, they should be better placed to bring it back and adapt it to the needs of their respective organisations. The following sections describe the main components of this extended course in popular education methodology: they are based mainly on the detailed documentation – the 'memories' – of the workshops run in 1995 which, with some adaptations (which I will leave the reviewer of this chapter to point out), is the general format still being used today.

Workshop 1: Starting from Practice: the 'Triple Self-Diagnosis'
True to the principles of starting and theorising from practice, the aim of the first workshop is to help groups explore beneath the surface and take an objective look at their practice. To this end, IMDEC has developed the 'Triple Self-Diagnosis', an extended exercise for examining the three dimensions of practice previously mentioned: concept, context and actual practice. It takes the following format:

CONCEPTION (of practice): firstly, the aim is to find out what people in any particular group/organisation *think* they are trying to do. The particular technique used to do this is normally a 'brainstorm with post-its'.
- Each participant receives 3 or 4 post-its
- They take a few minutes to think of the 3 or 4 main things they are trying to achieve (their objectives) in the organisation (or in their particular role in the organisation)
- They write these down on post-its, a separate post-it for each objective.
- Participants are organised into groups of 4 – 5. All post-its are laid out on the floor (some 16 to 20 per group) and the group spends a few minutes reading them.
- Groups then have to discuss all the objectives/post-its and see if they can group them into different categories or classifications
- On a large, blank poster groups draw a column for every category they decide on. They write the title of the category at the top of the column and place all the corresponding post-its below it
- Each group's poster, showing all the objectives and their classification, is put on the wall.
- All participants take time to walk round the room and see what each group has produced.

- The co-ordinator asks questions to encourage critical analysis: how do the objectives and their categorisation compare between groups? If they are different, why is that so? Are there any inconsistencies? Do some objectives conflict with others?
- If appropriate, the posters can be kept and written up for future reference.

At the stage of classification, it is the discussion which matters rather than the final outcome: there are no right or wrong answers. In thinking through possible categorisations for the objectives, discussions move from the concrete to the abstract, from practice to theory. The co-ordinator should not provide a set of ready-made categories beforehand: at this early investigative stage, the less the co-ordinators interfere the clearer an idea is obtained of the groups' own perceptions of what they are trying to do. When the exercise is finished, the collective view of what the group *thinks* it is trying to do, inconsistencies and all, is there, objectified, for everyone to see. (If the organisation has a written constitution or stated aims and objectives, it is important that these are not to hand. The list of objectives should not be pre-meditated but come from the heart).

CONTEXT of practice: participants now describe the social context in which they are trying to intervene. In groups of 4 or 5, according to similarity of role within an organisation, they 'brainstorm' what they see as the main elements of this context. The co-ordinator explains that these elements could be political, economic, cultural, organisational – anything and everything they see as important (though it is better to avoid giving examples as these may guide people to think in a particular way). Groups then follow the 'poster exercise' explained earlier and present their synthesised vision of the context for the larger group to de-code.

The small groups often interpret the context in different ways, some emphasising the local, others the regional, national or even international. The co-ordinator again asks questions to provoke deeper analysis: why are there different interpretations? Are they complimentary or contradictory? Would any group want to make changes, having listened to different interpretations? The posters can be photographed or copied onto smaller paper for future reference.

ACTUAL PRACTICE: again working in small groups, participants note down what they actually do in the organisation and how they go about doing it. This is then synthesised into a 'sociodrama' and presented to the whole group for interpretation and analysis. The co-ordinator guides a whole group discussion along similar lines as before: do the sociodramas reveal any problems with the practice? Do some examples of practice clash with others? Is there anything obviously needing done to improve this practice?

The final stage of the 'triple self-diagnosis' is to reunite the analyses of these three areas – concept, context and actual practice – in what IMDEC calls the 'CONFRONTATION'. What is consistent through the three areas?; what are the conflicts?; what requires remedial action? A full-group discussion revolves around the completion of a chart with three columns entitled 'Consistencies', 'Inconsistencies' and 'Knots' (ie something needing straightened out).

'Starting from where people are at' is an oft-cited mantra, not only in popular education but in adult education as a whole. The 'triple self-diagnosis' is designed to find out precisely 'where people are at', in all its variety and contradictions. When all aspects of a popular organisation's practice are laid bare and no assumptions taken for granted it provides the basis for discussion between educators and learners about the appropriate way to proceed with a programme of education and action. While participative techniques are useful for this exercise, they are not ends-in-themselves: it would be possible to do the triple self-diagnosis using a completely different set of techniques.

When the training is over, activist-educators go back to their own organisations and pay close attention to all aspects of their practice, possibly running or adapting the triple self-diagnosis themselves.

Workshop 2: Theorising Practice

The aim of this particular workshop is to encourage participants to step back and theorise (or, simply, 'think') about how to improve the practice of their organisation. The general theme to be followed is 'the dialectical perspective on the process of organisation and education'. Some activities covered are:

1. 'What Does It Mean to Theorise?': in small groups, participants discuss what this means and what obstacles prevent organisations thinking about their practice. Some recorded answers are 'not all reflection is theory but it can lead to theory', 'sometimes we theorise spontaneously', 'activism, pragmatism and the inability to involve groups' is an obstacle and 'we should plan time for theorising'.

2. 'The Dialectical Nature of Transformatory Practice': popular education is about thinking and doing (theory and practice). Consequently, it is concerned with both educational and operational-organisational considerations and the activist's dual role as an educator and as a leader.

Participants see a slide-tape show of a cartoon character called the 'desert rabbit'. A community of animals live under-nourished in an area of semi-desert. In the middle of the desert, surrounded by a barbed-wire fence, there is a beautiful oasis with fertile orchards and plenty to eat. However, it is home to a vicious tiger and its twenty-three cubs. The animals accept this situation as natural: the tiger is king of the land. One day the desert rabbit dares to go over the fence and steal some fruit from the orchard. Once there he decides to study the tiger for a while and notices that he never moves. When not even shouting and stone-throwing make him budge, he approaches the tiger, taps him on the shoulder and realises he is a hollow, paper maché model. He climbs onto the tiger and shouts to the other animals to come in, that the tiger is only made of paper. They all think the desert rabbit is mad; they have always been respectful of others, are afraid of God's anger and refuse to go in.

The co-ordinator throws out questions for discussion. What did they think of the leadership qualities of the rabbit? What were his strengths and weaknesses? What could he have done to encourage the other animals to reconsider their views of the tiger? This serves as an example of abstract theorising. In the next stage of the exercise, participants relate the theoretical issues to their own, concrete practice. Do the characters, and their actions, have real-life parallels? What issues does the story raise for leading activists in popular organisations? This slide tape is a good example of a popular education resource, problematising rather than providing solutions to an issue. It is followed up by practical and analytical work on skills of listening and communication.

3. Next comes the simulation game, 'Blindfolded and Tied-up' (Bustillos & Vargas, 1993: Vol 2, 8.28 – 8.34). With the exception of a few chosen 'observers', participants divide into two groups, one wearing blindfolds, the others with hands tied (loosely!) behind their backs. The blindfolded win the game if they manage to organise themselves collectively and produce a symbol of unity in the allocated fifteen minutes (but beforehand the co-ordinators prime three of the blindfolded to act as infiltrators and sabotage attempts at unity); those who are tied up are just told to participate in the game. Stage 1 lasts five minutes, no-one is allowed to speak, normally nothing much is achieved and the 'tied-up' are unsure what to do. In stage 2, also five minutes, participants are allowed to speak; accusations of 'infiltrator' are often made; the 'tied-up' are still unsure what to do but sometimes try and support the blindfolded. In stage 3, the blindfolds are removed. In leading a decodification of the game, the co-ordinator asks such questions as who do the blindfolded/tied up/infiltrators represent in real life, how did each group behave, what do the bonds symbolise, why was/was not organisation achieved? The game can be used as a reference for discussing the dialectical relationship between organisation and 'conscientisation'; the

'Stages' are also useful for discussing theories of knowledge, each Stage corresponding to a different way of learning; Stage 1 is about learning through perception and the senses, Stage 2 highlights the role of language and Stage 3 shows the importance of conscious action in trying to bring about organisation and unity.

4. 'Analysis of Reality and the Ability to Be Constructive': participants brainstorm and discuss the differences between selected social categories. In this example the categories were 'national', 'democratic' and 'popular', on the one hand, and 'economic', 'political' and 'ideological-cultural' on the other. They repeat the process, this time distinguishing between a 'dominant' and 'popular-alternative' political programme. In groups, participants receive a selection of statements prepared by the co-ordinators (eg: 'full respect for the state of law', 'a hard line on the conflict in Chiapas') and blank cards to add further statements of their own. Groups discuss the statements and colour-code them according to whether they feel they belong to a 'popular-alternative' or 'dominant' programme: the statement on respect for the law, for example, caused much disagreement. Some felt the law was an instrument of oppression while others saw it as liberating: the problem was that dominant classes could ignore it. In a plenary session, groups then place their cards on the appropriate box in a large grid (see below) and explain why they think this box is the most suitable category. The exercise provokes discussion of the integrated nature of reality and the blank cards for the 'alternative-popular' programme encourage participants to make concrete proposals which take all aspects of reality into consideration.

	National	Democratic	Popular
Economic			
Political			
Ideological/Cultural			

Workshop 3: In-Depth Analysis: Culture and Communication

Activists are often aware of the political and economic dimension to their struggle but discover, in the first two workshops, that they have thought little about the question of 'culture'.

1. 'Introduction and Reunion': a range of objects is placed on a table (jar, casserole, basket, guerrilla doll, bible and so on). Participants mentally select an object and think about what it means to them, either personally or in terms of its relevance to their organisation. All those who pick the same object come together and explain and exchange the multiple 'significances'

of the object. In a plenary discussion the co-ordinators argue that since the objects provoke a range of different sensations, this activity illustrates the subjective nature of culture; that the objects were neither good nor bad in themselves but what mattered was the value people gave them and the context in which they were placed. This is an important point, showing that the same experience means different things to different people. Or it can even work at different levels with the same people: we might criticise junk food but still eat it, for example. It is our relationship with each object which constitutes 'culture'. Symbols are a form of non-verbal communication and may be perceived through our emotional rather than our rational faculties.

2. 'Brief Diagnosis of Culture and Communication': participants are divided into groups according to their particular area of struggle ('indigenous group', 'urban group', for example). They discuss the 'culture' in which they work and try to capture this in a poster, collage of images or song and then present this to the full group. Co-ordinators and other participants ask questions, make comments and critically analyse the presentations of culture.

Some observations and questions to come out of this part of the workshop were: 'Are the oppressive elements always outside popular/ indigenous culture?' 'Why is nothing bad said about popular culture?' 'Women are oppressed, for example, and this should not be supported.' Many groups didn't identify the contradictory nature of culture. 'A *fiesta* can be a good thing or simply a drunken brawl.' 'Culture is our relationship with others and the value we project onto things.' 'The more objective we can be about culture, the better strategies for action will be produced'.

3. 'The Cultural Question': the objective here is to understand the concepts of 'dominant' and 'popular' culture and to recognise contradictions within the latter. It starts with the discussion of a slide-tape show, the 'Bilingual Parrot', a provocative, no-holds-barred comment on cultural imperialism, where a parrot refuses to learn English since it is the language of the oppressor. Points brought up for discussion are that it might be useful to learn English (for Mexican workers to communicate with low-paid US workers); that there are internal problems in Mexico too (such as racism against indigenous people); that culture is always changing and is affected by economic and political change; that there is no such thing as a 'pure' culture.

'Song and Dance': participants take a break and dance to the music of 'el tahur', a song telling of a *macho* man who kills his wife while she acquiesces in her own murder. Participants then see a news-clip about a similar, real-life incident and discuss the influence of *machismo* on popular culture. No-one mentioned that they had been dancing to 'el tahur' not long before: this led to a discussion of subtle and subconscious cultural influences.

'Cultural Jigsaw': one group has a jigsaw of a TV, another a jigsaw of mixed elements taken from 'popular culture'. The first jigsaw shows symbols of Hollywood films spreading the values of the 'American way of life' (ie the dominant culture); the second jigsaw shows similar symbols (a cinema, TV, a playboy) but also has an entirely different set (*fiestas*, organised action, community ideals and so on). The graphics are used as a focus for analysing the nature and content of popular culture: 'what is popular culture, what would we like it to be?'

'Study of Texts': participants analyse and discuss different texts addressing the issue of culture, one on the ideas of Antonio Gramsci and how they relate to popular education (Antillón, 1991) and one on a taped discussion between Eduardo Galeano, Raul Leis and Carlos Núñez on whether there is any such thing as a Latin American culture. General comments were that popular culture is ambivalent and that it is important to promote the positive aspects in the struggle against domination: to do this it is necessary, firstly, to find out what people think, feel, do, value and so on.

4. 'Popular Culture and Communication': participants examine and discuss a selection of educational materials on the 'critical recuperation and systematic giving-back' to people of aspects of their social reality: essentially this means encouraging people to take a step back and 'distance' themselves from their reality in order to think about it critically. One example is 'Martha and Mamerto', an audiocassette dealing with *machismo*, a story in which all social roles are reversed: women take on the role of men , the sun becomes the moon, the cockerel becoming a hen and so forth. After discussing the issue in the abstract, in terms of the story, participants then consider how it relates to real life.

In teams according to their area of work, participants then do a practical, creative project to acquire experience in using the methodology. Some produce a video, some a radio programme, some prepare 'invisible theatre': the final product is presented in a plenary for co-ordinators and others to discuss and collectively the group tries to highlight principles for producing good, appropriate educational materials.

'The Conception of a Dialectical Methodology and the Integrated Nature of Social Practice': this section goes back to the CDM, emphasising its integrated nature, and encourages participants to consider how it can be incorporated into their practice. They study a video and text which further explain the meaning of the CDM. Comments from participants at the end of this session included 'there's a lot of boring speech-making in our organisations'; 'the CDM highlights the contradictions in reality but also its integrated nature'; 'studying reality is difficult but it helps to keep going from particular examples to the general and then back to the particular'; 'the language in the texts is difficult'.

Workshop 4: Back to Practice

This workshop leans more towards the practical side of popular education, encouraging participants to consider research, planning, evaluation and systematisation when developing educational and organisational activities. It starts off with a review of all that has been covered in previous workshops and goes on to a mini-diagnosis of the conjuncture – the political, economic and cultural influences currently affecting their different areas of work.

1. 'The CDM and Methodological Instruments': this starts with a simulation exercise, the 'Ideal Community' (Bustillos & Vargas, 1993: Vol 1, 5.66 – 5.72). Secretly, a small group of participants are chosen to be members of a fictitious community and given different information on what it is like. In colour-coded cards this information is divided into the categories of (a) the objective and contextual (b) the subjective, how people view the community and (c) its historical development. In public, another group of participants is selected to be visiting 'promoters' or agents of change whose job is to design the 'ideal community' on the blank posters provided. They are told that all necessary information is to be found in the room. Two participants are chosen to act as observers. It is common for the 'promoters' to start designing this community in an unstructured way. The co-ordinators stir up the emotions of the community members, encouraging them to ask questions. Once a dialogue has been initiated between 'promoters' and community members, a new group of participants are asked to be promoters, to start again and avoid the mistakes of the first group. This is repeated a few times until all the information comes out and a structured, participatory approach is adopted. The whole group reflects on what happened and considers how it relates to actual practice. Important points which come out of discussions are, for example, (a) the importance of making contact with groups which are already organised (b) financial incentives should not be the starting point. Organisations can wither when the money disappears (c) local people, not the visitors, should be the 'subjects' of the project.

2. In two teams, participants then do a 'Treasure Hunt' (Bustillos & Vargas, 1993: Vol 1, 2.82 – 2.90) based on recommended steps for conducting 'participatory research'. Each team has five 'researchers', five members of the community 'being researched', two evaluators of the research process and an accompanying co-ordinator to ensure that all runs smoothly. Each 'clue' in the treasure hunt gives three options for the next stage of the research, one of which is considered 'correct' by the co-ordinating team. An example would be researching 'health problems in the community' where the three options in the first clue would be (a) do a community survey on the theme of health (b) define the aims and objectives of the research (c) describe how you see the importance of this theme (clue 'b' is correct). Participants choose an option and perform the task. If they make a mistake the co-ordinator lets them work for ten minutes before correcting them and guiding them to the correct task. When they complete the correct task, the clue to the following task is on the back of their envelope. Participants work through ten stages in participatory research, from defining the theme to conducting a final evaluation. At the end, the whole 'simulation' is discussed, starting with the views of the observers. Common themes are (a) the extent to which the 'researchers' involved the 'researched' in the process (b) how well they performed each task (c) how well they worked as a team. This is followed by study and discussion of different texts on how to carry out participatory research.

3. 'The CDM and the Organisational Process': participants see a slide-tape of *Cantimplora*, a project which engaged a community in post-revolutionary Nicaragua in the rediscovery of its culture (destroyed under the dictatorship of Somoza) and which illustrates the integrated, dialectic nature of reality. The community is seen to be in a process of constant change, driven on mainly by different conflicts; objective facts and subjective analyses inter-relate and cultural, political, social and economic developments go hand in hand. The co-ordinating team relate this back to the 'conception of a dialectical methodology'.

Throughout the whole training programme, participants and co-ordinators engage in a constant process of evaluation and structured documentation ('systematisation') of the workshops' proceedings.

Comment on the 'School of Methodology'

When I first encountered terms like the 'conception of a dialectical methodology' and 'the triple self-diagnosis', my first reaction was to laugh. A literal translation into English sounds ridiculous and any attempt to promote them in the UK would require careful linguistic and cultural adaptation. They caused difficulty to the trainees in Mexico as well, though in the end they had time to work them out.

The CDM anchors educational practice in a philosophical approach to understanding reality – dialectical thinking – in which the appropriateness of a particular technique depends on how it fits into this larger framework. Given time to work through its complexities, I think the distillation of so many ideas from philosophy, social science and education into an identifiable, named construct – the CDM – is a useful guide for educator-activists in their work and helps prevent a pick-and-mix approach to popular education, a common problem in the past.

To some extent, however, the acceptability of the CDM will depend on reactions to the notion of 'dialectical thinking'. It has drawn heavily on the legacy of the Marxist influence on popular education in the seventies and eighties though it would be wrong to see the CDM as some form of disguised Marxist propaganda. One of its principal architects, Carlos Núñez, is vehemently critical of left-wing apparatchiks posing as popular educators; Antillón has already shown how the CDM rejects 'preconceived, abstract theories' of action. Mejía (1990, 72; quoted in Gutiérrez Pérez & Castillo, 1994: 165), on the other hand, suggests that in popular education the word 'dialectic' has suffered a similar fate to 'Freirian education' or 'participative techniques' and has been co-opted by all and sundry, with its original meaning distorted. With their elevation of relative truths and their attack on all-encompassing, totalising explanations of reality, the ideas of postmodernism are also a clear challenge to the notion of dialectical thinking.

Alforja's work also illustrates the important role played by educators (in this case referred to as 'co-ordinators') themselves. Not only are they responsible for designing extended programmes of learning – their prepared contribution to discussions (such as the proposal of the CDM), the particular techniques (or texts) they choose to use, the questions they decide to ask – while they may not be in the business of telling people what to think, educators certainly have an important influence on what people are likely to think *about*.

Conclusion

In the past few decades, to many looking on from afar, the methodology of popular education in Latin America has been steeped in mystery and romance: the ideas of Freire, 'animators' for teachers, inspirational community drama, 'movements' as schools, high status among NGOs and so on. But perhaps it has not been quite so different as imagined. Learner-centred methodology has flourished in many parts of the world and in Europe the equivalent of participatory techniques can be found in anything from community education to management training. Now more than ever, with the ease of global communication, a cross-fertilisation of educational-methodological ideas seems to take place across geographical and disciplinary boundaries: I have seen the same techniques being used in popular education, communicative language teaching and development education, each discipline claiming credit for their invention. In Latin America, popular education has undoubtedly produced its share of innovative, inspirational practice but I am wary of exaggerated claims for its unique, unadulterated status.

It is also useful to distinguish, conceptually, between an educational methodology (a set of principles on how to put a particular philosophy of education into practice) and a collection of individual pedagogical techniques, adaptable to a variety of purposes. The critique of 'banking' education comes from many different quarters, not only popular education, and various currents in 'progressive' education – discovery learning (Hodkin & Robin, 1985), student-centred learning (Brandes & Ginnis, 1986), 'deep' as opposed to 'surface' learning (Entwhistle et al, 1992), 'andragogy' (Knowles, 1980) – all seek to engage students in participatory learning. While each can (and does) use similar techniques to those of popular education, they have different aims in mind. The intended learning outcomes may be open-ended, as with andragogy, a theory stressing the self-directed nature of adult learning; alternatively, a participatory approach may be seen simply as a more efficient method of transferring the educator's knowledge to the learner (as in some interpretations of 'deep learning'); in the case of the CIA or multinational companies in Honduras (Carr, 1990), we have even seen how a participatory approach can be used deliberately for the purposes of manipulation. Popular education has a different philosophy altogether and questions of methodology should always relate back to its fundamental aims and objectives: thus we have to look below the surface of what passes as method to discern what really goes on. Knijnik's work with the Landless People's Movement in Brazil (Knijnik, 1996 quoted in Coben, 1998: 210), for example, shows how what might appear, superficially, as 'banking education' could actually be something in which, ironically, learners are manipulating the 'teacher': peasants explain how they pretend to listen to the advice of government technicians, knowing it will open doors to important contacts and financial credit to which they normally have no access. Coben concludes that 'the elaborate game being played out leaves Freire's distinction between banking and problem-posing education, with its assumed transparency of motivation, far behind' (Coben, 1998: 211).

Crucial to a discussion of methodology is a consideration of the role of the educator. The Alforja example shows that popular educators are no mere facilitators of do-it-yourself learning. At all times, they have an interpretative, influential and necessarily interventionist role in the educational process and it would be disingenuous to argue otherwise. (The concern in popular education is not that it is directive but that it should not be manipulative or authoritarian). The quality of the educator, then, has an important bearing on the educational process experienced by learners. The appropriateness of various methodological techniques cannot be considered in isolation from the educator's ability to judge which technique to use, when and with what modifications. There is no magic to techniques in themselves. Indeed, learners' reactions to different techniques vary and in some contexts the educator may even judge it appropriate to start with a traditional educational approach, with which people are comfortable, before moving gradually towards more participatory learning, in consultation with the learners themselves. When I accompanied Mexican popular educators meeting for the first time with delegates from 'autonomous municipalities' in Chiapas, in 1995, they had organised a traditional, speech-making event, precisely for this reason. The same can apply to the UK: as an adult education organiser in Glasgow I have interviewed potential students who did not care which course they joined as long they 'didn't have to do role-play'! The choice of technique may require sensitivity and negotiation on the part of the educator: who knows what impression learners may have (legitimately) acquired through a previous negative experience of 'trendy' learning? Equally, good educators should not passively accepts the learners' wishes: if they feel there is a better approach to learning they must justify this to learners, encourage them to try it and involve them in an on-going evaluation of the learning process. Poor educators could make a mockery of an exciting, participative methodology; good popular educators can do wonders with the least appropriate and dullest of government-produced educational materials (cf Archer & Costello, 1990: chapter 6). For all the variety of educational techniques available, a planned programme of popular education will be greatly enhanced by the participation of good-quality, highly-skilled educational practitioners.

More critically, in their assessment of the recent past in popular education, Gutiérrez Pérez & Castillo collate some harsh judgements on what has passed for methodology: 'the idea caught on that anyone could be a good popular educator as long as they had the will, social commitment and a manual of techniques to hand' (Torres, 1998b: 25; quoted in Gutiérrez Pérez & Castillo, 1994: 142). In the majority of cases 'pedagogy' was reduced to 'the strictly methodological which, in turn, was reduced to the appropriation and manipulation of particular techniques' (Mejía, 1988: 45; ibid: 143). The authors make two fundamental critiques. Firstly, they claim that the rhetoric surrounding methodology is one thing, reality another. 'when people claim that popular education is dialogical, participative, critical... etc., what they really mean is that it *should* be dialogical, participative, criticial... etc' (Torres, 1988b; ibid: 140). Secondly, they argue that for all its concern with methodology, popular education has failed to deal adequately with questions of teaching and learning: it has focused too much on politics, mobilisation and action and needs to address and monitor what people actually learn, how they learn it and what educators can best do to help. That 'pedagogy' should outrank 'methodology' is an important challenge for the current practice of popular education.

In conclusion, then, there is certainly much to learn from the methodology of popular education in Latin America and it has produced a plethora of imaginative ideas which could inspire educators in a variety of contexts. But we should not get carried away: similar techniques are also found in other areas of education. Nor should we be over-obsessive about methods: good popular education need not consist of a constant stream of dynamic, participatory techniques. An appropriate methodology should always relate to the aims and objectives of popular education as well as making an effective contribution to learning; it should be neither rigid nor formulaic but constantly reinvented in practice. In the final analysis, the knowledge, skills, adaptability and sensibilities of educators are a crucial variable in determining the quality of any planned, educational experience. Accordingly, today, the development of proper training for popular educators is considered a priority.

Review of Chapter 3: The Methodology of Popular Education

Roberto Antillón has been the coordinator of IMDEC's 'school of methodology' since 1985. He has run training programmes throughout Latin America on a wide range of themes related to popular education, such as participatory research, conjunctural analysis, participative techniques and popular communication and culture. He is the author of several texts, including 'Gramsci and Popular Education' (Antillón, 1991), 'What Are the Basic Elements of the Conception of a Dialectical Methodology?' (Antillón, 1994) and 'A Methodological Approach to Impact Assessment' (Antillón, 1999). He has been coordinator of IMDEC's education sector since 1997 and represents IMDEC on several national and regional networks.

The purpose of the following commentary is to enter into dialogue with the author – from the standpoint of our own experience in Latin America – and to contribute ideas which might enrich the content of the text. We would indicate at the outset that after an initial reading we readily identify with the points it raises: in terms of the information and opinions we now offer, we see these as a contribution which is complementary and in no way antagonistic to the author's work.

One of the main contributions of this chapter consists of the interest it stimulates in the many possibilities afforded by the use of 'participatory techniques' as educational tools. Possibilities which we Latin Americans often fail to exploit, perhaps because they are now such a part of our culture that we do not give them a second thought. The variations and adaptations presented here alert us to the need to be more pedagogically diligent and demanding in our use of participatory techniques; the examples offered by the author from his own experience give us clues and concrete evidence of how to link enjoyment and reflection without losing pedagogical rigour, as in the case of 'The Mail', 'Lifeboats' or 'Statues'.

Another contribution of great value is the emphasis given to dialectical thinking as a key element underpinning popular education methodology. In certain contexts this is no longer given its due importance, given the tendency to be carried away by 'intellectual fashions', as with the belief that Marxism, in its entirety, is a thing of the past, an outdated paradigm. We believe that new paradigms certainly continue to emerge; but that need not necessarily imply that everything which came beforehand is redundant. At several events where the crisis of paradigms has been debated, the Marxist dialectical approach has been considered one of the principal contributions which continues to be relevant and the arguments developed in the text strengthen this particular viewpoint, one which is crucial to the philosophical foundations of methodological design.

The principal critique which could be made of the chapter relates to what it communicates, indirectly, through its discussion of participatory techniques and the methodological framework within which they are put into practice. The general impression given by the author is a bit paradoxical since, on the one hand, he makes it clear on several occasions that participatory techniques have no meaning in themselves yet, on the other hand, he emphasises the detail of these techniques, particularly in his account of the 'school of methodology' workshops in Mexico, while allowing deeper methodological aspects to take second place.

For example, it is important to add that three pivotal themes run through the four workshops of the school; their function is to give sense and direction to the different reflections emerging from the discussions stimulated by the participatory techniques themselves. These pivotal themes are selected when an educational event is being designed, they are shared with the participants and it is an aspect of the methodology which operates as a guide to the coordinating group, a constant point of reference to prevent rambling discussions.

In the case of the 'school of methodology' the three pivotal themes suggested were:

- the CDM and strengthening the identity of subjects of change
- the CDM and the capacity to propose actions for change
- the CDM and new ways of doing politics.

At the beginning of the chapter I think it would be good to have a diagram giving an overview of the course design, showing how all the different elements link up. Moreover, in highlighting the planning of particular moments of reflection, it would be important to include the organisation of group dynamics, participation and democracy in the workshop, the dialogue which takes place both among participants themselves and, under the guidance of the coordinator, around the subject of pre-established theories of social change; and within all of that, the role of participatory techniques as an instrument for generating dialogue.

This initial, methodological design would be consistent with the rest of the content since, as the chapter develops, the ideas just mentioned are already explained within the framework of dialectical thinking, the basis of the so-called 'Conception of a Dialectical Methodology'.

Regarding any corrections, I think there are two types: some have to do with updating the programme of the 'school of methodology', since between 1995, the point of reference, and 1999, some changes have been made, especially from 1996 onwards when there was an *encuentro* of graduates' from the previous five years, an event which provided important feedback. The other corrections are more a question of detail.

On updating the school of methodology programme, we would mention that amongst a series of minor adaptations and changes, one in particular has acquired some significance. This has to do with incorporating the role of popular knowledge into the processes of theorisation; this is done explicitly and the methodology is designed to take it into account. While in 1995 the theme of culture was not addressed directly until the third workshop, we now work on the relationship between different forms of knowledge from the second workshop onwards and, as a result, the idea of theorising from practice is assimilated much more easily.

The other corrections of detail relate to the procedures of a couple of techniques described in the text; though apparently very simple, they do influence the logical development of group dynamics. The most relevant is the following:

In the self-diagnosis of the 'conception', we have found through experience that it is better to begin with one card chosen at random, which is then shared among the group, and we ask if anyone else has a card of similar content. In this way, a group gathers clusters of cards, organises them into columns and only then tries to think of a name or concept which would describe them. In other words, they work from the particular to the general. The procedure suggested in the text ends up confusing the participants because they see all the cards at the same time and that makes it more difficult to think logically.

Another aspect to be considered is the composition of the working teams. If there is a group of 30 to 40 people, as in the school of methodology, the workshop goes better if participants are divided into groups of 12 to 15. Groups of 4 to 5 participants mean that the plenary sessions become lengthy, repetitive and tiring.

All things considered, however, we repeat, in conclusion, that we readily identify with the general thrust of the arguments developed in this chapter.

Roberto Antillón

Chapter 4
Popular Education and the Landless People's Movement in Brazil (the 'MST')

"HE SAID IT WAS HIS LAND BECAUSE HIS ANCESTORS HAD FOUGHT FOR IT. So I SAID 'RIGHT I'LL FIGHT YOU FOR IT!' "

'Perhaps this song arrives
too late. Perhaps our
silence is too great.
Perhaps our awareness too slow
to awake. Perhaps willingness alone
is too little.
Let us look for
a path to peace and stop
the violence which kills too much.
...
Who knows if one day you will
raise your head in freedom
Latin America I love you too much.
Perhaps your suffering is
too great. Still they want
me to be quiet. Too late'.

From the 1st National Congress of the MST, 1985 (Caldart, 1987: 43)

'In the world of football, Brazil are the oppressors and Scotland the oppressed. In two weeks time, when they play each other in the world cup, if Paulo Freire had been alive he would surely have been supporting Scotland?' When I made this suggestion in São Paulo, in May 1998, at a public celebration of the life and work of Freire, hundreds of Brazilians shouted 'no way!' in response. It was different, though, when I went to a Landless People's Movement 'encampment' in Viamão, outside Porto Alegre: a large group of male and female football aficionados were emphatic that they wanted Scotland to win, though this had nothing to do with our 'third-world' footballing status. 'If Brazil do well in the world cup', they argued, 'the president will bask in the glory and land will disappear from the political agenda. We've worked too hard for that to happen'. Football-mad Brazilians supporting Scotland? This was a memorable example, for me, of the advanced levels of 'critical consciousness' reached by members of the MST.

At a time when disputes abound over the prospects for large-scale social change (Betto et al, 1993) and there is a reassessment of the relationship between popular education and the state, a case-study of outstanding significance is the educational work of 'O Movimento dos Trabalhadores Rurais Sem Terra', the 'MST', literally 'the landless rural workers' movement'). One of the major social movements in Latin America, the MST continues to harbour ideals of profound structural change, explicitly recognises the importance of popular education to its struggle and has developed its own, large-scale, independent educational programme, albeit maintaining, in the process, a difficult dialogue with the state. This chapter outlines the history and struggle of the MST, examines its educational programme and considers its wider contribution to popular education in Latin America.

The MST and its Struggle
The Land Question in Brazil
The focus of MST struggle is the (mis)use and ownership of land: a familiarity with the history of conflict over land is essential for understanding the MST today.

In colonial Brazil, all land belonged to the Crown and with the exception of the slaves, people using land productively were entitled to live on it. When slavery was abolished in 1850, those who ran large estates had a problem, for freed slaves would expect to work for themselves, thus depriving estates of their labour. To pre-empt this, a 'Land Law' was decreed to allow the sale of land into private ownership, in effect gifting large parts of Brazil to a select group of private landowners (Martins, 1997: 14). Lacking capital assets to buy land, freed slaves had no choice but to labour for former masters, though thousands joined together to form the earliest movements for agrarian reform (Sérgio & Stédile, 1993).

The interests of owners of large estates have had little to do with the needs of the wider population. Geared towards profit, the best land was – and remains – used for growing export crops at the expense of foods for local consumption. From the 1950s onwards, forced off the land by the modernisation of agriculture, millions of rural labourers migrated to *favelas* in the cities: the problems of urban Brazil were – and remain – tied up with the misuse of land. Inevitably, new organisations arose to demand land of their own but these were quashed by a military coup in 1964. When the military offered financial support to landowners, new economic groups became interested and, subject to intense speculation, land became an investment, bought and sold for profit, not for productive use (Martins, 1997).

Today, while some thirty two million Brazilians, are undernourished (MST, 1998), the government's own statistics (INCRA & IBGE, 1986, quoted in ibid) show that one percent of landowners own almost half of Brazil and the vast majority of privately owned land is either badly used, under-used or not used at all, though the Federal Constitution allows for the expropriation of land not performing its 'social function'. Yet Brazil is one of the least densely populated countries in the world and one of the few in which land reform could still bring enormous benefit to its population (Martins, 1997: 57). The MST struggle is 'pushed' by poverty and injustice, 'pulled' by the immediate, visible gains which land reform could deliver.

Origins, Aims and Identity of the MST

With the demise of dictatorship in the late 1970s, impoverished peasants carried out spontaneous land occupations all over Brazil. At first localised and isolated, these groups met up through the efforts of the 'Pastoral Commission on Land' of the Catholic Church: (the progressive church has had 'enormous influence on those living off the land, raising awareness of the need to become organised' (Sérgio, 1999: 3). In 1984 they formally united to become the MST, a movement currently comprising some three hundred thousand families (Stédile, 1999), and agreed on three major aims: land, land reform and a just society.

The first aim, 'land', appeals to both human justice and the law: as stated in the Constitution, land not performing its 'social function' should be expropriated and redistributed to those who are willing to work it.

The second aim, 'agrarian reform', acknowledges that redistribution of land is of limited value unless accompanied by comprehensive mechanisms of support. To control large landowners, prevent speculation and stimulate production for need rather than profit, land needs to be democratised. Land

The Novo Canudos (new tubes)
encampment, near São Paulo
Photographer: Morven Gregor

reform would support co-operatives, provide accessible credit and plan the development of industries and technologies appropriate to the countryside. However, throughout Latin America the cry of 'agrarian reform' has long struck terror into the hearts of land-owning elites and such a proposal is always fought tooth and nail by 'those who, there's no denying, have everything to lose' (Dalton,1985).

The MST argues that these aims cannot be achieved unless their struggle is geared towards more generalised, structural change and broadened to include other marginalised groups in Brazil. Accordingly, the third aim is for a 'just society' and throughout its campaigning the movement constantly attempts to engage the public in dialogue about the future of Brazil and the nature of desirable change. The MST hopes to achieve this through 'popular mobilisation' and the eventual existence of a 'popular, democratic state'.

The MST is a 'social movement, composed, basically, of the rural poor, those who have been robbed of everything' (Stédile, 1997): land tenants; owners of small holdings; landless rural labourers; inhabitants of *favelas* wishing to return to the countryside. While many are illiterate, some will have attended secondary school and a few even gone to university: leadership roles often fall to children of traditional peasant families who have acquired a formal education. An integral part of Brazilian rural culture, religious belief remains important to almost all members of the MST. Sérgio (1997) identifies five different tendencies within the movement, from Lutherans and Pentecostalists to three different types of Catholic, though the majority of activists and leaders are influenced by Liberation Theology. Those working in administrative or leadership roles receive no formal pay but a basic 'help with costs' (Bellé, 1998). The MST has no formal links to a political party but the Workers Party, in general, is supportive of its aims.

The MST's work has been recognised by a range of institutions. In recent years it has received 'the Vladimir Herzog national award for human rights, the Chico Mendes medal for its struggle against violence in the countryside, the Alternative Nobel Prize from the Swiss parliament in 1991, an Honourable Mention in the King Baldwin Award, from Belgium, in 1994 and the UNICEF Prize in 1995 for its education work with young children' (Betto, 1997: 216).

The Nature of the MST Struggle

The first stage in the MST struggle is to find out where there are areas of land failing to fulfill their 'social function' as required by the Constitution. A legal campaign then begins to acquire this land for MST use.

If straightforward campaigning leads nowhere, hundreds of members then occupy the land, set up an 'encampment' and intensify the battle for ownership. MST encampments offer a precarious existence. Protection against the elements is minimal, food is scarce, they can last for years and danger is ever-present. When I visited an encampment near Porto Alegre, the weather was cold, it had been raining, about 200 people seemed to share a thatched roof on stilts and others had little more than plastic bin-bags for shelter. An encampment needs to organise itself well to survive and many consider the collective organisation and struggle in encampments their major formative experience.

If successful in acquiring land the 'encampment' then becomes a 'settlement' and a new phase in the struggle begins (by 1996, 146 thousand families were living on some 1564 settlements). For the MST, the real challenge is now to prove by example, in the way settlements are run, that alternative models of rural development are possible. I visited the '30th of May' settlement in Charqueadas, in Rio Grande do Sul, and was stunned by the quality of the housing. To anyone struggling in an encampment, a settlement like this is considered the 'promised land'. Most settlers were trying to work as a co-operative – there was even a free, communal restaurant – though some families chose to work alone. While there were indications of 'normal' problems – personality clashes, persistent gender divisions – grassroots democracy seemed to be taken seriously, power and responsibilities were widely diffused and, a significant achievement, women had been elected to major leadership roles. I found the enthusiasm and excitement of the settlers inspiring. Not all settlements are as

The lush pasture and spectacular, self-built housing of an MST settlement in Charqueadas, southern Brazil, an example of what can be achieved when the campaign for land is successful. Compare to the conditions in an MST encampment.
Photographer: Liam Kane

successful, however, and even here, given the wider context – the lack of 'agrarian reform', no 'just society', no previous experience in self-management – it is a constant battle against the odds.

Organisationally, in encampments and settlements, all decisions are made at assemblies in which all men, women and children participate (Stédile, 1998). Co-ordination teams for specific tasks are elected at these assemblies. At a higher, state level (the MST operates in twenty-two of Brazil's twenty-six states), a general meeting of the MST takes place every two years prior to which settlements decide who should attend (this is proportional to the number of families) and who should be recommended for state leadership. This bi-annual state meeting is the maximum authority in the MST. It decides the general political line to be followed, elects twelve people to a state directorate and one more to the national directorate. Financially, the MST receives support from European Non Governmental Agencies (such as Oxfam and Christian Aid) and from the progressive wing of the Catholic Church. Encampments also organise 'work teams', half of whose earnings go to the MST, and settlements too make financial contributions.

On the surface, there appears to be a high level of participatory democracy within both encampments and settlements. However, some people are clearly more influential than others and the interplay between leadership and democracy, I suspect, is varied and complex. Navarro suggests that in settlements, the 'exaggerated' promotion of collectivism causes tension and works against genuine co-operation and solidarity (Navarro, 1997: 126-127) and Madeiros & Leite (Leite, 1997: 167) argue that even elected representatives can exert subtle forms of control. On the other hand, D'Incao (1997: 210) sees the MST as 'one of the most important manifestations of the process of democratisation of Brazilian society' and Petras (1997: 227) claims that 'this new democratic model of building society from below is the MST's principal contribution to the Latin American left'. Gilmar Mauro, a national MST co-ordinator, makes it clear they are 'not a movement of angels but a movement of people and wherever you have people you have problems' (TVE, 1997). For me, there is convincing evidence of genuine commitment to bottom-up development: the mass-based nature of the struggle, an education programme designed to enable participation, lack of uniformity between encampments and settlements, an openness to society and collaboration with many different agencies. Thus far, the urgency of the MST struggle also prevents institutionalisation: the career path of an MST leader leads to danger rather than riches and power.

Predictably, the MST's struggle has provoked hostility from governments, the media and powerful conservative interests. Leaders have been assassinated or jailed, landowners hire gunmen to break up occupations and there have been major massacres such as the murder of nineteen people in April 1996 in Eldorado dos Carajás. On the other hand, the achievable objective of acquiring a piece of land is a powerful motivation for people to take action, land is now at the top of the political agenda and the example of settlements exerts constant pressure on government to pursue reform. By its nature, struggle engenders solidarity, seen most clearly in the wake of repression when there is immediate response and increase in MST action throughout Brazil (Bellé, 1998). Most significantly, 'the greatest progress we have made has been in the conscientisation of the whole of society' (Stédile, 1997:109), with polls showing 85% of the population supporting agrarian reform (ibid). Initially, however, the target of 'conscientisation' is the membership of the MST itself and here the role of education has become a primary concern.

The Educational Work of the MST
The MST as a School
As the guest of a popular education centre with no links to the MST, I was taken to the town hall in Porto Alegre to hear a debate by a group of experts on the future of Brazil. I was surprised to see the public gallery packed with MST members from the nearby encampment. At the end of the speeches, in their red

Maria Antonia Delgada Nity, who has just learned to read and write in the encampment of Viamão. Photographer: Liam Kane

and white T-shirts and traditional, baseball-style hats, with great humility and respect, these ordinary people, of whom many were illiterate, stood up and debated fearlessly, in public, with a host of eminent politicians and academics before going home to their makeshift, plastic, bin-bag tents. Confidence and skill of this nature comes from involvement in a movement rather than sitting in a classroom. First and foremost, for the people in the MST, the major educational experience comes from active participation in organised struggle: de facto, the MST is itself an enormous school.

I was told that encampments in particular, at the sharp end, provide a crash course in political awareness, collective values, participatory democracy and a range of specific skills. There were around 1400 people in the encampment I visited in Viamão. They had organised into 37 groups of 30-50 people, each electing a representative to a co-ordinating committee for the whole encampment. In their groups, everyone discusses the issues relating to the organisation and strategy of the encampment and representatives take their views to the committee. Through this structure, drawing membership from several groups, the encampment had organised different teams to look after areas such as food supply, health, sanitation, sport and recreation, education and so on. As I walked through the fields of the encampment, there was a constant hive of meetings in progress as different teams and small groups planned their next move. To me, the level of participation was impressive but hardly surprising: only highly motivated people would put up with the physical conditions in encampments.

Clearly, life in an encampment stimulates creative, critical thinking and a need for new skills. Discussion of news items relating to the MST, for example, fuels a demand for adult literacy. The conflict between media reporting and the 'truth' ensures that literacy skills, when acquired, are endowed with critical analysis. In organising schooling for children, volunteer teachers and parents meet weekly to discuss appropriate curricula. Of necessity, volunteers learn to teach on the job but their demands have led the MST to run tailored courses in teacher-training. When encampments become settlements, attempts at collective organisation continue but individual families often choose to return to their tradition of farming for themselves. Some, as in Charqueadas, develop high levels of co-operative enterprise, participation and collective self-management and this leads to a continuous demand for education and training. In the best scenario, the experience of collective struggle and organisation in the MST leads to increased self-confidence, conscientisation and empowerment – classical ingredients of popular education.

Early in the MST's development, however, the need to tackle educational demands in a more systematic fashion became urgent. Firstly there was the problem of what to do with children. Makeshift schools were set up but it was unclear who should teach and what should be taught. There were debilitatingly high rates of illiteracy among young people and adults. For settlements to have any chance of success, it was crucial to develop technical and commercial skills related to agricultural production as well as competence in democratic, co-operative management. Finally, there was a concern to sustain the political education of all members and develop leadership training for key activists. With all this in mind, the MST set up a National Education Sector in 1987 to systematise its response to educational concerns.

New Schools, New Pedagogies

For the education of children, the MST runs around 900 primary schools (including encampments and settlements) catering for 85,000 children and employing some 2500 teachers (Bellé, 1998). While much of the curriculum ostensibly overlaps with that of a traditional state school, the experience of struggle created the desire for a 'new school' and 'new pedagogy' in harmony with the wider ideals of the MST. Quoting thinkers like Freire, Gramsci, Marx and Martí, the education sector developed its own philosophical and pedagogical principles (MST, 1996), the first being 'Education for Social Transformation', to work for 'a new social order whose principal pillars will be social justice,

democratic radicalism and humanist and socialist values' (ibid: 6). Accordingly, education should be:
- committed to the interests of the 'working and popular classes', starting with the MST
- available to everyone
- 'of' as opposed to 'for' the MST
- to prepare people to take action as 'subjects' of change
- open-minded about issues and values affecting social change (ibid).

Other philosophical principles are that education should:
- relate to working the land
- develop the spirit of co-operation
- encompass all dimensions of human need
- be for and carried out with humanist and socialist values
- be a lifelong process of training and social transformation.

Among a longer list of pedagogical principles are the importance of:
- the relationship between theory and social practice (the curriculum should rise out of the problems faced by a school's community)
- a common methodology for 'training' and 'teaching'
- social reality as the basis/fountain of all knowledge
- a socially useful curriculum
- an organic link between political and educational processes (i.e. while all education is political, all manifestations of a political process – the way settlements are organised, for example – also have an educational dimension)
- an organic link between the educational process and the system of production
- democratic management
- self-organisation by learners.

A final 'ingredient' (with echoes of both Liberation Theology and Che Guevara) is 'love' : 'those who do not love life cannot teach how to live' (ibid:24).

While these principles grew organically out of the MST, articulated by its educational sector (though aided by prominent, sympathetic educationalists), their successful translation into practice is variable: 'saying the word "sugar, sugar, sugar" doesn't make your coffee sweet' runs a Brazilian proverb, quoted by Caldart (1997:138). Knijnik (1997:269) argues that one of the education sector's strengths is its awareness and on-going analysis of gaps between principles and practice.

Teacher Training

The MST has a national, residential training school in the village of Veranópolis in the southern state of Rio Grande do Sul. Here, members who have been selected by encampments and settlements from all over Brazil come to participate in the MST's own teacher-training course. Its three main objectives are:

1. To train 'educators for Agrarian Reform' and 'active participants in the MST'
2. To train and qualify teachers to work in MST schools
3. To develop both the general educational programme of the MST and a specific programme for rural workers' schools (Caldart, 1997:109).

Training is understood as 'a process through which educators develop the social, political and technical skills necessary for their creative participation in transformatory action carried out by, through or with the MST in the specific area of education' (ibid:109).

In line with its educational principles, however, it is a teacher-training course with a difference. Reflecting MST aspirations of co-operation and democracy, students are organised into a large co-operative from the start: 'encouragement, welcome...and that was when, handing over the educational plan for the course, the animator looked us firmly in the eye and said: get organised!' (ibid:69). In conjunction with the co-ordinating educational team – composed of some three to six persons – students are expected to take collective responsibility for managing all aspects of educational and domestic tasks such as deciding on timetables and curriculum, participating in collective forms of assessment, organising the cooking and cleaning and running commercial activities for subsidising the course. Through regular dialogue, the co-ordinating group's job is to help students analyse, discuss and work through difficulties as they arise.

The course lasts over two and half years and is divided into six different stages, each composed of 'course-time' and 'community-time'. 'Community-time' is important in helping students articulate their own training needs, as well as the changing needs of the MST, and feed these into curriculum planning for the next part of their course. The last stage is based on a practical research project designed not just to help the individual student but to offer new, systematised 'really useful' knowledge to the MST and contribute creatively towards the resolution of its problems. In terms of curriculum content, much time is spent analysing the reality in which people find themselves and identifying what ought to be learned. Dellazeri (1998) – of the educational team – says that though the course revolves around the varied, changing contexts to which students will return, so far the demand for traditional subject disciplines remains high: understanding the history of land struggle, mathematical and economic

*Carlota, a graduate
of the MST's own
teacher training
courses
Photographer:
Liam Kane*

understanding, how to produce quality art and literature – all are valued as fundamental to the MST struggle and student collectives insist on their inclusion in the curriculum.

Given the novelty of such an approach, it is also a profound – sometimes frightening – learning experience for the educational team itself (ibid), a group which seems openly honest about difficulties and failures. In one cohort, during a classroom discussion, students complained of a lack of democracy on the course, believing that those elected onto the students' collective always sided with the co-ordinating group. A major rebellion followed and the co-ordinating group was aghast at the presence of a 'them-and-us' mentality: in the end it led to a collective rethink of the course and was seen as an important step forward in the development of 'subjects', albeit causing discomfort to the 'trainers' at the time. On other occasions, when assessing students' community practice, settlements have complained that teacher-trainees can be too focused on schools, not enough on the wider struggle (ibid).

Other Courses

Another important initiative is the Technical and Administrative Course for Co-operatives (TAC). While this is driven by the same educational principles, its aim is to help people in settlements survive economically. The course centres on 'co-operative firm management', mixes 'education' with technical 'training' and seeks to promote the growth of organic intellectuals within the MST. The six main areas of focus are:

1. technical skills related to general administration
2. political/pedagogical/ideological issues, to encourage class-consciousness among workers and consideration of their educational role in the settlements
3. pedagogical skills and techniques
4. ethics: humanist and socialist values for a new society
5. skills related to organising and running a co-operative
6. technical skills related to agricultural and agro-industrial matters (Cerioli, 1997).

Like the teacher-training course, it is a period of experiential learning in which learners form a co-operative and live through its trials and tribulations. A co-ordinating team helps them reflect on problems as they arise. Conservative buzzwords like 'markets', 'enterprise' and 'business-studies' abound, students also engage with the ideas of revolutionaries like Marx and Guevara.

Three other initiatives are, firstly, a national training course for local, grassroots leaders (many of whom are weak in basic education). Leadership training 'always has one foot in school' (Bellé, 1998), involves considerable travel to acquire a broader, national perspective on the struggle and includes organising campaigning events such as a '17th of April' march (commemorating the massacre of Eldorado dos Carajas) in which participants are supervised and assessed. The second is the effort put into the teaching of literacy skills to young people and adults. In encampments and settlements literacy 'monitors' promote basic education throughout the movement but their level of formal education is often minimal and they require constant support. Finally, the MST publishes an increasing number of educational materials which are in high demand, even from teachers outwith the MST.

The MST and State Education

So far, I have painted the MST as an independent organisation doing its own, political education work in opposition to standard state provision, a classic example of the popular education of the seventies and eighties. In fact, however, the picture is more complex and the MST has links with state education in several different ways.

Firstly, only national governments have the resources to bring education to everyone and in the new 'just society' envisioned by the MST, state education is considered a fundamental right, even though it should have different educational aims. Accordingly, the MST supports all public campaigns for better state education. It also attempts to win official recognition and financial support for its own schools and teacher training courses. While this is not always easy – and the results vary regionally within Brazil – it is surprisingly successful. Some of the mobile encampments have even acquired recognition for their 'itinerant schools'. In some settlements, the school is financed by the state, including the salary of the (MST-trained) teacher. In others, the state may also supply the teacher, though initially a 'settlement' post can be seen as highly undesirable by state employees. While there can be problems between government-trained teachers and an organised settlement community with its own articulated educational demands, many state teachers are inspired by the experience. The work of MST teachers in settlements has also attracted the interest of state educationalists and, as in the case of the Charqueadas, governmental trainee-teachers can sometimes visit settlements as part of their course.

In its own teacher training courses, the MST also tries to meet the demands made by government for official teacher qualifications. In Rio Grande do Sul, for example, the course is validated externally and evidence shows that in addition to the alternative and experimental work in which they are involved, students also do well at conventional exams. Moreover, the MST course accepts students who are not part of the MST and the mixture has been dynamic, with non-MST participants overcoming previous prejudice and sometimes becoming activists themselves (Dellazeri, 1998). Though it may appear paradoxical to look for state recognition for such an alternative – if not revolutionary – project, the desire for formal recognition emanated from course participants themselves.

Whether as advisers, teachers, trainers or researchers, state-employed educationalists have also played an important role in the MST from the start. While some academics collaborate with the MST education sector, others work on its teacher-training courses. Subject specialists make specific contributions on request and PhD students can be at the heart of research and documentation (eg: Caldart). However, as Knijnik points out (1997: 265), it is a very particular relationship in which the MST is clearly in control. 'Professionals' must be invited to help and, a priori, sympathetic and politically committed to supporting the MST. It can also be difficult for established educators to work in such a different environment, whether putting up with mosquitoes and poor accommodation or coping with unusual roles, as educators responding to – rather than pronouncing on – student needs.

It might be objected that, as with the Workers' Education Association in the UK, for example (Westwood, 1992: 230-233), or in other scenarios in Latin America (Archer & Costello, 1990: 96-113), when radical educational movements seek state support they end up being compromised, co-opted and stripped of their radical vision. In time this may prove to be a problem but at the moment the MST seems very much in control. Firstly, their education work is a response to the needs and demands of a struggle which is alive and kicking: it has to relate to that struggle or it loses its raison d'être. Secondly, state support appears to be a prize won from below, through the strength of the MST, rather than a gift bestowed from above. Finally, the inadequacies of state education mean that it has little alternative to offer and 'devolving' education to the MST may be the simplest (and cheapest) way to carry out its responsibilities.

The MST and Popular Education

The MST's educational work shows strong continuity with the recent, radical past in Latin American popular education. All education is considered political and whether it happens to be campaigning, organising co-operatives, tackling illiteracy or running specialist courses, every aspect of MST practice is underpinned by the desire to politicise, raise critical awareness and encourage the emergence of 'subjects' of change. Articulated in its philosophical and pedagogical principles, its practice often seems classically Freirean and not dissimilar to the popular education of the seventies and eighties.

The MST experience raises important issues about the relationship between political ideology and the role of the popular educator, an area in need of improved theorisation (see chapter 6). Ideological differences matter, for although popular education should have no truck with transmitting pre-packaged ideology, the political orientation of educators affects all aspects of their practice, from planning programmes of work to 'speaking their own word' in any educational dialogue. In the practice of popular education, wherever it takes place, the educators' ideology is an issue which ought to be honestly and openly addressed.

In the case of the MST, the predominant ideology has been characterised as eclectic, inspired principally by 'Marxism, popular religiosity and rural, communitarian practices' (Petras, 1997: 275). Leaders and militants have been strongly influenced by Liberation Theology (Sérgio, 1997). With other peasant movements in Latin America, the MST has been considered 'the human face of revolutionary politics in the post-Communist, post cold-war world' (Petras, 1997: 272). Unlike (much of) the contemporary left, it refuses to accommodate itself to the supposed inevitability of neo-liberalism: the vision of a radically different society – an achievable 'utopía' – is clearly a prime motivational force in the MST, explicitly acknowledged in its literature and confirmed repeatedly in discussion by MST members. Its radicalism has been bolstered by the experience of struggle, its success in turning encampments into settlements, its growing strength and confidence, its popularity with the wider public and the belief that in the context of Brazil, land reform offers real potential for achievable, large-scale social change. While it continues to place 'class' at the centre of social analysis and talk explicitly of 'socialism' – though it also addresses issues of identity and difference – the MST is a different beast from traditional left-wing organisations. It is a popular movement born out of struggle, neither a political party nor guerrilla army. 'Socialism' is conceptualised as a project of self-liberation, not a gift to be handed down from above. High value is placed on grassroots democracy and participation (ibid: 273) whereas many Marxist organisations are considered hierarchical and intolerant of dissent (Núñez, 1993). Moreover, the fundamental thesis of the MST – the need to repopulate the countryside – has been attacked by the orthodox left as backward and anti-modernist (Martins, 1997).

Some might object that with its talk of socialist values, Marx and Guevara, the education sector of the MST is really involved in old-fashioned, leftist propaganda, with an 'educated' leadership out to manipulate a vulnerable majority. Firstly, it is undeniable – and unavoidable – that the ideology of the education sector influences the educational experience of the learners. This applies equally to all educators, however, of whatever political hue. Like any other educational practice, popular education is never non-directive, a point repeatedly emphasised by Freire, among others, in despair at perceived mis-readings of his own work (Freire, 1993). Secondly, there is considerable evidence against accusations of crude manipulation. The education sector is arguably more democratically representative of its members than any ministry of education: it is not a 'closed shop' but co-operates with many outwith the MST; learners attending courses – and the camps and settlements which choose them – clearly have a say in the curriculum; problems are openly acknowledged, including an awareness of gaps between rhetoric and practice. However, there is still no place for complacency: we have seen how one of the problems acknowledged by Dellazeri (1998) related precisely to learners' perceptions of manipulation.

The MST – commonly referred to as a 'popular social movement' – is a prime example of how in Latin America a 'movement' is considered the 'school' in which popular education takes place. In the wake of Freire's earlier work, the creation of this umbilical link between popular education and popular movements, where the demand and infrastructure for collective learning are already in place, was the key development in popular education. It is a concept to which all initiatives in radical education must surely attempt to relate.

But times have changed in popular education. In many instances, from a previous position of clear-cut opposition to the state, space has opened up for dialogue and there is a growing awareness of the limitations of popular education regarding large-scale transformation. Throughout Latin America, people formerly engaged in popular education have now joined the state sector and in Brazil, in particular, much is being done to see how the experience of adult,

Clemí Marcón stands at the entrance to the impressive 30th of May MST settlement in Charqueadas
Photographer: Liam Kane

popular education can be adapted to the context of children in state schools (Do Vale, 1992). While it would be absurd not to take advantage of this new space in an emergent civil society, it clearly has its dangers: Latin American authorities have a long history of combining 'populist' discourse with effective co-option of dissent.

On the evidence so far, the MST appears to have maintained its radical edge while taking full advantage of the changed political conjuncture. It is clearly in charge of its own education programme, with its own educators, courses, schools and materials, and, from a position of strength, has managed to negotiate (limited) state support and recognition without yielding autonomy. But its relationship with the state is dialectical, not merely a question of opposition, and through the various courses and schools opened up to non-MST educationalists – students, teachers or researchers – the MST both makes a contribution to state education and engages the whole of society in a wider educational debate.

Knijnik (1997) argues that there are several innovations brought to popular education by the MST, the first being that 'relative to the history of other social movements, one new development is itself the high degree of importance which the MST has come to attach to education over the last few years' (Knijnik, 1997:263). As a university academic responding and lending support to the MST, rather than trying to guide it, she argues that the role of the intellectual has changed from one of a generalist working for 'conscientisation' to that of a specialist akin to Foucault's 'specific intellectual'. (While this may be true for those intellectuals outside the MST, to me it seems that the process of 'conscientisation' remains a priority and in this the role of the MST's own generic, 'organic intellectuals' is clearly important). Another novelty is that its work has repercussions beyond the MST. Its very practice throws out a challenge to the state regarding the purpose of education and highlights state inadequacies of scale and quality of provision. The interest in the MST shown by state-employed teachers and the widespread dissemination outwith the movement of its education materials are examples of this. Finally, she argues that unlike some examples of popular education practice, though the MST properly respects the place of 'popular' knowledge and culture, it also engages with 'academic' and 'scientific' knowledge. While this is encouraging, I would question its novelty as the critique of 'basismo' (loosely translated as 'grassroots-ism'), an extreme reaction against academic knowledge in favour of *all* popular knowledge (discussed in chapter 1) , has been around for some time (Núñez, 1992: 56).

Conclusion

For me, the strength of the MST's work in education lies in a combination of three factors. Firstly, hegemonic within the MST is a radical political culture which links the particular with the general, makes a structural critique of capitalism and aspires towards the transformation of the whole of society. It is not a single-issue campaign working in isolation from other struggles nor does it focus on issues of identity and difference to the exclusion of all else. Though it tends not to use precisely the same vocabulary, it clearly has a 'conception of a dialectical methodology', discussed in the last chapter, at the heart of its practice. This culture is important in framing the type of questions pursued within the educational context. Secondly, in actively promoting the principles and practice of popular education – imaginatively adapted to a changing social context – I believe the MST makes genuine efforts to promote democracy and participation, not feed people a 'party line' from above (as has happened in other left-wing organisations). This combination of open-ended educational enquiry and the politically and culturally radical environment in which it takes place is powerful. Thirdly, the education work is tied to a specific struggle which has the advantage – through the 'carrot' of a piece of land – of offering tangible benefits to its protagonists, a strong incentive for participation. The struggle for land and, when acquired, the attempt to work it successfully, inevitably leads to a questioning of wider, political realities and increased motivation to learn.

However, from experience, people in the MST are aware of their movement's limitations (hence the importance of broadening their struggle), including what it can expect to achieve through education. It has powerful enemies: education is only one weapon in a much wider political battle. Nevertheless, at a time when the struggles of ordinary people are frequently written off, the scale of the MST attempt to engage so many in the struggle for a radically better world is uplifting: the unprecedented prominence given to popular education makes it a case study of world-wide significance. Finally, contrary to much fin-de-siècle preaching on the demise of radical alternatives, the MST shows that the vision of a radically better world continues to be a great motivator for change and that the role of popular education is as important as ever. It is a heartening message for all educators and activists working for change.

Review of Chapter 4

Gelsa Knijnic teaches on the Post-Graduate Education Programme of the University 'do Vale do Rio dos Sinos' in Brazil. For over ten years she has been working collaboratively with the MST in the area of mathematics education. Her research with the MST is guided by an approach called 'Ethnomathematics'. She currently co-ordinates the Popular Education Working Group of the National Association of Post-Graduate Studies and Research in Education. Among her many publications are 'Exclusion and Resistance in Brazilian Struggles for Land: (Underprivileged) Women and Mathematics Education' (Knijnik, 1998), 'Indigenous Knowledge and the Ethnomathematics Approach in the Brazilian Landless People's Education' (Knijnik, 1999a), 'Ethnomathematics and the Brazilian Landless People's Education' (Knijnik, 1999b) and 'Ethnomathematics and Political Struggles' (Knijnik, 2000).

I was honoured to receive the invitation to review chapter 4 of Liam Kane's book. It has challenged me to rethink many of the issues at the heart of my activities over the last decade as an educator working alongside the Landless People's Movement. As I started to think about my response, which began to take shape today, the 2nd of May 2000, it was a time of mourning for the MST and for all of us who are so ashamed of our military police who massacre agricultural workers just because they want to stay in the countryside, grow food, educate themselves and live their lives with dignity. The images of violence (see the newspaper Folha de São Paulo, 3/5/2000) bear witness, once again, to the harshness of their struggle for social justice in a country where the unequal distribution of wealth reaches the most perverse levels the world has seen.

Liam Kane's chapter provides a broad-ranging, in-depth illustration of the many dimensions to the MST's struggle, particularly those ideas which have inspired its work in the area of Popular Education. Supported by a diverse and representative body of the most recent literature on the Movement – and on empirical data collected on his visit to the south of Brazil – the author has constructed a text in which the many dimensions of this struggle are neither simplified nor glorified but presented in all their complexity. Here we have one of the great merits of the work I am currently reviewing: it doesn't stop at describing the struggle of a popular social movement but also sets out to 'problematise' it. His discussion of the organisational aspects of the MST and 'participatory democracy within both encampments and settlements' is exemplary in its critical and ethical stance in problematising the Movement's struggle. His astute educator's eye has singularly and sensitively captured the heterogeneous world – constantly changing, constantly in motion – of the MST. Kane asserts that 'while it continues to place "class" at the centre of social analysis and talk explicitly of "socialism" – though it also addresses issues of identity and difference – the MST is a different beast from traditional left-wing organisations'. In my view one of the crucial elements which makes the Movement 'a different beast from traditional left-wing organisations' is precisely the fact that 'it also addresses issues of identity and difference'. Among such issues I would highlight the question of gender. From the mid-1990s onwards, 'MST women's collectives' began to organise in the encampments and settlements (Knijnik, 1998). More recently, these went on to constitute the 'Gender Sector' which holds a similar position to that of the 'Education Sector' in the national, organisational structure of the MST. In April 2000, in Brasilia, this Gender Sector organised the 1st National Congress of Women Agricultural Workers and attracted 3000 participants: its agenda covered a wide range of topics and reflected the importance given by the MST to this particular issue. The importance of this development is highlighted in the testimony of one young woman, a state coordinator of the Gender Sector who points out that for her '*machismo* is also present amongst us in the Movement because the whole of society is geared towards men'. And she adds: 'the Movement has taken important steps towards ensuring that women form an integral part of the decision-making process in the Movement...This means that today it is guaranteed that in all training courses 50% of those attending should be women and at least one term of the course should be used for discussing gender-related issues'. As Kane asserts, how to deal with issues of identity and difference is also an integral part of the MST's agenda, indicating that other themes of domination, in addition to those of class, have been a focus of attention in their struggle.

In this struggle, Education has become one of the priorities, clearly illustrated in the section entitled 'The Educational Work of the MST', where the author carries out an impressive, wide-ranging analysis of the Movement's different areas of activity. More recently, a new element was added: the first degree-level course in MST Teacher-Training, taking place at the University of Ijuí in the northeast of the state of Rio Grande do Sul. The introduction of this course represents one of the Movement's efforts to acquire proper qualifications for its teachers (as the author has shown, this also happens at other stages in the educational work) and its view that in the search for certification it is also necessary to occupy the spaces provided by formal institutions. This has been one of the original traits of the Movement. At the same time as it pressurises public governmental bodies to carry out effective land reform – one which will go much further than simply an egalitarian distribution of land – the MST builds alternative spaces for education and seeks to have them legitimised by the appropriate bodies within the country's education system. As Kane illustrates well, this has occurred throughout the history of the Movement and, allowing for specific, regional variations, has generally been a very successful enterprise. In training their own teachers, while affording them access to a university education, the Movement makes it possible to control its own educational project, maintaining its own pedagogical principles, in its different areas of activity. This also means that increasingly it is the Movement's own members who will be in charge of its Education. Moreover, when they feel confident and qualified to represent themselves – and this has already started happening – these are the voices which will be heard in Popular Education forums and academic conferences throughout the country. I also find the MST an innovative popular movement in its defence of the symbolical, the right of representation.

This certainly has repercussions for redefining the role played by we intellectuals who work alongside the Movement. As I discuss at greater length elsewhere (Knijnik, 1996) – a point to which Kane also makes reference – I consider our position as intellectuals very compatible with that announced by Foucault in his notion of 'specific intellectual', distancing himself clearly from the Gramscian concept of 'organic' intellectual. I fully agree with Kane, however, when he affirms that my argument is relevant when referring to 'intellectuals outside the MST' but that 'it seems that the process of "conscientisation" remains a priority and in this the role of the MST's own generic, "organic intellectuals" is clearly important.'

Important not only to its struggle for Education. Today, in a country characterised by social exclusion, unemployment, hunger and extreme poverty, the MST is a mass movement which needs leaders who can advance its struggle for social justice. Ethical and committed intellectuals like Liam Kane are important allies in this struggle.

Gelsa Knijnik

Chapter 5
Popular Education and the Politics of Identity: Women's and Indigenous Peoples' Movements

Popular education is best conceptualised as a generic activity relating to a wide range of grassroots struggles for change. In chapter 3 we saw that whatever the initial concern leading to learning and action, popular education seeks to locate this 'generative issue' within a wider, integrated reality, paying particular attention to the interests of the 'oppressed'. Increasingly in Latin America, in addition to more material, class-based concerns, issues of identity and difference such as ethnicity or gender – those at the heart of 'New Social Movements' in Europe and the USA – also take on this initial generative role. Many theorists argue, however, that in Latin America the interpenetration of these 'newer' concerns (those of 'social' movements) and more traditional, material, class-based concerns (those of 'popular' movements) is often, though not necessarily, more immediately visible and acute (see Hellman, 1992; Foweraker, 1995).

This chapter examines the case of two social movements which are organised, at least ostensibly, around issues of 'identity' rather than 'class'. It explores the relationship between 'consciousness-raising'within these particular movements and the broader, generic practice of popular education in Latin America.

Women's Movements and Popular Education
Background on Women's Movements

'Three times I cheated on you
At first, out of anger
Then, on a whim
And finally, just for fun'
(Paquita La del Barrio, a woman from a working class neighbourhood, who to great acclaim produces popular-feminist songs in the normally male-chauvinist tradition of Mexican country *ranchera* music: La de Barrio, 1996)

Given the cultural-ideological diversity of organisations run by and for women, and the further diversity within them, in the context of Latin America it is meaningless to talk of a single 'women's movement'. These organisations include mothers of the 'disappeared' confronting the military in Buenos Aires and Santiago; 'El Poder Femenino' (feminine power), a right-wing organisation supporting the overthrow of Allende in 1973; women who organise communal 'popular kitchens', 'glass of milk committees' and 'mothers' clubs' in Peru; ex-guerrillas in Central America who now struggle for women's' rights in the post-war context of frustrated revolution; workers in the sweatshops of multinational companies; the hundreds of organisations sending delegates to the biannual conference of Latin American women, from revolutionary socialists to lesbian rights activists, hotly disputing the meaning and relevance of feminism.

Outside exclusively women's groups, moreover, there are few grassroots struggles for change which do not have many (or even mainly) women as the key activists, a fact I find reinforced with every visit to Latin America. In addition, the testimonies of individual campaigners like Rigoberta Menchú (1991), Elvia Alvarado (1989), Domitila Barrios de Chúngara (1978) and Benedita da Silva (1997) – from Guatemala, Honduras, Bolivia and Brazil respectively – have reached a world-wide audience. Given the strength and permeability of *machismo* (male chauvinism) in Latin America sooner or later, in any movement for change, the issue of gender and women's rights inevitably has to emerge.

Today, women's involvement in the public sphere 'is a leap forward of such proportions that it could scarcely have been imagined in 1972' (Franco, 1998). But this increased participation has not been unproblematic. Firstly, since the 'second wave' of feminism in the late 1970s, there has been a history of tension between 'feminist' movements (whose starting point is to question the patriarchal structure of society) and 'women's' groups which form part of the popular, social movements campaigning for human rights or improved social services. Feminists have criticised women's groups for only fighting for short-term demands and for not openly challenging the traditional role of women; in their turn, women's groups have rejected 'the feminists' attempts to claim ideological leadership of the women's movement' (Villavicencio, 1994: 59) and have seen feminism as far too middle-class (a stereotype of feminism also promoted by both right and left-wing political parties). In time, however, there has been a rapprochement between these two positions. On the one hand, through participation in particular struggles and campaigns, many women's groups, such as the Mothers of the Plaza de Mayo in Argentina 'without trying to change patriarchal ideology or abandon their femininity, produced a transformation of the traditional feminine conscience and its political role' (Feijoo, MDC, quoted in Stephen, 1997: 11): paradoxically, it was precisely by playing on the traditional role of motherhood that their political struggle was so effective, leading the Mothers to adopt roles which were anything but traditional. Similarly, women have found their traditional roles simultaneously challenged and reinforced when they become active in urban popular movements in Mexico City (Díaz-Barriga, 1998). Chinchilla (1992: 41) argues that the experiences women gain in such struggles 'often create fertile ground for links between a gender-specific consciousness; what Molyneux (1986) calls "women's practical interests", feminist consciousness ("women's strategic interests") and social consciousness (consciousness of class, social sector, nation etc'. Equally, when feminists have involved themselves in supporting the popular struggles of non-feminist women, this has sometimes broadened their understanding of feminism from one with an exclusive focus on gender-specific issues, such as reproductive rights and equal opportunities, to encompass wider social and political concerns. On the other hand, when women from the popular movements started to attend the Latin American and Caribbean Feminist *Encuentros* started in 1981, both sides had the chance to debate the significance of feminism and come to a modus vivendi. To the initial disputes over feminism and socialism, each *encuentro* seemed to add something new:

- a consideration of race as well as gender and class (particularly in Brazil, 1985, when a busload of mainly black women from a favela in Rio were refused entry to the *encuentro*)
- the 'coming-out' of lesbian groups
- the participation of women from Central America, with their experience of revolutionary struggle
- a gradual acceptance that feminist ideas need not be the exclusive preserve of 'bourgeois ladies' and that a woman can be 'doubly-militant', both a political and a feminist activist
- 'a transition from the small group of feminists to a large, broad-based, politically heterogeneous, multiracial movement' (Sternbach et al, 1992: 227).

At the same time, discussions and debates on the 'women's question' were already taking place within left-wing political parties and the broad-based, social and popular movements themselves. It was commonly argued, both by men and women activists, that gender issues were secondary to the main struggle for a more egalitarian society, that they would be dealt with after the revolution (when, in any case, patriarchy, being a product of capitalism, would wither away of its own accord) or that to dwell on issues of difference would only serve to weaken the struggle. As time went on, the holes in this argument became increasingly obvious and women who started off as political activists saw the need to tackle *machismo* and patriarchy even within their own popular organisations. These tensions were particularly fraught in Central America (Aguilar et al, 1997). In Nicaragua the Sandinistas controlled the women's revolutionary organisation *AMNLAE* until they lost the elections in 1990: only then did women activists feel released from their Sandinista straitjacket and the women's movement has flourished ever since (Montenegro, 1997; Stahler-Sholk, 1999). In the southern cone too, after years of campaigning on the streets, in the words of one activist 'when the democratic government took over, the men around here said, "It's okay, Rosa, you can leave it to us now". We thought, "have they forgotten everything we did during the dictatorship?"' (Fisher, 1993: 30). In the current context, there is a general acceptance among women political activists that gender issues must be addressed within the popular movements themselves. In some cases, as in Chile and Peru, emphasising their class-orientation, women have formed themselves into '*popular* feminist organisations' (Schild, 1998).

In her study of women and social movements in Latin America, Stephen (1997) concludes that it is no longer useful to dichotomise between 'feminine' and 'feminist' groups, 'practical' and 'strategic' interests or 'political' and 'feminist' activists. Her interviewees suggest that the borders between social, cultural, political, domestic and public spheres are all blurred and that within any group – and within individual women themselves – multiple, complex and frequently contradictory identities coexist. The contradictions relate to the wider socio-political structure and the range of competing ideologies to which women are exposed (including, for example, the influence of both the traditional-conservative and popular-progressive church). Rather than an expression of a collective, abstract identity, then, Stephen sees women's movements as embedded in very specific political and social contexts in which, despite many differences and arguments, women are able to co-operate and unite around a specific struggle at a particular moment in time. But there are persistent tensions around issues of social class. In considering the current, specific context of Latin America, where feminism is being absorbed (or co-opted) by new 'democratic'

BOX 5:2 'Clementine' (from Mexico)

'We sent them back, armed with a single match. How did I feel? The same as everyone else. Nobody wanted to go out. The bullets were buzzing in the hall and some idiot stuck his head out the window. The kids were piled up in bed with their parents standing in front of them. We knew that out there a crime was being committed against those boys but what could we do? Swallow our anger and hope they wouldn't come and mess us up too. There wasn't even any electricity in the neighbourhood. It was dark everywhere and we couldn't see a thing. Nobody spoke or ate. The kids were hunched up on the floor and if any of them started playing we'd say "shut up, for Christ's sake, they're killing people out there". All the neighbours had a trunk behind the door. The only way they were going to get us out would be at the point of a gun. But then the students started running into the neighbourhood. Imagine it. They ran around the street shouting in desperation, knocking on the doors like madmen, begging us to let them in. Do you think anybody wanted to let them in? No way. The boys were battering the doors but people just acted daft. Then I thought to myself "fuck the soldiers! I'm going to let them in". So several boys came in and hid beneath the bed, in the wardrobe or wherever. Me and a few others shouted to the rest of the neighbours to stop being bastards and help the students out. Then they started opening their doors and all the students got in. And you know what, son? That's when the soldiers arrived, right where you're standing, and they went into the houses. They knocked the trunks out the way with their rifles. They went in and started beating people up. It made no difference, us being women and children, though the men came off a bit worse. They wanted to take away anyone who might look like a student. We were really scared but the poor students were shitting themselves. All of us – men, women, children and the students went out to the square and the battle began. The soldiers were knocking lumps out of us. And then, I don't know where the idea came from, son, but I began to shout "Turn on the gas! Turn on the gas!" And then we all opened those gas tanks you can see in the square. That was when I grabbed a box of matches, took one in my hand and said to the soldiers "Right, you're not taking anybody. If you do we're all going to get blown to fuck". I made as if I was going to light the match and all the soldiers jumped backwards. Picture the scene. By this time all the neighbours had matches in their hands. The soldiers backed off and went away. And we stayed that way all night, son, holding the matches, just in case the soldiers came back.'

From *The People Know Best...Anecdotes and testimonies from Latin American popular educators* (Núñez, 1990)

governments, where many ex-activists have become *femócratas* (bureaucratised feminists), where elite NGOs promote professional rather than 'popular' campaigns, where the feminist cause is pushed more at UN conferences than in the streets and *barrios*, both Franco (1998b) and Álvarez (1998) question whether these particular expressions of feminism have any legitimate claim to be representing the interests of poorer women.

The Relevance of Popular Education

On the face of it, it is obvious that the principles and practices of popular education should be relevant to the vast majority of women and women's movements in Latin America. Victims of both the 'feminisation of poverty' (Quiroz Martín, 1997) and a deeply ingrained *machista* culture, even in progressive conjunctures where 'heroes and revolutionaries in the line of fire can be total despots at home and no-one thinks it's wrong' (Montenegro, 1994: 174), women are clearly a large sector of the 'oppressed' in whose interest popular education purports to exist. By definition, some argue, it is inconceivable for 'popular' education not to be 'feminist' at the same time (La Comisiona, 1996) and even feminist critics of Freire – who denounce his early use of sexist language – have acknowledged the contribution his ideas have made towards the emancipation of women (Weiler, 1996). Freire himself came to apologise for his earlier oversights and took up the feminist cause with enthusiasm.

But reality is not so simple. In its earlier days popular education focused on issues of class oppression but was oblivious to matters of gender. It was only after the women's conference in Mexico City in 1975 and the subsequent growth of feminism that it began, very slowly, to consciously address the issue of gender inequality (Guzmán, 1994 & Celiberti, 1996). Since then, the importance given to gender has depended on a number of factors: pressure from funding NGOs from the north, the strength of feminist ideology, its relevance to poor and working-class women and the vagaries of particular political conjunctures. While Central America was considered the bedrock of radical popular education in the 1980s, the stifling of feminism by both *Sandinismo* and the Salvadorean guerrilla affected popular education too (Barndt, 1991; Vásquez, 1996). After 1990, the popular education movement in Latin America started to take gender issues more seriously. Partly, this was due to the force of a newly unleashed feminism in Central America which had politically radical credentials; partly because the demise of the revolutionary dream led to a general crisis in popular education which, after a period of reflection and reconstruction, began to look more positively at the potential of 'new' social subjects of which the women's movements were one (REPEM, 1994). However, outside of women-only groups, there is a long way to go before gender issues can be genuinely considered integral to the practice of popular education. It is easy to pay lip-service to what may be considered a development buzzword or the latest NGO fashion (Vários, 1994) and even where good, progressive popular education centres do take it seriously, many are honest enough to acknowledge it is a hard nut to crack (CIAZO, 1997): I know of popular education centres where the critique of sexist language is highly developed but page-three type pin-ups can still be seen on the walls.

In trying to understand the dynamics of any popular education project with women, it is useful to examine the ideological and cultural standpoints of both learners and educators prior to the project's initiation. How do women identify themselves within their particular context? To what extent do they see themselves primarily as poor people, mothers, wives, workers, black or indigenous people, for example? What are their main concerns? How much, if at all, do they consider men to be the cause of their problems? Good popular education should really be doing this anyway, of course, even if not driven by a strong gender awareness: tools like the 'triple self-diagnosis' described in chapter three are ideal for bringing out self-perceptions, with all their variety and contradictions, and the 'conception of a dialectical methodology' would encourage analysis of the interplay between these different aspects of identity. And to what extent do the educators start from a perspective which emphasises the 'popular' over the 'feminist', or vice-versa? Some organisations may have little predisposition to tackle gender in a different way from any other issue; others may consciously choose to tackle it within an integrated, holistic approach to popular education. But there are also many Latin American NGOs and centres which are now staffed by women, work only with women, have developed an explicitly feminist approach to popular education and who argue from a feminist perspective in their discussions with grassroots organisations, albeit, if they are good educators, within the framework of a dialogical and participatory approach to education (cf DIGNAS in El Salvador; Valenzuela, 1999). Like many Marxists before them, some feminists stand accused of just trying to tell people what to think (Vega, 1999). And there are also different currents and sometimes contradictory positions within feminism itself (Mendoza, 1997), particularly regarding biological interpretations of gender and the relationship between sexes. An extreme position is 'the perception that women possess certain characteristics that make them better than men, simply because they belong to the female sex' (Lamas, 1994:161) though many (most?) feminists reject this as 'womanist' and agree with Jaquette that 'women are neither "naturally" democratic nor "naturally" conservative' (quoted in Vargas, 1994:5). Mediated by the context in which it takes place, the dialectical relationship between groups of learners and popular educators, with all their variations, give rise to very different practices of popular education within women's movements.

In her analysis of the history of NGO projects promoting popular education with women, Guzmán (1994) divides these into two broad categories, those which focus, initially, on welfare and those which focus on equality. While both types are similar methodologically, the initial objectives of 'welfare' projects are to increase women's self-esteem, help satisfy their immediate needs (including coping with domestic and motherhood-related tasks), promote democratic organisation, encourage links with the wider popular movement and increase their capacity to put pressure on the state. 'Equality' projects, on the other hand, centre on themes highlighting feminine subordination such as sexuality, domestic work, remuneration, power relations within and outside the family and so on. Initially, as part of the gender versus class debate, these two categories were considered to be in conflict, but in time it became clear that both categories 'generate a process which transcends their proposed objectives, creating the conditions for convergence between both types of project as well as between feminists and popular educators' (Ibid: 137). It has often been the case (Eber, 1999) that as a result of poverty and hardship women are drawn initially to welfare-type projects through an inability to adequately perform their traditional roles as mothers, wives or household managers (the initial 'generative' issue) and once immersed in a process of popular education and struggle, end up challenging the very roles they sought to fulfil in the first place, in some cases, as with 'popular feminine organisations' in Peru, eventually taking on, face to face, such high priests of patriarchal authority as mayors, civil servants and congressmen (Villanueva, 1998). It does not do to be complacent, however: there is always a danger that where educators lack a feminist consciousness, projects initially focusing on women's welfare may end up reinforcing, rather than challenging, traditional roles.

Since popular education is part of a wider process of organising for change and operates at different levels – with individuals, groups, large communities and national movements – it can be difficult to isolate and measure the precise effect of what is purely 'educational' (the theme of evaluation is examined in chapter 7). However, there are countless examples of projects with women which have been considered successful and in which popular education has played an important role:

- Perú Mujer and the Centre for Women's Action and Promotion (CEPAM) in Ecuador, both educating on issues like domestic violence, discriminatory violence and family law. They work at grassroots level but also campaign at government level for institutional change (see Fink, 1992)
- the Honduran Federation of Peasant Women (FEHMUC) which pressurised the Honduran government for agrarian reform (Ibid)
- the 'Women's Movement 2000', in Colombia, which brings together black, indigenous, peasant and urban women to analyse their concept of gender, based on their own experience as community leaders, and relate this to an understanding of the social-political order in Colombian society. This movement grew out of community leadership training provided by the Colombian Pedagogical Society (Lozano, 1998), an NGO specialising in popular education

- in El Salvador, the NGO 'Mujeres por la Dignidad y La Vida' (generally known as 'DIGNAS'), set up by ex-guerrilla fighters turned feminists, has received positive results from their wide range of educational initiatives with women from the popular sector, including courses in technical training, midwifery, literacy, education for citizenship, basic gender education and, most successfully, a 'school of feminist debate' running at three different levels (Vásquez, 1996)
- the 'Women's Network' in Brazil, which connects around 3000 groups throughout the country, works in campaigns against poverty and hunger and promotes an education for 'a new relationship between men and women' in all areas of life by (a) strengthening the self-esteem and self-organisation of women (b) providing specialised training (c) helping with income-generating activities and (d) advising on the creation and management of projects (Viezzer & Moreira, 1995; see Websites)
- in the 'Santa Barbara Women's Educational Project' in Honduras – based on an 'egalitarian and feminist' philosophy' and the belief that even the most severely conditioned rural women can become empowered to take charge of their lives – when one external evaluator saw the women in action she commented 'I was very moved. Here were women whom I'd met in 1986, and who at that time couldn't speak without covering their mouths with their hands and saying "I'm very nervous about speaking", addressing the camera or a crowd of women. And they had become people who were assertive, and as strong as they'd always potentially been, but now able to live and project this strength; and that was just fantastic. I've not seen anything like it in any other popular education work' (Rowlands, 1997: 94).
- At the continental level, the Latin American Council of Adult Education (CEAAL) plays an important, co-ordinating role through 'REPEM' (Eccher, 1998), a 'Popular Education Network for Women in Latin America and the Caribbean'. Much of this work focuses on income-generation projects. This is important but on the evidence of reports submitted to international journals, to me it seems that some of the work comes dangerously close to 'enterprise' rather than 'popular' education' (see Repem, 1998).

Methodologically, the approach to popular education with women should follow the same principles and procedures outlined in chapter three, though the subject matter and content is likely to differ. It is often said that suffering in isolation, women blame themselves for their hardship and the first problem to be tackled is a lack of confidence and the need to build self-esteem (Castillo, 1998). This may be due to general cultural factors, explains Angela Hernández, a popular educator in the Dominican Republic, saying that 'if a woman feels ugly because she is mulatta, because her hair is course...if she doesn't identify with her Caribbean physiognomy...if she feels that her way of speaking is inappropriate, that her skin colour isn't beautiful, that her traditions and images are inferior...It's a huge obstacle. That's why the cultural work of popular education is a very energising factor' (quoted in Fink, 1992: 178). It is also a result of having internalised the belief that women are inferior, and a common exercise early on is for women to identify the total amount of (paid and unpaid) work for which they are responsible and to compare this to men's: on its own, without any comment from educators, women can find this revealing, a first step on a path towards increasing their sense of self-worth. Significantly, popular education work with women has highlighted the importance of dealing not only with critical analysis at the rational-cognitive level but also affective, non-rational knowledge like 'emotions, sensations, feelings and free associations' (Mazo, 1996): these have a cognitive dimension too, however, since 'appropriate' feelings are often learned responses.

Other examples of popular education methodology with women would be:

- drawing and naming the reproductive organs of both sexes when dealing with the topic of sexuality. This can reveal ignorance and myths which need to be tackled urgently (Bosch, 1998)

- a game provoking critical thinking on gender roles. Groups have a deck of cards containing 'stereotypical phrases about female and male gender roles and a board with two squares, one showing a man and the other a woman. Players take turns picking up cards and reading aloud the phrases written on them. Then they decide whether each phrase refers to a woman or a man and place each card on the appropriate square. Players have to justify the decision they make and other players may or may not agree. In indecisive cases, cards are placed in the middle. The objective is to raise awareness about gender stereotypes and the discrimination they help perpetuate. The game is also designed to motivate participants to suggest ways of changing this situation' (ibid: 174)

- in a mixed workshop on domestic violence which I recently attended in rural Nicaragua, men and women were divided into separate groups and asked to produce a visual representation of their experience of being on the receiving end of violence. When they came back together, men had to de-code the women's drawings before hearing the 'true' explanation and women did the same with the men's (see box 5:1). In this way real-life (but unattributed) incidents were critically analysed in a collective search for causes, effects and solutions (though there was some dispute among educators over the appropriateness of having a mixed group at all)

BOX 5:1 Mixed Workshops on Violence in the Home and Community

POSTER A

These posters were produced in 1999 by groups of men and women near Jinotega, in Nicaragua, when popular educators asked them to draw their experiences of being on the receiving end of violence.

Poster A, drawn by women, shows a man beating a woman to provoke an abortion, a drunk woman abusing her children, a man chasing his wife and children out the house, an abandoned woman being left with all the family responsibilities and a woman seeing her husband with his lover. In their discussion of the poster the women said that when men are out late, they also hide knives and dangerous implements in case the men try to use them when they come home.

POSTER B

Poster B, drawn by men, shows a father forcing his son to work on the farm (this was common to all the men, who felt they had missed out on their childhood), a scene from the war against the *Contras* when someone walked non-stop for 11 days and came across the massacre of 16 children, a boy being tied up by his mother for not behaving himself, children being exploited financially and working with men in a culture of violence.

Remaining in single-sex groups, the participants went on to consider (a) the underlying causes of this violence (b) what they could do to reduce levels of violence and (c) what they needed from their partners to help achieve this. Men and women then came together to discuss their findings collectively.

- appendix 5:1 outlines the thematic content of a popular education programme carried out with Indigenous women in Chiapas (see Hernández & Mendoza, 1999).

Finally, many tensions surround popular education work with women. The first is the effect it may have on their domestic lives, particularly regarding relationships with husbands or partners: 'the increasing ability of women to articulate their needs and play an effective role in projects tends to draw conflict over traditional sexual roles into the home, as men perceive women's involvement as a threat to the hierarchical structure of the household' (Fink, 1992: 185). Sometimes these domestic pressures are so strong that they win out in the end, finally forcing women to leave organisations; sometimes it is the reverse and women flee their domestic situation. On other occasions the conflict is solved in a way which is advantageous to women and, as men are forcibly re-educated by the practical consequences of their wives' new-found skills, particularly where this produces material improvements, can even lead to improved all-round relationships. There is also an issue about whether or not popular education aimed primarily at women should be done in women-only groups or should also try to involve men. Opinions on this vary and may depend on the circumstances: Rowlands (1997) makes a strong case for women working alone, to begin with, until they develop the confidence not to be intimidated by men in a mixed group. In some pioneering work in community-based popular education, the Nicaraguan popular education centre CANTERA runs separate workshops for men and women and then brings them together to hear, analyse and debate each other's deliberations: they have been conducting serious research into the long-term impact this has on the attitudes of men (Welsh, 1997; see also chapter 7). A challenge for educators is how to balance a respect for women's popular knowledge and culture, though this may promote gendered roles and values with which they have little sympathy, with a process of challenging women to think about how things could be different: if women already have a low sense of self-esteem it does no good to jump in with both feet, rubbishing the traditional roles which may be their only source of pride. The use, or not, of the word 'feminism' in popular education is also a hot potato, even for educators who perceive themselves as feminists, and while some prefer to use it regardless, others argue that concepts, rather than words, are what count and feel that since 'feminism' is a word surrounded in misunderstanding and prejudice, it can be better to avoid it altogether and talk in general terms about gender (Mendoza, 1997:137).

Conclusion

In a wide variety of social and political settings in Latin America there exists a heterogeneity of women's groups, which are composed in turn of individuals with different needs and concerns. Popular education with women, accordingly, takes on a multiplicity of forms. A central focus of analysis is the extent to which popular education can be considered to have absorbed a feminist perspective into its practice. If directed at an undifferentiated category of 'women' in general, however, as opposed to those belonging to the poorest sectors, it ceases to be 'popular' education, properly speaking, becoming, instead, feminist pedagogy or gender training (see Walters and Manicom, 1996:8). In general terms, popular education directs itself towards all those men and women who collectively make up the politically and economically 'oppressed'. While recognising the specific, multiple oppressions particular to women's experience, popular education with women would not turn its back on the more structural oppression of which men from the poorest sector are also victims. Popular educators, feminists included, do not set out to foment war between the sexes but in tackling all forms of oppression aspire to make life better for everyone. Those who still wish to emphasise the sexist nature of oppression may choose to identify themselves more precisely as 'feminist popular educators' (ibid).

Indigenous Peoples' Movements and Popular Education

Background on Indigenous Peoples' Movements

(Note on terminology: for centuries, Columbus's mistaken belief that he had reached India meant that native Americans in Latin America were known as 'Indians'. While this term is still commonly used today, organised native Americans generally prefer the term 'indigenous peoples', 'indigenous' being more geographically correct and 'peoples' conveying a plurality of indigenous cultures which other terms conceal. But 'correct' terminology is an ongoing topic of debate (see Yúdice, 1998: 370)).

'Oh curse of Malinche, when will you leave my land, when will you set my people free?'
(Ochoa, 1979)
Thus concludes Amparo Ochoa's well-known song which captures the history of Mexico in two simple verses and laments the colonial legacy of anti-'Indian' racism which persists to the present day. Malinche was the indigenous lover-interpreter of the Spanish conquistador, Hernán Cortés, and her name is synonymous with 'traitor'. The song argues, in the first verse, that in the beginning, at the time of the conquest, native peoples were enchanted by mirrors and beads and believed the Spaniards to be gods: when they realised their mistake

it was too late. In the second verse, Mexicans continue to be seduced by foreigners (this time North Americans) and their goods and while any northerner is welcomed with open arms into a Mexican *mestizo* household, native peoples of Mexico continue to be treated like dirt. The song encourages *mestizos* to value indigenous peoples and stop selling their souls, like Malinche, to the foreigner (though for all its good, anti-racist intentions, it perpetuates a one-dimensional view of both Malinche and indigenous peoples. She had little choice in her fate, having been sold to Cortés as a slave by a native *cacique*, and Cortés was only able to conquer Mexico by allying himself with indigenous peoples who were already victims of an imperial power, the Aztecs).

Some studies estimate that there are over sixty million indigenous people in Latin America and the Caribbean today – over 13% of the region's 460 million inhabitants – though they are much more highly concentrated in some countries than in others. Indigenous people make up 30% of the population of Mexico, 55% of Peru, 66% of Guatemala and 71% of Bolivia, for example (Maduro, 1992, quoted in Quintanilla, 1998: 26). The effects of the conquest – war, the spread of disease, enslavement and hard labour – all wreaked havoc on Latin America's indigenous peoples, some of whom, like the Caribs of the Dominican Republic, were wiped out entirely. According to some estimates, at one stage this havoc caused the indigenous population of the Americas to fall from 112 to a staggeringly low two million (Wearne, 1996: 3). The legacy of centuries of exploitation (see Galeano, 1973) is such that today even 'the World Bank and other development agencies indicate that Indians remain the poorest and most destitute of the region's population, with the highest rate of infant mortality and childhood malnutrition and the lowest rates of literacy and schooling' (Davis & Partridge, quoted in Domínguez & Lowenthal, 1996:97). Indigenous people clearly come into the category of the 'oppressed' for whom popular education ought to have something to offer.

Linked to basic material demands, questions of cultural identity have always been at the heart of indigenous peoples' struggles. It is a complex area, however, with many competing interpretations as to what constitutes authentic indigenous culture. In the 1930s and 40s, in a movement known as *indigenismo* (Indigenism), sympathetic, left-wing, *mestizo* politicians drew attention to what they saw as the positive aspects of Indian culture. It became a fashionable area of study, with *indigenismo* almost a synonym for 'anthropology': an old Mexican joke said that 'a typical family in the highlands of Chiapas is composed of a mother, a father, four or five kids and an anthropologist' (Carlsen, 1999:51). In effect, despite some useful anthropological contributions, *indigenismo* was a dialogue about Indians carried out by *mestizos*, was essentially paternalistic and mostly developed into governmental policies geared towards assimilating indigenous peoples into nationalist states.

In opposition to *indigenismo*, by the 1970s, as indigenous peoples themselves became increasingly active in a wide variety of organisations, from trade unions and political parties to Christian base communities, a new way of thinking emerged, *indianismo* ('Indianism'), 'a philosophy which emphasises that indigenous peoples should lead the struggle for recognition of their own culture, needs and rights' (Wearne, 1996: 173). (Ironically, and confusingly, though the word 'indigenous' is considered more progressive than 'Indian', by contrast 'Indian*ism*' is more progressive than 'Indigenism'). While indigenous peoples now saw the need to become 'subjects' rather than 'objects' of their own destiny, there were different ideas within *indianismo* of how to relate to the wider world. An early trend saw *indianismo* as part of a wider, left-wing political project. When indigenous people continued to experience racism, however, even from left-wing *mestizo* colleagues, they sought to ignore political questions of right and left and to concentrate on cultural issues to which only indigenous peoples could relate: ethnicity was to take precedence over class. Currently, the dominant trend is for indigenous peoples to do their own, independent organising but make tactical alliances with non-indigenous groups when and where appropriate.

A legacy of *indigenismo* and its assimilationist tendencies is that indigenous communities have often been conceptualised as survivors of a previous age, a culture frozen in the past, rather than one (or many) which has also adapted and evolved with changing circumstances and contact with other cultures. In its need to accentuate the positive in the battle against racism, there is even a danger that *indianismo*, too, might present an unproblematic, even mythologised view, of indigenous communities. While there are undoubtedly elements common to most indigenous communities – the central importance of land, the naturalist and environmental values emanating from a rural lifestyle, a system of customs and laws in which collective rights and community participation are highly valued – there is no such thing as a 'pure' indigenous culture. Indeed, the very notion of a generic 'Indianness' is a European construct. There are currently more than 800 different ethno-linguistic groups in the Americas (ibid) and notions of identity, constantly changing both within and between these different groups, cannot be easily pinned down.

Some indigenous people wear traditional dress, for example, while others prefer jeans and sweaters; some fight to preserve their own language, others argue the need to learn Spanish or Portuguese, the languages of power; some live in isolated rural communities using traditional farming techniques – or even modern agricultural machinery – while others live in cities and vie with the Internet and mobile phones. People might also adopt different identities for different occasions. Never static, identity is engaged in a process of constant reconstruction in which there are both continuities and ruptures with the past. Despite the need to redress the balance of centuries of racism and promote all that is positive in indigenous cultures – an important step in self-affirmation – it would be a mistake to resort to simplistic romanticism. Indigenous cultures too, like any other, have their share of problems, complexities and contradictions. There are important debates within indigenous communities themselves over gender roles, for example, or the balance between individual versus collective rights (Carlsen, 1999). Depending on the particular context, indigenous groups too can be as capable of environmentally damaging practises as anyone else (Bebbington, 1996). Recent discussions among popular educators in Mexico found that "'there are indigenous cultures in which men hit women and this is considered acceptable by both". This started an important discussion, for while it is true that in the past there was an over-emphasis on the classist vision at the expense of other sources of identity, it is also true that today there is a manipulation of culturalism which turns culture into an entity considered to be sacred, static, essentialist and immovable and which has to be defended because "'it is good"'" (Mendoza, 1997: 56). However sympathetic the aim, attempts to eulogise without problematising indigenous cultures ultimately do the cause of indigenous people a disservice.

In the 1980s and 90s, with the state unable to fulfil the most basic of welfare functions and with the parallel rise in *indianismo*, indigenous people started to take matters into their own hands and campaigning organisations appeared all over Latin America. In Brazil alone, 48 indigenous organisations emerged between 1982 and 1990 (Wearne, 1996). Though they often seemed to arrive from nowhere, they were usually the result of painstaking 'ant-like' organisational work which had been going on for years (Regino Montes, 1999: 27), building on previous, less visible networks of resistance. Starting from the bottom-up, many of these organisations went on to collaborate in federations at local, regional, national and even international levels. In Ecuador, the Shuar-Achuar Federation helped found the Confederation of Indigenous Nationalities of Ecuadorean Amazonia which, in turn, became part of the international Coordination of Indigenous Organisations of the Amazon Basin, the largest indigenous organisation in the Americas (Wearne, 1996: 170). With the approach of 1992 and the 500th anniversary of Columbus's 'discovery', indigenous organisations acquired a massive international profile and succeeded, more or less, in subversively converting all the planned, official celebrations of the 'discovery' into a celebration of '500 years of resistance' instead. This international visibility was given its maximum expression with the awarding of the nobel peace prize to the Guatemalan human rights activist, Rigoberta Menchú.

As with other social movements, though they may appear self-contained and homogenous from the outside, from the inside looking out indigenous movements too have a diversity of goals, strategies, representatives and networks (Yashar, 1996) and while some concentrate on affirming the importance of their pre-Columbian roots, others are more concerned with how to interact with the non-indigenous cultures which surround them (Klesing-Rempel, 1999). Common to most, however, is a dual concern with improved material well-being and the defence of cultural values. In practice these translate into campaigns for land and resources, on the one hand, and (varying degrees) of self-government and autonomy on the other (Kearney & Varese, 1995), albeit within, rather than independently of, existing national states. Apart from increasing the profile of indigenous people's concerns, the movements have had various successes: the Shuar-Achar Federation in Ecuador and the Indigenous Regional Council of the Cauca in Colombia have reclaimed land, run transport and education services, on a large-scale, and almost operate as a parallel government within their respective nation states (Wearne, 1996: 167). In Chiapas, Mexico, at the San Andres talks in 1996, the Zapatistas also achieved recognition for more than 30 'autonomous municipalities'. As with many other battles fought by indigenous organisations, however, legal rights are one thing, having them respected is another.

Popular Education

'Don Gino: All this talk, in these modern times, about interculturality and popular education is nothing but 'mental masturbation'.

Don Quispe: All this ignorance, in these modern times, of the importance of interculturality and popular education is nothing but 'modernism taken to extremes'.

Don Gino: You sir – with all due respect – wish to turn back the clock of modern history.

Don Quispe: And you sir – with all due lack of respect to what you're saying – are dismissing out of hand our experience of 500 years of Latin American history.'
(Subirats, 1993: 66)

Some argue that given the widespread poverty and oppression of which they are victims, albeit with the additional factor of ethnic discrimination, in essence the problems of indigenous peoples are not so different from those of other popular sectors (Quintanilla, 1998). Until recently, this has been the line generally taken within popular education too. When indigenous people have taken part in popular education initiatives it has been as part of an undifferentiated popular sector, in the context of urban or rural grassroots organisations, for example, or in Christian base communities. It is only with the recent increase in activity from indigenous peoples' organisations themselves that the Latin American popular education movement has been forced to think more deeply about how popular education should relate to the specific concerns of indigenous peoples. In its 'global plan' for 1998-2001, for example, CEAAL (1999) recognises its lack of experience in this field and its need to develop, from direct experience, conceptual and methodological guidelines for working within the whole area of 'interculturality'.

In Latin American educational circles, 'intercultural education' is the term most frequently used when discussing issues of ethnicity. Except, increasingly, within the framework of modern language teaching (Mughan, 1999), where it mainly refers to the inter-relation of *national* cultures, it is seldom heard in the UK, where the dominant concepts – hotly debated over the years – have been 'multicultural' and 'anti-racist' education, though it is commonplace in Spain (Ruiz Abascal, 1998) and is becoming popular in Europe too (Council of Europe, 1999, Teacher: 5). In looking at the educational demands of indigenous groups in Mexico, Rockwell (1998) argues that as it is currently understood, the concept of intercultural education in Latin America is a qualitative break with the preceding *indigenista* and assimilationist tradition of 'ethnic' or 'bicultural' education. Intercultural education is for everyone, not just indigenous peoples, and aims to foment 'respect, knowledge and mutual understanding' between all the different groups in any one nation (Merkx, 1993: 56). Klesing-Rempel (1999) emphasises that in addition to learning about other cultures, intercultural education requires people to reflect critically on and reconstruct their own cultural identity. It is often quoted alongside other terms such as 'bilingual education' and Subirats (1993) even talks of 'Intercultural and Bilingual Popular Education'. The provision of appropriate, formal 'intercultural' education for the children of indigenous communities has been a main demand of indigenous organisations, in fact, and they have often succeeded in both organising their own schools and forcing the state to fund them (García Bravo, 1993).

But just as there is debate about what actually constitutes indigenous cultures, there has also been a history of disagreement about the relative importance of purely 'cultural' as opposed to 'class-based' issues in popular education. There is a real need for cultural affirmation, for indigenous peoples to openly assert and take pride in the cultural values which centuries of oppression have aspired to demean and subdue. This is a necessary prerequisite for an authentic sense of identity and the confidence to become 'subjects' of change. On the other hand, if disconnected from a specific historical and political context, an over-emphasis on culture can divert attention away from fundamental issues of power and control. Accordingly, many ruling groups (such as those governing Mexico for most of the century) have been happy to indulge in populist, *indigenist* rhetoric and espouse the values of indigenous peoples' cultures. In itself this poses no real threat to their power and has even allowed them to pose as champions of the oppressed.

A specific example is the case of linguistic diversity. With 30 million indigenous people in Latin America speaking around 400 different languages (Merkx, 1993), when popular education has been involved in literacy projects, there has often been tension over which language should be the focus of study. Language is the main vehicle for encoding and articulating culture so the preservation and promotion of indigenous languages is essential to the exercise of self-affirmation, an antidote to the cultural imperialism of the language imposed by colonial oppressors. However, to reject Spanish and/or Portuguese and promote an exclusively monolingual indigenous culture is to be cut off from what has become the language of power. It also robs different indigenous peoples of a 'lingua franca' enabling the co-ordination of political activity. Archer & Costello (1990: chapter 8) document one such example in Guatemala, in the 1980s, where twenty-two different indigenous languages are spoken and where, with some financial support from the government, a project of cultural reclamation by the Mam people (centring on radio broadcasts in Mam) was seen by other indigenous groups in the Guatemalan peasants union as being divisive, since Spanish was the only feasible medium of communication between the different indigenous groups struggling against the brutalities of dictatorship. While the radio programmes were successful in promoting self-affirmation through the increased status given to the Mam language, the peasants' union felt that since the programmes failed to address 'generative' issues like land reform – mainly because the government would neither have supported nor tolerated such broadcasts – then indigenous culture was becoming, effectively, a tool for domestication rather than liberation. While continuing to recognise the value of their own indigenous languages, others such as Rigoberta Menchú or literacy students in El Alto, Bolivia (ibid: chapter 9) also emphasise the importance of having access to the language of power in the struggle for change. Although there can be problems in transcribing certain indigenous languages which have no history of being written down, it is now generally assumed that while literacy should start primarily with people's first language, it can be acquired simultaneously in another language as well (Jáuregui, 1993).

Given their history of oppression and marginalisation, on the face of it there appears no theoretical reason why the principles and practices of popular education, as outlined in chapter one, should not be immediately applicable and beneficial to indigenous peoples in Latin America. The normal procedure would be to start from people's perceptions of their own reality, encourage deeper analysis and attempt to find connections with wider structural forms of oppression. Within this approach, if discrimination or cultural concerns were the 'generative' issues, then it should be natural for the practice of popular education to draw these out from the beginning: it should certainly not try to suppress them. However, as the Don Gino/Don Quispe dialogue and CEAAL's global plan reveal, in practice it has not proved so straightforward. Many indigenous groups feel popular educators have been insensitive to the cultural needs of indigenous peoples, mistakenly seeing them as separate from more generic, class-based concerns. While this should not and need not be the case – there is nothing contradictory about dealing simultaneously with cultural and class-based issues, indeed they are dialectically interconnected – it is another indication of how, in spite of the participatory and learner-centred nature of popular education, the ideology of the educator still has an important influence on the eventual educational experience of learners (see next chapter).

However, the popular education movement has now been sensitized into reflecting more deeply on this aspect of its practice and the future will hopefully bring greater theoretical and methodological awareness of the most effective ways for indigenous communities to engage in popular education. In Mexico, groups of popular educators (including indigenous people themselves) have already started to analyse this aspect of their practice and have identified particular areas of difficulty which need to be worked on, including (a) dealing with divisions and conflicts within indigenous communities (b) how indigenous communities relate to the outside world (c) what unites and differentiates one community from another and (d) the balance between individual and collective rights (CEAAL, 1996: 26). The work of the Asociación Mayalán (see Appendix 5:1) provides a contemporary example of the popular education work carried out by indigenous communities themselves.

A Word on The Zapatistas

On the first of January 1994, the same day that the North Atlantic Free Trade Agreement between Mexico, Canada and the USA came into force, the Zapatista Army for National Liberation (EZLN) – a guerrilla army of indigenous peoples from Chiapas, the poorest state in Mexico – captured the town of San Cristóbal de Las Casas and made a series of demands of the Mexican government regarding the granting of land, autonomous powers and the provision of services to indigenous communities. Twelve days later, the EZLN declared a cease-fire, without laying down its weapons, and entered into negotiations with the

The 'autonomous community' of Oventic in the state of Chiapas, Mexico, one of the five
Aguascalientes (cultural centres) set up by the Zapatistas and where many underwent education and
training for the national exercise of 'popular consultation'
Photographer: Liam Kane

government. Though these negotiations remain on-going, they have been
characterised by governmental backtracking, constant harassment by the
Mexican army and paramilitaries (including the massacre of 27 women and
children in the village of Acteal in December 1997) and a parallel dialogue
between the EZLN and Mexican (as well as international) 'civil society'.

Though this is not the place to discuss the EZLN in any detail (see Harvey,
1998; Urzúa & Taulis, 1994; Kampwirth, 1998; Zermeño, 1997) it is worth
mentioning that the EZLN does not correspond to standard stereotypes of a
left-wing guerrilla army, has no ambitions to conquer state power and does not
see itself as a vanguard leading the masses towards a utopic future (Holloway,
1999; Bruhn (1999) makes a comparison between the EZLN and Mexico's
other, more traditional guerrilla force the 'Popular Revolutionary Army'). With
its preference for dialogue over violence, its lack of conventional revolutionary
rhetoric, its emphasis on issues of identity as much as class (ibid) and its use of
the internet to communicate with the world from the heart of the Lacandón
forest, journalists sometimes refer to the EZLN as a 'postmodernist' guerrilla
army (see Esteva & Prakash, 1998), though we should be wary of simplistic,
superficial labelling. It has a massive following among the indigenous
communities of Chiapas and collectively the EZLN and its active but non-
guerrilla supporters are known as the Zapatistas.

It is striking that so many of the communiqués and actions of the Zapatistas coincide with the theories and practices of popular education. As yet, however, I have come across no systematised account of any aspect of Zapatista practice explicitly referred to as popular education. Perhaps this is no surprise given the EZLN's relatively short-lived existence and the daily pressures of its struggle with the state. In September 1999 I was due to visit one of the five *Aguascalientes* – villages which had been designated 'cultural centres' by the Zapatistas (*Aguascalientes* being a reference to the famous convention of the Mexican Revolution, in 1914) – where I was due to visit the early stages of an experimental programme in popular education which had, apparently, got off to an exciting start. In the event, at the time of my visit repression around this particular *Aguascalientes* became severe and I was prevented from doing any research. A proper, thorough study of popular education under the Zapatistas is a piece of work crying out to be done. In its absence, I think it is worth highlighting a few aspects of Zapatista practice which are popular education in everything but name.

The first is the relationship between the Zapatista leadership and the rest of the Zapatista movement. Unlike most political movements, both from its communiqués and actions, the evidence suggests that rather than dictate policy 'from above', the Zapatista leadership is in constant dialogue with popular knowledge 'from below' and its decisions are made after extensive consultation and discussion with indigenous communities (part of the rationale for wearing balaclavas in public is to prevent any visible distinction between leadership and the rest of the movement). In Zapatista discourse this is known as the concept of *mandar obedeciendo*, to lead or 'govern by obeying' (Ceceña, 1999). This goes back to the origins of the EZLN itself, when a group of traditionalist revolutionaries had planned to organise a rebellion but were gradually educated by indigenous people of the need to listen to communities and work for mass participation before taking any action. When the EZLN finally went public, in fact, it was through the 'consensual decision-making of hundreds of communities' (Harvey, 1998: 228), when these communities said the time was right, even though the armed guerrillas – including the main EZLN spokesperson, sub-comandante Marcos – felt differently (ibid: 197). This dialogical approach to revolutionary leadership corresponds exactly to the recommendations made by Freire in chapter four of *Pedagogy of the Oppressed*.

Secondly, the EZLN does not confine itself to attacking the government but tries to engage the whole of 'civil society' in a dialogue about the future of Mexico and in its promotion of participatory democracy – articulated in the 5th Declaration of the Lacandón Forest (Hernández Navarro, 1999) – attempts to mobilise the wider population into becoming 'subjects' of change. As part of this process, the EZLN organised a National Democratic Convention prior to the presidential elections in August 1994 and over 6000 delegates from civil society organisations attended and debated how to improve (or initiate) real democracy in Mexico. Having organised the convention and raised the issue of democratic participation, the EZLN then deliberately opted to 'step to one side' and let the others do the talking, popular education on a large-scale. In response to a massive national and international exercise in 'consultation' in 1995, the EZLN then tried to organise a civic front for unifying popular struggles around the banners of democracy, freedom and justice, 'a new political dynamic ... not interested in taking political power but in building a democracy where those who govern, govern by obeying' (EZLN, 1996; quoted in Harvey, 1998: 209). With the Mexican government disrupting and stalling the Peace Process, another massive exercise in public consultation was organised in 1999 in which thousands of Zapatistas travelled all over Mexico to promote further dialogue and action (see box 5: 3).

It is worth looking at how the Zapatistas address educational issues within the spaces which they themselves control, such as the thirty-two 'autonomous municipalities' (López Monjardín & Rebolledo Millán, 1999) which the Mexican government officially recognised in 1994 (though it is a concession they seem to have regretted). On a previous visit to Chiapas, in 1995, I accompanied a group of popular educators up sickeningly winding roads to the autonomous municipality of Jototol where some sixty people from surrounding villages converged to spend a day examining how, in this new political context, the autonomous municipalities could be run in a democratic way (as opposed to the dictatorial methods of the former local authorities). The attending educators had been working for some time in the area of popular education and local government. The set-up was unusually formal for a popular education event, with representatives from each community giving a speech on developments in their locality and the 'educators' making a presentation on key issues relating to democratic self-management. Individuals could then make comments from the floor but the whole process meant only one person spoke at a time and there was no opportunity for in-depth group discussion. At one stage I thought the educators lacked awareness of a participatory methodology. However, they argued that since this was the first contact between the indigenous people and these particular NGOs, they did not want to do anything culturally inappropriate and in their various community assemblies, this was the format with which people were familiar. The educators hoped that future events would be more participatory, but only after they had a chance to work with the communities and explain and negotiate the changes. Again, a good example of how techniques are only tools for the job and of the important, mediating role of the educator.

BOX 5:3 Zapatista *Consulta Popular*

With the government ignoring the demands of indigenous peoples in Chiapas, after months of preparation with popular organisations the Zapatistas organised a 'consultation of the people' in March 1999, a massive exercise engaging civil society in discussion (and action) on the nature of democracy and the rights of indigenous peoples in Mexico.

In preparation for the *consulta*, thousands of 'brigades' were set up all over Mexico with 28,000 voluntary *brigadistas* organising a nation-wide programme of public meetings and campaigning events. 5000 delegates of ordinary Zapatistas (with equal numbers of men and women, none with any significant rank in the EZLN) dispersed through the whole of Mexico to tell their stories from Chiapas, counter the government's propaganda, answer questions and hear the views of the wider public. This was a major educational event for the Zapatista delegates themselves (who attended preparatory training courses beforehand), many of whom had never even visited the capital of Chiapas, San Cristóbal (Castro, 1999).

On the day of the *consulta*, the brigades asked the public to answer 'yes', 'no' or 'I don't know' to four key questions, two of which were

1. *Political Participation*: Do you agree that with all their strengths and richness, indigenous peoples should be included in the nation's future, playing an active role in the building of a new Mexico?

4. *To Govern by Obeying*: Do you agree that ordinary people should organise themselves and demand that the government *governs by obeying* in all aspects of national life?

Almost three million people voted in the *consulta* with an estimated 65 million coming into contact with Zapatista delegates altogether (figures taken from CIEPAC, 1999). Evaluations showed that the exercise was considered a success in creating the space for a dialogue between the Zapatistas and civil society and 'a great lesson...for those who participated' (ibid: 3), though weaknesses in the overall organisation were also identified (ibid).

But apart from the popular education work of NGOs, '*zapatista* organisation itself has been a major contributor to the socialisation of all types of basic knowledge: the significant use of the written word, knowledge of other cultures and societies within and beyond the country, an understanding of national history and citizenship' (Rockwell, 1998: 44). In other words, like the MST, the movement is the school. The lack of governmental help has meant that many communities have appointed their own schoolteachers. These have recently come together to exchange their experiences and some expect that in the long run this process will generate a whole new debate about what kind of public education system is desirable for the whole of Mexico (ibid).

Two final observations: firstly, the convergence of Zapatista political practice and the principles of popular education can be explained by the synthesis of three major influences on Zapatismo: (1) the Marxist analysis brought to the movement by revolutionaries from other parts of Mexico (in the aftermath of the national upheavals of 1968) (2) the history of large-scale organising and critical reflection carried out by catechists of the radical, popular church in Chiapas (3) the traditional importance already given to collective, democratic decision-making which was present within indigenous communities themselves. Secondly, for all that there is much to admire in the dignified way the Zapatistas engage in politics, perhaps their movement highlights some of the problems, paradoxes and limitations of a 'popular education approach' to large scale political and social change. García A (1998) shows how five years after the uprising, 'civil society' has not lived up to the Zapatistas' expectations. Despite all the support they receive, the organisation of a strong, united front has not been possible, umbrella groups keep fragmenting and the Zapatistas have come to recognise the ambiguous, 'heterogeneous and conflictive nature of "civil society"' (ibid: 108). Bruhn (1999) concludes that while the Zapatistas have certainly had a massive impact on popular consciousness, in terms of bringing about any real change they have come to an impasse. She argues that instead of organising consultations and dialogues around wooly agendas, the Zapatistas really need to work on the content of specific political proposals; instead of appealing only to 'civil society', they need to grasp the nettle and work out how to relate to political parties. These issues reappear in the following chapter.

Conclusion

From the examples of the women's and indigenous peoples' movements in Latin America we can see that popular education has something both to offer and to learn from social movements focusing primarily on issues of identity rather than material deprivation. With their experience of attempting to help ordinary people become 'subjects' of change, there is much which these social – sometimes *popular social* – movements have been able to appropriate from the theory and practice of popular education. In turn, the movements have impacted on popular education themselves, highlighting particular areas of oppression which were generally ignored in the 60s and early 70s and helping to make ethnic and gender issues areas of 'cross-curricular' concern (see CEAAL, 1999b). Arguably, however, in many places the job is far from complete.

But while there may be much in common between popular education and the consciousness-raising of social movements emphasising issues of identity, there are also points of divergence. Firstly, however vaguely defined, there is clearly a concern with social and economic class at the heart of popular education and those sections of the women's movement ignoring this, for example, could not claim to be engaged in popular education. Theoretically, the same would apply to indigenous groups (see Grueso et al (1998) and Warren (1998) for further discussion of ethnicity versus class) though in practice this is less likely as indigenous peoples are also, almost invariably, the poorest of the poor. Secondly, as illustrated in chapter three, popular education encourages a holistic, integrated approach towards thinking and acting on social reality. Social movements (or parts of them) which isolate individual issues from a wider social, political and economic context would be ignoring basic popular education principles. Thirdly, we have seen that in themselves, social movements are constantly changing and are by no means homogenous. They often encompass a variety of tendencies and currents of thought, some of which are closer to popular education than others: it can be difficult to make generalisations. (The environmental movement provides another example of significant internal divergence, with groups varying from the middle-class and 'conservationist' – having little in common with popular education – to those whose concerns are simultaneously political-ideological and linked to the struggles of poor people to satisfy basic needs – everything to do with popular education (see García, 1992; Collinson, 1996 & Reyes Ruiz, 1999)).

Properly speaking, then, popular education is conceptually distinct from the particular, focused consciousness-raising promoted by those movements ostensibly built around themes of social identity. In the context of Latin America, however, where material disadvantage is so visible and widespread, inevitably, the specific concerns of these 'social' movements often intersect with broader, 'popular' attempts to bring about social change. In this scenario, the particular emphases and expertise of social movements can have a big impact on the more generalised practice of popular education. Whenever the concerns of popular education and these movements do converge – when the 'social' coincides with the 'popular', when a movement's 'generative issue' becomes a catalyst for wider, politically-committed reflection and action – it has always proved an enriching experience for both.

Review of Chapter 5

María del Carmen Mendoza Rangel graduated as a social worker from the National Autonomous University of Mexico (UNAM) and has a Masters qualifiction in Pedagogy. She is the founder of the Mexican Social Workers' Association (ATSMAC) and author of various texts on social work including 'Training through Reflecting on Practice' and the 'Methdological Notebook' for Indigenous Women's Education. Curently she is involved in several activities. She lectures in UNAM on the History of Social Work and the Theory of Community Development as well as being an adviser on curricular studies; she is a training consultant in the methodology of Community Intervention, Popular Education and the Systematisation of Practices;

she is the Coordinator of the Regional Plan for Chiapas of the Mexican NGO 'Service for Development and Peace' (SEDEPAC) and is regional director of CEAAL (the Latin American Council of Adult Education).

Grouped into five sections, our response to this chapter attempts to reinforce much of what the author says, debate aspects of his particular focus and include additional interpretations of our own.

1. From Indian Dominion to Oppressed and Exploited Class

When Christopher Columbus arrived in America in 1992, thinking he was in India, he gave the name of 'Indians' to its population. Since then, Latin America has been the land of the Indians, the men and women who gradually, over centuries, would be reduced from the original owners and sole inhabitants of these fertile, exhuberant lands to being isolated to a fraction of each country's territory.

As the author points out, from being lords, owners and governors of their own destiny, Indians were to become the dominated, the exploited and the oppressed. In the 16th century the wealth found in the land motivated many more Europeans to come in search of their fortune. The paternalistic attitude which considered these Indian peoples unfit to govern themselves led to an extension of royal powers to secure the vice-royalty of New Spain, with governors and their families being sent out from Spain. The resulting three centuries of Spanish domination profoundly modified the original composition of the population; their persecution forced them to flee to inaccessible and unproductive lands – which is where they are now mostly to be found – and to become a source of exploitable slave labour.

Liam Kane rightly highlights this as an important element in the characterisation of Indian peoples. They invariably constitute the poorest sector, live in the worst conditions and have the highest rates of mortality, illiteracy, malnutrition and marginalisation; more than 70% are monolingual and have no possibility of making any progress within the wider world of white people, creoles and mestizos.

After Latin American Independence and the consolidation of national states, the strategies designed for dealing with Indian Peoples turned into what the author calls an anthropological and cultural movement. Later given the name of Indigenism, this tendency was consolidated in the 1950s with the creation of the Latin American Indigenous Institute, the result of the 1st Interamerican Indigenous Congress, celebrated in Mexico, in 1940, with delegates attending from 19 countries. However, Indigenism was never capable of overcoming paternalistic attitudes or the attempt to acculturalise, assimilate and integrate

Indian communities into what Indigenist political programmes assumed to be 'civilisation'.

Among the many legacies of Indigenism, the author rightly highlights the 'vision of the ancestors' of which Indian peoples are assumed to be the inheritors and survivors. This vision is of a nostalgic culture, one 'frozen in time', whose subjects are passive and whose institutions appear intent on uncritically preserving their practices, traditions and customs; the reality, however, is that both people and institutions have changed over time in response to different historical moments and through their relations with other cultures.

However, despite living and surviving in the worst of conditions, one central, permanent element is the Indians' relationship with nature and mother earth. From this, argues the author, there emanates a naturalist vision of the world, a set of environmental values and a social system whose customs and laws place a maximum value on collective rights and community participation. It is central to indigenous people's identity because it represents the objective, material basis of their social being and, therefore, the element which defines their culture, the ways in which they speak and communicate, their language and creativity, their social customs, their traditions and celebrations. The value of these social customs constantly govern their way of life and though on occasions they are swapped for others, the change may not be a 'preferred option' but simply a means of survival. And those other elements which do not disappear, which are authentically their own, retain their importance and have a mystical, spiritual value.

However, we agree with the author that these new practices and relationships make a contribution towards Indigenous people's own, developing and changing identity, this 'process of constant reconstruction, of continuity and rupture'. This needs to be understood in developing an appropriate methodology for working with indigenous groups.

2. From Oppressed Class to New Social Subject

We agree with the author's analysis of the emergence of indigenous peoples' movements in the 1980s. In addition to the important examples he offers, we would add the formation of Councils of Indigenous, Black and Popular Resistance which were built up at local, national and international levels – even at the level of ethnic groups themselves, within each region – and were the backbone of the mobilisation which allowed indigenous people to make an impact at national level within each country; they became new subjects of change with a renewed self-belief, with their own demands and identities – beyond that of social class – and with aspirations to become a new social force, capable of playing a major role in the shaping of the future.

3. The Dilemma of Indian Women's Struggle

In reference to the dilemma constantly facing women's movements, the author describes differences and tensions between a gender-specific and feminist consciousness, fully justifying women's involvement in Popular Kitchens, for example, even though this doesn't modify the role history assigned us in the service of others. Indian women, he suggests, are still closer to a social rather than a feminist consciousness. And even at that, indicates the author, women's progress is experienced as a threat to the family structure and, we would have to add, the organisational structures and established order of communities. For that reason, women's involvement in organisational structures is strongly challenged by their husbands, their families, the collectives and, as if that wasn't enough, by women themselves who are afraid to break their daily routines. These domestic and community pressures are one of the main reasons why women often retreat into their private lives and abandon the idea of participation in public life. It means that opportunities for practising leadership are only sporadic and prevent women having access to government posts or community leadership.

The author describes many varied educational experiences of women in Latin America. However, in a point which we consider of great importance, he indicates that the first challenge is to strengthen women's self-respect and self-esteem, especially when their only source of pride is the 'fulfilment of their traditional roles'. (We have recently been working on a process of systematisation in a Women's Aid Centre in Tláhuac, responding to the policies of the current local government of Mexico City ; in doing so we have concluded that the main focus of attention in gender education should be 'Women and their Basic Relationships').

4. The Contribution of Popular Education to Women's Struggles

The author then considers how far the practice of popular education in Latin America has adopted a feminist perspective, given that the themes dealt with in educational work with women normally relate more to their status as people who are 'poor and oppressed', where projects firstly seek to bring about basic economic improvements. And though feminism can recognise multiple, specific oppressions, questions are asked of its relationship to the structural oppression of which men are also victims.

So the author brings us to the heart of a debate which feminism has not yet been able to resolve. In the meantime, civil organisations drive ahead in their educational work with women, starting from their needs, searching for alternatives, promoting reflection on their own particular identities, strengthening their self-esteem and raising awareness of their rights. In their (our) work with indigenous peoples, we have to accept that though they may not appear explicitly on our educational agendas, themes such as ethnic identity, cultural diversity, intercultural dialogue, spirituality and indigenous people's 'cosmovisions' are now taken much more seriously.

And we agree with the author that these themes require theoretical and methodological clarity or it will not be possible to trace the roots of identity and culture and allow us to build and rebuild social subjects capable of making changes to their daily lives, both within the family and the community. This is the greatest challenge facing any educational process which aims to strengthen these particular social subjects: and it has to be done without losing sight of 'the popular' which, as indicated by the author, offers the only possibility of providing a broader, political perspective.

5. The Zapatista Project: An Historical Opportunity

The chapter concludes with the proposals made by the indigenous peoples of Chiapas to the rest of the Mexican nation through the Zapatista Army of National Liberation (EZLN). These have made a strong impact on popular and civil consciousness even when it seemed that the Zapatista struggle was at a dead-end.

We'd point out that the EZLN is not a traditional vanguard guerrilla army. Its emergence and declaration of war was preceded by a long process of consultation, discussion and decision-making at community level. The public communications they make to the nation are more impregnated with the cosmovisions of indigenous peoples than with the political-military speeches of guerrilla groups. The Zapatistas do not want war; they rose up to make their voices heard and to communicate their word; to say to us 'enough is enough', after the centuries of exclusion, poverty and slow death which they have endured.

The Zapatistas broke both their and our silence and called on the whole nation to stand up and search for democracy, peace, justice and a life of dignity. Their contribution to history was to have made us recover a capacity for surprise and wonder; more importantly, they mobilised civil society, the left, popular groups, civil organisations and political parties around the series of initiatives which they have been presenting over the last six years and which have taken centre stage in the struggle for national change.

Their calls to build human 'circles' of Peace (most notably around the cathedral in San Cristóbal de Las Casas) to rescue the first few months of dialogue; the declaration of 19 Autonomous Municipalities in October 1994; the National Democratic Convention and the Committees for Dialogue in 1996; the International Encuentros of 1997 and the formation of national and international committees to discuss the transition to democracy; the National

Consultation accompanied by the symbolic capture of the Nation in March 1999 when more than 5000 Zapatistas sat down to 'dialogue' with millions of Mexicans all over the country. Through all this activity they have established a historical precedent. Without their contribution, without their calling to order, we would not be the same nation as we are now, transgressors of the institutional order, mobilised and full of ideas in the struggle for local, municipal and national power. Without the Zapatistas we would not have a progressive council in the largest city in the world and we would not have the utopic vision necessary to continue in the construction of a society sustained by democracy, peace, justice and dignity for all.

To conclude, it is important to indicate that the great contribution of this text is that both in terms of its theoretical and methodological analysis, the author very successfully tackles one of the key issues of the relationship between 'popular' and 'women's' education: its complexity. For the British public to examine our social reality should be an enriching exercise for both parties: long may it continue and I hope it makes a positive contribution towards the generation of respect and dignity for women in both societies.

María del Carmen Mendoza Rangel

Appendix 5:1 Thematic Outline of a Training School in 'Leadership and Participation for Indigenous Women' in Chiapas, Mexico:

First Module: The Personal and the Family
Theme 1: Identity, Self-esteem and Self-affirmation of Women
Theme 2: The Participation and Leadership of Indigenous Women
Theme 3: The Exercise of Power within the Family
Theme 4: Our horizons: Towards a View of Gender
Theme 5: A Consideration of Methodological Procedures

Second Module: The Community and the Municipality
Theme 1: Community Identity
Theme 2: Community Participation and Women's Leadership
Theme 3: Community Organisation
Theme 4: Indigenous Women's Views on Gender
Theme 5: A Methodology for Community Work

Third Module: The Organisational and the National
Theme 1: Organisational Identity
Theme 2: Participation and Leadership of Women in Organisations
Theme 3: The Exercise of Power in the Organisations

Theme 4: Views on Gender from a National Perspective
Theme 5: Building a Strategy for Going Forward Together
(Hernández Pérez & Mendoza Rangel, 1999)

Appendix 5:2 Asociación Mayalán

Asociación Mayalán is a popular organisation working with fourteen different Mayan communities in the northwest highlands of Guatemala. Its aims are to foster unity, organisation, education and sustainable economic development in rural communities. An extract from its publicity on popular education says:
'Informal or popular education has many uses in our communities:
- To rescue and preserve our Mayan customs and traditions
- To raise consciousness on social, political and economic issues
- To teach skills that will help us improve our immediate living conditions (health, nutrition, etc.)
- To improve our technical abilities – for example in production and management of our economic projects

To achieve these objectives, Mayalán organises training and workshops in our 14 communities on a variety of subjects... The following is a list of some of the workshops and training we offer:
- Domestic Violence
- Self-Esteem and Women's Rights
- Political Education (women's groups and mixed groups)
- Implementation and Enforcement of the Peace Accords
- Constitutional Reforms and the Popular Referendum (in preparation for the Popular Consultation on May 16th, 1999)
- Mayan Calendar and Cosmovision
- Microenterprise Management
- Production and Design Techniques for Artisanry

These themes have been developed based on the needs and requests of our members, in response to the problems and priorities felt in our communities. We are flexible and willing to develop and facilitate other workshops according to the interest and participation of our membership'.
(From Mayalán, 1999)

Chapter 6
Popular Education and Ideology

"WE'RE GOING TO DIVIDE INTO TWO GROUPS NOW: MARXIST, FEMINIST, CATHOLIC AND NATIONALIST POPULAR EDUCATORS OVER THERE .... PROTESTANT, ENVIRONMENTALIST, SOCIAL DEMOCRAT AND MACHISTA POPULAR EDUCATORS OVER THERE "

I am increasingly convinced of the urgency to recognise, explicitly, that the practice of popular education is inevitably influenced by the ideological orientation of the educator(s). I believe that a reluctance to address the relationship between popular education and mainstream ideologies is a weakness in popular education – though it may be rooted in the desire to avoid the traditional schisms of the left – and a source of confusion to anyone trying to grasp the dynamics of the popular education movement. In a major piece of research into popular educators' practice, the limited response to queries on ideology led the researchers to conclude that 'with such a highly ideological discourse; with a debate in progress founded on different ideological positions; in an area of work where educational materials are necessarily ideological in content, it is curious that so little importance was given to this topic (ie 'ideology') and that it is generally treated with such superficiality' (Núñez et al, 1992: 54).

By 'ideology', I refer to the particular set of ideas and beliefs – political, cultural, philosophical – held by a group (or individual) and used to interpret reality. Though there are core values which should be common to all authentic popular education practice (such as a political commitment to oppressed groups and a participatory methodology) these still allow people with a wide range of ideological motivations to feel included. The ranks of popular educators have been swelled by Catholics and atheists, social democrats and Marxist revolutionaries, feminists and *machistas*, nationalists and internationalists, with many and varied combinations in-between. In the recent past, in times of dictatorship, the differences may have seemed unimportant as people struggled against an immediate and obvious source of oppression, the state. In the past ten to fifteen years, however, there have been major social and political changes in Latin America such as

- transitions from dictatorship to formal 'democracy'
- the growth of 'civil society'
- 'structural adjustment' of the economy, in return for debt rescheduling
- the dominance of free-market economics ('neo-liberalism')
- the privatisation of many state functions
- the increasing impoverishment of the majority of the population
- the Vatican's assault on Liberation Theology
- intellectual confusion and the belief, among many, that with the fall of the Berlin Wall and defeat of the Sandinistas there no longer exists an alternative, socialist model of development

(See Petras & Morley, 1992; Carr & Ellner, 1993; Halebsky & Harris, 1995; Domínguez & Lowenthal, 1996; Veltmeyer et al, 1997)

In this scenario, different ideological orientations take on a more obvious significance. They lead to a variety of ways of interpreting the changes and, consequently, of how they ought to be handled; it also presents problems for any attempt to conceptualise current theory and practice in popular education.

This chapter analyses a range of ideological positions within popular education and explores the connections between ideology and educational practice. It concludes by suggesting a conceptual framework for interpreting the confusing and often contradictory signals in much of what is currently said and written about popular education. First, though, a detour: since this chapter argues for openness and honesty in matters related to ideology, readers are due an explanation of the ideas and beliefs influencing the author's own analysis. In making these transparent, allowing them to be taken into account, readers can then 'adjust their sets accordingly' and arrive at their own, independent conclusions.

The Author's Cards on the Table

While I am as prone as anyone else to confusion and contradiction, with a reluctance to be pigeon-holed by precise definitions – and have an aversion to all fundamentalisms, religious and political – I broadly describe my ideological orientation as humanist-Marxist. 'Marxism', however, means a thousand different things to as many people – and there are many schools of Marxist thought – so a brief explanation is required.

First, there are interpretations of Marxism I reject, as when the words of Marx, Engels, Lenin or Trotsky are touted, quasi-religiously, as ultimate truths. The classic Marxist texts, and analysis of their meaning and relevance, are immensely important but too much deference leads to an uncritical, mechanical, fundamentalist and dogmatic approach to Marxism. In particular expressions of Marxism-Leninism, this fortifies the elitism of self-proclaimed, vanguard revolutionaries who, considering themselves enlightened possessors of superior knowledge, assume the task of leading the ignorant masses blindly to their socialist destiny. Without denying the important role of leadership in any organised movement for social change, such combinations of elitism and dogma, for me, are extremely dangerous.

Then there is an exaggeratedly economistic interpretation of Marxism which reduces all human activity to an economic foundation. Ideologies like liberalism, conservatism, Protestantism, Catholicism – or social prejudices like sexism, racism and homophobia – can all be explained by economic structures and developments. Rather than battle intellectually against ideas, then, the thing to do is change the economic system and new ideas corresponding to the new system will emerge and become the norm (so, with the advent of socialism, racism and sexism will wither away). Taken to extremes, it becomes a deterministic philosophy in which history is programmed by immutable economic laws, with little scope for human subjectivity. Historical materialism (explained in chapter three) is interpreted to mean that on their own, the contradictions of capitalism will inevitably lead to its downfall and replacement by a socialist-communist mode of social organisation. In the last chapter we saw that it can be an excuse to avoid more immediate responsibilities, with *machista* Nicaraguan Sandinistas refusing to answer feminist critiques until successful revolution had been achieved. For me, the search for an underlying economic explanation of social change is a (the) major contribution of Marxism: when it becomes reductionist, however, when it is the only explanation, when all human subjectivity is squeezed out of the equation – it becomes dry, mechanical, off-putting and not a great deal of help to anyone.

Then there is the interpretation which equates Marxism with the political systems (and regimes) of the former Soviet block, Communist China, a few other countries round the globe, Cuba, and communist parties everywhere which slavishly followed the Soviet line. Not being old enough, myself, to have witnessed the birth of these regimes and invest them with personal emotion, I never had any difficulty in seeing, for example, that the ex-Soviet Union was a place run by an elitist, totalitarian regime (though each country and regime would have to be judged on its merits). There is no denying that Marxism suffers from its public association with the likes of Stalin, Ceaucescu and Pol

Pot but to blame Marxism for the atrocities of these particular tyrants is like blaming Christianity for those of Pinochet in Chile, Ríos Montt in Guatemala or Ronald Reagan in Central America. While right-wingers everywhere have conveniently (and successfully) perpetuated and promoted this image of Marxism as a despotic, anti-democratic and economically inefficient philosophy, for decades there have been Marxist organisations speaking out against such distortions of their beliefs. As early as the Spanish Civil War, from 1936-1939, when Stalin was more interested in crushing authentic revolution than in combating fascism, it was clear to many on the left that the Soviet government's agenda was its own self-interest (Orwell, 1989 & Morrow, 1974). Likewise, when Russian tanks entered Hungary in 1956, their identity as an imperial global power – not a liberator of the oppressed – was further confirmed. For me, then, the idea that socialism died with the fall of the Berlin wall is an absurd conclusion to take from the events of November 1989. Certainly this symbolised an important change in the make-up of statist, geo-political alignments but the idea that the Soviet Union was an authentic, socialist utopia to which Marxists could aspire was already dead and buried by 1939, if not before.

My understanding of Marxism is that it is a flexible, methodological approach for interpreting the world though famously, of course, 'the point, however, is to change it' (Marx, quoted in Engels, 1950: 99). It combines a rigorous class analysis of political and economic change with an attempt to grasp social reality in its totality, the belief that human subjectivity is an important factor in change (so ordinary people do have the power to intervene in and shape the course of history, though 'they do not make it under circumstances chosen by themselves' (Marx, quoted in Elster, 1989: 277)) and that subjugated classes themselves must be the prime agents of radical social change: a Marxism which is profoundly democratic but recognises that poverty and the unequal distribution of wealth and power effectively prevent the exercise of real democracy. I also believe this is what truly reflects the principles of the original Marxists (see Harris, 1992, especially his discussion of Marxism and democracy, for an analysis of different strands within Marxism and how these are reflected in the Latin American context).

Since I question the thesis which equates the fall of the Berlin wall with the death of socialism and believe that the current social and economic changes known as 'globalisation' are simply the latest stage in the development of capitalism, for me, in their humanist variety, the principles of Marxism continue to be as relevant as ever. In Latin America, this is not a particularly popular position to defend (even less so in the UK, where New Labour has declared the class war over) but I think there are three main problems with the currently fashionable, whole-scale rejection of Marxism.

Firstly, anti-Marxist critiques generally stereotype and equate Marxism with those interpretations denounced at the beginning of this section, a Marxism seen as dogmatic, elitist, vanguardist, economistic, deterministic, formulaic and dependent on the former Soviet block for its inspiration. Unfortunately, it appears that in popular education in Latin America, this kind of Marxism has made its presence felt all too often: it is absolutely right that it is censured. To condemn this particular type of practice is one thing, however, but to confuse it with Marxism *per se* and conclude that Marxist tools of analysis should be abandoned altogether is to throw a giant out with the (albeit contaminated) bathwater.

Secondly, though the inhumanity of the neo-liberal agenda is widely attacked, the general downgrading among intellectuals of 'class' as an issue has led to a shift in thinking which mistakenly, I believe, allows great hope to be placed in the potential of formal 'democracy' – free from rigged elections – and an invigorated civil society to bring about qualitative social change. While these developments are to be welcomed, particularly where they have replaced totalitarian dictatorships, those with economic power still manage to pull the strings and 'democracy' is singularly failing to improve the living conditions of the poor. To ignore underlying class struggles is to see neo-liberalism as a de-politicised, technical development plan which is failing to deliver (and therefore needs to be adjusted) rather than a set of policies deliberately promoted by particular classes to defend their own economic interests (and therefore needing to be completely rejected) which, in its own terms, is working very effectively: (see Veltmeyer et al, 1997, for a full analysis of neoliberalism and class conflict in Latin America). Equally, civil society is not a homogenous entity but is sometimes highly fragmented, with many groups pulling in different directions and the analysis (some might call it 'postmodernist') which simply sees these groups as expressions of different, disconnected identities, with no structural or economic explanation of how and why such identities and differences arise – or how they inter-relate in a single, common reality – is one which, to my mind, only strengthens the hand of neoliberalist advocates. Susan George illustrates this chillingly in asking 'who will make sure the good guys win, in so far as business interests, gun lovers and the Ku Klux Klan also figure in civil society?' (George, 1996: 372).

Thirdly, in mistakenly equating socialism with the ex-Soviet Union, and thus proclaiming its death with the fall of the Berlin wall, those who would argue that the socialist dream of radical change has been destroyed (Castañeda's (1994) 'utopia unarmed'), that capitalism is here forever and that the best we can hope for is to minimise its negative effects – they spread a dispiriting and defeatist message which encourages restricted thinking, dampens ambition and takes radical change off the agenda. Like an incompetent teacher who tells children they are stupid, the danger lies in the possibility that the message is believed, turning into a self-fulfilling prophecy (though encouragingly, children have a nasty habit of proving their teachers wrong). This does not mean we should indulge in pie-in-the-sky idealism, as if imagining a different world will bring it into being, nor that the gargantuan nature of the task involved in effecting radical, structural (some call it 'revolutionary') change should be underestimated. Realism is essential. However, as Allman and Wallis argue in an important essay on radical education, there are two kinds. One, common to many social movements in the UK, remains at the level of localised and fragmented resistance to oppression, 'the realism of the postmodern condition, a realism which spells the abandonment of the search for common and, therefore, potentially shared human goals' (Allman & Wallis, 1995: 19). Another, though starting necessarily with these differentiated expressions of resistance, considers them the first step in a long, arduous struggle in the direction of total, social transformation.

Fourthly, I am against the kind of Marxism which, in reducing cultural attitudes and identities to a mere reflection of economic development, patronises movements which fight racial or gender oppression, for example, just because they lack a wider, economic and structural analysis. On the other hand, in the aftermath of the discrediting of Marxism (based on a stereotyped version of what it supposedly represents), within a so-called 'post-Marxist' or 'postmodernist' framework, the pendulum appears to have swung the other way, economic and class struggles have been demoted and attention is focused, instead, on bringing about cultural change, with 'culture' perceived in the abstract, disembodied from specific material realities. The thoughts of the Italian Marxist Antonio Gramsci are often cited to justify this 'culturalist' orientation. In a reaction against economic reductionism, Gramsci emphasised that in addition to revolutionising the economic 'base' of society, it was also important, at the 'superstructural' level (ie 'civil society'), to engage in the struggle for ideas which would challenge the 'hegemony' – domination by consent – of the ruling classes. Gramsci has had an enormous influence on Marxism and, indeed, on radical adult education in general, but I think that his representation as a 'culturalist' ignores his insistence on the dialectical relationship between culture and the relations of production (see Allman & Wallis, 1995, for an analysis of the misrepresentation of Gramsci in adult education). Others are even more emphatic: 'the fate of Gramsci ... is to have become, as historian T.J. Jackson-Lears put it, "the Marxist who's safe to bring home to Mother". Gramsci has become safe, tame, denatured, – a wisp of his revolutionary self. Academics seeking to justify their retreat into highly abstruse theories have created fanciful illusions about their "counterhegemonic" activity. They have created a mythical Gramsci who holds views he never did, including an opposition to revolutionary socialist organisation of the sort that he, following upon Lenin, held indispensable' (Phelps, 1995: 54; quoted in Holst, 1999: 409-410). In my view, then, while the cultural practices of any group or movement of resistance need to be respected, and should be the starting point of engagement, a popular education which fails to encourage an investigation of how a particular struggle relates to a wider context and the dynamics of class struggle overall – albeit without imposing its views – is one with severe limitations.

In summary, then, I fully endorse the critique levelled at many so-called Marxist organisations in the past – and they ought to learn from this. But I also believe it is wrong to reject the tools of Marxist class analysis for the idealism which sees progress in terms of a heterogeneity of disconnected groups (some of which are reactionary) engaging, within civil society, in a struggle for cultural meaning. Though it may not be immediately imminent, I do not think we should begin to entertain the defeatist notion that large-scale, structural change – some would call it 'socialism' – is impossible: given the conditions in which the majority of humanity live, it is surely a struggle which can never be abandoned?

Ideological Diversity within Popular Education

This section examines ideological diversity within popular education and its implications for practice. It begins with a selection of quotations (chronologically ordered) from individuals who have been prominent in the field. With the caveat that they do appear out of context, the quotations nevertheless illustrate a range of ideological positions within popular education and serve as useful reference points for the analysis which follows.

A

'Through a process of the collective production of knowledge, the specific contribution of the educator is to try and help with the construction of popular class-based organisations which are broad, united, democratic and capable of carrying forward the great task of building socialism in this country'.

Pedro Pontual (Faria et al, 1988: 21) in a debate on popular education in Brazil.

B

'Never before in the history of humanity have so many of us lived through such a short century; dreams, illusions, utopias which began to appear real on the 17th of October 1917 and which collapsed in November 1989 with the symbolic and profoundly material fall of the Berlin Wall. The consummation of the fall of communism dragged down with it every type of Socialism, including the Democratic, weakening the power of critical, progressive thinking and creating the certainty that there is no place on earth where it is possible to harbour suspicions, doubts or alternative thinking'

Marco Raúl Mejía (Colombian) in an article on 'rethinking the basics' in popular education (Mejía: 1993: 7)

C

'...we discussed whether it was true that people's dreams had been destroyed and that the paradigms were in such crisis that there was no point in building them any more...We all agreed that this was not a viewpoint we shared...It is not true that hope has died; only the arrogant moderation of those who essentially defend economic interests, no other value, can dare to suggest that history is over, that ideologies no longer exist and that capitalism, that unjust model which keeps us all in misery, has triumphed and is there for the rest of eternity'.

From the cover of a published discussion on the continuing relevance of ambitious plans and dreams ('utopías') in Latin America (Betto et al, 1993), involving Frei Betto (Brasilian), Fernando Cardenal (Nicaraguan), Orlando Fals Borda (Colombian) Jorge Osorio (Chilean) and Carlos Núñez (Mexican).

D

'In this text, the analysis of the (Lord's Day) Movement as a case-study in popular education will focus on the religious. This is because for the people in the movement, both the *campesinos* and the author of this book, religion is integral to the way they read the world. It is at the heart of all the reflection and action which takes place within the movement'.

Pedro Benjamin García (Brazilian) (1993: 9) in his book 'Liberation as the plan and dream of God and Man: An experience of popular education in a rural area'.

E

'A number of experiences of popular education fell into a kind of fundamentalism. For many, the concept of dialectics wasn't clear and it was used mechanically...Course outlines were used which were ideologically loaded; we launched ourselves into teaching about contradictions but we were less interested in educating than we were in taking power'

Gutiérrez Pérez & Castillo (1994: 173-4) in their critical revision of popular education up to 1994.

F

'With all the errors, limitations and inconsistencies which the experiences of popular education may have had, it is undeniable that in the most diverse corners of Latin America they constituted a dynamic and effective accompaniment to the popular sector, helping in the process of understanding and transforming that reality, with an essentially dialectical and democratic methodology and with a pedagogy which was critical, dialogical, creative and liberated people's potential to both produce new knowledge and new conditions of life...Today, old and new ideas confront each other. Therefore, in our desire to build a new society (...) we need to emphasise that there are still some fundamental values and viewpoints which have not lost their validity'.

Oscar Jara (Costa Rican), speaking on the continuing relevance of popular education (Jara, 1994c).

G

'The new social actors are women, homosexuals, citizens' movements, consumers, authorities and well-intentioned businessmen with whom we ought to establish relations, though we hold on to our different identity. In that way, popular education should be better able to integrate the popular sectors into society and be more inclusive towards these new actors with whom we can have a dialogue and debate about education'

Rosa María Alfaro (1994: 19) in an article entitled Popular Communication or Education for Citizenship?

H

'The pedagogy of popular education – theoretical and practical knowledge – manifests itself today as a knowledge which is de-centred and characterised by pluralisation and fragmentation. Thus, just as there are multiple options and ways of thinking about the context, there are also several options and ways available on how to recognise, understand, evaluate, systematise and express our pedagogical knowledge'.

Alfredo Ghiso (Argentinian-Colombian) in a book on the educational implications of postmodernity (Ghiso, 1997: 65)

I

'From the "basic learning needs" perspective of Jomtien and the "lifelong learning" of Hamburg, with regard to developing new forms of relationship and management between government and society, there opens up a vast field of action for Popular Education in our countries'

Carlos Zarco Mera (Mexican), secretary general of CEAAL, commenting on the UNESCO Declaration of Hamburg regarding the education of adults and young people (Zarco Mera, 1998: 18)

J

'However, here we can see a profound convergence between the concerns raised by humanist Marxism, such as that of Che Guevara, and those expressed by a popular education of liberation. I wonder whether it is through the interaction and inter-penetration of these two approaches that the new revolutionary theory will emerge...So popular education for liberation turns into a critique of authoritarianism and economism, not only of capitalism but also of dogmatic Marxism and really existing socialism. At the same time it is critical of vanguardism, which identifies not the people but a self-proclaimed vanguard as the true revolutionary subject...'

Giulio Girardi (Nicaraguan) speaking on the ethical and political challenges of popular education at the start of the 21ˢᵗ century (Quintanilla, 1998: 62)

Analysing Ideological Diversity

Inevitably – given popular education's left-wing roots, its concern for the oppressed and its desire for structural social change – in any attempt to map out the range of ideological positions of its practitioners, a key indicator is the degree to which these might (or might not) be considered Marxist (though as we have seen, Marxism itself provokes different reactions and interpretations). For our immediate and particular purpose, if we take a Marxist analysis to be a mode of enquiry characterised by a critique of capitalism, a belief that political, social and economic developments generally arise from the attempts by different social classes to promote their interests (the results depending on the outcome of inter-class struggles), that the ideas dominant in society are those propagated by the most powerful class (though the degree to which they are contested also depends on the intensity of class struggle) and that the task for humanity is to build a new system of social organisation run by and for the many, rather than the few (socialism) – then if we examine the above citations within this framework of reference we see a considerable degree of ideological diversity.

Pontual (quote 'A') is clearly of a Marxist persuasion, openly linking popular education to socialism. While this comment was made in 1988, at a time when socialism appeared to have more public credibility than today, of the six popular educators taking part in this debate Pontual was alone in arguing such a clear-cut line. In quote 'B', Mejía gives all the indications of an ex-socialist who has abandoned his beliefs as irrelevant to the current situation. In equating the fall of the Berlin wall with the collapse of the socialist-communist dream, Mejía seems to accept, uncritically, that the political system of the former Soviet Union and Eastern Europe was genuinely socialist. As we have seen, this view is disputed by other socialists who saw it as Stalinism rather than socialism and who, as socialists, celebrated its downfall. Mejía's analysis leads him to extreme pessimism regarding the possibilities of structural change. In quote 'C' Betto et al make a severe attack on the type of thinking Mejía seems to represent, arguing that it only serves the economic interests of the powerful. This debate about paradigms, whether hope and the possibility of large-scale social transformation still exist or whether, as Fukiyama (1992) would have it, we have reached the 'end of history' in which capitalism reigns supreme, is an important backdrop to issues of ideology in popular education (a debate in which Freire himself intervened, with his book *Pedagogy of Hope*, crtiticising ex-Marxists for abandoning the concept of class struggle).

For me, García's comment in quote 'D' raises an important issue which as yet I have never seen properly (or even casually) addressed in the literature on popular education. Given that a great deal of popular education has taken place within the context of the progressive church and the influence of liberation theology, how is it possible to reconcile the proselytising mission of a religious organisation with the attempt to promote critical, independent thinking? There is little doubt that much of this work has made an important contribution to the development and strengthening of grassroots movements. Religious popular educators – whether priests, nuns or catechists – encourage a political reading of scriptures and a search for spiritual support for the struggle to be free of oppression. Politically, this can be extremely radical. Instead of the traditional, preacher-centred service, the Catholic 'Mass' can be an animated centre of collective discussion with a mixture of spiritual, humanist and political commitment known to have moved the most resolute of socialist atheists. I have heard of priests who, in their urgency to promote collective organisation have declared from the pulpit that 'only people who are organised will be able to enter into heaven'! (Kane, A, 2000) Whatever we think of such comments, it is clear that many in the radical church are and have been worthy upholders of the interests and self-organisation of the popular classes: from Camilo Torres to Oscar Romero, Christians have been martyred for earthly rather than celestial causes. On the other hand, the discussion and analysis they promote takes place within the boundaries of a clearly-defined religious-ideological framework. While the interpretation of scriptures can be discussed, the underlying assumptions of Christianity and Catholicism are not in dispute. If popular culture and beliefs are strongly religious, then of course it makes perfect sense, in popular education, to start from there and broaden out to wider considerations. However, these religious beliefs do not just happen to be there by accident. The same priests, nuns and catechists who take on the role of popular educators are important agents in spreading these beliefs in the first place (though why they are so readily accepted is a different discussion). There is a paradox here which, if it cannot be resolved, should at least be openly acknowledged: while they may well be promoters of critical reflection and action, religious popular educators are also simultaneously engaged in a process of banking education and ideological persuasion. The extent to which this might also apply to non-religious educators is discussed later on.

In quote 'E' – and in their book in general – Gutiérrez Perez & Castillo make a number of sideways critiques of Marxism, linking the notion of a 'dialectical' methodology to (Marxist) ideological fundamentalism. Their book is a thorough and enlightening examination of popular education in Latin America but I think they are sometimes guilty of confusing the quality of educational practice with the ideological orientation of the educator, two separate issues (see Diagram 6:1, Box D). If an educator goes around dispensing lectures on ideology (unless specifically requested to do so) or always resorts mechanically to a particular set of methodological tools, regardless of the occasion – this would be poor practice: it would be condemned by other educators who are opposed to ideological imposition (even if they happen to agree with the content of the 'lectures') and who make appropriate use of the same tools. However, though the practice is clearly manipulative, this is a separate consideration from the soundness or otherwise of the ideological beliefs of the (clearly very poor) educator. Nowhere in their book do the authors draw the same conclusions about religiously-based popular education, for example, which is arguably the most ideologically up-front popular education of all. Similarly, it is a loaded statement to say that 'course outlines were used which were ideologically loaded':

A mass for returned refugees in El Salvador. Urging people to keep the community strong, in his sermon the priest said that only people who were organised would be able to enter into heaven. Photographer: Anne Kane

to give the authors the benefit of the doubt, they may have been thinking of exaggerated, manipulative attempts to direct people's thinking. But even in good popular education practice, that which draws out people's own knowledge and encourages debate and discussion, it is impossible for a course outline to be ideologically neutral. Moreover, the essence of popular education is that it cannot and should not be neutral. Consciously or otherwise, I think that the authors take advantage of the poor educational practice of some Marxists (of which, it would appear, there has been a lot!) to attack the philosophy of Marxism rather than poor educational practice, *per se*. They also imply that such ideological zeal was geared towards taking power, presenting an elitist, vanguardist image of Marxism which, though often accurate in Latin America, would not be supported by Marxists who see ordinary people – not an intellectual leadership – as the agents of radical change.

In the past, having been one of the most explicit in linking popular education to a class analysis (see Jara, 1994), in quote 'F' Oscar Jara hangs on to some of his earlier ideas but accepts they are being challenged by new ones. In this and other writings (Jara, 1998), while he continues to criticise neo-liberalism and argue for structural change it seems to me that in general he now emphasises the importance of new social actors (such as women's and indigenous peoples' movements) and looks for new openings for popular education (such as within local authorities) while quietly dropping the language of class analysis. In quote 'G' by Rosa María Alfaro, I was surprised to find 'well-intentioned businessmen' as a sector with which popular education would seek to co-operate. While there is clearly an awareness here that the popular sector is something different from the other movements she mentions – presumably based on its class – I think this quote reflects the views of the many who, in the aftermath of repression and the lack of formal democracy, have placed great faith in the potential of a newly emerging 'civil society' to deliver social change. Much of the literature on new social movements takes this view and we have already seen (in chapter five) the importance of civil society to the struggle of the Zapatistas, though they are aware of its limitations. A Marxist view, on the other hand, takes a more critical look at civil society, seeing it not as an even playing-field but another site in which the class struggle is played out. While supporting the particular struggles of movements which focus on issues of identity (and having learned from them), a Marxist analysis would seek to explain the source of (and solution to) these struggles within the wider, structural framework of capitalism and class struggle, not as isolated examples of indiscriminate oppression based on abstract prejudice.

In quote 'H', though it is not immediately clear whether he approves of or is merely describing the situation as he sees it, Alfredo Ghiso paints a 'postmodernist' picture of the current state of popular education in Latin America. He goes on to celebrate this diversity (in the same article) and the ability of popular education not to be sucked down by its older, ideological roots, of which Marxism was one. After welcoming the fact that popular education now extends to groups which reject a class analysis, he concludes that if there is to be a 'unity in diversity' regarding popular education today it will be neither imposed nor premeditated but will emerge naturally from the 'systematised', collective educational experiences of all these different groups. Aside from his separation of 'identity' from 'class' and his representation of Marxism as a somewhat outdated philosophy, Ghiso's postmodernist stance differs from a Marxist analysis in that he seems to abstain from any attempt to understand and explain the dynamics of such 'pluralisation and fragmentation' and the ways in which the different groups, identities and movements inter-relate, dialectically, within one political system. Elsewhere, Ghiso (1993) argues eloquently on the importance of a 'dialogue between knowledges' – without doubt an important concept in popular education – but his postmodernist exposé leaves the impression that 'true' knowledge is relative and that he is not prepared to argue the validity of one set of systematised knowledge against another. If popular education is merely what groups and movements happen to do, if there are no essentialist claims to what it *ought* to be, then almost anyone could claim to be doing it, even – why not? – humanitarian, right-wing neo-liberalists.

Being familiar with both the ideas of Freire and the recent past in Latin American popular education, when I first began to research the more academic publications of CEAAL (the continent-wide umbrella group for popular education), I was often confused by articles of the type from which Carlos Zarco Mera's statement (quote 'I') was taken. From a literature focusing on 'popular classes', grassroots organisations, participatory democracy and attempts to transform the whole of society, I suddenly found myself immersed in a world of governments, bureaucracy and UN conferences where the discourse, much gentler now, was the uncontroversial, mainstream educational jargon of terms such as 'basic learning needs' and 'lifelong learning'. What did this have to do with popular education? Older and wiser now, my reaction to such statements is ambivalent. On the one hand, given that the state is generally much less (directly) oppressive than before and spaces have indeed opened up for civil society to make its influence felt, it would be absurd of the popular education movement to ignore this opportunity and press home its case for radical educational change. Accordingly, if there is no compromising of values, an engagement with formal education and the state's agenda is a perfectly valid option. Moreover, as popular education went through its own auto-critique from the early 90s onwards, one of the weaknesses to emerge was that too much concern had been focused on political organisation, not enough on bread-and-butter pedagogical issues. Attempting to address this legitimate concern, what some called the 'pedagogist' wing of popular education (see Núñez, 1993) sought to inform themselves better of the developments in formal educational research. As a result, in current writing on popular education it is more common than before to encounter discussion of mainstream educational issues, whether in the form of the latest, specialist jargon or the ideas of well-known educational thinkers like Rousseau, Piaget or Vygotsky (Mariño, 1993; Grossi, 1993 & Hernández, 1995). On the other hand, Latin American states have a long tradition of co-opting radical movements, a tradition which, according to some, is particularly vibrant in the current climate with neo-liberal states contracting-out services to non-governmental organisations (the traditional financiers of popular education), obliging them to compete for funding but ignoring those which are not flexible enough to bend to the neo-liberal agenda (Petras, 1999). In the struggle to secure survival and financial viability, many succumb. Moreover, as a counter-claim to the 'pedagogists', some have argued that while their contribution has been necessary and important, at times it has gone to the other extreme and downplayed the political and organisational aspects of popular education (Núñez, 1993). Faced with the type of argument suggested by Carlos Zarca Mera, then, I think it pays to be open-minded about discussions of mainstream educational developments but also alert to the possibility of internal sub-texts and ambiguities.

Quote 'J' is taken from a book by Giulio Gerardi, a liberation theologian, ironically enough, who argues against the defeatist pessimism of those who would turn their backs on revolutionary politics, asserting that 'Marxism is now more relevant than ever' (Quintanilla, 1998: 110-111). He makes a clear distinction, however, between a Marxism which is dogmatic and economically deterministic, leaving no place for human subjectivity – which he considers moribund and associated with the former Soviet Union – and the Marxism he defines as 'popular, humanist... critical, heuristic, participative and liberatory' (ibid: 106-107) which he defends.

We can see, then, that for all its common discourse on siding with the oppressed and enabling people to be agents of social change, there is still a wide variety of ideological leanings among those who in their various different contexts assume the role of popular educator. Fundamentally, these differences relate to different forms of political analyses, a reflection of the wider confusion and crisis in which left-wing politics in Latin America has been immersed for a number of years. While the diversity may be partly due to straightforward ideological disagreement, it can also be a manifestation of specific forms of political organisation in a particular time and place. Orellano (1999), for example, explains how in El Salvador different popular education centres have clearly grown out of and reflect different ideological 'tendencies' of the *FMLN*. Cutting across the political-ideological spectrum of centre to far-left politics, of social democracy to revolutionary Marxism (and we have seen that even here there is disagreement on what these terms represent), come a whole, other range of '-isms' – nationalism, feminism, *indianismo*, environmentalism, popular Catholicism, postmodernism, for example – all of which influence, to varying degrees, the final ideological make-up of educators.

Occasionally the ideological differences are openly recognised, not merely submerged in the sub-text of complex educational debate. In his discussion of *CEAAL*, for example, argues that 'multiple understandings of popular education have fostered contradictory projects, some with an explicit analysis of the state and social class...and others appearing prone to legalistic and ultimately populist constructions of those same institutions' (Austin, 1999: 44). Looking at two of CEAAL's affiliates, he contrasts the neo-Marxist perspective of the Federation of Cuban Women (*FMC*) with the ideological confusion of the Latin American 'Women's Popular Education Network' (REPEM) who 'restrict change to that which is congruent with the current dominant regional state project, in this case neo-liberalism'(ibid: 57). He argues that 'they are to that extent susceptible of the Petras/Morley hypothesis' (ibid): this refers to a critique, sustained by Petras and others throughout the 1990s, that many Latin American intellectuals – whether NGO employees or those of the stature of Carlos Fuentes and Jorge

Castañeda – have made far too easy an accommodation to neo-liberalism (see Petras & Morley, 1990 &1992; Veltmeyer et al, 1997).

In Bolivia, in their attempts to square up to popular education's problems in a neo-liberal context, the movement of popular educators attempted to identify its own deficiencies and ideological divisions. Among those mentioned were (a) a purely 'phenomenological' perception of neo-liberalism: educators are immersed in its negative effects but have only a superficial analysis of its causes (b) a lack of historical awareness and the abandonment of 'old' tools of analysis, with nothing new to take their place (c) that educational objectives range from those which are clearly ideological and political (to transform reality, to support popular organisations in their historical project, 'liberation') to the more pragmatic objectives of improving people's living conditions and analysing possible solutions to real problems (d) 'as is well known, there is currently an absence of political references to which Popular Education can relate (on account of the fall of the Berlin Wall, the failure of really existing socialism, the globalisation of the economy, the internationalisation of culture…) this means that Popular Education proposals lack a proper foundation and lead to the uncritical acceptance of the neo-liberal model. Pragmatism becomes the norm, even in popular organisations themselves' (Colectivo CEAAL-Bolivia, 1994: 106 & 113).

Clearly, then, explicitly or otherwise, there is a wide range of ideological influences – and a great deal of confusion – at work within the popular education movement. It is now time to consider how this translates into practice.

Problems related to Ideology and Popular Education

Though popular education makes no pretence of political neutrality – quite the opposite – it should never be in the business of feeding learners a particular political line, encouraging them, instead, to think for themselves. From my own reading of popular education, however, I think it is unavoidable that the particular ideological orientation of the educator – whatever this might be – has an impact on many aspects of the educational process.

Take, firstly, Freire's notion of 'critical consciousness'. If educator-activists aim to develop this faculty in learners, and they themselves are supposed to possess it already (leaving aside, for the moment, the question of how they are meant to acquire it), then their only way of recognising critical consciousness is through their own, particular ideological construction of what this actually means. But 'critical consciousness' for some could be 'naïve consciousness' for others. Freire (as well as Marx and Gramsci) talked of how oppressors try to present inequality as a natural phenomenon and that the role of education is to unveil the ideological manipulation behind the dominant, hegemonic ideology.

But in Latin America, if someone currently believes there is no alternative to neoliberalism and that 'democracy' is the key to progress (socialism now being a utopian dream), is this 'realism' or a lack of 'critical consciousness' (given that this is what the defenders of neoliberalism encourage people to believe)? In 1999, the UK and US governments offered a humanitarian rationale for going to war in Yugoslavia. This was accepted by many people on the left who would presumably claim to posses a degree of critical consciousness; others who examined the different class-interests involved, however – information not readily available in the mainstream press – could have argued that an acceptance of the humanitarian rationale showed a complete lack of critical consciousness. This is not the place to rehearse the respective arguments (see Chossudovsky, 1996 or Chomsky, 1999): the point is simply that the understanding of what constitutes critical consciousness, an important concept in popular education, is something which varies dramatically, in accord with more generalised political and ideological beliefs.

Secondly, the ideological beliefs affecting perceptions of critical consciousness also impinge on the commonplace popular education exercise of 'conjunctural analysis' or 'naming the political moment' (see Arnold et al, 1994: 52-61), the attempt to map out the interplay between political, social, economic and cultural developments at a particular moment in time, an important preliminary step in deciding upon courses of action to be taken. This activity is carried out both among educators themselves, in their various centres, and in conjunction with the organisations with which they work. Essentially, however, these conjunctural analyses are subjective interpretations of reality and are dependent on the intellectual and analytical tools of the participants, mediated by their particular ideological orientation. In Latin America, one 'conjunctural analysis' sees the advent of formal democracy as an opportunity for real change, leading popular educators to move into the state sector or put their efforts into electoral politics: this happened in Mexico in the early 1990s, with the rise of the *Partido de la Revolución Democrático*, which had begun to challenge the ruling *Partido de la Revolución Institucional*, in power since 1928. Another would guard against the danger of 'democracy' being used to distract 'popular classes' from pursuing their own independent forms of struggle and organisation (in Mexico the popular movement was significantly weakened by the exodus of activists into electoral politics; whether this was a price worth paying also depends on how the conjuncture is analysed). In 1995, when I attended an exercise in conjunctural analysis with the staff of the 'Mexican Institute of Community Development', it was clear that several conflicting analyses were vying for supremacy, all based, fundamentally, on different ideological orientations. Similarly, within the Popular Education Forum in Scotland, much work is being done to address the opportunities for change presented by the recently inaugurated Scottish parliament. But within the Forum, whose members, undoubtedly, are all committed to radical change, there are many different ways of analysing this particular conjuncture, from scepticism that the parliament can make any difference to an unequivocal optimism linked to a sense of national pride and achievement. Though the Forum has yet to address the issue squarely (it will, sooner or later), it is clear that social democratic, Marxist, nationalist, religious and other beliefs and values are all bubbling beneath the surface, reflected both in the kind of educational activity in which different members opt to engage and in the underlying ideological assumptions implicit in the educational materials they produce.

Thirdly, while popular education seeks to 'problematise', rather than present solutions, and the methodology is one in which educator-activists encourage discussion and analysis by posing questions, rather than giving speeches, it is an illusion to think that questions are inherently more ideologically independent than statements (powerfully illustrated for me when, after a state ban on any mention of homosexuality in schools, a gay rights group in the US leafleted pupils to 'ask about lesbians': all day long teachers had to answer 'please miss, what's a lesbian?'). As they interact in any group discussion, the questions occurring to educators will depend on how they happen to see the world in the first place. Although they should be open-ended, neither leading to conclusions nor dictating what people should think, they do, however, have a great deal of power to suggest what people should be thinking *about*. In Nicaragua recently, when I attended a popular education workshop for people who had been traumatised by Hurricane Mitch, the participants took part in a simulation exercise in which different groups held different degrees of power. In the debriefing session, it was clear that different educators instinctively tended to ask different types of questions, some leaning more towards 'structural' political questions, some more towards the 'personal'. In the Scottish context, working with a group in an area of urban deprivation, one educator might be inclined to ask, 'what can the new parliament do to bring about change? What can we do to make sure it happens?'; another could ask, 'do you think the parliament has the power to bring about real change? Should we put any effort into lobbying parliament or concentrate on other activities?'; or another, 'whose interests will the parliament seek to defend? How will it behave if big business flexes its muscles?'. These are different sets of questions, each prone to push the discussion in different directions. The three educators could be highly-skilled practitioners with a genuine political commitment to social change: inevitably, however, their different ideological positions inspire a diversity of questions which are likely, in turn, to lead to different educational experiences for learners.

In the same vein, while dialogue, as opposed to knowledge-transfer, is at the heart of popular education's methodology, what an educator-activist actually says in the course of any dialogue must have some influence on its outcome. There will be times when educators are called upon to explain and state clearly what they think of whatever is being discussed and while this should not be presented as objective truth, but a contribution towards a collective search for understanding, again, particularly if educators argue their case well, it should affect what people are going to think *about*. In the workshop in Nicaragua, as well as the questions they asked, educators also contributed their own interpretations of what the simulation represented. The extent to which anyone might agree with the educator's views is one thing, and will depend on a number of factors (the way in which this connects with the learners' experience, the credibility accorded to the educator, the strength of views of the learners themselves and so on), but it is inescapable that the different ideological orientations among educators are bound to result in different experiences for the learners. It matters, then, what the educator happens to think.

But the dynamics of any dialogue cannot be reduced to a formulaic exchange of views (between educator and learners and among learners themselves) in which dispassionate human beings rationally select the best of each argument and weave them into a whole new personal philosophy. Dialogue involves argument, debate and passion in which people are likely to start by defending their current view of the world until they are persuaded to think (or feel) otherwise. And herein lies the contradictory role of the popular educator. On the one hand, educators aim to encourage independent critical thinking; on the other, in the midst of a collective investigation into the best way to bring about change, they will endeavour, naturally, to recruit people to their own particular point of view. Even though they may be open-minded, if they have strong, well substantiated views, what they might really want, ideally, is that learners become independent, critical thinkers and then, of their own volition, arrive at the same conclusions as themselves! This tension – though it can be creative – is particularly evident in organisations with both a campaigning and an educational wing. Currently, for example, Friends of the Earth Scotland runs an exciting popular education programme around the theme of environmental and social justice (Samson & Scandrett, 1999) but the unpredictability of the educational process often clashes with the campaigning imperative to encourage people to take specific forms of action, immediately, if particular negative developments (in the view of FoES) are be averted. Sometimes the particular ideological bias or content of the educator's contribution is obvious, either in the educational materials they use or in their own personal or institutional identity (religious activists, 'feminist popular educators', NGO personnel or party political members, for example); sometimes it will be more subtly embedded in the details of their everyday practice. In either case, learner-centred methodology or not, Freire is surely right to have claimed (in response to the critique that he saw the teacher's role as too stand-offish) that to a greater or lesser degree, 'all education is directive': in assessing in which particular direction, a consideration of the educator's ideological orientation is of primary importance.

Finally, though popular education respects the value of 'popular' knowledge, only an educational practice rooted in *basismo* would expect popular movements, purely from their own experience, to come up with the best ideas for taking their struggle forward. Popular education has to bring 'popular' and scientific, academic or 'systematised' knowledge into contact – the 'dialogue of knowledges' – to maximise the potential of education's contribution to change. Educators have a key function in determining to which particular 'systematised' knowledge a group will be exposed, either through their own views, the educational materials they select or the people and resources they can bring into contact with the particular group or organisation. And though in popular education new knowledge should be presented for analysis, discussion and possible rejection – not for uncritical consumption – it matters very much, I believe, what this new knowledge happens to be. Whether it comes wrapped in a technicist, religious, feminist, Marxist, social-democrat, nationalist or environmentalist (etc) ideological package, it will undoubtedly have a variable, though not deterministic, effect on the educational outcomes.

Popular Education and Ideology: An Analytical Framework

Putting the educator at the centre of the picture, Diagram 6:1 represents the ways in which questions of ideology relate to the practice of popular education.

The line at the bottom of *Box A: Ideology* represents the political spectrum, from far right to far left. Anyone to the right of centre is really at odds with the fundamental precepts of popular education. Though they may genuinely feel for those who suffer hardship, whatever their explanation for its existence it does not include the belief that the system is basically designed to favour those who control it: the notion of a 'right-wing popular educator' is a contradiction in terms. The ranks of popular educators are undoubtedly filled by those from the left though, as we have seen, this incorporates a wide range of beliefs, from socialist democrat to Marxist revolutionary. The bottom line, however, is that all see the system as unjust and poor people as the victims of oppression: the differences lie in the analysis of what needs to be done. But the picture is more complex than finding a position on a standardised line of political affinities. Many other ideologies, from nationalism to the ethos of a particular NGO,

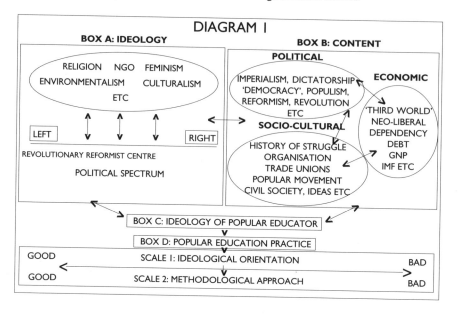

can cut across this line, at any point, interacting with the more traditional forms of political identification and resulting, at the end of the day, in a myriad of different ideological outlooks.

Box B: Context shows ideological orientation not as an abstract phenomenon but as dialectically linked to a specific social context. This context has political elements (from Pinochet's dictatorship to the Cuban or Nicaraguan revolutions), economic elements (such as the degree of crisis or interference by the *IMF*) and socio-cultural elements (like the strength of the popular movement), each having an influence on the other. The Sandinista government was constrained by outside interference and economic crises, for example, and when they lost the elections in 1990 the new government of Violeta Chamorra was in turn restricted by the strength of grassroots organisation. Different ideologies spring from different contexts: the early days of revolution in Nicaragua and Cuba inspired great hope that radical change was possible while currently, as we have seen, the apparent triumph of neoliberalism has led many to abandon radical politics altogether. But ideology also influences, as well as responds to, the social context (indeed, ideas *are* part of the context). The ideologies of the MST, the Zapatistas, the traditional Church, liberation theology, the media and so on – all make significant but differential impacts on the context (while at the same time having to respond to it).

Having distilled his or her own views from a complex interaction between a multiplicity of ideas and a particular social context (*Box C: Ideology of Popular*

Educator), the popular educator duly sets off to work. Whatever format this personal distillation of ideas takes – and it will vary widely from person to person – it will unavoidably influence the individual educator's practice. *Box D: Popular Education Practice* shows that in any popular education practice the educator has both an ideological and a methodological contribution to make. In one sense these contributions are completely unrelated, running in parallel (hence the parallel lines of Scales No 1 and No 2): no matter their ideology, educators could be highly or poorly skilled in a methodological approach. In another sense, since learners experience this practice in its totality, they are also inter-connected (hence the arrows between the lines). However, in assessing the value of any particular practice of popular education we should distinguish between the educator's ideological orientation and his or her application of methodological procedures. What merits a 'good', 'bad' or 'somewhere-in-between' on the ideological Scale (No 1) depends on who is doing the judging: social democrats would be likely to give Marxists a 'bad' and vice-versa, though other values (feminist, nationalist, environmentalist, religious etc) will cloud the issue. On the methodology Scale (No 2), people who try to manipulate, abuse their power or go on ideological rants would be down towards the 'bad' end; those who start from people's specific concerns, promote genuine dialogue, use appropriate and imaginative pedagogical techniques and contribute their knowledge without trying to dominate – these would be up towards the 'good'. An outside evaluator could well judge an educator to be 'good' on one Scale, 'bad' on the other.

Conceptually, I believe that this distinction between the ideological and the methodological is extremely important, though mostly absent, in discussions and debates about popular education. Firstly, the two are frequently lumped together. We have seen, for example, that Marxist popular educators have been accused of being over ideological (see Gutiérrez Pérez & Castillo, 1994, and quote 'E') when, in fact, I would suggest, they are no more or less ideological than Christians, social democrats or anyone else: the target of such criticism should be the educators' bad *practice,* because they are being manipulative, not their *ideology,* though there would be some logic to the argument if the (mistaken) interpretation of Marxism is that it is inherently manipulative *per se.* But anyone, of any ideological orientation (within the limits already defined), could engage in good or bad practice: social democrats, Catholic activists, revolutionary socialists – all have the potential to be exemplary or woeful practitioners of popular education. If the purpose of critique is to point to deficiencies in practice with a view to making improvements, that is all to the good; if it is to discredit a particular ideological viewpoint, then the critique should move to different terrain altogether, to the purely ideological-political, and leave popular education, temporarily, to the side.

Secondly, if, as I have argued, it does have an effect on the educational process, then ideology matters. Educators have to take it seriously, constantly re-evaluate their thinking and be conscious of the role ideology plays in their work. This can raise problems. In certain contexts, if there are strong, political rivalries, the promotion of explicit, ideological debate could be delicate and run the risk of being counter-productive. Nor would it be appropriate, normally, for educators to declare their beliefs at the start of a project as the motives could be easily misinterpreted: suitable timing is required. In any general discussion or analysis of popular education, however, if at all possible, at some stage the question of ideology should be dealt with openly and honestly so that the educator's position is clear and political-ideological debate can be distinguished from discussions on the quality of educational practice.

Conclusion

There is an ideological diversity within the popular education movement in Latin America which is both symptomatic and reflective of social, political and cultural developments in society at large, particularly with regard to the crisis of the left. I have argued that the educator's particular ideology inevitably impinges on practice and that the relationship between the two requires greater, explicit clarification. Popular educators can find themselves in paradoxical roles, with a (potentially creative) tension between encouraging independent thinking and the urge to persuade others to their own particular views. Finally, in any analysis of popular education it would be helpful, conceptually, to draw a clear distinction between a critique of ideology, on the one hand, and a critique of methodology, on the other.

Review of Chapter 6

A graduate in education with a Masters in teacher-training, for the last 10 years Marleny Blanco has been working for CIAZO, a popular education foundation in the Salvadorean capital, San Salvador. This work has included adult education, the production of educational materials (for adult literacy) and the training of popular educators and community leaders. She is currently working in the areas of institutional management and political campaigning. She has the personal satisfaction of working in something which (a) makes a positive contribution towards communities (b) reflects her own views of the world and (c) offers substantial professional development. She also teaches on education courses run by the University of El Salvador.

First of all I'd like to say that I feel passionately about the subject I am about to discuss, not only because I experience the ups and downs of popular education in my daily life but because I am also convinced popular education continues to have validity and relevance for the transformation of our communities. With great humility and due respect to the readers and Liam Kane, the author, I'll now dare to examine his thoughts on popular education and ideology.

While it is true that we can understand ideology as the interpretation people have of the world, we cannot do so without also taking into account the context in which this interpretation is developed. So as well as asking about an educator's own ideological inclinations we have to inquire about the context which led them to become involved in educational activity. From the previous chapters it should be clear that the emergence of groups of popular educators in Latin America corresponds to the developing struggles of social movements and their efforts to change society.

Regarding the analysis of ideological diversity, it is appropriate, as the author has done, to do so from a framework of reference – and I am able to share the view that 'in their humanist variety, the principles of Marxism continue to be as relevant as ever' – though this does lead to a particular way of looking at the world. And just as there can be no neutral interpretation there can never be any single conclusion either so, in the end, each new analysis leads to an ever greater ideological diversity.

I must say that it is not very usual to examine isolated statements from different authors, though it is one way – within the limitations of a text, of a logically developed argument – of drawing readers' attention to the particular status and recognition accorded to these particular authors. So when it is suggested 'we were less interested in educating than we were in taking power' it is important to contextualise this statement because though the emphasis might well have been placed on political-ideological, rather than technical-methodological-pedagogical aspects of popular education (in the case of El Salvador, for example, we might place this in the decade of the 80s), the emphasis would currently be the reverse. For that reason I do not believe we should talk about popular education as if it belonged to the past: it continues to be relevant and I fully support the argument that its basic philosophy and values have not lost their validity. By that I mean that its aspirations and ideals of struggle remain relevant; what happens, though, is that they are applied to new contexts, as societies evolve and develop. However, we have to recognise that some practices have not been able to adjust to these changes and their vision can be either too limited or too ambitious.

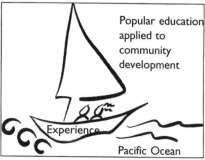

This image illustrates whether or not popular education is out of step with changes in context or whether, by contrast, it is open to the enormous opportunity for further development and enrichment. Obviously, to achieve maximum potential effect, all aspects of popular education have to be strengthened.

It shows the diversity of experiences and the different approaches which have developed. However, we have to be aware that 'not all diversity is connected'; in other words, diversity can also lead to a lack of unity in the struggle for transformation and it can happen – we still see cases – that when we find obstructions on our path, instead of clearing them away we rearrange them so that no one else is able to pass.

On this unfolding path of opportunity, we come across new forms of relationship between government and society. It has to be said that it is not due to the kindness of governments that these new spaces emerge. They are the result of the popular movements' struggle, not only of protest and pressure but also their ability to make positive, concrete proposals for change.

In the midst of these opportunities there emerge 'new social actors' (women, homosexuals, consumers and so on) towards whom popular education has to be inclusive; this is a logical progression, given both the changing social context and the developments within popular education itself. Nor can we ignore this new scenario of so-called 'globalisation', a phenomenon which we have to resist; we cannot sit arms-folded and pretend it isn't there. We have to be well prepared to fight it.

Taking all these considerations into account, I share the author's concern (and invitation) to review the potential impact which popular education might have, a review which, in addition to the variety of ideological influences, might also consider the possible opportunities, issues, new scenarios, outstanding/unpaid accounts, confusions and challenges which it faces.

Regarding the question of ideology and popular education, I would highlight the importance of three particular elements: critical consciousness, ideological belief and the role of the educator. While it is true that the methodological approach of the educator sets out to 'problematise', the end goal is different: it is to influence social change by enabling people to analyse and identify appropriate action to take in whatever circumstances they may find themselves. It is important to ask, then, how well the experience of popular education is able to do this.

Undoubtedly, when popular educators stand in front of a group they are in a position of power. While 'all education is directive', in the words of Paulo Freire, we also have to ask: towards what end? For whom? How is it carried out?

Currently in Latin America there are educational projects using the REFLECT-Action approach (Box 2:1), a way of working which, among other things, emphasises the importance of power relations embedded in structures, procedures, attitudes, roles and so on: that is why we have to constantly analyse whether we see ourselves as facilitators, advisers, teachers, guides or something else.

Whichever role we choose to adopt in life, it will necessarily be rooted in some ideological conception of what we are trying to achieve. If we opt to be a 'popular educator', we have to be clear that what we do will still be influenced by our own personalities, by whatever functions we are prepared to carry out – or changes we are prepared to make – as a result of our developing relationship with a group or community.

Finally, a word on the author's 'analytic framework' for considering popular education and ideology. It is indeed important to highlight these two areas – the methodological and the ideological – in which popular educators (might) exert an influence on practice. And however we might engage in this kind of work, we have to do so with sincerity: people easily perceive whether or not we are fully committed to the process.

To conclude, I commend the exercise to invite Latin Americans to review this book and I consider this chapter's contribution – as well as the rest of the book – to be of value. The important thing, now, is that the book becomes an analytical tool for improving popular education practice.

Elda Marleny Blanco

Chapter 7
Assessing the Impact of Popular Education at Micro Level

"HE SAID HE WANTED TO MAKE AN IMPACT SO I WAS HAPPY TO OBLIGE"

In 1989, on an Oxfam trip to the Caribbean, I visited the small rural village of Dupetit in the north-eastern corner of Haiti. Liaising with other NGOs and the local radical church, Oxfam supported the training of a number of villagers in the basics of popular education. When I met with the people of Dupetit and these trainees – known locally as *animateurs* – I asked what difference, if any, they felt popular education had made to their lives. They cited the case of the former *Duvalierist* magistrate who had been terrorising the village for years. When the *animateurs* began their work, encouraging people to analyse problems and consider action for change, the villagers decided to run their despot out of town and prepare for the inevitable backlash of repression. Each time the *tontons macoutes* visited the village to retaliate, its inhabitants fled and remained hidden till it was safe to return. Eventually the *macoutes* gave up, villagers elected their own magistrate and were elated at the immediate change in their lives. I was impressed. If popular education could make a difference under the brutality of (an albeit dying) dictatorship, then surely it had something to offer oppressed people everywhere?

But occasional anecdotes are no basis on which to draw grandiose conclusions. In looking realistically at what popular education might be expected to achieve, this chapter examines:

- the problems involved in evaluating its impact

The new, friendly judge who replaced the previous despot in Dupetit, Haiti, an achievement attributed to popular education.
Photographer: Liam Kane

- methods of evaluation
- success and failure in local, community or micro level projects. This section focuses on examples of detailed evaluations, partially-evaluated case studies and the views of popular educators.

Chapter 8 then examines the impact of popular education at a national or macro level.

Problems with Evaluation

'Not everything that counts can be counted.
And not everything that can be counted, counts.'
Albert Einstein (quoted in Roche, 1999: v).

'It is impossible to evaluate the manifest results of popular education comprehensively because neither the outcome to be measured, nor the population exposed, nor an appropriate comparison group is well-defined'
(Hammond, 1998: 157).

In the world of formal education, the assessment of learning has become a jargon-laden, specialised field: behavioural and expressive objectives, intended learning outcomes, construct validity and reliability, formative/summative/continuing/peer/self-assessment and so on. These concepts and tools are available to non-formal education too – along with others tailor-made for the job –

though some have argued that in an over-reaction against formal assessment (criticised as oppressive, manipulative and individualistic), adult education is often woefully lax in self-evaluation (Rogers, 1992). Within popular education in Latin America, in the past – though not so much now – the systematic analysis and evaluation of learning has also been inadequate (Rivero, 1993: 130). In researching for this chapter, I was struck by the little space devoted to evaluation in popular education publications. However, given that the aims and objectives of popular education go beyond classroom learning and seek to have a positive effect in a wider social context, though they remain useful, the standard means of measuring and evaluating educational progress are insufficient. The evaluation of popular education necessarily becomes part of a broader approach to understanding and measuring social change, commonly referred to by development agencies as 'impact assessment'.

But there are many reasons why making generalised statements about the effectiveness, or otherwise, of popular education is a speculative business. First, in any organisation working for change, the border between 'education' and other activities such as 'communication', 'organising', or 'campaigning' is frequently blurred. While popular education is the deliberate and planned attempt to promote learning in the midst of collective action, as Brandão (1989:73) points out it 'is neither based exclusively on (explicitly) educational events nor gives priority to any particular educational mode' and 'turns both reality and the process of transformation themselves into educational events'. Due to the linkages between many different types of cultural action it can be difficult to isolate what is uniquely 'educational' from the rest.

Second, there are many causes of social change and the role played by popular education is seldom clear cut (making it difficult to compare the merits of one educational project with another). Externally, every context in which popular education attempts to intervene is different, each enmeshed in a wider social reality which is itself in constant flux. Positive changes occur where there is no popular education; negative changes resist the best that popular education can offer. The example from Haiti was successful but it could have been otherwise. Though popular education played its part, other factors, too, were important. Had the same actions been taken earlier, when the dictatorship was stronger, or had the *tontons macoutes* been more persistent and intelligent, it might easily have ended in bloodshed. Internally, within educational projects, similar variables are at play. It makes a difference whether the members of any movement or organisation form a homogenous group or pull in different directions, whether they are already politicised by struggle or still immersed in 'naïve consciousness', whether they actively seek to increase learning or need to be coaxed. And no group of learner-activists is an undifferentiated, collective mass: groups are

Church in Dupetit, Haiti. In French Creole, the sign says 'up with the gospel of liberation, down with the gospel of resignation'
Photographer: Liam Kane

composed of people whose different personalities and abilities may lead to radically different individual experiences of learning.

The skills and experience of popular educators, too, are an important variable (Hammond, 1999). While popular education is fine in theory, some argue that in reality, due to the pressures of poverty, the range of demands on time and lack of access to educational opportunities and training, the majority of grassroots popular educators are too poorly equipped to put the theory into practice (Archer, 1994: 229). The success or failure, then, of (what is intended to be) popular education may be greatly affected by the abilities and attitudes of individual educators. Do they encourage independent thinking or subtly seek to persuade? Are they able, pedagogically, to create an appropriate climate for learning? Do they have adequate interpersonal skills (technical competence alone being insufficient)? How does their political understanding influence the questions they ask and the contribution they make to discussions?

Third, some argue that difficulties in evaluating popular education are rooted in the vague and open-ended nature of its aims: 'Criticisms of the Freirian method, and disillusionment with what has passed for popular education, have generated scepticism amongst some educationalists and NGOs. Evaluating the impact of social education programmes has proved difficult, to some extent because their goals were over-ambitious, or simply too vague. Ideological commitment alone will not transform unjust social and economic structures' (Eade, 1997: 80).

Fourth, it is difficult to know beforehand what the outcome of popular education should be. The normal procedure in educational assessment is to have an initial set of aims and objectives against which progress can be measured. It is good practice in popular education, too, to be as clear as possible about what it is hoped will be achieved. However, 'the processes of social development cannot always be understood in terms of expected and visible results. The inherent processes lead to unexpected results which may not comply with the predetermined goals and anticipated outcomes of initiated projects/outcomes...The major difficulty with objectives like enhancing the participation of women and their empowerment lies not in characterising them, but in predicting the outcome at the outset of the projects' (Sonpal & Acharya, 1995: 53-54). In other words, since the whole point of popular education is to help people take control of their own future, it is a contradiction in terms to pre-determine what this future ought to be. On the other hand, how can we tell if popular education is worth the effort if we have no idea what it is meant to achieve in the first place? As we shall see, this dilemma is partly addressed by ensuring that evaluation is both participatory (where learners themselves are involved in deciding how the effectiveness of popular education should be assessed) and qualitative (where it is not only the extent of change that is measured but the significance that this has for learners). Evaluators need to be sensitive to the possibility of changes taking place in unanticipated areas.

Fifth, in the aftermath of an educational project 'many benefits will remain invisible and do not lend themselves to easy measurement' (Cernea, 1992: 59; quoted in Nelson & Wright, 1997: 17). The results may be intangible for 'empowerment... is a state of being and not easily observable' (Meyer & Singh, 1997: 59). Hildebrand argues that since 'adult education and training often deal with invisible learning processes...one should look not only for quantitative, visible outcomes, but also for qualitative impacts, which may escape immediate visibility' (Hildebrand, 1995: 9-10). While it might appear, on the surface, that an educational project is having little impact, it is possible that important changes are actually taking place but either go unnoticed or fail to produce visible results till a later date, when evaluators have gone home. Attempts to evaluate a legal rights programme, for example, 'can ignore the fact that a person who is now sufficiently aware and confident to use the legal system may consider this a significant change in his or her life, even if it does not immediately lead to a positive legal result or a demonstrable change in the quality of their life' (Roche, 1999: 23). Furthermore, 'although impact assessment is about systematic analysis, it is also centrally about judgements of what change is considered 'significant' for whom, and by whom; views which will often differ according to class, gender, age and other factors' (ibid).

Sixth, there are also practical obstacles to assessing popular education's impact. The planning, monitoring and evaluation of projects for change – and the collection and analysis of (appropriate) quantitative and qualitative data – requires both time and considerable expertise: hard-pushed educators struggle to cope. Also, since evaluations are mostly carried out by Non Governmental Agencies, or popular education centres funded by NGOs, the particular agendas of different NGOs inevitably impinge on the process of evaluation and how this is perceived by the recipients of funding. Mulusa argues that due to the dynamics of power in play, 'all along the NGO or government extension service ladder there is intrinsic fear and distrust of formal evaluation' (Mulusa, 1995: 23) and that it can become a public relations battleground for different vested interests: 'often one comes across comments such as "with this kind of report our funding will surely be discontinued", "we need a good evaluation report", or "top executives have no time for such detailed reports, just summarize the main achievements of the programme in a few pages". Clearly, the emphasis is not on how learning takes place or what role participants have played, but on how far stated programme objectives have been achieved, and whether or not the NGO has made a positive impression to the funding agency and the host country' (ibid: 19). In this context, in reporting on what they have learned during a project in popular education, learners may well be tempted to say what they think evaluators would like to hear – thus attempting to procure continued funding – as opposed to speaking the whole truth. The danger is that '"consciousness raising", like institutional development, can be a means to ensure that participation occurs only on the non-governmental organisation's terms' (Hussein, 1997: 176). It would be naïve to ignore that in the current climate in Latin America, with governments eager to contract-out social services, even the more progressive NGOs are tempted by government funding and feel pressure to engage in the types of evaluation favoured by governments (ie those which show quick results and positive cost-benefit analyses) rather than those more suited to a genuine assessment of the effectiveness of popular education (Gideon, 1998). In a nutshell, there is a constant danger that evaluations can be designed and conducted for the benefit of NGO managers – inappropriately aping the managerial practices of businesses – rather than for those whom development projects are supposed to serve (Wallace, 2000).

There are other complications. Evaluations are likely to be good when aims and objectives are modest, bad when they are ambitious or risk-laden; long-term evaluations are difficult to conduct. But the picture is clear: while evaluation is an essential component of good popular education practice, it is complicated, seldom clear-cut and inevitably influenced by the subjective judgements and values of different evaluators.

Methods of Evaluation

The process of evaluating any social intervention involves clarifying what the project is attempting to achieve (its aims and objectives), deciding on appropriate 'indicators' of change, monitoring any changes which occur, analysing indicators against the initial objectives and making a final judgement on the effectiveness of the project. Appendix 7:1 shows suggested indicators for the REFLECT programme, an attempt to promote popular education through literacy (see Box 2:1). In view of the problems already described, good evaluators are never enslaved to pre-ordained procedures. They are flexible, self-critical and sensitive towards invisible and unanticipated change; initial objectives and indicators require constant reviewing and adjustment. Rowlands illustrates the point well in her discussion of women's empowerment: 'because empowerment for each person or group is in a sense, a unique process, indicators must be flexible and wide-ranging, and are likely to change, possibly quite radically, over time. For a woman for whom it is a major challenge to attend meetings, initially her presence at meetings might be the measure of her empowerment; later, it might be her regular active contribution to discussion; later still, it might be her ability to initiate group activities. Given the often intangible and nebulous psychological and social processes involved, it can be easy, too, to miss the significance of particular events or inputs. Sometimes the impact of an activity will not be felt for some time. Yet conversely, it can be tempting to attribute a particular advance to a specific activity, with no evidence whether it would have happened anyway. Organisations should be humble about the work they do, and accept that it is not possible to define and measure every detail' (Rowlands, 1997: 140).

Broadly speaking, there are two main approaches to evaluating the outcomes of projects for change. One focuses on objectivity, 'the standard paradigm of seeking quantitative facts in an objective, technocratic manner. Emphasis is placed on measurability; and reviewing timeliness, efficiency, and value for money is standard. Analysis is generally objective and scientific, reducing reality to its smallest possible components' (Meyer and Singh, 1997: 60). This is probably the most common understanding of evaluation. It is often carried out by personnel external to the project and tends to meet the needs of funding agencies or project managers seeking to justify expenditures. A second – though not mutually exclusive of the first – focuses on more subjective, qualitative dimensions of change. To account for invisible and unexpected changes and to isolate a project's achievements from what would have taken place anyway, it is essential that the intended beneficiaries are involved in identifying and measuring what, for them, are appropriate indicators of change: 'the development of (qualitative) criteria is a political and educative activity in its own right and cannot just be left to the "experts"' (González, 1993: 41). This is now commonly known as 'participatory evaluation'. If 'popular' knowledge is to be respected and people encouraged to be 'subjects' of change, then their views on the significance of what they are learning is essential.

Evaluation can take place at different levels. For popular education, the simplest – and, some would argue, the only one usually considered (Tandon, 1995) – is the evaluation of explicitly educational events such as 'workshops' and training courses. This should now be standard practice in popular education. Generally speaking, it seeks to discover from participants (a) what they felt was good, interesting or useful about a particular course or workshop (b) what was not so good, dull or a waste of time (c) suggestions for improvement (d) their overall evaluation and (e) any other comments they wish to make. (Having experimented with many types of course evaluations myself, including sophisticated charts for scoring every activity, I find that these five open-ended queries provide by far the most useful information). There are several ways of doing this: individual questionnaires asking focused and open-ended questions, small-to-large group discussions noting the main points on paper or more creative activities like drawing, sociodrama, games, spoof letter-writing or allegorical book reviews (Maceira Ochoa, 1998). In longer sessions, learner representatives might meet regularly with the educators to make on-going adjustments where appropriate (as we saw with the MST). While these evaluations provide evidence of how learners see their progress and give an important insight into popular education's impact, its most useful function is to enable educators to become 'reflective practitioners' and improve their practice. Again, results should be treated with care: it may be too early to assess how useful the learning will be (making evaluations too negative) or participants may fear hurting educators' feelings or losing potential support (too positive).

Having worked out provisional indicators of change, there are a variety of techniques for collecting the information required. Before any activity takes place, the first task is to establish baseline measurements against which future changes can be compared. Sometimes relevant information already exists – statistics on health, education, incomes, numbers participating in community organisations, for example – and can be obtained from governmental, community or project records, though much of it has to be deliberately sought out. In many cases, educational activities themselves supply *de facto* the necessary, preliminary information. In providing both a description and analysis of what any group thinks it is trying to achieve, what it actually does and how it relates to its wider context, the results of an initial 'triple self-diagnosis' (see chapter three) serve as a benchmark for measuring future changes in attitude. The same applies to diagnostic tools used in 'participatory rural appraisal' (Box 3:1), where people create informative calendars, social maps, historical timelines and so on in the process of analysing their communities (Shah, 1997; Archer & Cottingham, 1996). The REFLECT programme offers an example of 'a Table/ Matrix showing participation in community organisations – which lists all the organisations in the community and asks people whether they are members/ attend meetings, whether they feel involved in the decision-making process or whether they have any position of authority (eg secretary, treasurer or chair). Each question can be asked for the time before the REFLECT circle and the position after the circle. In the El Salvador pilot this showed impressive results, with more than 60% of participants having assumed positions which previously they had not held' (ibid: 73).

Roche's research asserts that 'simply talking, and listening, to people is probably the most common and useful way of assessing impact. This does not mean to say that it is easy. In the case studies these discussions happened in a variety of ways: individually and in groups; formally and informally; using pre-defined questionnaires, semi-structured interviews, and workshops; and simply by chatting' (Roche, 1999: 108). He goes on to discuss the imaginative use of 'focus groups', how to learn from 'direct observation' and the technique of 'impact flow charts', where, using arrows to indicate the direction of change, people produce diagrams showing what, for them, have been the consequences of particular interventions. Herrera Menchén (1998) discusses how to observe, record and evaluate relevant 'slices of life' using (a) field diaries, with detailed description and analysis of evaluators' observations and (b) 'anecdotal recordings', where people are asked to explain and interpret interesting or unusual developments.

Assessing the impact of popular education raises other questions:

- the feasibility of a control group (of people not participating in the project) against which the effect of popular education could be compared
- the validity of the sample used – in relation to age, gender, status and so on – when it is not possible to record the views of everyone involved
- the amount of intrusion which people will tolerate for the sake of evaluation
- ensuring that everyone is heard and recorded, not just the most articulate.

Notwithstanding the problems discussed at the beginning of the chapter, it is clear that impact assessment is a complex area which requires time, resources and expertise. It is no surprise, perhaps, that in popular education, evaluation is seldom as thorough as it might be.

Success and Failure in Micro-Scale Projects
'The current context challenges popular education to refocus on what is specifically educational about its practice and, in particular, to evaluate its results... Many experiences of popular education have been successful in

providing the necessary knowledge for solving the aforementioned (ie everyday) problems.' (CEAAL, 1995: 136)

'In Latin America an important debate is taking place on the theoretical and methodological aspects of popular education. Two criticisms commonly heard are that popular education quickly becomes too ideological and that many of the changes it sets out to achieve fail to materialise. Despite that, the contributions and intuitions of this particular pedagogical endeavour can be seen everywhere.'
(Martinic, 1995, quoted in ibid).

Examples of Detailed Evaluation
Well-evaluated case-studies provide insights into what popular education can achieve. The REFLECT programme in El Salvador set out to use literacy as a means of empowering communities. Measured against the indicators in Appendix 7:1, the findings from the initial evaluation of REFLECT (see Appendix 7:2) showed, for example, that:

- 100% of learners felt the project had improved their self-confidence (compared to 42% in a non-REFLECT control group)
- 80% of newly-trained *facilitators* said they were now more active in community organisations than before, with almost half holding new positions of responsibility
- 77% of learners said they were now actively involved in decision making in community organisations whereas beforehand they had been passive (an observation corroborated by people not involved in REFLECT).

In Nicaragua, the popular education centre CANTERA evaluated the impact of its courses on 'masculinity and popular education' carried out between 1994 and 1997 (Welsh, 1997), a novel piece of work prompted by the demands of the women's movement, grassroots women's experiences of trying to implement change (ie men's resistance to it) and advances in gender theory (see also Broadbent, 2000).

1. The study covers this four year period and examines the case of two hundred and fifty male participants from different backgrounds. Each participated in four workshops over a period of a year. Each workshop lasted four days.
2. A year after the end of their courses, CANTERA carried out a detailed survey of 112 of the men. The questionnaires asked them about their attitudes and behaviour in both the year prior to and following the course.
3. They were asked 118 questions covering areas such as self-perception, the consumption of drugs, tobacco and alcohol, their participation in household

chores, decision-making within their relationships, domestic violence and communication and relationships in the community.

4. Meetings were held with the men to discuss and assess the impact of the courses on their lives.

5. In parallel, a different questionnaire was answered by 45 women who were close to the men (wives, sisters, mothers, or work colleagues) and they too met to discuss the impact of the course.

In its detailed, analytical breakdown, this particular evaluation would delight the most enthusiastic of statisticians. Appendix 7:3 shows only a selected sample of the principal findings, two of which were that:

• 66% of the men felt their perception of themselves had changed either a lot or significantly as a result of the course. This was corroborated by the women, with 62% attesting to the same

• 80% of men said they felt more solidarity with women after the courses and 84% of women also felt this to be true.

The evaluation went on to articulate and categorise precise manifestations of these changes, from the frequency with which men now washed dishes to the numbers who participated in different types of community organisation. The particular details of each claim need to be critically analysed but even as they stand, they do provide an overall view of how both men and women felt the impact of this particular course, outwith the confines of the educational workshop and over a substantial period of time. Several lessons were drawn about the future direction of this work, one of which was the need to 'open up more spaces for reflection on the political implications of work which focuses on the theme of masculinity' (Welsh, 1997: 110).

Examining such detailed evaluations, I find myself reacting in different ways. First, with so much data collection and analysis, they seem to require a level of professional expertise in applied social sciences that even to competent and well-qualified educators, the exercise must often seem daunting. Second, they obviously demand a great deal of planning, work, time and money. Third, the evaluations are usually tied to a specific project with a view to making it more effective in the future: the degree to which they might hold lessons for the wider practice of popular education will vary (though REFLECT is an exception as it explicitly sets out to draw lessons for practice on a global scale). Fourth, they do not usually make for exciting reading. Personally, I find the easiest approach is to read the conclusions first and only then, if inspired, to dig deeper. As a counterweight to the standard, academic presentation of results, some centres are exploring more creative methods of monitoring and evaluation – video diaries, for example – which could be more accessible to all project participants (Archer, 2000). Fifth, however much detail is presented, a dose of healthy scepticism (but not cynicism) is required. Important information may be missing, unknown even to the evaluators, and other agendas and interests may have (consciously or not) influenced the proceedings. Interview questions can invite particular answers, people may fill-in questionnaires too quickly, factors other than the educational project may have influenced the participants' behaviour. And the purpose of the evaluation needs to be ascertained. Does this in any way influence the results? One centre (La Cuculmeca, 1998) categorises the exercise into:

- 'self-indulgent' evaluation (strictly academic, with no practical application)
- 'enforced' evaluation (because funders demand it)
- 'defensive' evaluation (as a means of justifying mistakes and/or blowing your own trumpet)
- 'punitive' evaluation (to allocate blame and punish people) and
- 'productive' evaluation (which can produce results which will be beneficial to future work).

Sixth, despite the limitations inherent in any evaluation, the exercise is important for (a) reflecting on and improving educational practice (b) introducing evidence and rigour into claims regarding its effectiveness. Instead of relying on assumptions, impressions, anecdotes or hearsay (though they too have their place), systematic evaluations of this nature undoubtedly enable more accurate assessments to be made on the degree of success or failure of popular education.

Less Detailed Evaluations: A Selection of Case Studies

Though it does not provide the same detail as the examples just examined, for me, one of the most informative books on popular education in Latin America remains Archer & Costello's (1990) collection of case-studies in literacy and empowerment. Selected from all over the continent – urban Mexico, rural Honduras, highland Bolivia – they take place in a variety of political contexts, from dictatorship in Chile to revolution in Nicaragua. Their approach is to give (a) an introduction to the social, political and economic background in which the educational project takes place (b) a detailed description of the project (c) an analysis of the project's strengths and weaknesses and (d) an attempt to draw general conclusions from the comparison of different projects. (Surprisingly, there seems to be a dearth of this type of material produced within Latin America itself. Much of the best-known writing on popular education – Gadotti & Torres (1994), for example, or the journal *La Piragua* – is in my view too theoretical and abstract, ironically ignoring its own oft-repeated mantra to 'theorise from practice').

Archer and Costello's (1990) case-studies provide evidence of how popular education:

- ...promoted solidarity among Salvadoreans in refugee 'camps' in Honduras. Children who could read helped teach adults. Classes encouraged collective responsibility: nobody could move up a grade until everyone had passed. Literacy was linked to organisation and women became the predominant activists in the camp's committees. People chose to learn skills which would be useful to them on returning to El Salvador. Popular education was seen as a threat by the Honduran authorities: they tried to impose their own teachers but solidarity in the camp was strong enough to resist this.

- ...had problems even when the context of political revolution, in Nicaragua, was ostensibly in its favour. In Batahola, a district in Managua, local people saw Sandinista educators as too political, finding the education offered by the popular church more relevant. People wanted to learn how to read and write, not discuss politics. Traditional ideas in education prevailed, both among learners and teachers, and popular education was often considered inferior to formal education. Arguably, economic desperation was so great that it destroyed collective values and 'people were more interested in eating than in building a new society' (ibid: 52)

- ...led to better organisation among rural co-operatives in Honduras. This, in turn, led to increased economic well-being – as *campesinos* were able to by-pass profiteering middlemen – and improvements in health. It helped, too, in successful struggles for land – 'we saw the literacy process and the reclamation of land as inseparable' (ibid: 72) – though some later suffered reversals. Promoting women's participation also proved difficult.

- ...was co-opted by the Mexican government working in a shanty area of Mexico city, promoting 'pseudo-Freire for a pseudo revolution' (ibid: 105). But this was recognised by the community itself which was already well organised. People ended up using the government's (conservative) education materials for themselves but adapted to their own ends: 'the materials themselves don't matter, it is how you use them' (ibid: 109).

- ...was carried out clandestinely, under Pinochet's dictatorship in Chile, with women in a laundry. Their interest in soap operas inspired a project on visual literacy. A cultural-educational centre produced a video on human rights and asked the women to provide the narration, a process through which they became sensitive to ideological perspectives in film. Locally produced videos were then distributed throughout popular neighbourhoods and visual literacy was seen as playing 'an important part in breaking the culture of silence' (ibid: 125) and in promoting the growth of organisations.

Rowlands' research into the Women's Educational Programme in Santa Barbara, Honduras, showed that despite the significant obstacles to be overcome (poverty, isolation, pressure to stay at home), women gained substantial empowerment at the three levels of the personal (acquiring the courage to leave home and speak out in public), in their relationships (becoming less subservient to their husbands) and collectively, described by one witness as 'for example, this problem of needing marketing of basic grains. So they think about it and decide whether to do it or not do it. The problem they have now with the priest: other groups wouldn't have faced up to the problem; a CARITAS group that has problems stops meeting and ends; but these groups have maintained themselves, and are achieving a strong maturity. In the face of problems, they look for solutions, they don't ask others for the solutions or abandon the group because of the problem...they've taken the decisions. They see what's necessary and look for how to achieve it. They're walking on their own two feet' (Rowlands, 1997: 85). The group's empowerment produced (modest) economic gains and impacted on the wider community as others emulated their action and women became inspired to seek leadership posts in other community organisations. This particular experience challenges the conventional notion that people have 'to have their basic needs met first and then they can give themselves the luxury to think about human rights' (ibid: 97-98). In this case, self-dignity was a greater motivator than material improvement. It also shows the importance of beginning with small steps. When participants saw that popular education quickly engendered small changes in their lives, within their families or in their own personal esteem, they were encouraged to go back for more. The quality of key activists/leaders/educators was identified as central to the programme's success. Strong personalities managed to keep the group motivated but knew how and when to stand back and encourage others to take on greater responsibility, important interpersonal skills which can elude the best of us.

From my own experience, I was impressed with popular education in the coffee-growing community of Cañadabonita, high in the mountains of the Dominican Republic. To avoid being exploited by middlemen and moneylenders, a number of communities formed a coffee-producers' co-operative. They successfully by-passed the middlemen within the Dominican Republic – though not internationally, a much more difficult task – and significantly increased their share of the profit on coffee. Some of this went to individual families and some to improve communal facilities. Popular education related to the desire for democratic and participatory organisation: positions of responsibility were constantly rotated so that all members would acquire a variety of skills. Literacy and numeracy were vital for the maintenance of accounts, understanding the coffee trade and making sure the co-operative was not

A popular education poster from a coffee-growers co-operative in the Dominican Republic. It shows agricultural workers being bled dry by money-lenders, usurers, the banks, middlemen, the government and the International Monetary Fund
Photographer: Liam Kane

exploited. Effective participation required an ability to analyse a changing situation and offer opinions on how the co-operative should develop. In an atmosphere of change, drama groups started to challenge the traditional role of women. My lasting image is of sitting with the coffee-growers round a stove in one of the hilltop shacks (don't let the brochures fool you, the Caribbean can be cold!). With no electricity or running water, these families presented the classical image of poor, 'third-world' peasants. Yet here they were debating percentiles, market-shares, fluctuations and future trends on the New York exchange: I couldn't cope and had an early night.

The Views of Popular Educators and Researchers
Important evidence for judging success and failure is the testimony of popular educators themselves. As witnesses to practices unlikely to result in published evaluations and as participants in debates on how to react to changing political realities, the documented reflections of popular educators – either as individual thinkers or in group discussions – provide useful insights into the highs and lows of popular education practice. Here are some examples.

1.   In the mid 1990s, in the midst of continent-wide debate on the continuing relevance of popular education and its relationship to pedagogy, the educators of Alforja discussed what was positive and negative in their own and others' practice and wrote up their deliberations in 'the thousand and one mad ideas which occurred to us concerning the debate on pedagogy' (IMDEC, undated). While defending the validity of much of what was done in the name of popular education, they also listed a number of weaknesses (see Appendix 7:4) among which were that:

- On many occasions we understand the 'subject' as a homogenous group and fail to see that there are individual personalities and different levels of learning within the group.
- Some practices of popular education have understood subjectivity to be synonymous with political consciousness, negating other aspects like feelings, aspirations etc
- There was a lack of criteria for measuring the impact of popular education.
- There was a need to document experiences of popular education in a systematic way and make sure they receive a wider circulation (cf ibid)

2.   In an article giving an overview on developments in popular education, the general secretariat of CEAAL (1995) cited some of the positives as:

- many experiences of popular education have been of real practical help to people, contributing substantially to the development of their critical consciousness, organisation and ability to take action
- in the new, less dictatorial climate in Latin America in which the transformation of state education is under discussion, the accumulated experience of popular education has a lot to offer
- potentially it is a dynamic force for strengthening civil society and the development of active citizenship

and some of the negatives as:

- sometimes it has been too ideological
- the practice has not always been as good as the theory
- there is a need for more 'systematisation' of experiences in popular education (ie proper documentation which describes, analyses and evaluates these experiences)

3.   From his work with *campesinos* in Mexico, in his proposal for a 'participatory and self-managed model of *campesino* education', Mata García (1994) argues that given the nature of the obstacles in the way of liberation, popular education has to be prepared for a long haul. If done properly, it has an important contribution to make in enabling popular *campesino* organisations become 'self-managing' and capable of taking action, the only possible chance

they have, no matter how remote, of changing their circumstances for the better. Among internal and external barriers to success he mentions:

- 'The idea that organising collectively for economic improvements, in itself, will lead to political struggle has for the most part been untrue...Why? ...The answer is not easy, since that depends on the circumstances of each situation. However, in the majority of cases the main problem has been that when people have not managed to develop a political consciousness, organising becomes extremely difficult' (ibid: 77-78)

- Because communal organisational work requires patience, sacrifice and takes a while to produce results, many people, especially the poorest, who have most to gain, give up.

- The lack of homogeneity in any organisation, where members have diverse and sometimes even conflicting interests

- 'One of the great, unsolved problems with popular, self-managed, peasant organisations remains the lack of a long-term objective giving a global vision to the struggle, thus avoiding the break-up of groups when immediate objectives have been achieved' (ibid: 79).

In discussing the role of educators – though he mainly has governmental, rural extension workers in mind (for whom Freire (1974b) also wrote an important essay) – Mata García adds that 'one of the main political errors of many educators has been to give more importance to economic rather than political work. The problems already mentioned, such as individualism and lack of solidarity, can only be overcome when, right from the start, economic organisation is directly linked to political organisation and the latter is the driving force'(ibid: 82). He goes on to list a series of possible methodological failings, from paternalism to a desire for quick results, all boiling down, basically, to the theories of popular education being insufficiently translated into practice.

4.   On NGO efforts to promote 'participatory development', researchers have commented on how the concept of 'participation', central to popular education, is much more complex than at first appears. Hussein argues that participation 'has become the dominating ideology in contemporary thinking in both non-governmental organisations and governmental/inter-governmental organisations ... and that "participation" is a multidimensional concept meaning different things to different people' (Hussein, 1997: 170). Some point to 'a tendency for those who use the term participation to adopt a moral high ground, implying that any form of participation is good' (Pretty and Scoones, 1997: 159). They argue the need to define the term more precisely as studies have shown that for some NGOs 'participation simply implied local people doing what planners wanted' (ibid). Echoing both other researchers into NGO activity

(Tendler, 1982) and the testimonies of popular educators themselves, in an article on theory versus practice in participatory development, Lane argues that 'it may be more appropriate to label such self descriptions (ie *participation*) as "articles of faith" rather than accurate representations of NGO activity' (Lane, 1997: 182). Highlighting, again, the lack of systematic evaluation of participatory development – of which popular education can be considered a part – she discusses one of the few studies into levels of participation in development projects (Broadhead, 1988): this found that 22% of people did not participate at all, 24% had a low level of participation, 36% a moderate level and 18% a high level. Soberingly, for popular education, she concludes 'that both "NGO" and "participation" are dangerously close to becoming buzzwords, rhetorical terms without theoretical clarity or practical content' (Lane, 1997: 190).

5.   Among internationally renowned educationalists, La Belle (1986) has argued that in practice the reality of popular education does not match up to the radicalism of the rhetoric. Where there was political action, he claimed, this was 'often narrow and controlled by the dominant sectors' (ibid: 214, quoted in Torres, 1990: 273) and that part of the problem in bringing about structural change was that popular education programmes 'lack the theoretical frameworks to guide their implementation in the face of adversity and opposition' (ibid). Torres concurs with La Belle regarding the limits to popular education's success and while he recognises internal weaknesses, he lays more stress on the wider, contextual factors which operate as constraints: 'the degree of success or failure of a paradigm of popular education will be related to several factors including (a) the historical configuration of the social formation according to its position in the world capitalist system, and hence the relationship of dependency/interdependency of this society, (b) the degree of political struggle in a given social formation, and (c) the organisational quality of the social movements and classes. If, in spite of what technocratic thinking is encouraged to believe, a fundamental feature of educational practices is it political character, the nature of the political system and the State ought to be taken into account when explaining the success or failure of popular education' (Torres, 1990: 274).
Finally, in talking to activists in Latin America, it is clear that for many, some form of popular education was instrumental in their initial engagement with political activity. Two outstanding illustrations of this are the Guatemalan nobel peace prize winner, Rigoberta Menchú (1991) and the Honduran peasant-union organiser, Elvia Alvarado (1989).

Conclusion

From the (insufficient) evidence available it seems clear that in small-scale projects for change, with the right combination of factors – a good project, good educators, a relatively harmonious organisation, a context in which there is room for manoeuvre – then popular education has the potential to bring about qualitative change in the lives of some of the least well-off people in the world. It has managed to be beneficial in a range of social-political contexts, from dictatorship to revolution, and has brought about positive changes in areas like economic development, self-esteem, the strengthening of organisational solidarity, collective action and increases in the general quality of life. Even those most critical of popular education (though not politically opposed to its aims) usually qualify their critique with praise for its many examples of success.

On the other hand, there is a consistency about the comments on its shortcomings. Most notable is that while the lofty goals of popular education are fine in theory, they have proved much more difficult to achieve in practice. Perhaps this is to be expected: given the lack of opportunities for sustained, in-depth training and the persistence of hostile cultural traditions (sexism, authoritarianism, 'banking education' and so on), the variety of skills demanded of popular educators is daunting. There is also a need for greater attention to bread-and-butter pedagogical issues, including the importance of systematic evaluation and an awareness of different, individual learning requirements. Another critique is that popular education has often been considered too 'ideological' and insufficiently rooted in real needs, though as I have argued elsewhere (chapter 6), I believe this has more to do with methodological malpractice than with ideology.

There are also grey areas. It often appears that minimal material needs must be met before people can relate to (the luxury) of learning. On occasions, however, the promotion of increased self-esteem and group solidarity is experienced as empowering in itself, even when little or no economic improvements ensue. Though the critique of ideological zealotry is well-founded, the other extreme – where popular education only engages with a group's perceived needs, avoiding dealing with ideology altogether – is also problematic. Finally, given the difficulties in impact assessment and the number of variables involved, from events in the wider world to the abilities of individual educators and learners, it is perhaps meaningless to make sweeping generalisations on the success or failure of small-scale projects in popular education: each has to be judged on its merits.

Appendix 7:1

Selection of indicators for monitoring and evaluating a REFLECT programme in literacy and empowerment

Monitoring/basic outputs

- attendance
- drop-out
- content and quality of participant's books
- participant's ability to read and write (including numbers)
- participant's self-evaluation of progress in reading, writing and numeracy;
- development of literate habits (who reads what/how often)
- the quality of each graphic produced
- level of participant's ability to analyses/interpret their graphics
- level of participation in, and quality of, discussions
- the number of people from the lowest socio-economic groups who are involved in circles
- effectiveness of the facilitator/ relevance of training to facilitator's needs
- costs

Evaluating outcomes and impact

- self-confidence/dignity/self-esteem
- ability of circle to resolve internal conflicts
- number of actions taken by each circle (and number of participants/ level of success of each action)
- membership of REFLECT participants in other community organisations (where they were not involved before)
- changing role of literacy in community organisations
- changes in local literacy 'events' and 'practices'
- impact on children's education (increased enrolment/ attendance of REFLECT participant's children?)
- impact on participant's income / control over income
- new areas of knowledge
- change of behaviour / habits / attitudes (in respect of agriculture / resource management / health etc)
- mobility of women
- status of REFLECT participant in family / community
- patterns of intra-household decision-making
- impact on facilitators themselves
- cost effectiveness

From Archer & Cottingham (1996b: 72)

Appendix 7:2

Selected Results from an Impact Assessment of the REFLECT Programme in El Salvador

- 100% of learners felt the project had improved their self-confidence (compared to 42% in a non-REFLECT control group)
- 80% of newly-trained *facilitators* said they were now more active in community organisations than before, with almost half holding new positions of responsibility
- 77% of learners said they were now actively involved in decision making in community organisations whereas beforehand they had been passive (an observation corroborated by people not involved in REFLECT)
- the literacy circles initiated many actions, from setting up medicinal-plant nurseries to successfully campaigning for increases in school enrolments
- over 40% of learners said that being involved in the circles had led to changes in their working practices on the land, such as analysing soils for crop suitability or using organic fertilizers and pesticides
- personal testimonies indicated that the programme had had a large impact on the local economy
- one notable problem was that the information on indicators of empowerment had not been broken down by gender, something to be corrected in future evaluations (Archer & Cottingham, 1996b: 52-72).

Appendix 7:3

Selected Results from an Impact Assessment of CANTERA's Courses on 'Masculinity and Popular Education'

- 66% of the men felt that their perception of themselves had changed either a lot or significantly as a result of the course. This was corroborated by the women, with 62% attesting to the same
- 61% of the men felt the course had made them either a lot or significantly less violent, though the women were less enthusiastic with only 49% agreeing
- 49% felt they drank less alcohol now, though only 29% of women agreed
- only 45% of men felt they had improved either a lot or significantly in their contribution to domestic chores. Interestingly, slightly more women than men (49%) felt this to be true
- 80% of men said they felt more solidarity with women after the courses and 84% of women also felt this was true
- 56% of men felt the courses had helped them either a lot or significantly in their relationships in the wider community. Substantially more women (71%) felt this to be true

- After the course, there was an increase from 18% to 35% of men who said 'I participate in/or support activities organised by women in defence of their rights'
- After the course there was an increase from 16% to 32% of men who were part of a men's discussion group or a 'men against violence group'. There was no notable change in the number of men participating in community movements, neighbourhood associations, trade unions, or political parties.

From Welsh (1997)

Appendix 7:4
Popular Educators' Views On Common Weaknesses in Popular Education Practice

- Often, the starting point of some practices in popular education is objective reality rather than the way a specific group understands, perceives and experiences that reality
- On many occasions we understand the 'subject' as a homogenous group and fail to see that there are individual personalities and different levels of learning within the group
- Some practices of popular education have understood subjectivity to be synonymous with political consciousness, negating other aspects like feelings, aspirations etc
- Popular education has produced few materials for dealing with the theme of subjectivity. The most important experiences in this area have been developed in relation to workshops on gender issues
- We often limit the education process to workshops and organised educational events
- Although we are clear about what we should do in theory, in practice we often fall into situations where (a) we look for unanimity in plenary sessions, pushing groups towards consensus, since we're not sure how to handle debate and differences (b) group-work and reporting-back is not sufficiently supervised by the educator so quite often we don't achieve the objective of producing collective knowledge and reaching conclusions
- A need to open a dialogue with different 'pedagogists' to overcome some of our own weaknesses
- Problems in keeping contact with those who have participated in popular education training
- A lack of criteria for measuring the impact of popular education.
- A need to document experiences of popular education in a systematic way and make sure they receive a wider circulation.

From 'the thousand and one mad ideas which occurred to us concerning the debate on pedagogy' (IMDEC, undated).

Chapter 8
Assessing the Impact of Popular Education
at Macro Level

"HE SAID HE WANTED TO MAKE AN EVEN BIGGER IMPACT THIS TIME"

At one end of the scale, we can try to assess the impact of popular education in the context of individual, localised projects (see previous chapter). In the middle, we can examine larger, single movements like the MST or the accumulated impact of smaller projects within any one region or country. At the other end, there have also been attempts to promote social change through single, large-scale, co-ordinated projects in popular education. Inevitably, at this end, the relationship between popular education and the state comes into focus.

This chapter examines the relationship at its closest, in the earlier years of the Nicaraguan revolution, with particular reference to the 'Literacy Crusade' and 'Popular Basic Education'. Having assessed popular education's impact in this revolutionary conjuncture, the next section considers its potential to effect large-scale change within more conventional settings; in the process, it examines historical changes in how the popular education movement has perceived its relationship with the state.

Popular Education in Revolutionary Nicaragua
The aftermath of the Nicaraguan revolution in July 1979 offered an opportunity in Latin America for large-scale popular education. Having deposed the tyrannous Somoza dynasty, in power since 1936, both the Nicaraguan people

and the revolutionary Sandinista government were keen to promote massive change throughout the country. It was a climate of liberation, expectation and hope. Education was a priority, seen as an essential human right, a pre-requisite for economic development and a means of encouraging mass participation in the revolutionary process. Though education had also been important to the Cuban revolution, this had generally consisted of 'banking' education with a left-wing content (not until the 1990s did Cuban organisations start to engage with the Latin American popular education movement). By 1979, however, the theories of popular education were widely-known in Latin America. With the revolution in Nicaragua it appeared that, for the first time, a national government not only wanted popular education to succeed but saw it as central to its policies.

From its inception, however, the Nicaraguan revolution was beset with problems. A desperately poor country of only three million people, half of whom were under fifteen years of age, Nicaragua was nonetheless considered the 'threat of a good example' (Melrose, 1985) to United States interests and throughout the 1980s presidents Reagan and Bush used every available means to bring Nicaragua to its knees, including economic destabilisation and the illegal funding of a counter-revolutionary war. By 1990, this, plus a growing disillusionment with the government's handling of the crisis, led to the loss of the 1990 presidential elections (Harris, 1992; Gonzalez, 1990). By the year 2000, the Sandinista party had little radical left to offer: it had made pacts with conservatives, stood accused of betraying its principles, prominent Sandinistas had become wealthy, activists left the party in droves and their leader used parliamentary privilege to avoid beeing tried for the sexual abuse of his daughter. Debt, increasing poverty and the ravages of Hurricane Mitch had left the Nicaraguans worse off than ever, a scenario which cannot be ignored in any critical assessment of the long-term impact of popular education in the revolutionary period.

The Literacy Crusade

Within two weeks of coming to power the Sandinistas set in motion a campaign to wipe out illiteracy. In language that could have come straight from Freire, the minister in charge of the campaign, Fr. Fernando Cardenal, made it clear that education was much more than the acquisition of skills: 'we believe that in order to create a new nation we have to begin with an education that liberates people. Only through knowing their past and their present, only through understanding and analysing their reality, can people choose their future. Only in that process can people fulfil their human destiny as makers of history and commit themselves to transforming that reality' (quoted in Miller, 1985: 113).

An army of *brigadistas* – volunteer literacy tutors, mainly secondary school or university students – were given intensive training in Freire's method of teaching literacy, with the 'Revolution' as the principal generative issue (though two departures from Freire's method were to use a national primer, rather than locally produced materials, and the use of short, generative sentences rather than single words). Their job was to disperse through the country and teach people how to read and write, promote discussion and analysis of the revolution and collect the social histories of different communities. The 'Literacy Crusade', as it became known, took place between March and August of 1980.

The crusade remains a highly significant event in the history of Nicaragua and its achievements have been widely praised. According to official figures, 95,582 *brigadistas* took part, 406,056 Nicaraguans became literate and illiteracy was cut from 50% to 13% (INIEP, 1995: 7-9). By any standards, given the lack of time, resources and trained personnel, this was an amazing accomplishment, deserving of the Literacy Prize it received from UNESCO. Not only did it spread technical skills of literacy to hitherto neglected communities, in touching the lives of approximately a quarter of the population, the crusade was effectively a 'massive school for the people' (Guido, 1999), a grand-scale cultural exchange between town and country, old and young, (lower) middle-class and the desperately poor. It was a formative experience for the thousands of *brigadistas* who had never previously left the city and had no idea of life in rural communities. At times the testimonies of learners and *brigadistas* reflect precisely what popular education is supposed to be about:

'Eventually it began to work. My students learned how to write *machete* and I learned how to use one'
Rodríguez, *brigadista* (Archer & Costello, 1990: 31)

'I thought the methodology used for teaching literacy was good because it motivated people to talk about the structure of Nicaragua and the hard reality of its history of dictatorship. No-one had ever organised a literacy campaign before or asked why *campesinos* were marginalised and exploited'
Rodolfo, *brigadista* (INIEP, 1995: 71)

'For me the Crusade was the best school, the best workshop, the best study circle we ever had. Instead of being told about how the *campesinos* had to live, we went to see it and experience it for ourselves'.
Oscar, *brigadista* (INIEP, 1995: 114).

'How can you believe in the revolution and not join the literacy brigades? Last year I took up a gun, this year it's an exercise book, but I don't see any real difference. It's all part of a war to liberate our country'
Unnamed *brigadista* (Barndt, 1991: 61).

'Do you know I am not ignorant any more. I know how to read now. Not perfectly, you understand, but I know how. And do you know, your son isn't ignorant any more either. Now he knows how we live, what we eat, how we work and he knows the life of the mountains. Your son, ma'am, has learned to read from our book'
Campesino speaking to a young *brigadista's* mother (Cardenal & Miller, 1981: 26)

'The literacy classes helped us to discuss the possibility of having our own land and enabled us to organise into a co-operative structure in order to obtain it'
José, literacy student (Archer & Costello, 1990: 34),

Brigadistas also linked their literacy work to development projects, gathering important information about agricultural practices and patterns of health as well as rescuing popular culture by recording stories, songs, legends and histories wherever they went. In 1990 it was 'estimated that perhaps as many as 8,000 children may be alive today as the result of having mothers who participated in the campaign and gained skills that enabled their children to be healthier' (Arnove, 1994: 187). Researchers claim that the crusade 'produced some clear and significant results, which have endured. It was critical in reducing the high degree of inequality between countryside and city, males and females, and the Atlantic and the Pacific coasts. It mobilised previously marginalised populations into new roles related to national reconstruction. It strengthened mass organisations, notably the Sandinista Youth Organisation, the teachers' association (ANDEN), and the Nicaraguan Women's Association (AMNLAE). It was the first national task in which women had equal participation, and it provided the opportunity for women to take the lead in other activities...It initiated the process of administrative decentralisation of the country, dividing it into nine regions and delegating substantial authority to local government entities and to the mass organisations' (Carnoy and Torres, 1990: 338).

While evaluations of the crusade unanimously highlight its achievements, it is clear that there were also serious problems. Firstly, there is debate about the validity of the statistics and the rigour with which they were collected. One study found people (a) who had been wrongly recorded as literate (b) for whom the crusade had reinforced and developed existing literacy skills rather than introduced them for the first time (Sandiford et al, 1994). In the long-term, due to the war and continuing economic crisis, it proved impossible to develop a society in which literacy skills became integral to a normal lifestyle. For want of practice, many of the skills acquired started to wither away: sadly, in a sample of three and a half thousand women who had been declared literate in 1980, by 1990 46% could no longer pass the simplest of tests (ibid: 44). Secondly, again, the practice of popular education often (maybe even usually) deviated from theory. There were criticisms – not only by political opponents – that the purpose of the crusade seemed less about encouraging authentic liberation, more about enlisting support for the Sandinistas. The literacy primer, 'Dawn of the People', clearly promoted the Sandinistas in a positive light, highlighting the role of the army in the revolution, personality profiles of Sandinista heroes and the benefits of Sandinista land and welfare reforms – a political line entirely defensible but, nevertheless, an educational programme meant to persuade rather than 'problematise'. The content was off-putting to many students – the opposite of an authentic, generative issue – and frequently ignored. Nor did *brigadistas* find it easy implementing a non-traditional approach (Hirshon, 1982). Confused and frustrated, they often abandoned any discussion of social themes altogether and resorted to traditional forms of rote drilling, especially as deadlines for national testing drew near. Arnove argues that 'the major political thrust of the National Literacy Crusade resided not in the generative themes and emotionally charged words of the primer but in the very context of the mass mobilisation. For the most part, the instruction and learning I observed were very traditional' (Arnove, 1994: 27).

'Popular Basic Education' And Other Initiatives

As a follow-up to the literacy crusade, and running in parallel with the formal educational system, the Sandinistas also set up a national programme of basic, adult popular education (*Educación Popular Básica*). This was intended to consolidate and develop skills acquired in the crusade, reach out to those whom the crusade had bypassed and, progressing upwards to six (later nine) different levels, introduce other skills related to language, mathematics, arts and social sciences. It was to engage the participation of grassroots organisations, start from generative themes, involve all participants as both teachers and learners and promote critical analysis of reality with a view to taking action for change. Relying mainly on Sandinista mass organisations, the programme was delivered through the creation of 'Popular Education Collectives' (CEPs). These were flexibly structured learning groups, meeting when and wherever it suited people most, usually for two hours, five evenings a week. Much like the crusade, they were co-ordinated by youthful 'popular teachers' many of whom had still to complete primary education themselves or were even recent graduates of the crusade. Popular teachers were given on-going training at weekends.

By 1986 there were 17,428 Popular Education Collectives and 17,203 popular teachers (or co-ordinators) reaching some 195,000 learners throughout Nicaragua (Arnove, 1986; Barndt, 1991). Backed up by radio programmes, newspaper articles and specially produced materials, the educational guidelines were taken straight from popular education theory:
'Each lesson in the national texts thus followed three steps:
   Step 1: We observe our reality
   Step 2: We interpret our reality
   Step 3: We transform our reality.
In Step 1, for instance, a photo is used to reflect the key theme of the lesson; participants are asked to link the situation presented in the photo to their own experiences. A sample lesson on "corn" is used with questions to guide the discussion.
   In Step 2, the class begins to analyse the problem, deepening an understanding of it through reading and writing practice.
   In Step 3 students are encouraged to organise some kind of community action around the issue discussed.'
   (Barndt, 1991: 71).

'Lesson plans of the various texts frequently call upon students to write letters, send telegrams, talk to friends, and put into practice ideas that they have read about or discussed in the CEPs. A number of the CEPs use sociodramas or role playing, small group discussion, development of class montages of newspaper and magazine clippings to illustrate and explore social issues' (Arnove, 1986: 50).
   However, the war caused over 800 popular education collectives to close and disrupted the training of popular teachers – of whom more than 300 were killed in counter-revolutionary violence (Arnove, 1994: 188). Like health workers, popular educators were a potent symbol of the revolution which the *Contras* (counter-revolutionaries) set out to destroy. Though the numbers the programme reached were impressive and learners seemed to prefer 'popular' teachers to 'professionals', once again there were problems putting theory into practice. While the willing participation of so many committed volunteers was admirable, and arguably one of the strengths of the programme, when faced with 'mixed-ability' groups of learners and subject matter of which they themselves had little knowledge 'the abilities of popular educators appear to be stretched beyond the breaking point' (Arnove, 1986: 55). In difficult times educators tended to fall back on the traditional forms of education with which they were most familiar. Arnove's study of the national texts also suggests that, once again, a particular political line was being promoted. Learners were often

inhibited from speaking out, feeling there was meant to be a 'right' answer to the questions. Barndt asserts that the lack of training meant many popular teachers 'stuck mechanically to the texts, without encouraging more dynamic discussion or connecting the content to local experiences' (Barndt, 1991: 70). The physical demands of working all day and, for many, being involved in other revolutionary activities, led to high dropout rates among both learners and teachers. By the end of 1984, with national pressure for economic development and the need to develop skills quickly, grades had been standardised with formal education and the Popular Education Collectives were often seen simply as a different way of gaining qualifications. Archer & Costello (1990: chapter 3) describe the problems faced by one Popular Education Collective even when conditions seemed relatively favourable.

Both the Literacy Crusade and Popular Basic Education were projects co-ordinated by the Ministry of Education. But popular education is a generic practice relevant to many (all?) areas of social action: 'popular education was everywhere…in the health brigades, in the work of the Defence Committees, in the communities, even in homes…people recognised that you don't need experts, that education is about people with experience, your mother, my aunt, sharing what they know. Popular education lives in the people: it is the revolutionary process' (Victoriano Artiaga, Director of Adult Education, ibid: 42). Barndt (1991) describes a number of different popular education initiatives such as:

- Training programmes in popular communications for would-be photographers, artists, radio journalists, writers and so on. The programmes involved trainees doing participative research in communities, learning their skills by producing materials and having these analysed by fellow-participants and community members themselves.

- To promote preventative health care, the Ministry of Health organised Popular Health Campaigns in a similar fashion to the Literacy Crusade. Some 24,000 health *brigadistas* were trained through a multiplier system (10 educators trained 12 people, each of these trained another 10 who trained another 10 in their turn). At the grassroots, Popular Health Councils were set up in 1981 and co-ordinated by representatives from all the major mass organisations (women and youth organisations, trade unions etc). Catchy cartoons connected with popular culture ('you can't learn baseball by sitting behind a desk and the same applies to health'), gave out important information and challenged people to think. Training was designed not for *brigadistas* to go about imparting information but, through a popular education approach, to involve grassroots organisations in deciding the best way to promote good health and prevent disease: 'What's basic to the popular education we've developed is that the people have been given the right not only to learn about health, but also to participate in planning the programmes so they adapt to their needs... Popular education has done this: it has proved that organised people can prevent diseases... Popular education is a liberating process which allows popular organisations to link health and sickness to their historical, structural causes, and to participate in decision-making, management and control of health programmes, in order to transform their environment and improve their conditions' (Dalila López, Ministry of Health, ibid: 98-99).

Similarly, the ideas of popular education (and the multiplier system of training) permeated other state agencies and large-scale grassroots organisations, from those concerned with land reform and rural co-operatives to unions concerned with safety and workers' rights. Barndt (ibid) goes on to describe case-studies of the role played by popular education in women's education, Christian Base Communities and the training of community workers.

General Comments

On the surface, with a fully supportive government and a population crying out for change, revolutionary Nicaragua offered a unique opportunity for popular education to prove itself on a large scale. If its impact is evaluated simply by comparing social welfare indicators prior to 1979 with those of today then it was a failure. But this would be unfair. The revolution was under siege from the start, security and economic survival took precedence over education and popular educators themselves became targets of violence. Judgements vary widely between those who consider popular education in revolutionary Nicaragua to have been a failure and those who think that given the circumstances, it was extremely successful (Carnoy & Torres, 1990). Though perfectly open about internal Sandinista mistakes, in retrospect the former Minister for Education, Fernando Cardenal, still emphasised that 'the military aggression was the greatest obstacle to developing a truly popular education' (Barndt, 1991: 166).

External aggression aside, the case of Nicaragua shows likely limits on the effectiveness of popular education even in a revolutionary context. First, the constant internal opposition to both the Revolution and popular education presented the new government with difficult choices though Harris (1992) and Gonzalez (1990) argue that in its attempt to placate rather than confront private capitalist interests, the Sandinistas made a fundamental mistake. The persistence of private education, which could afford to pay higher wages and rob the state of qualified teachers, was one way in which popular education was hampered. Second, in their early education work, to consolidate the revolution and inform the population of the changes taking place, the Sandinistas leaned heavily towards propaganda. To their credit, this was later recognised and modified, but in a context of dramatic social change, where political structures are fragile and reactionary interests ready to pounce, it is perhaps no surprise that the desire to persuade conflicts with the promotion of open-ended dialogue. It is paradoxical, indeed, for any government, revolutionary or otherwise, to promote authentic critical thinking when this could be turned on the government itself. Third, the lack of economic resources, infrastructure and trained personnel prompted a centralised and hierarchical form of organisation, with many educators frustrated by the officialdom of lower-level bureaucrats (Arnove, 1994: 43). Fourth, by 1983 there was a shift in emphasis away from popular towards formal education as by now 'there was a much more urgent need to increase material output, and this, in turn, seemed to require more specific skills' (Carnoy & Torres, 1990: 353). Finally, as with smaller-scale projects, it was clearly not easy to translate theory into practice and given the inexperience of so many educators and the limited training available, then the extent to which popular education actually happened was variable.

Nonetheless, we have seen that considerable achievements were undoubtedly made. Despite his detailed criticisms, Arnove could argue in 1986 that 'it is very much the case that tens of thousands of previously illiterate and poorly-skilled individuals are now playing important roles at all levels of the society, from co-op to national legislative bodies' (Arnove, 1986: 68). The revolutionary context unleashed an enthusiasm and energy for change not seen in apparently more settled societies. That so many were prepared to suffer hardship and volunteer for the public campaigns is surely an inspiration to radical educators everywhere? Independently of the impact on targeted learners – and this had its successes as well as failures – the thousands of *brigadistas* experienced a massive exercise in popular education, engaged, as they were, in an on-going analysis of their social reality and an attempt to do something to change it. The combination of the revolutionary political conjuncture, the opportunities for action it created and the promotion of popular education led, arguably, to a widespread, enduring culture of participation. Many saw the defeat of the Sandinistas in 1990 not as the death of a revolution but the considered choice of a politically aware electorate who rightly saw the vote as the only way to stop the war (as well as to register dissatisfaction with aspects of Sandinista behaviour). As we saw with the women's movement in chapter 5, grassroots organisations experienced a second liberation, freed from the straitjacket of always defending the Sandinistas, and were now able to be more authentic 'subjects' of change. This subjectivity was expressed often in the 1990s – student protests, worker's strikes, community action and, famously, the blocking of national roads in 1991, when president Chamorro

Marta Ligia López and Jaime Guido, veterans of the Nicaraguan Literacy Campaign, outside a popular education centre in Mateare, on the outskirts of Managua, where they continue to work as volunteers.
Photographer: Liam Kane

was unable to travel through the country – as different movements took direct action to thwart attempts to reverse the gains of the revolution. Nor are the Sandinistas themselves spared: as they make compromises in parliament which prejudice their erstwhile, popular support, they have been as likely as the government to be on the receiving end of protest. In a visit to Scotland in March 2000, the co-ordinator of the Nicaraguan Community Movement in Matagalpa, Sergio Sáenz, claimed that the legacy of popular education in revolutionary Nicaragua was its lasting impact in creating an active and participative citizenry. Three indicators stood out. Firstly, he could reel off a number of contemporary examples where, through a process of popular education, communities in Matagalpa had achieved high levels of participation and action and won a number of local campaigns. Secondly, he argued that given the taming of the Sandinistas, the high level of activism of popular movements was the only effective opposition which the current government faced. And finally, he reminded me that barely an election takes place in Nicaragua which does not have a turn-out of at least 90% of voters. 'Tell me another country where you see that level of voluntary, political participation', he said mischievously, as someone introduced him to a Member of the new Scottish Parliament.

Popular Education and the (Non-revolutionary) State

But revolutionary Nicaragua was a unique example, in Latin America, of an authentic attempt to run a national, governmental programme of popular education. Mostly, the state plays a different role. The degree to which it is hostile, tolerant or supportive of movements for change affects the ability of popular education to operate on a large-scale.

A Historical Perspective

Popular education has attempted to function within every type of state. In dictatorships it goes underground, often taking refuge in the Church. The double identity of the Catholic Church – traditionally conservative and 'respectable', but partly radical and 'popular' – has afforded a certain amount of cover. People also find imaginative ways to elude the constraints of dictatorship (Archer & Costello, 1990), though it is clear that under extreme authoritarianism, the promotion of overt, large-scale popular education is impossible.

In more liberal contexts, the picture varies. The Institutionalised Revolutionary Party (PRI) of Mexico has generally allowed popular organisations a degree of freedom to agitate. Towards the end of the 1980s, the Mexican popular movement posed a threat to the continuing hegemony of the PRI and at a crucial point, activists chose to work through a new political party – the *Partido Revolucionário Democrático* – rather than remain outside formal politics. Though it is difficult to measure – and I am unaware of any relevant evaluation – since a great deal of popular education had been done with the organisations belonging to the movement, it is reasonable to speculate that it did achieve some large-scale impact. If we accept that popular education has influenced the practice of the Zapatistas (see chapter 5), then this impact continues to the present day. Again, however, there are limits: the PRI and its allies have demonstrated a willingness to engage in mass repression, if necessary, to frustrate any radical change and as yet it remains unclear how the Zapatista conflict will be resolved (at the time of writing the PRI had just lost control of the presidency for the first time in its history). It seems, then, that where it has become a well-organised movement itself, popular education is likely to have a large-scale impact when the wider popular movement is able to pose a threat to existing power relations.

Some ostensibly progressive (though non-revolutionary) governments have even been prepared to promote a popular education, of sorts, by themselves. In 1988, in its wish to pay back some (but not too much) 'social debt', the social democratic government of Rodrigo Borja in Ecuador attempted to organise a literacy campaign of the type run in Nicaragua in 1980, linking it to issues of human rights and social justice. The campaign was co-ordinated by Rosa María

Torres, who had been active in Nicaragua herself and who argued that 'if we remain on the margins of the state, we only have marginal possibilities of making marginal change...we are left working on a small-scale' (in ibid: 78). But because the campaign was independent of a wider social project, conflicting, in many ways, with the government's political philosophy – it had no intention of tackling vested capitalist interests nor supporting the struggles of popular organisations – it was not too difficult for private interests and reluctant educationalists to frustrate its more radical pretensions (ibid: chapter 5).

The tradition of 'populism' is infamous in Latin America. Populist politicians seek a strong power base among the poor, presenting themselves as champions of their interests, often with fine, radical rhetoric. They maintain power by wrestling concessions from the most powerful, on the one hand, thus appealing to a grassroots constituency, but ruling with an iron rod on the other. In effect, they referee class conflict and block any real, structural change. The archetypal 'populists' were Getulio Vargas in Brazil, Juan Perón in Argentina and Juan Velasco in Peru, prominent from the 1940s to the early 1970s, a time when Latin American economies were expanding and the state had a surplus for distribution. Less strong today, the tradition still survives in various guises, often in local politics. The period of João Goulart's populist government in Brazil (1961-1964) illustrates the possibilities for popular education in such a context. Albeit with a view to capturing the radical vote at a time when his position was shaky, Goulart supported an early form of large-scale popular education. Freire was invited to organise a national literacy campaign which, had it been completed, would have enfranchised millions since people were denied the right to vote in Brazil if they were illiterate. In one year alone, the Movimento de Educação de Base (with state support) trained as many as 3,870 educators and had 111, 066 graduate learners (see Box 1:2). However, within a populist, non-revolutionary context, state-led popular education has in-built contradictions and limitations. In Brazil, when threatened, those defending powerful economic interests (supported by the United States) staged a coup in 1964. Popular education was immediately repressed. The evaluation of popular education here, then, is problematic. On a large scale, initially, it was successful enough to be a threat to dominant interests (which it should be); the reaction it (partly) provoked, however, was disastrous. Since then, Freire always maintained that the state – and the oppressors – effectively set the limits to popular education's room for manoeuvre. La Belle (1986) goes further and concludes that except in the context of a guerrilla army, popular education can only work for political reform, rather than revolutionary change, despite its radical rhetoric.

Contemporary Thinking

The desired relationship between popular education and the state has been a source of recent debate. Suppressed by hard-line governments and influenced by the rise of revolutionary struggle, in the 1960s and 70s the popular education movement in Latin America was an oppositional force whose political-pedagogical project seemed to have no place within state education which, it was believed, ultimately sought to defend the privileges of the oppressors. Popular education was (and remains) commonly understood as an activity external to the state, the domain of progressive NGOs and popular organisations. From the 1980s onwards, however, stark, uncompromising, anti-statist positions have been questioned. Some argue (Torres, 1990; Gadotti, 1992) that knee-jerk, anti-government resistance is based on simplistic notions of the state; that rather than a mere extension of the oppressors' power, the state is a site of social, political and economic struggle in which there is room to agitate for change. In attempting to achieve maximum impact, popular education, they believe, cannot refrain from battling its corner and exploiting contradiction in the state arena. The issue was central to the 'rethinking the basics' debates of the early 1990s, especially how to make the most of less authoritarian governments and, increasingly, of more progressive local authorities.

The outcome of the debate is that the popular education movement is currently much more willing to engage with the state than before. On the one hand, there are real dangers in this course of action. As discussed in chapter 6, contemporary neo-liberal states in Latin America are keen to sub-contract social services to NGOs, co-opting them away from more radical agendas. Engagement with the state on these terms, some would argue (Petras, 1999), connives with rather than challenges oppression. Popular education NGOs operating within this scenario run the risk of having a net negative impact.

For me, Gadotti articulates the mature position to take, arguing that the popular movement and popular education should strive to have one foot within the state apparatus 'but it has to be only *one foot, inside.* The other foot should be outside. *Tactically inside, strategically outside...*Maintaining this dialectical relationship between being *outside* and being inside is important for the movement's own survival. The *negotiating* strength of the movement within the State depends on its capacity for *mobilisation* outside it' (Gadotti, 1992: 71).

This particular position was illustrated in São Paulo between 1989 and 1992 when the Workers' Party (the 'Partido dos Trabalhadores', PT) won control of the city council. Freire was made Secretary of Education and Gadotti one of his chief assistants. Arguing now from within the state, and for 'popular education through popular participation' (ibid: 68), Gadotti outlined three requisites for the democratisation of decision-making: (a) the autonomy of social movements and their organisations in relation to the administration (b) the opening of channels of participation by the administration and (c) administrative transparency/the democratisation of information. In São Paulo, 'popular councils' were formed to provide a midway house between the State and popular movements, a place for the latter to place its 'one foot' inside the former. These were not 'talking shops' but decision-making organs of democracy. Though their novelty inevitably sparked resistance, in the end they were considered a great success in promoting popular participation. In a similar vein, an adult education forum was created for popular movements to meet with and make demands of the state, both in terms of physical resources and the types of educational experiences to be offered. Gadotti claims that this had a big impact within São Paulo in its ability to 'strengthen popular movements without binding them to the State' (ibid: 76).

It was also an opportunity for Freire to promote his ideas within formal education, to create a 'Public Popular Education' for São Paulo's 678 schools, 700,000 students and 33,000 teachers (Wong, 1995: 122). His administration 'made an explicit political choice to place public education at the service of poor and working-class communities' (ibid: 125). It promoted a reorganisation of the curriculum around 'generative' themes (teachers and students would research their communities to find out what these were) and the practical application of newly acquired knowledge. It encouraged teacher and community participation in curriculum development (teachers were given 10 paid hours a week to meet together, analyse educational issues and have their thinking challenged) and devolved much decision-making to the schools, even allowing them to opt-out of the administration's reforms. In an attempt to evaluate this experience, Wong argues that despite the challenges, 'some schools managed to confront, overcome, and transform their struggles into full implementation and fulfilment of many of the Municipal Department of Education's goals. Observations of these schools revealed classrooms abuzz with student activity, students eagerly participating in discussions and unabashedly questioning ideas and concepts, and teachers actively working with other teachers....Other schools, however, remained somewhere between partial implementation of the project and outright resistance to it. In these schools, teachers struggled with the underlying concepts and ideas, at times expressing frustration or even outright resistance to its various premises' (ibid: 130). For Wong, the experience illustrated the difficulty of changing entrenched attitudes towards education, the impossibility of achieving radical change in all schools and the need to do popular education with teachers around their own social reality (as opposed to thinking only of the children's). It also highlighted the limits and complexities of state-initiated popular education in that (a) since the project did not spring from popular movements themselves, grassroots commitment had to be won over and (b) even when schools and communities opted in, sometimes this was less through a genuine concern for change and more through a desire to keep in with authority.

Albeit within a context in which national and global capitalism still reigns supreme, with all the contradictions which that presents, when progressive local authorities seek to open up spaces for the genuine participation of popular movements in the struggle for change they offer important opportunities for popular education. Famously, the PT municipal government of Porto Alegre, in Brazil promotes an exercise in 'participatory budgeting' (Abers, 1996) where, after an extended process of community debate and discussion, the popular movement decides how 40% of the municipal budget should be spent (the other 60% being decided by the council). In the town of Gravataí, in the state of Rio Grande do Sul, the department of culture and education has produced a book on popular education for teachers which is radical enough to contain a chapter entitled 'the importance of Che Guevara' (Genro, 1999). In the small town of Cuquío, near Guadalajara in Mexico, when the new, local Partido Revolucionário Democrático won the municipal elections – the first time the ruling PRI had ever lost – they asked for popular education training from IMDEC to help them promote community participation and avoid the elitism of their predecessors. Subsequently, they organised many forums for collective dialogue which produced some notable results. When they had to decide on the location of a health centre, for example, having heard all the viewpoints face to face, the people in better-off 'wards' voted against their own self-interests and in favour of the poorest – to the great surprise, even, of the councillors.

General Comments

When popular education attempts to have a large-scale impact, it necessarily engages with the state. Its greatest opportunity has been when working in tandem with a revolutionary government, though even here there were numerous obstacles to success. Increasingly, the state is seen less as a monolithic representative of powerful interests, more as a site of struggle in which popular education needs to be embroiled. In optimistic scenarios, progressive States (or local authorities) create considerable space for large-scale projects; more normally, states will attempt to co-opt popular education and concessions are only won when the popular movement is strong. It can be argued that in many instances, popular education has managed to have a significant large-scale impact though it is also true that the same problems impeding success on a small-scale continue to apply.

Conclusion

Given its overlaps with other forms of social and political action, assessing the impact of popular education is problematic. The larger the scale of the project, moreover, the greater the complications though the practice of proper, systematic evaluation increases regardless. While each case must be judged on its merits, evidence suggests that where circumstances are favourable and the quality of popular education is high, it undoubtedly contributes towards progressive social change. It is a constant challenge, however, to make practice live up to the promise of theory.

After a period in which anything seemed possible, the popular education movement in Latin America has learned of the limits to what it can achieve. On its own it will not change the world: other social, economic and political dynamics are more powerful. Nor can it provide the type of macro-service which is the responsibility of the state: in addition to its work with popular movements, it now campaigns for free, public, 'popular' state education for all.

But to recognise the limitations of popular education is not to question its *raison d'être*. It is one of many contributions to the struggle for social change and committed educators and activists battle on, constantly striving to narrow the gap between theory and practice. Regardless of the difficulties faced, wherever social and political injustice exists, popular education will remain a necessary, honourable and sometimes catalytic endeavour.

Review of Chapters 7 and 8

Brought up in Northern Ireland and Scotland, Patrick Welsh was briefly a teacher in Nigeria before moving to the Nicaraguan war zone of central Zelaya, in 1986, to work on the 'Casas de la Cultura' project for the promotion of popular culture and education. From 1991-1993 he was projects officer for Latin America and the Caribbean for the UK-based NGO CAFOD. From 1993-1999 he was based in CANTERA (a popular education centre in Managua), developing methodologies for gender work with men. He is currently a development worker with ICD/CIIR, promoting gender training for men on issues of masculinity and violence in Honduras, El Salvador, the Dominican Republic and Ecuador as well as providing support for the newly created Association of Men Against Violence in Nicaragua.

In my experience as a popular educator in Nicaragua during the last 15 years, attempts to assess and evaluate the impact of Popular Education have proved to be complicated processes, often presenting more challenges than concrete results. As such, I think that chapters 7 and 8 are well researched and a clear and honest portrayal of the issues associated with assessing the impact of popular education in Latin America. On reading these chapters, it was comforting to discover that popular educators in other Latin American countries have faced similar difficulties to the ones that we have encountered in Nicaragua. Comforting but also disconcerting and surely an indicator that much more effort needs to be put into the development of theoretical frameworks and practical methodologies for assessing the impact of Popular Education.

Perhaps one of the major obstacles is the imprecision with which Popular Education is itself understood and expressed in conceptual terms. When asked to define 'popular education', many popular educators, ironically, find it easier to explain what it isn't. Indeed, one of the most common maxims that I have consistently come across over the years is: 'Popular education is not just a set of methods and techniques for working with the poor and marginalised', which, when stripped down and critically examined, eventually leads to a precise conceptualisation of what popular education is. When evaluating popular education and measuring its impact, therefore, it is important to differentiate between processes orientated towards incrementing people's capacity for critical thinking that leads to empowerment, and the adaptation and incorporation of popular education methods and techniques into development projects or programmes as a means of achieving specific goals.

Popular participation in vaccination programmes, for example, that envisage the training of health *brigadistas* on a massive scale will undoubtedly have positive effects on the epidemiological control of disease. Success can be measured in relation to coverage achieved and even related to the popular education methods and techniques employed for the *brigadistas'* training. There is no guarantee, however, that people's awareness will have been raised as regards the causes of the diseases they are being vaccinated against nor that they will have become sufficiently empowered to actively participate in their future prevention. To reach these goals, people have to be enabled to challenge ingrained cultural values and centuries' old practices, (not only related to health) that simultaneously entails the critical appraisal of their perceptions of themselves and their world. Methods and techniques associated with popular education may have been successfully incorporated into the vaccination programme, as a means to specific ends, but popular education per se and the utopian ends that it pursues have scantily, if at all, been taken on board.

The evaluation of popular education, and its successes, are intrinsically related to visions of reality and concepts of development. In recent years many international funding agencies, NGOs and government entities have increasingly begun to adopt the 'logical framework' as a useful tool for the planning, execution and subsequent evaluation of development projects. The underlying premise is that once a specific problem has been identified, a strategy that incorporates the definition of precise goals, indicators, etc., can be elaborated to enable that problem to be solved and thus improve the quality of life for the beneficiaries of the project. Evaluation thus becomes a fairly straightforward, technical exercise to measure results in relation to the previously established stated aims and expected results.

Within the framework of the Conception of a Dialectical Methodology (see chapter 3), however, reality is conceived of as a complicated and interrelated network of social systems (and systems within systems) within which a diverse and complex array of human beings take part, in a variety of ways that are determined, in turn, by their own particular social condition(s): class, gender, race, sexuality, age, etc. Popular education proposes the systematic, critical analysis of reality in order to expose the power relations and structures that exist and that sustain and prolong injustices and inequalities. The aim is not so much to solve a problem, but rather to 'problematise' reality and generate viable, ethical proposals to transform that reality. The evaluation, therefore, of popular education per se becomes a complex and often daunting task, given that it is primarily concerned with radical shifts in people's perceptions of themselves (attitudes, values, conduct, etc.) and their relationship to existing power structures at all levels. The application of the 'logical framework', then, presents serious shortcomings for the evaluation of programmes and projects conceived of and carried out within the philosophical framework of popular education.

It could be argued that the extent to which power relationships (on micro and macro levels) have been significantly altered as a result of the promotion of processes of popular education, is a major indicator of their impact. History teaches, however, that power, even in its most benevolent forms, ultimately seeks the control and domination of those who are subordinate to it. Power, in general, changes only to preserve itself. To what degree then can governments, albeit revolutionary or progressive ones, truly promote popular education? By their very nature they exist to exercise governance and not to promote people's capacity to critically analyse power. As has been seen in this chapter, the processes of popular education promoted by the Sandinista Revolution enjoyed mixed success. Undoubtedly related to the war and economic embargo imposed by the US Government, their impact was also severely limited by the hierarchical social structures that continued to permeate Nicaraguan society and which, as a whole, were not readily subjected to critical analysis. The promotion of popular education once again takes second place to the utilisation of popular education methods and techniques for specific pre-established objectives, and the systematic analysis of power, its uses and abuses, is minimised if not totally neutralised.

In recent years, the incorporation of gender analysis into popular education has widened and deepened the debate on power. Throughout the 1980s, women within the Sandinista Revolution resorted to popular education as a means to promote critical awareness and improve women's economic situation. By the end of the 1980s and throughout the 1990s much of the analysis has been centred on power relations between women and men and popular education methodology has continued to be widely adopted, within civil society, in the struggle to empower women and obtain gender equity. The unequal, socially constructed power relationships that exist between men and women and which lead to women's systemic subordination and exploitation are mirrored in other social relationships (class, race, age, etc.) and political structures (trades' unions, political parties, state institutions, civil society organisations). Power, when attained, is to be used to control and dominate other beings considered in some way inferior; mechanisms, often including the systematic use of violence, must be developed to ensure the propagation of power. The paradigm of power that leads a man to beat his wife is similar to the one that motivates generals and politicians to start wars.

If social transformation is to be achieved, the challenging and transformation of power in all its many dimensions and manifestations (not just political power) must become a central concern for popular education and appropriate evaluation techniques developed to measure real change in power relations and structures. In debates on gender and popular education in Nicaragua, it has been proposed that the power socially allocated to men as a result of their gender socialisation represents one of the greatest challenges for popular education. Men, after all, continue to dominate public and political life. How then can external social and political power structures be transformed if they continue to be dominated by individual men whose conception and internalisation of power, independent of their political ideology, is one characterised by the control and dominance of others? Indeed, how can popular education propose social transformation if gender analysis is not an integral part of its philosophy and practise?

To seriously challenge and transform power, however, organisations that promote popular education must deepen their understanding of how power is conceived and exercised not only within social institutions and between individuals in society but also within the organisations themselves. Ironically, mistakes committed in the past on a macro level more than two decades ago (by the Sandinsta Government for example) tend to be emulated on a micro one today. Many organisations that promote popular education theory and practise in the projects and programmes that they support and accompany, fail to incorporate the same principles internally. As such their organisational structures and institutional cultures continue to reproduce hierarchical structures and internal power relationships that are marked and marred by discrimination and marginalisation based upon gender, class differences, racism, ageism, sexual orientation, etc. Cultural stereotypes, prejudices, ignorance and fear lead to the reproduction of power relationships that oppress, exploit and subordinate. These are contradictions that must be recognised and exposed to a critical analysis that goes beyond objective reality, incorporating the realms of each individual's subjectivity. If the evaluation of traditional popular education projects and programmes that have dealt mainly with political consciousness and action have been difficult in the past, the challenges for the future are immense.

Gender analysis, of course, is the most advanced incursion into subjective reality that popular education has so far dared to experiment with. A recent piece of research carried out in Nicaragua (D'Angelo, 1999) discovered that the levels of critical awareness and empowerment of women who had taken part in (popular education) training courses on gender issues were in general greater than those who had not. Whilst both groups rejected blatant affirmations that openly propagated women's inferiority and subjugation to men's power, in practise the women who had had access to workshops and courses where they were able to collectively analyse their gender condition, demonstrated a greater capacity to take control of their own lives and to instigate concrete changes to improve life's quality. A central issue was the arrival at a clear understanding of the social construction of male and female gender identities and power relationships.

Whilst the scope of the study, however, did not attempt to validate particular elements of the methodologies used and their relationship to the changes reported by women, this was carried out to a certain degree by the impact study on the masculinity and popular education courses carried out by CANTERA in 1997 and referred to in chapter 7. The following elements were considered 'extremely or very important' by more than 75% of the men who took part in the study:

- The fact that men's own reality is a starting point for analysis
- The emphasis put on group work
- The variety of methods and techniques used
- The collective articulation of proposals for change
- The new spaces for reflection and analysis that are opened up.

The impact study, in fact, formed part of a wider attempt to validate the effectiveness of popular education in the promotion of changes in men that also included the development validation of a training manual. In 1999, 'The Meaning of Maleness' was piloted in six communities in different parts of Nicaragua. A total of 18 local promoters were trained in the use of the manual, whose implementation was meticulously monitored by members of the

CANTERA team through the systematic application of 10 previously prepared instruments. This enabled a precise evaluation of the methodology, its scope and limitations and permitted the incorporation of modifications to the manual. It also facilitated the articulation of a series of methodological, pedagogical and theoretical "lessons learned" and points to take into consideration for the implementation of processes of popular education with men on issues of gender and masculinity which have been incorporated into the second edition of the manual.

A third element was the systematisation of the courses on masculinity carried out by CANTERA between 1994 and 1998. Adopting the systematisation model developed by ALFORJA, this exercise enabled the 'theorisation of the process' to take place and permitted a deeper analysis of the relationship between gender and popular education and its particular application to processes of awareness-raising with men orientated towards 'the unlearning of *machismo*'.

As stated in chapter 7, many organisations do not have the time, money and personnel necessary to carry out exhaustive integral evaluations of popular education processes and the major emphasis is invariably put on the evaluation of educational activities (workshops, seminars, etc.). Furthermore, in many situations, the day-to-day pressures and practical demands on popular educators lead to excessive, albeit necessary, activism, that can lead to inadequate time dedicated to evaluation and systematisation. As a result, these are often experienced as a disturbance. In some cases, even when time is allocated for evaluation, little emphasis is put on the preparation of the evaluation and over-zealous educators invariably feel frustrated and sometimes even guilty that they are not in the field doing something more useful! CANTERA's main aim, in carrying out this unusually strict process of evaluation, validation and systematisation of its gender work with men, was the development of a thoroughly tried and tested practical methodology that can be easily multiplied in a variety of different contexts. Whilst it may seem a 'luxury' and it most certainly meant the allocation of time, money and trained personnel, the end result is that other organisations interested in promoting processes of awareness-raising with men on issues of gender and masculinity, in Nicaragua and other parts of Latin America, will not have to reinvent the wheel. They have a basic methodological and theoretical framework within which to begin their work. They will, of course, have to evaluate and measure the impact of that work, and develop appropriate methods and techniques to do so. Furthermore, the systematisation of future processes of popular education between men on issues of masculinity and gender will undoubtedly generate new 'lessons learned' to enable methodologies to be improved. Such is the dynamic of the Conception of a Dialectical Methodology.

Every popular educator has a utopian dream of social justice and a firm belief that popular education can lead to the transformation of the unjust external and internal pressures, structures and mechanisms that subordinate, dominate and exploit. The more we learn to evaluate and systematise our personal and collective experiences, the more lessons we glean from our popular education practise and its theorisation, the greater will be our contribution to social justice at both a macro and micro level. Our learning is a continuous process only in as much as we cultivate the spaces necessary for its fruition. Evaluation, impact assessment and systematisation are, therefore, indispensable dimensions of popular education and an important means to maximising our learning and contribution to social justice. It is our opportunity as popular educators to 'make practice live up to the promise of its theory' since it enables us to develop and improve methodologies aimed at personal, social and political transformation. As the author points out in his concluding paragraph, 'to recognise the limitations of popular education is not to question its *raison d'être*... Regardless of the difficulties faced, wherever social and political injustice exist, popular education will remain a necessary, honourable and sometimes catalytic endeavour'. And popular educators will be ever present to critically reflect and analyse, to propose and implement strategies for transformation and of course to evaluate, assess the impact of and systematise their experiences no matter how daunting and complex the task may appear to be.

Patrick Welsh

Chapter 9
'Rethinking the Basics' of Popular Education: Current Practice and Future Directions

"SHE SAYS THE UNITED STATES IS GOING TO STOP INTERFERING IN LATIN AMERICA, THE IMF IS GOING TO CANCEL THE DEBT, EVERYBODY'S GOING TO HAVE A GOOD STANDARD OF LIVING, THERE'S GOING TO BE NO MORE RACISM OR SEXISM AND POPULAR EDUCATORS ARE GOING TO STOP USING BIG LONG WORDS THAT NOBODY UNDERSTANDS "

There were important, wide-scale attempts in the 1990s to 'rethink the basics' of popular education in Latin America, a process known in Spanish as *Refundamentación*. This chapter (a) considers the contextual background which prompted this review (b) examines the process of *Refundamentación* and its effect on current practice (c) speculates on the future directions of popular education and (d) explains my own understanding of the recent changes. Recurrent themes throughout the sections are:

- the 'crisis of paradigms'
- the extent to which popular education should work inside or outside the state
- the relationship of popular education to 'new social actors'
- moving from 'protest to proposal'
- whether the concept of the 'popular' requires amplification or, indeed, continues to have any relevance.

But at this point, before attempting to reach any conclusions, it is important to mention the areas not explored in this book and to consider the problems associated with making generalised, sweeping statements on popular education in Latin America.

Problems of Generalisation

Latin America is a vast, geographical expanse with an infinite variety of political, economic and cultural formations. Independently of how it feels to be male, female, white, black, *Mestizo* or indigenous there are worlds of difference between living in Mexico City, the coast of Cuba or the highlands in Peru. Even within one country, far less the whole region, there may be so many different contexts that the understanding of what constitutes popular education is localised rather than national (Eccher, 1996). This book leans heavily on Mexico, Brazil, El Salvador and Nicaragua; the rest of Latin America is under-represented and each country easily merits a book to itself.

Attempts to generalise on a grand scale inevitably rely on information gleaned second-hand from documentation. This means that those individuals and organisations best able to document, publish and disseminate their experience are those whose opinions are most widely-known. Eccher explains the problem: 'we are people of action, so we write very little. So because we write little, no one knows what we're doing... So there we have another problem: how to get our work known because the work we do is at a grassroots level, it's more about running workshops, about face to face interaction' (ibid: 5). In terms of documentation, CEAAL is the most visible organisation in the region, but I know popular educators who feel remote from its orbit and whose perception, rightly or wrongly, is that it is too academic. A lot may be happening in the real world, then, which never becomes common knowledge: there is a tentative nature to all generalised conclusions.

There are also important practices which this book has been unable to cover. A larger project would describe cases-studies of popular education within trades unions, political parties, local authorities, environmental or young people's movements, for example; or case-studies based on particular specialisms, such as *systematisation*, video production or community radio. Due to the lack of clear demarcations between popular education and other types of political-cultural activity, moreover, many relevant experiences may be classified as something else. Confusingly, I have met human rights activists who do not consider themselves popular educators – criticising the latter as too 'ideological' (a critique discussed in chapter 6) – but produce provocative film-documentaries on local generative issues, show these in the streets, on screens attached to vans, and creatively encourage community-wide discussion and action: imaginative popular education by most definitions.

The Background to 'Refundamentación'

The process of *Refundamentación* was instigated by political and economic changes taking place in Latin America. From the late 1980s onwards, one of the two principal characteristics of Latin American states is that they are formally more democratic than in previous decades, when military dictatorship (Chile, Brazil, Argentina), civil war (Central America) or an all-powerful state apparatus (Mexico) formed seemingly insurmountable obstacles to progressive change. Former warring factions now oppose each other at the ballot-box, less frequently with bullets, though whether on account of the left's disunity and lack of credible, radical alternatives or the wealth and resurgent populism of the right, conservative political parties frequently remain in control, despite their discredited past (Winn, 2000; Mejía, 2000). Greater openness and democracy has undoubtedly brought benefits. As governments seek to convince the world of their democratic credentials, it becomes a legitimate public activity to challenge the abuse of human and civic rights; candidates put forward by civil and popular movements have won local elections (Mendoza, 1997: 149) and some see the decentralisation of power to local level as a potential new 'utopía' for democratic participation (de Brito, 1997); 'civil society' has expanded and new organisations, movements and 'social actors' have space to promote their particular visions of progressive social change. But enthusiasm for democracy has to be tempered by reality. Beneath the democratic veneer, authoritarianism is ever ready to pounce and traditional elites use every trick in the book to maintain privilege and avoid being tried for their crimes of the past. Parodying former US policy in Central America, it is a situation sometimes described as 'low intensity democracy'(Cendales et al, 1996: 121).

The other characteristic is the predominance of the so-called 'neo-liberal' model of economic development (Green, 1995), Latin America's experience of end-of-the-century, global capitalism (see Harris, 2000). Relying on the market for economic development, neo-liberalism promotes the privatisation of state enterprises, the withdrawal of subsidies for basic commodities, the free flow of capital in and out of countries and the ever-increasing process of globalisation in which giant enterprises dominate over the sovereignty of national states. With devastating social consequences, it abandons the vulnerable to their fate and the view that 'democratisation is impossible under neo-liberalism' (Cendales et al, 1996: 120) on account of the *de facto* 'dictatorship of the market' (Betuto Fernández, 1998: 75) is one which is easy to defend. Among the consequences of neo-liberalism, Betto (2000) lists (a) a depoliticisation of society, as people are told there is no alternative (b) a shift towards localised struggles, people feeling powerless to effect national or global change (c) a concern with results rather than theory, 'more action and fewer meetings', with struggles focusing

Nativity scene made by de-mobilised URNG fighters, celebrating Christmas and the first anniversary of the signing of the Peace Accords in Guatemala in 1997. Each traditional character is given a label: Mary is the URNG, Joseph is the army and government, a shephard is civil society, the devil lurking in the background is neo-liberalism, the Baby Jesus is the peace process, the angel represents international observers and the (invisible) star above was labelled hope.
Photographer: Morven Gregor

on immediate benefits like jobs, land or housing rather than abstracts like socialism or revolution (d) the predominance of personal over social concerns and an increasing attraction towards spiritualist escapism.

All of which has led, ideologically, to disorientation and a much-heralded 'crisis of paradigms' on the political left: if socialism or revolution is no longer considered feasible, or even desirable, what should former left-leaning political movements be setting out to achieve? With or without a 'paradigm' for change, however, the basic structural problems in Latin America continue to provoke widespread grassroots struggle against injustice and in favour of greater social and economic equality. Many consider the MST (chapter 4) an important guide to new styles of action as it manages to link personal benefit (a piece of land) to a struggle for national political change in which members experience for themselves the viability of alternative forms of collective organisation (Betto, 2000). The Zapatista struggle in Chiapas also challenges neo-liberalism and has proved a positive inspiration throughout Latin America. More recently, the highly organised indigenous popular movement in Ecuador has wrestled many gains from the neo-liberal agenda, was responsible for the removal of two presidents and even jointly governed the country for a period of twenty-four hours (Collins, 2000). These and other movements face enormous difficulties in their attempts to bring about radical change; they experience contradictions in trying to reconcile anti-government protest with specific proposals requiring dialogue and negotiation. Nevertheless, they continue to inspire and challenge the apathy of the neo-liberal mantra that 'there-is-no-alternative'.

Two other changes to note are, firstly, an increase in delinquency and drug-related crime. With the implementation of the Peace Accords in El Salvador, for example, thousands of ex-combatants from both the army and the guerrilla have found themselves de-skilled and jobless, seeing little option but to turn to crime to survive. To help deal with past and current traumas, social psychology is now an important concern throughout Central America (Bickel, 1999). Secondly, with the neo-liberal 'rolling back of the state', there has been spectacular growth in the number of Non Governmental Organisations working in areas of welfare and social work normally considered the responsibility of governments. While some of these have a history of radicalism which they strive to maintain, many others stand accused of operating out of self-interest, happy to legitimise and strengthen the neo-liberal model in the process (Ponce, 1999; Mendoza, 1997: 53; Petras, 1999).

Refundamentación and its Effect on Current Practice

It was inevitable that these changes would impinge on the practice of popular education which had seemed to promise so much in the seventies and eighties. Now seen as part of a failed political project of total transformation, its credibility was threatened and the years 1990 to 1993, in particular, were a time of major crisis and disillusionment within a popular education movement unable to interpret the new reality (Ponce, 1999). While this necessarily forced popular educators to reconsider their assumptions, at its biennial conference in La Havana in 1994, CEAAL pro-actively set up a region-wide process of 'rethinking the basics' – refundamentación – to confront the difficulties. As well as individual publications attempting to address the crisis, a series of 'workshops' took place over the next few years in which popular educators from all over Latin America came together to analyse the problems and attempt to put popular education back on a surer footing. The documentation of these discussions (such as Dimensión Educativa, 1996; CEAAL, 1996 and Mendoza, 1997) gives an important insight into understanding the changes eventually taking place.

Grappling with Paradigms and Ideological Crisis

In chapter 6 I argued that a variety of ideological orientations are present within the popular education movement. While the discussions around refundamentación are framed in terms of how popular education should progress, there are clearly different political analyses bubbling beneath the surface. From Costa Rica, Jara (1996; 1998) argues passionately against allowing confusion to degenerate into nihilism, against the 'paradigm of resignation' and the 'profoundly mistaken' idea that neo-liberalism can bring peace and prosperity to Central America'; as well as taking advantage of the openings which the new situation offers, he defends the need to continue pursuing structural change. Rebellato (1998) argues that what he calls Latin American 'critical theory' has now emerged from the crisis stronger and more mature than before, having been able to integrate new dimensions such as 'the component of uncertainty, the recognition and defence of diversity – specifically cultural or multicultural diversity – and the strategic importance of the public sphere and civil society' (ibid: 61). But he also emphasises that neo-liberalism is not simply an economic model but an ideological vision. Not only should it be resisted, but 'paradoxical though it may seem, I think it is necessary not only to affirm the current importance of Latin American critical theory but that we need to make it even more radical than before... however, the priority to find an economic alternative must be recognised, for unless there is a transformation of the economic structures, all other alternatives are futile' (ibid: 60-61). From Bolivia, hinting at deeper problems, Betuto Fernández (1998: 76) tellingly suggests that 'neo-liberalism does not fight against popular education, it just seduces its educators'. From Cuba, González Rodríguez (1998) considers contemporary Latin American popular education a 'bat-like' concept in that some see a bird where others see a mouse. She argues against those strands of thinking which 'limit horizons to extending the sphere of active citizenship, to restoring and improving a democracy wounded by neo-liberalism' (ibid: 91). Instead she defends the 'majority tendency' which believes in building an alternative participatory democracy from below. In doing so, she continues, it is important to maintain a critique of the whole of the capitalist system, not isolated bits and pieces.

On the other hand, Cendales et al (1996) observe that 'the option for democratisation, the recognition of the plurality of subjugated social actors and the broader range of themes which today express alternative and emancipatory aspirations – together with the exhaustion of the classist paradigm – have brought a certain distancing from the concept of "the popular" and there are now few references to the "impoverished" actors in our countries' (ibid: 117). Moreover, they also see a decline in the 'visionary dimension of popular education, the commitment to alternative forms of social organisation. With socialism's loss of prestige, everything would seem to indicate that the current liberal democracies are the desired form of state organisation and political and social fulfilment. It would seem that many have turned their backs on the visionary dimension which was so fundamental to the original discourse of popular education' (ibid: 118). They go on to argue that popular education has to do more than just be supportive of democracy, that the social structures originally giving rise to popular education are still in place – and have even been exacerbated – and that while issues like democracy, citizenship and human rights are important, there is also an urgent need to 'reclaim and prioritise the sense of the "popular" in popular education' (ibid). Elsewhere, others invoke Freire's later writings to support their conviction that popular education needs to hold on to its visionary dimension or 'utopías'(Mendoza, 1997: 9).

Others suggest that the so-called crisis of paradigms needs to be kept in perspective. Many practices in popular education are started and sustained 'not on account of any consistent theoretical proposition but because they are driven by convictions, hopes, feelings or by other "ingredients" which have not been properly studied in this process of rethinking the basics' (Cendales et al, 1996: 108). One group of educators came to question whether 'popular education is really based on these paradigms at all and maybe we are getting caught up in a dilemma which isn't really ours. Maybe those who worry about looking for new paradigms are academics searching for theoretical consistency...we came to the conclusion that we shouldn't get too worked up. We've committed ourselves passionately and optimistically to the popular struggle and the building of new knowledge. Maybe that's the paradigm that keeps us going' (Mendoza, 1997: 61).

So there are mixed, confusing and sometimes contradictory messages in how the popular education movement has reacted to this period of ideological disorientation. My own reading of the situation is that though there remains a problem with paradigms – if by that we mean that the popular education movement no longer has the same, singular vision as before – the element of crisis has subsided and there now reigns a modus vivendi among three currents of thought. While still critical of neo-liberalism (those who are not have effectively abandoned popular education altogether), one group of educators concentrates its attention on the 'new spaces' which have appeared and now talks the language of democracy, civil society and citizenship; another has a more problematic understanding of these concepts and while it explores all new opportunities and acknowledges the importance of issues of identity and difference, it continues to see class and structural change as the central concerns; another gives up on ideological paradigms altogether and hopes that by immersing itself in grassroots work, the most effective ways to progress will make themselves apparent.

Before and After 'Refundamentación'

All chapters in this book have made reference to how popular education has evolved over the last thirty years. Ideological paradigms aside, this is an appropriate moment to recap on the major differences in practice since before and after the process of *refundamentación*.

Popular education used to be considered an alternative to state education, most of the struggles in which it was involved saw the state as the source of its problems and, not infrequently, the longer-term goal of helping a new revolutionary state come to power lay in the background. Taking advantage of new democratic openings, the popular education movement now has a less monolithic view of the state and, where possible, looks to co-operate strategically, particularly at local level, to achieve maximum impact. Nor is the state, in its new, trimmed-down, less-interventionist format, seen any more as the prime culprit: that role has passed to neo-liberalism, though its amorphous, intangible nature makes it a difficult target to pin down. Ironically, as we saw with the MST, with the increasing privatisation of public services, popular education can now even be considered a defender of the state, albeit one which maintains a critical posture (Martin & Shaw, 2000, discuss the same theme in the context of the UK). It remains a problematic area, however, and some educators still believe that the dangers of co-operation turning to 'co-option' make it too risky a course of action (Ponce, 1999). For me, Gadotti's notion of 'one foot *inside* and one foot *outside*' the state makes perfect sense (see chapter 8), provided the ability to mobilise support 'on the outside' remains intact.

Before *refundamentación*, oppression was understood primarily in terms of class and popular education's contribution focused on the struggles of those groups which were least economically well-off. While this remains a priority, the scenario is now more complex. Oppression is seen to cover a far wider range of themes – democracy, human rights, citizenship, gender issues, interculturalism, environmentalism – and popular education is considered relevant to the organisations and movements involved in their corresponding struggles. CEAAL illustrates the point in its global plan for 1998-2001: 'in our countries the emergence of the theme of citizenship with the rise of national movements for democracy and respect for human rights presented us with a series of themes and dimensions which our previous educational offerings had never considered... the experience of the plebiscite in Chile, the campaign for democracy in Paraguay, the movement for peace in Colombia, increasing awareness of indigenous issues in Mexico and Ecuador... constitute concrete experiences of broad participation which have necessitated national awareness campaigns and education for citizenship' (CEAAL, 1999: 35). Popular education is now more sensitive to the existence of a plurality of 'social subjects' and takes place in a wider variety of settings: as opposed to simply helping mobilise against the state, it is now considered relevant to all areas and concerns of civil society (Arruda, 1999). In the process, some emphasise that 'the fact that today we recognise that there exist different identities and processes giving rise to different social subjects does not mean that social classes no longer exist – we should not end up at the other extreme. In Latin America the processes of social differentiation, subordination and exclusion are tied to economic subordination. By that I mean that people are simultaneously black and exploited, indigenous and landless. In my view the category of "popular" is still valid though we have to consider widening out our understanding of what we mean by "popular sectors" and "popular subjects"' (de Brito, 1997: 92).

Popular Education and Pedagogy
Pedagogically, there are three main differences between popular education pre and post *refundamentación*. The first, as Cendales et al (1996) point out, is that the broader discipline of pedagogy – the research into the principles, practice or profession of teaching – is now taken seriously whereas beforehand it was considered part of formal education and, consequently, the system of exploitation. The popular education movement historically emphasised the political and methodological aspects of its work at the expense of the 'nuts and bolts' of learning: 'in any analysis of the practice of popular education, the pedagogical component gradually became watered down, causing it to become routine, superficial and devoid of content. This led to a decrease in the quality of popular education...Pedagogy became confused with politics and in practice the educational element, properly speaking, was unclear and lacking in focus' (Osorio, 1996: 10). It had little or no dialogue with mainstream theories on teaching and learning such as constructivism (how the mind develops through different stages of complexity and makes sense of the world outside, an area of research mostly associated with the Swiss psychologist Jean Piaget and, increasingly, the Russian psychologist Lev Vygotsky) or behaviourism (where learning is geared towards, and its success judged on, changing people's behaviour patterns. Associated predominantly with the figures of Ivan Pavlov and Burrhus Skinner, these theories have caused considerable controversy – famously savaged by the US linguist and radical intellectual Noam Chomsky – but have been enormously influential on education worldwide (see Tennant, 1997, for an excellent introduction to different learning theories in adult education). Popular education has 'come in from the cold' and now seeks to debate with and learn from mainstream pedagogical theories both to assist its courtship of formal education but also to enrich its adult education practice within social movements. However, it is a reciprocal process in which popular education has challenged

conventional pedagogy in its turn. Freire's emphasis on placing people's welfare at the centre of education has had an important influence on humanistic theories of learning (such as those proposed by Carl Rogers, see O'Hara, 1996). The political aspect of popular education, and the critical thinking it encourages, have influenced the development in the United States' formal education sector of 'critical pedagogy'. Among others, this is associated with educational thinkers like Peter MacLaren (1996) and Henry Giroux (1996), both of whom were close friends of Freire. It is ironic that as it searches for ways of engaging with formal education in this new context, popular education in Latin America is seeking to learn from the experience of US 'critical pedagogy' for which it was partly responsible in the first place.

Secondly, popular education has started to pay more attention to the individual dimension of learning. Partly this is due to its recent dialogue with conventional pedagogy, which has always focused on how individuals learn; partly it is a result of its own self-critique, recognising that in working for the collective good of popular organisations, it has often treated groups as homogenous entities and ignored questions of individual subjectivity altogether (IMDEC, undated). While popular education still aims to work for the collective, common good – there is no question of promoting the meritocratic individualism of (much) conventional education, where the talented prosper and the rest are abandoned to their fate – it now has to concern itself with the progress of the individual members of any group, both in terms of their intellectual understanding and their subjective reactions to the educational experience.

The concern with subjectivity leads to the third element, an acknowledgement that people do not learn by their capacity to reason alone. In the past, popular education has concentrated on developing critical consciousness, on the intellectual processes of understanding the causes of oppression and rationalising what could be done to change them. Now there is greater recognition of the affective side of learning, the need 'to be able to understand people's experiences in terms of their knowledge, dreams, intuitions and sensibilities. We cannot look at real-life experiences simply in terms of how we theorise them; if we really want to be subjects of change, we cannot restrict ourselves to the intellectual aspects of popular education, we also have to examine our frustrations, our dreams, our joys, our tears and our sensibilities. Entering into critical dialogue is not simply about producing rational knowledge; it is also about confronting how we feel about the challenges we have to face in the future' (Jara, 1996: 93).

But the significance of the dialogue between mainstream pedagogy and popular education goes beyond an instrumentalist concern with making popular education more effective; it has a political and ideological dimension too. While most popular educators recognised the need to engage with and learn from broader-based pedagogical research, some began to emphasise the pedagogical at the expense of – even criticising the previous weight given to – its political and ideological aspects. They became known as the 'pedagogists'. In turn, others felt that while the 'pedagogists' had an important contribution to make, they were pushing the pendulum too far the other way (Núñez, 1993). There were regional variations to the resolution of this debate. The 'pedagogists' were particularly strong in Chile where a de-politicised discourse fitted well with the devolution of state services to favoured NGOs. In Mexico and Central America, Ponce (1999) feels that the different 'tendencies' are a lot calmer now and that the political dimension of popular education has survived and been enriched by the 'pedagogist' contribution. In Brazil, where the relationship between public and popular education is highly developed, Haddad (1999) argues that though the basic political aims of popular education are still in place, they have lost some of their symbolic force and there has been a general shift in concern towards questions of 'knowledge' as opposed to 'ideology'. Orellano (1999) cuts through much of the debate, observing that 'pedagogical differences are really political differences' at the end of the day.

The Future of Popular Education

I earlier suggested three currents of thought apropos the role of popular education in the contemporary social context (one concentrating on democracy, citizenship, new spaces and social actors; one still focusing on class and structural change while sensitive to issues of identity and difference; one less concerned with theory, more with throwing itself into the struggle). Inevitably, these also engender different visions for the future. And given the importance of context, these visions will necessarily adjust to developments in the political, economic and social spheres in Latin America, whatever these happen to be: *refundamentación* is an on-going process. For the moment, I think a consideration of popular education's future can be divided into developments which are already underway and attempts to engage in crystal-ball speculation.

Changes in Progress

With new spaces opening up for democratic participation and the widening of popular education's horizons to include all aspects of civil society, there is much talk now of social movements, accompanied by popular education, moving 'from protest to proposal' (Fals Borda, 1992: 305). In Guatemala, for example, 'the Peace Accords opened up a range of possibilities but the dilemma for the popular movement lies in the need to change the direction of our actions and discourse, to move from an adversarial stance to making concrete proposals. Until recently, our activities were always about confrontation but now the situation is different. Now we need to become specialists, learn how to influence the political process, how to lobby and how to develop proposals for new legislation. We have our own particular needs and the spaces exist in which we can participate: if we do not occupy those spaces we will be leaving the popular movement to participate in a political vacuum' (Mendoza, 1997: 5-6). Similarly, in a collection of papers on 'Popular Education in the 21st Century', Jara argues that popular education has to 'motivate and channel participatory citizenship into strengthening local governments and exercising new mechanisms of opinion-forming and decision-making which will break with *clientelismo*, co-optation and corruption in the exercise of power. To move on from a logic based purely on confrontation, protest and demand to a logic which includes dialogue, negotiation and making proposals' (Jara, 1998: 31). He argues that 'as popular educators we are called to contribute what skills we have towards promoting the radicalisation of democracy and democratic relationships; towards ensuring that from now onwards, the democratisation of society really responds to the interests of the majority, to the popular interests' (ibid: 33).

In the same collection, Núñez argues the need for more visible political involvement, citing the example of the 'Civic Alliance' in Mexico, a movement 'created from within the popular education networks. It was the first time there was ever any "electoral supervision" to challenge the many kinds of electoral fraud which have always existed in Mexico' (Núñez, 1998: 46). A major figure in Latin American popular education, Núñez himself is an interesting case: moving from 'protest to proposal', he was briefly a 'politician without a party' in the Mexican national congress, one of several civilian candidates supported by the PRD (Democratic Revolutionary Party) which was keen to introduce new thinking into the political system. 'And I wasn't the only one; in fact, the party proposed that 50% of the candidates should be citizens who don't belong to any party. With all the limits and opportunities that this entailed, other comrade 'citizens', party militants and myself battled away for three years presenting proposals and ideas expressing our different way of understanding politics, not the old traditional, bureaucratic style – with its power quotas, prima donnas and so on – but the other way, the one we've been talking about' (ibid: 45). Núñez's temporary move into formal politics was only agreed after heated debate within IMDEC, the popular education centre which was his base: they were aware of the potential for co-option which such a move represented (Kane, 1995).

While this danger is ever-present, when the link to the popular movement is strong it holds enormous potential. For me this was illustrated clearly in

1995 when I accompanied a group of popular educators on a long, sickening trip up the hairpin bends of Chiapas to the village of Jototol. One of the Zapatista 'autonomous municipalities', it was hosting a popular education event on the theme of 'local democracy'. I learned, to my surprise, that one of the happiest educators present, seemingly oblivious to all the discomforts, had also briefly served as a deputy in congress. But he had done so with the single purpose of acquiring *inside* knowledge, which he could then use *outside,* of the obstacles, opportunities and pressure points for increasing local, participatory democracy. He was now delighted to be back out, with a great deal more to offer. I was impressed. Maybe the idea will catch on among Members of the Scottish parliament!

One outcome of rethinking the relationship with the formal sector is that the popular education movement increasingly addresses its potential relevance to children: 'when we develop popular education strategies we generally think in terms of the conscientisation of adults. And although it is well known that popular education is not synonymous with adult education, in practice the bulk of our experiences only account for this particular age group. If we want to develop a popular education appropriate to the new millennium, the first thing we need to do is broaden our educational horizons and overcome our current prejudices. It will serve no purpose to think about rebuilding the social fabric of society, fragmented by the modernising strategy of neo-liberal capitalism, without unleashing the creativity of children and young people. If we are talking about new ways of doing politics then we have to include their particular view of the world too, one which lacks the experience of adults but is free from many of its better and lesser known vices' (González Rodríguez, 1998: 92). The concern with children and young people as 'subjects' of change has an obvious overlap with the issues of pedagogy and state-sector schools (see also Rigal, 1994) though it is not restricted to the formal sector: popular education increasingly works with young people's organisations, drop-in centres for children and in the more extreme contexts of urban deprivation is developing a 'pedagogy of the street' (Graciana, 1997).

Given the difficulties in putting popular education theory into practice (see chapter 7), it is no surprise that many argue for a future in which popular education will be strengthened by more sustained, systematic training of popular educators than has been available in the past. De Souza argues that 'professionalisation is fundamental. We cannot continue with voluntarism and communitarian action; we cannot simply demand generosity, dedication and commitment. We need to be able to count on educators who operate as professionals, who are both competent and effective in their work' (de Souza, 1996: 104). In the new context of negotiated engagement with the state sector, he and others believe that in developing training for educators, the popular education movement would gain by forging closer links with progressive university departments; this would also improve its capacity to engage in research. The benefits of such a relationship have already been seen in relation to the MST in Brazil and it is increasingly common to find NGOs and popular educators seeking to develop such links.

The View From CEAAL

Probably the most complete overview of the general directions in which popular education is heading is to be found in the regional plan (1998-2001) of the Council of Adult Education in Latin America (CEAAL). Bringing together an increasing number of centres involved in popular education throughout the region, CEAAL defines its mission statement as:

> 'To improve the all-round training of popular educators, strengthening their capacity to have an influence on (a) the actions of people, groups and social movements in the various areas in which they are involved in educational work (b) the promotion of liberatory socio-cultural activity and processes (c) the development of public agendas and policies which favour both the democratic transformation of our societies and the conquest of peace and human rights' (CEAAL, 1999: 23).

The affiliates of CEAAL agreed to set up a number of common priority projects to put its strategic objectives into practice: 'from the perspective of Popular Education – both learning from its past and assessing its potential future – these projects seek to respond in an appropriate and effective manner to the perceived, principal needs of Latin American reality' (ibid: 3).

Appendix 9:1 provides a thematic overview of these projects, with details of their individual aims and objectives. Though the different strands have many overlaps, Projects 1-4 generally reflect the view that popular education now has a much wider application than before and is relevant to all areas of civil society, not just the strictly 'popular', economically poorer sectors.

Strand 2 is closer to the type of activity traditionally associated with popular education. The 'actors' specifically mentioned are indigenous people's movements, *campesino* movements, popular movements and political parties (ibid: 42).

Strand 3 is about influencing the course of public debate and the educational policy of governments. It examines national educational reforms from the perspective of 'successful experiences and new concepts in popular education' as well as the 'Education of Young People and Adults'. The agencies involved are governments, multilateral organisations, organisations and movements with experience in popular education, UNESCO and academics working in the area of the Education of Young People and Adults.

All in all, CEAAL's regional plan reflects the themes examined so far, albeit the different interpretations of popular education remain in the background.

In August 1999 I attended a workshop in El Salvador run by the Central American network, Alforja, a prominent affiliate of CEAAL. Educators were grouped according to the organisations in which they worked and asked to produce a draft 'strategic plan' of their organisation's future activities (currently much training relates to organisational aims, objectives, short and long-term strategic planning. While these ideas have largely emanated from the worlds of the military and big business – hardly the bedfellows of popular education – they are still considered useful tools when adapted to progressive causes). After discussing each organisation's draft plan, there was consensus among the larger group that in looking towards the future it is important to conduct a thorough analysis of the current social reality, think creatively and ambitiously about the changes desired ('dream about the future but don't leave reality behind') and then act with both 'realism and audacity', a fitting catchphrase, I feel, to take popular education forward, though with 'audacity', hopefully, the slightly dominant partner.

Speculative Thinking and Concluding Remarks

As well as having high hopes for the future of popular education in Latin America, I confess to some reservations as well. Let me deal with these first. When first drawn to the subject I was inspired by the combination of its political radicalism and its concept of ordinary people as 'subjects' of change. It seemed to offer a radically different way of thinking about education and politics from anything I knew in the UK. In the 'mother of all democracies', political participation meant voting once every four or five years and letting politicians get on with it, and significant numbers did not even bother to do that. No matter the party in power, powerful economic interests held sway and with some justification the least well-off could relate to the cynical cliché that 'if voting ever changed anything they would abolish it'.

When I see so much hope invested in 'democracy' in Latin America I feel that much potentially radical energy will be directed away from grassroots organisations towards governmental institutions and political bureaucracies which will then set out to frustrate, co-opt, redirect or seduce its exponents in the attempt to minimise their threat. Popular education's current discourse seems to place much faith in an unproblematised concept of 'civil society' and 'citizenship': taking the UK as an example, it is debatable whether either, on its own, does much to promote progressive change. Interpretations of 'citizenship' can be far from radical (Patterson, 2000). Indeed, it was the Conservative government of John Major which introduced the Citizen's Charter in the UK and it has been the most conservative components of civil society – the supporters of the homophobic Clause 28, for example, which bans schools from dealing openly with homosexuality – which have made their presence felt in the supposedly 'democratically renewed' Scotland.

I am not suggesting that popular education should hold back from engaging with the state, civil society and the themes of democracy and citizenship; far from it, particularly as these are obvious 'generative' issues. But for me it has to do so with a clear understanding that social inequalities – including 'newer' concerns like racism, sexism and environmentalism – have their roots in the wider, structural relationships which capitalism prescribes; that while contemporary society may appear more complex than before, with a greater variety of social actors and representations, it must continue to identify – and retain a clear political commitment towards – a structurally oppressed, 'popular' sector or class. If not, as with former expressions of radical education in the UK (Westwood, 1992), it might easily be absorbed into mainstream education and political systems which pose only the smallest of threats to existing power relations. My concern is that this may already be happening. Many educators referred to in this book (Núñez, Jara, Cendales and so on) make impassioned pleas, in the new political context, not to abandon the class-based concerns inherent in the concept of the 'popular': their voices are powerful but it is a worrying sign that they feel required to speak out in the first place.

On the other hand, there is also ample cause for optimism. Many of the recent changes were desperately required and I look forward to learning from an increasing number of properly 'systematised' and evaluated projects in the areas of 'interculturalism', environmentalism and gender education, not simply case-studies of political activism but projects which also take seriously the 'pedagogist' critique. Where the popular education movement manages to keep one foot firmly outside the state sector, it will be enlightening to find out what it can achieve on the inside; the MST could be an inspiration to other movements. And the move from 'protest to proposal' is a healthy development in avoiding a spiral of negative thinking. Many left-wing movements have promoted a culture of protest – understandable and necessary, given the extent of capitalist domination – but which can also lead to feelings of disillusionment and powerlessness if nothing positive, concrete and achievable is offered in return.

Ultimately, in the future, I believe that the term 'popular education' will be applied to so many different practices in Latin America that without closer examination it will be hard to tell exactly what it means. These practices will be roughly divided into those of the three currents of thought mentioned earlier. One will be so intertwined with mainstream education and the discourse of governments, emphasising pedagogy over political commitment, that it will run a constant danger of losing its 'popular' roots. Another will consciously maintain its political vision and commitment, adapted to the demands of each new political conjuncture. The other, though not too clear on how to interpret the ideological debates, will maintain its political commitment through its practice of figuratively rolling up its sleeves, joining the popular struggle – in whatever form this takes – and working out what to do as it goes along. For me personally, it is the latter two groups which will continue to be inspirational. While political and economic systems continue to produce the degree of injustice and inequality which exists in Latin America today, they will inevitably produce, simultaneously, movements of ordinary people struggling for change. Education, alone, cannot provide the solutions but, if authentically 'popular', it will continue to be present wherever these struggles take place, doing what it can to ensure that the 'movement' is also a 'school'.

Conclusion

This chapter has examined the changes taking place in popular education over the last decade, particularly as a result of the recent, on-going process of 'rethinking the basics'. It has shown how in the context of more widespread formal democracy and an expanding civil society, while the term 'popular education' has lasted the pace, the significance of the concept 'popular' is in dispute: some choose to drop the word altogether (considering it a relic of old-fashioned, class-based politics), some argue for a broadening of its meaning to include 'new' social actors (as opposed to only those of low economic status) while others defend its use much as before (albeit agreeing that 'popular education' now needs to relate to a wider constituency). Within the popular education movement, responses to recent developments in Latin America have varied: I have suggested they can be divided into three rough currents of thought which, after an initial period of dispute, currently co-exist harmonically. Speculating on the future, on the one hand popular education faces a danger of being absorbed into the mainstream, with its commitment to radical change either compromised or diluted; on the other, it will undoubtedly learn from its past mistakes and exciting developments are to be expected.

Review of Chapter 9 and the Postscript

Maria Clara Bueno Fischer worked for several years in a popular education centre in the south of Brazil. She briefly moved to the UK, gaining a PHd in Education at the university of Nottingham with the thesis "Radical Trade Union Education in Practice? A Study of CUT's Education Programme on Collective Bargaining". She now teaches and researches on the Post-graduate Programme in Education at the university 'do Vale do Rio dos Sinos' (UNISINOS), in the state of Rio Grande do Sul, Brazil, with a research-focus on Basic Education and Social Exclusion. She is a member of the international Popular Education Network for academics and continues to work alongside NGOs and popular social movements as a researcher and adviser in popular education.

It is a great opportunity and a pleasure to engage in this dialogue with Liam Kane. An opportunity because, as Paulo Freire has taught us, a dialogue presupposes a mutual commitment to whatever is going to be talked about; in this case, the author and myself are both committed to the theory and practice of popular education in Latin America and its existing or potential relevance for other countries, particularly the United Kingdom. And a pleasure because the seriousness with which the author has written this book stimulates curiosity, both politically and epistemologically, a basic ontological component of our development as human beings.

Having accepted the invitation to engage in dialogue with the author, I must make clear that I do so from a specific 'location'. I spent a number of years working in a Popular Education Centre in the south of Brazil; several more years studying the concept and practice of popular education in the 'new' trade unionism in Brazil (represented by the 'CUT' – the Workers' Central Union – whose conception of education has deep roots in popular education) and, more recently, working in the university, where I have been studying and researching the relation between education, work and social exclusion; I am also trying to apply what I learned through social and popular education movements to my current work in academia.

Liam Kane's treatment of the foundations and perspectives of popular education and its relevance for other countries is accurate, condense and his arguments well-founded. He adopts a position of non-neutrality in his analysis, something which is extremely positive. He also demonstrates a quality I consider very encouraging in my British colleagues, a certain sceptical pragmatism which, were it to combine with our Latin American optimism, would contribute much to our common, visionary project of building a just and democratic world. That said, I'll now comment on some of the points he raises.

The first thing I would emphasise is the need to understand popular education in a historical perspective. It is conceptualised and practiced by individual and collective 'subjects' at a particular moment in time and operates within the constraints imposed by its historical context. This is acknowledged by the author when he calls attention to the dangers of making generalisations, when he recognises key moments in Latin American history with which popular education is linked and when he insists on identifying what a range of different voices have to say. I have selected a few points on which to comment: the relationship between education, conscientisation and organisation; popular education and the current wave of vocationalism in adult education; political aspects underlying popular education; other pedagogical considerations.

In the history of popular education the relationship between education and political conscientisation has been an integral part of its identity and has therefore come to occupy a distinguished place in history. This relationship has taken on different forms throughout its history. In Brazil, in the 1960s and part of the 70s, it was strongly linked to the grassroots work of the Church but was also highly present in the political activism of sectors of the left which, after frustrated, tentative efforts at armed struggle, found in this double-barrelled concept a possible way of broadening the struggle for change to more actively include the popular sectors. And here an important element should be highlighted: popular education offered (and still offers) the possibility of working *with* people as opposed to *on their behalf*. At the end of the 70s and early 80s – I talk from my own experience here – education and political conscientisation became strongly associated with a third element, 'organisation'. Education's relationship firstly to conscientisation and then to organisation emerged in different contexts, when the popular forces in Brazil were confronted with different types of challenge. The first was associated more with localised, clandestine, grassroots action in times of military dictatorship; the other was linked to a moment when organised popular movements started to come out and reclaim democracy, when the discussions and reflections of the small groups of the previous period would contribute a great deal to how these organisations saw themselves. The symbiotic relationship between 'education, political conscientisation, organisation' was, for some time, the basic guiding light for those involved in popular education. Clearly it was assumed that education – even conscientisation – on its own does not change reality and people need to organise collectively to be 'subjects' of change, to be able to take action and put forward proposals. But this has to be done in a particular way and understanding the role of 'education' helped popular organisations see that the various aspects of their practice – their leaders' behaviour, the everyday life of grassroots workers, the proposed organisational structures, the decision-making procedures, personal motivations

– all educate, or un-educate, people on a daily basis: accordingly this practice requires constant analysis and revision to be educationally beneficial, and some of it can be carried out in the context of systematic, formal courses.

All of which is associated with 'praxis', a concept still possessing analytical vigour and the power to mobilise, and, I believe, one of the highly revolutionary lessons popular education has to offer. It leads many popular educators to avoid romantic and naïve notions of education with regard to both the transformation of consciousness as well as overly-academic diversions. This profoundly dialectical relationship between organisation and education is clearly present in the philosophy and practice of the Landless People's Movement (MST). It is fundamental to understanding the Conception of a Dialectical Methodology.

The author develops highly pertinent arguments regarding the need to re-emphasise the principle of the integrated nature of people's everyday experience, especially when considering subjectivity and culture in the groups with whom we are working. In this, undoubtedly, the concept of experience developed by the English author E.P. Thompson has been of help to popular educators in Latin America.

I would draw attention to one aspect only briefly mentioned in the text (the postscript) with regard to the wave of vocationalism in the current practice of adult education. The author identifies this as an important space for the mobilisation of 'radical educators'. I think this area provides an enormous space for dialogue among popular educators throughout the world; it could even be called a 'generative theme', given its potential to stimulate an understanding of contemporary economic, political and social relations and to restart an unresolved debate between 'adult' and 'popular' educators on the relationship between technical, vocational and instrumentalist training, on the one hand, and general and political education, on the other. This leads us to another important area for popular education, at least in Latin America, and that is the present demand for technical and political training within what has come to be known as the popular, solidarity-based economy which includes, among others, the experiences of self-managed enterprises and co-operatives.

I would also like to comment on the political horizons of popular education. The author identifies three currents of thought: educators who act with reference to the 'new spaces' opening in the present context, in which democracy, civil society and citizenship are seen as fundamental; a second group which, though taking advantage of the new spaces, maintains the dimension of social class and structural change as its central concern, though recognising and taking account of issues of identity and difference; and a third group which turns its back on ideology, concentrating on grassroots work as the most effective way of making progress.

Though such a division is useful in the sense that it captures the basic political differences existing on the horizons of popular education practice, I think it might suggest a simplistic way of reflecting the situation. I refer to the disassociation, or perhaps subordination, between the struggle for (and the achievement of) a democratic society, a strong civil society and the rights of citizenship, on the one hand, and structural change on the other. From a historical viewpoint, especially in Brazil, popular education emerged from and developed within a civil society which was struggling for democracy inside and outside the state apparatus and had a vision of capitalist society being transformed to favour the interests of the popular classes. As I see it, then, this articulation between democracy, civil society, citizenship and structural change was always present, though with different emphases. The issue today, however, where there are political leaders sympathetic to the popular education movement at local and sometimes even at national level, is the practical challenge of how to govern 'for everyone', independently of their social class, though from the viewpoint of the popular classes, when the fact is that the capitalist state has not yet collapsed. In this context the concept of citizenship takes on a new meaning, with political horizons. This might or might not be contradictory with structural change, depending on different political analyses and practices. Certainly, a systematisation of the recent practices of popular-democratic governments, including their proposals for public education, could be informative with this regard. It is important to remember that other social movements which are not clearly classified as 'popular' have raised important issues which popular movements, too, have subsequently addressed. This creates the need for new alliances and makes the political horizons of the popular classes' struggle more complex.

Finally I would like to emphasise that popular education undoubtedly inaugurated a change of paradigm in the history of education and politics which, I believe, as it develops further, will continue to make its mark both inside and outside the system, in formal and non-formal education. I refer to the recognition that education is not neutral; to valuing the collective construction of knowledge; of the attempt to construct a relationship in which the educator is also a learner and the learner is also an educator; that it is not a question of acting *on behalf of* but acting *with*; that since education takes place everywhere, it is also necessary to change the wider context; that education for liberation largely emanates from the oppressed, from the popular sectors of society; that the meaning of 'popular', among other things, includes all those who live off their own labour. It is important to be aware that popular education still aspires to universality and irreverence for it is inextricably linked, in its guts, with the oppressed sectors of our Latin American societies.

Maria Clara Bueno Fischer

Appendix 9:1
1998-2001 Regional Plan of CEAAL
(the Latin American Council of Adult Education)
Common Priority Projects
Focus No 1: Building Citizens' Power

Strand 1.1 Strengthening the Process and Initiatives of Organised Civil Society.

• Project 1: *An Encuentro on "Civil Society in Latin America and the Caribbean"*
... aims to stimulate and strengthen regional networks of NGOs so that organised civil society is visible at a Latin American level and can have a stronger influence over governments.

• Project 2: *The Systematisation of Experiences in Citizenship Education in our Countries*
... seeks to analyse and learn from the growing practice of 'education for citizenship' which has posed a challenge to the original concepts of popular education.

• Project 3: *An Encuentro on the Theme of Civil and Social Organisations and the Exercise of Governance*
... aims to promote a process of critical reflection among those who have been key figures in strengthening civil organisations but have now also had a chance to participate in government posts.

• Project 4: *A Consultative Exercise on Communication and Education in Latin America*
... explores how the values of popular education can be promoted in the context of mass communication and new technologies.

Strand 1.2 Strengthening Popular Movements

• Project 5: *The Systematisation of the Experience of Popular Movements which Have a National and International Influence*
... recognises that the effects of neo-liberalism have been so devastating that in many cases, poor people can look no further ahead than their daily survival. In other cases they have managed to develop organisations which have had a national impact. This project focuses on the three experiences of the Landless People's Movement in Brazil, the Zapatistas in Mexico and the Communities displaced by violence in Colombia. Researchers and movement activists are to collaborate and reach conclusions on what these experiences can teach about political activity in Latin America.

• Project 6: *Training Related to Awareness-Raising among the Wider Public*
... aims to train 250 people in 5 countries on how they can raise their concerns in the public sphere, encouraging others to take a more active role rather than

leave decisions to governments. Training will be based on what comes out of the analysis of the 6 specific experiences of trying to raise awareness about (a) the indigenous problem in Mexico (b) building peace in Guatemala (c) the role of women in Peru (d) policies of participatory citizenship in Bolivia (e) processes of sustainable agriculture in Brazil and (f) educational policies in the Dominican Republic.

• Project 7: *Learning how to Build 'Local Power' in Latin America*
... aims to collate, disseminate and run training around the best practice in popular education and participatory local government. With around 16,000 municipalities in the Continent and many leaders of progressive social organisations now taking part in and winning local elections, there has been a growth in what could be classified as a 'municipalist movement'.

Strand 1.3 Influencing Public Debate on Educational Policy

• Project 8: *Follow-up to the Conclusions of the 5th International Conference on Adult Education and their Application to Latin America*
... aims to strengthen governmental support for this area: only Bolivia, Colombia and Mexico have governmental institutions of adult education, for example. CEAAL has been a key player in stimulating governments into following up on the UNESCO international conference and it is felt that this is an important opportunity for Popular Education to make an impact on educational discourse and policy (see Pagano et al, 1998, for a debate among popular educators on the significance of this conference). Almost all Latin American countries are engaged in reforming their education systems, and it is formally recognised that the theme of human rights has to be taken seriously in a modern society:

• Project 9: *Human Rights and Educational Reform in Latin America*
... is about capitalising on this shift in perspective, bringing into play the accumulated experience of Human Rights organisations in this area.

• Project 10: *Consultation on Literacy in Latin America*
... is about using popular education's accumulated expertise in teaching literacy to influence governmental attempts to promote literacy.

• Project 11: *Latin American Seminar on "Multicultural Societies and Intercultural Education"*.
... recognises that 'historically linked to the poorest sectors, Popular Education has only recently started to include an intercultural perspective as a central component of its political and educational project' (CEAAL, 1999: 59). By examining the concrete experiences of CEAAL – members in Bolivia, Ecuador, Guatemala and Mexico, in particular – and in conjunction with the reflections of international organisations like UNESCO, it hopes to produce both

theoretical analyses and practical proposals for including intercultural perspectives into educational projects.

• Project 12: *Latin American Seminar on "Popular education and Environmental Education"*

... seeks to collate and synthesise the best practices of Popular Education in the area of environmentalism – again, a recent development – to work out how popular education can best contribute to the development of environmental education and influence the practice in this area of governmental and multilateral organisations.

Adapted from CEAAL (1999). The other part of the Regional Plan, 'Focus No 2', aims to make CEAAL a more effective learning organisation for its members.

Conclusion

Popular Educators' Union
Honduras
December 2000

BBC
London / Glasgow

Dear Points of View,

Imagine our disbelief — — —
— wish to complain — — — satellite T.V. — — —
— — BBC review of — — — L.A.B. book on
popular education in Latin America — — author —
— arrogant — — pompous — — ivory tower — — — —
caber-tossing academic — — — no idea — — who
does he think he is? — — — never showed his
nose around here — — — we don't tell him
how to make whisky — — — — L.A.B. — — ashamed
— — — disgraceful — — never again.

Disgusted of Tegucigalpa

The Response from Latin America

Let me begin on a personal note. Firstly, when I suggested it would be a good idea for different popular educators in Latin America to review each chapter – and that the reviews should be included in the book – the Latin America Bureau were sceptical: it could be an organisational nightmare and what if the feedback were negative? I too was worried, on both accounts, but once conceived the idea was compelling. If popular education is about a 'dialogue of knowledges' and acting *with* as opposed to *on behalf of* people, then within the confines of this publication it seemed a good way of demonstrating these principles in action – as well as compensating for the non-Latin American status of the author. So, given the risks and labour involved, I am proud that we went ahead.

Secondly, it was a nervous time waiting for reviews to arrive. Some of the reviewers I have never met, others only briefly and the remainder over a period of days, at most: I had no idea what to expect. My overwhelming feeling, at the end, is relief that it has not led (yet) to public humiliation.

Reading the reviews it is clear that while they have much in common they also emphasise different aspects of popular education and illustrate some of the ideological differences discussed in chapter 6. I do not want to abuse the position of author and respond further to what has been written: I leave the last word with the Latin Americans. In the end, the reviews achieved what I had hoped for: there is enough positive feedback on my own analyses to accord them respectability, enough criticism to show a range of interpretations and encourage deeper thinking and enough new material to add qualitatively to what each chapter has to offer. Phew!

A Simple Complexity

I have reached the conclusion that popular education in Latin America is both an extremely complex and wonderfully simple phenomenon.

Complex, because it begs familiarity with a range of academic disciplines:

- different branches of philosophy for understanding Freire's notion of 'ontological vocation', for example, or how people perceive and experience the world or the ways in which knowledge is acquired
- history, politics and economics:- for understanding the different contexts in which popular education takes place. Together with sociology, these disciplines inform the practice of *conjunctural analysis*
- sociology:- for understanding a broader range of social phenomena, from the significance of religion or *machismo* to different theories of social movements. This leads to additional areas of complexity, like postmodernism, post-structuralism and so on
- psychology:- for understanding concepts like the 'culture of silence' or different theories of learning.

And the language of popular education, too, is difficult, either on account of its jargon – which sounds even worse in translation – or because it reflects the complexity of the ideas being examined. Jargon is sometimes unavoidable and complex ideas require effort but some of the literature on popular education remains unnecessarily exclusive. People with a basic knowledge of Spanish or Portuguese should still attempt the original texts, however: forewarned is forearmed and it pays to be selective.

But ultimately, it seems to me, the strength of popular education lies not in complex, academic formulations but in a few key, simple yet powerful ideas. It...

- demands a political commitment in favour of the 'oppressed'
- attempts to enable ordinary people to become 'subjects' of change

- recognises many types of knowledge
- requires a methodology which allows these different 'knowledges' to be shared

Simple or not, the significance of these ideas is enormous, sometimes standing conventional notions of education on their head. Their implications for practice are summarised in the Addendum, a checklist for educators, activists and 'cultural workers' on implementing a popular education approach to their work.

And finally...

Anyone seeking to discredit the record of popular education in Latin America will find ammunition. They could reject its political and philosophical premises, criticise gaps between theory and practice, point to examples of failure or defend, instead, other, more conventional ways of pursuing political change: whoever said 'no revolution ever came about as a result of a popular education workshop' had a point.

But to compile a list of failings serves little purpose. No one involved in popular education claims it is the solution to the world's ills: clearly, there are limits to what it can be expected to achieve. But it does, undoubtedly, have a contribution to make to all organised attempts to promote progressive social change. And in so far as educational processes will take place anyway – whether informally, as the 'hidden curriculum' of political action, or more explicitly, in 'workshops' and courses – popular education can help to make them more appropriate and effective. Weaknesses and failures, moreover, are seldom inevitable: learning from the past, gaps between theory and practice can be progressively reduced, if not entirely closed.

In the end, I believe, the Latin American experience of popular education offers an exciting challenge to all educators and activists – no matter the context, the group of learners, the subject, theme or action being explored – to fundamentally rethink what they do and why they do it. It offers a host of practical ideas for galvanising potentially boring talks or lectures into dynamic, participatory, educational events. It shows educators how to engage in radical, political education without becoming propagandist (a common problem on the left), to consider the role of power in any educational encounter and to respect learners' knowledge while unashamedly putting forward their own. Most of all, perhaps, in the current political climate, when grassroots activism is often discouraged and superficial, pre-packaged, 'conservative' ideologies are handed down from on high, popular education offers an alternative approach to thinking about politics, one in which people become thinkers and 'actors' for themselves, not simply passive consumers of spin. And that can't be a bad thing, now, can it?

Postscript
Lessons for The Rest of the World?

"THEY SAY NONE OF THIS IS RELEVANT
BECAUSE EUROPEAN EDUCATION ISN'T POLITICAL!"

'The fallacy of neutrality in education:
*Antonio: It's a rather complex issue, because our academic life in Chile was a life of
total involvement in a political context...*
Paulo:...which has not been the case here in Geneva...
*Antonio:...so that for us in Chile teaching was bound up with political positions,
with a political struggle, with changing reality. Whereas the European context has
been completely different and has not had this political dimension. And for that
very reason my work has been fundamentally "neutral" in that respect (laughter).
In fact, I believe that it has been even more political than what was overtly political
in Chile. Here politics consists in denying the political dimension, thereby removing
all analysis and all thinking from the concrete political context of social struggle'.*
(Paulo Freire & Antonio Faundez in conversation: Freire & Faundez, 1989:
30-31)

This postscript examines the impact of Latin American popular education on
the rest of the world. With particular reference to the UK/Scotland and my
own personal practice, it also considers further potential lessons to be learned.

But two points need emphasised beforehand: first, especially in times of
accelerating globalisation, there is no such thing as a pure, unadulterated, regional
culture. In Latin America, popular education has always been influenced by
ideas and practices from elsewhere: from European philosophers (ancient and

modern) and Russian psychologists to African revolutionaries and popular movements the world over (Steele, 1999). Second, since political and social environments condition educational practice, ideas need to be reinvented – not simply transplanted – from one context to another.

Evidence of Existing Impact

At a global level, the influence of popular education in Latin American has undoubtedly been greatest through the writings of Paulo Freire. His *Pedagogy of the Oppressed* ranks as one of the all-time classic texts to address the concerns of the 'Third World'. In Africa, his contribution has been widespread (Godono, 1998), even personal, having briefly worked in Guinea Bissau, Tanzania and Cape Verde. Produced in anglophone Africa, the widely-acclaimed Community Education handbooks, *Training for Transformation* (Hope & Timmel, 1999), are explicitly based on Freire's ideas, albeit with a strong religious interpretation. In an ironic inversion of *triangular trade*, these are now published and used in the UK too, such has been their success. Just as in Latin America, radical educators throughout the globe have been inspired by Freire even if they have learned of him second hand and found some of his ideas difficult (Duke, 1990: chapter 8). He has influenced a number of educational projects in the UK (Kirkwood, 1989), is a central point of reference for 'critical pedagogy' in the USA (Giroux & McLaren, 1994; McLaren, 1995) and is frequently discussed with reference to feminist and anti-racist education. While his influence is enormous, we should not forget that he is also interpreted, misinterpreted and co-opted in so many different ways that each attempt to put Freire's ideas into practice has to be judged on its merits.

As opposed to the more theoretical writings of Freire, the everyday practice of Latin American popular education is less well known internationally. In the English-speaking world, there is an obvious problem of linguistic accessibility, compounded by a lack of informed reporting on Latin America in the mainstream press. As a result, I believe, unless people happen to have developed a particular interest in the region and taken steps to become better, more critically informed, it can be difficult to see beyond the stereotypes of Latin America. Inspired by images of Che Guevara, a radical Freire and a continent in permanent upheaval, it is not uncommon, in my experience, for educators in the UK to have exaggerated, sometimes exotic notions of popular education in Latin America: the problem is that the Latin American experience then seems too remote to have any relevance here.

However, there do exist useful attempts to make the broader Latin American experience better known. Canada, in particular, has had a significant exchange programme with Central America and Arnold et al's *A Popular Education*

Handbook (1983) – now somewhat dated but still helpful – and *A New Weave: Popular Education in Canada and Central America* (1994) offer excellent snapshots of Latin American practice, insight into its relevance to Canada and practical guidelines on implementation. Augusto Boal's work is becoming better known all the time, both through the publication of his books and the number of workshops he and his supporters organise around the world. Indeed, the evidence from the literature on adult education and development is that the 'participatory theatre' approach to education for change is in a healthy state wherever you look (Malamah-Thomas, 1987; Mavrocordatos & Martin, 1997). In Europe, it is no surprise that educators in Spain and Portugal are those most familiar with Latin American practice. In 1998 a major *encuentro* took place in Cádiz to compare the healths of European and Latin American popular education at the start of the new millennium (Andreu Abrio, 1998). The last three years have seen the birth, in Europe, of a popular education network for committed academics (see Martin, 2000; Kane, 2000b): this has now expanded globally and important Latin American presentations were made at its *encuentro* in Edinburgh, in June 2000.

The progressive wings of international, northern-based NGOs have also been influenced by the Latin American experience and this has filtered through to their domestic programmes. This influence is most obvious where NGOs have invested in 'Development Education' in their own countries, in the North. Focusing mainly – though not exclusively – on the South or 'third world', Development Education aims to challenge negative and simplistic stereotypes of people and places, give voice to the views of popular organisations and encourage an analysis of the causes of poverty (Development Education Commission, 1999). It is different from popular education – concentrating on other people's reality, rather than the learner's – but in its methodology and political commitment, albeit with the same ideological complications analysed in chapter 6, it also has strong similarities. As one of Oxfam's development education workers in the 1980s, though I have no proof to offer, I feel that our constant exposure to issues of grassroots development meant we learned from popular education by 'osmosis'. The influence was never explicit – the word 'conscientisation' was familiar and a few may have read Freire – but somehow the same ideas permeated development education. Box P:1, for example, describes a video-discussion exercise produced in 1985. It starts from people's own reality, provokes discussion, asks open-ended questions, brings new knowledge into the 'dialogue' and encourages follow-up action. It has the classical traits of a popular education approach (though we are immodest enough to claim a *'je ne sais quoi'* of our own) though none of us had either read Freire or heard of popular education at the time.

BOX P:1
Africa-Scotland Video

Learners are told they will see a video comparing life in Scotland with life in Africa. Beforehand, they jot down what they expect to see. The video then shows only the good about Africa and the bad about Scotland. The commentary on Scotland is arrogant and opinionated, delivered in an aristocratic English accent and deliberately designed to annoy Scottish people with its unbalanced representation. The educator asks three main questions: how do you react to this video, what did you think of the commentator and did you think it contained any truth? In discussion, while most Scots would be annoyed if this were presented as a true image of Scotland, they accept that what is said is actually true; it's what is *not* said that distorts the whole picture.

Turning the exercise on its head, learners then consider what they wrote about Africa. Almost always this consists entirely of negative images. The discussion then explores where these images have come from (from opinionated outsiders?) and why positive things are seldom heard about Africa. Follow-up work would encourage a survey of the media on 'third world' images and a campaign to promote more balanced reporting.

These are the influences already identifiable but, as a citizen of the UK or, more precisely, Scotland, in researching the Latin American experience I inevitably speculate on what else could be relevant to my own particular context. The following section, then, considers the benefits that a more deliberate, comparative study of popular education in Latin America might yield to British practitioners.

The Potential Relevance to Scottish-British Popular Education

I have no desire to overstate the importance of the Latin American experience. Radical educators in the UK already engage in good work, imaginatively exploiting available opportunities and there are aspects of theory and practice common to both regions, particularly in an age of digital communication. And perhaps what I take to be Latin American is sometimes less original, more international than I imagine. That said, there remain clear enough differences between radical education in Latin America and the UK to justify a comparative examination. With echoes of the 'Triple Self-Diagnosis' (chapter 3), I think this can be usefully divided into the three areas of 'context, conceptualisation and practice'.

Comparing the Contexts

Differences in context inevitably affect educational practice. The most obvious, in our case, is that the degree of 'oppression' in the UK is less severe than in Latin America and the sense of urgency regarding social change arguably weaker. On the other hand, social inequality undeniably exists. The 1990s saw increasing polarisation between rich and poor (Rowntree Foundation, 1995; United Nations, 1997), there is a 'third world' within the 'first world' and discrimination on the grounds of race, gender, disability and so on have far from disappeared.

In general terms the character of the state, too, is different. Since the second World War, UK governments have been willing and able to afford the provision of a minimum level of social services through the Welfare state, though perhaps this is now under threat; at the same time, mainstream ideology would have us believe that the UK is a 'democracy' and that established political institutions (parliaments, local authorities and political parties) are the appropriate agents of change. In the UK, we depend a great deal on the state. In Latin America, however, the state's failure to provide basic welfare means that people have had little choice but to form popular organisations and take independent action themselves. The problem with relying on the state – though this is not an argument for abolishing welfare – is that when it fails to promote progressive change, vulnerable people feel powerless: visiting the UK in the 1990s, popular educators from Latin American saw 'apathy' as a major problem they did not have to face at home.

Another difference is the type of social movement engaged in cultural-political activity. It has been argued that the more visible 'new' social movements around feminist, anti-racist and environmental agendas, for example, are generally more 'middle-class' than their Latin American counterparts, their concerns overlapping less with those of basic, material deprivation (Hellman, 1992; Patterson, 1999). We need to be careful here: Barr (2000) rightly highlights the dangers of allowing academics to define what counts as a social movement, arguing that throughout the UK there are a variety of groups which are active in poorer communities but seldom included in the 'social movement' category. Nevertheless, I still believe there is little in Scotland or the UK which can be directly compared with the popular movements of Latin America. Occasional broad-based campaigns have some similarities and there are fragmented grassroots organisations working for local change but there is an 'absence of an infrastructure of community-based organisations' (Killeen, 1999: 5), no coherent mass, organised activity in which the grassroots are 'subjects' of change. When Freire visited the Adult Learning Project in Edinburgh in 1988 he observed that the project should be more linked to the popular movement: ALP workers did not disagree but felt there existed no 'popular movement' to which it was able to connect (Galloway, 1997). In the early years of the new Scottish parliament, moreover, in the context of much acclaimed 'democratic renewal', it has been conservative social movements (in defence of the homophobic Clause 28, for example) who have by far made the greater noise.

With greater resources than its counterparts in the South then, the state in our 'democracy' is seen as the natural provider, both able and expected to organise basic welfare services, including education. There is currently no large-scale 'alternative' education outside the state. In Latin America the vacuum caused by the lack of state-organised adult education allowed popular education to flourish. Scotland and the UK has its own history of organised, independent radical education too (Westwood, 1992; Crowther, 1999), but this began to fade away in the 1950s following debates over the pros and cons of engaging with the state, the very issues recently being debated in Latin America. In the current political conjuncture, the resurrection of such a tradition – disengaged from the 'old', class-based, workers' movements to which it was tied – seems far from imminent.

What counter-hegemonic forces exist in Scotland, then, into which popular education could tap? Groups campaigning around issues of basic material demands are the most likely equivalent of Latin American 'popular organisations'. I am unaware of any systematic research into either the extent or potential collective strength of such groups but it is a piece of work crying out to be done. Trade unions are another possibility, though their existing educational work is directed at representatives rather than rank and file members and tends to focus on a 'narrow instrumentalism' and negotiation with management (Field, 1988; McGrath, 1999). In their comparison of Trade Union education between the UK and Brazil, Hannah & Fischer (1998) show the Brazilian CUT (Central Workers' Union) to be far ahead of its UK equivalent in reflecting the values and practices of popular education (Arruda, 1998, argues that the CUT's work in popular education ranks with that of the MST).

Within mainstream politics, we would not expect that political parties of the right, centre or of a nationalist persuasion would have any instinctive, ideological interest in popular education (though there would be room for manoeuvre in the latter two). While left-leaning parties do have elements in common – an analysis of social injustice and a desire for change – the logic of contemporary electoralism pushes all parties into the politics of persuasion, spin, sound-bite, populism and top-down leadership; when the heat is on, dialogue, debate, participatory democracy and the encouragement of authentic 'subjects' of change is no match for the imperative to secure votes. To me this rules out the (New) Labour Party in the UK and the principle parties of the recently-formed Scottish parliament as potentially serious 'schools' of popular education. (This is also true of political parties in Latin America with the exception, arguably, of the Workers Party in Brazil, jointly set up in the 80s by trade unions and social movements, though some maintain that it too has now allowed electoralism to eclipse grassroots activism: see Petras & Vieux, 1994). I do not mean to be flippant here. Electoralism can be defended and popular education is not the only way of working for change: between the two, however, there is undoubtedly a clash of values which are not easily reconciled. Further to the left, those parties not in serious contention for office, with a high degree of activism, which support progressive struggles wherever they take place and for whom electoralism is only one aspect of their work – potentially, I believe, they have much to learn from popular education. In particular, their *modus operandi* is often considered invasive and a healthy dosage of popular education could help their activists promote 'dialogue' rather than 'diatribe', to everyone's benefit.

Finally, as a reaction against the growing sense of powerlessness felt towards the end of the Thatcher-Major era and the increasing vocationalisation of adult education, there has been renewed interest in reviving the radical tradition in education. In Scotland, activists, community educators and academics set up the Popular Education Forum for Scotland in 1997 and its active membership has been growing steadily since (see Box P:2); the journal of Contemporary Community Education Practice Theory (CONCEPT) has a broadly popular education focus, including regular articles on Latin America; Crowther et al's (1999) *Popular Education and Social Movements in Scotland Today* is a landmark attempt to collate a wide range of disparate practices. It has one section on theorising popular education, another on historical perspectives and then a variety of contemporary case-studies which include campaigns against damp housing, trade union education and the disability movement's struggle for inclusion.

Conceptualising Popular Education

While there are similarities between Scottish-British and Latin American conceptualisations of popular education, there are also important distinctions. In Latin America's recent past, perhaps due to the degree of hardship and the strength of the popular movement, the political nature of popular education has been more sharply defined, the commitment to 'side with the oppressed' more openly spelled out. While the concept of politically committed education is not new to Britain either, its presence within mainstream education, at least, is marginal, where political 'neutrality' and uncritical vocationalism hold venerable status. Fundamentally, then, Latin American popular education challenges educators everywhere to consider the political aspects of their work;

at the same time, its self-critique on the dangers of 'ideologisation' should serve as a warning to over-enthusiastic political agitators.

Able to begin from any 'generative' theme but connect with so many different issues, the Latin American experience also demonstrates that popular education relates to all educators of adults, no matter their point of contact with learners. Translated into a British context, it means it is not the sole domain of generic community educators. It is relevant to anyone involved in adult education who has a commitment to social change. Health workers, training officers, trade union representatives, housing officials, campaigners, subject-based community educators (artists, local historians, linguists, flower arrangers and so on) and even university and FE lecturers: they may work under varying constraints but their subject matter, at least, is no barrier to engaging in popular education.

Above all, rather than an academic theory, popular education in Latin America is understood as the intellectual property of grassroots movements in which the notion of people as 'subjects' of change has a real meaning. This constitutes a powerful challenge to radical education in the UK where most work is carried out within the state and/or in isolated projects. The Latin American example suggests we look outwith the formal sector, seek out organisations already engaged in action for change and promote education work within them. Part of this work would be enabling organisations to network and learn from each other, helping build a popular movement from below. This is no easy task and is somewhat back-to-front with the Latin American experience, where popular education emerged from the movement. But it is worth pursuing. It has been the recommendation of many Latin American popular educators who, on visiting the UK, are impressed by the projects they see but dismayed at their segregation from a wider movement. This is being recognised within Scotland itself and while conditions may not be conducive to massive, Latin American-style popular movements, it is not unrealistic to consider taking small steps in that direction, as the 'Popular Education Forum for Scotland' is attempting to do.

With all its variety, then, Latin America is a valuable backdrop for understanding, in general terms, the dialectic between popular education and the state. This can stimulate new insights into the Scottish experience and even offer useful tools of political analysis. The concept of 'populism', for example, well entrenched in Latin American discourse, helpfully gives name to a particular type of relationship between state and people. A 'populist' regime (whether national or local) is a curious mixture: on the one hand it seems radical, claiming to be on the side of the poor (though appealing to all classes) with a handful of welfare policies to produce as evidence: it creates a climate in which the radical discourse of popular education can resound. But it is simultaneously conservative, attempts to diffuse and co-opt genuinely radical movements and is perfectly capable of authoritarianism if required. In their struggles with the state at various levels, popular movements in Latin America have become sensitised to the existence and dangers of populism. Foweraker (1995) argues that provided such awareness exists, movements can still make tactical gains even within a statist strategy of co-optation.

Though seldom referred to by name, 'populism' is a useful concept for identifying – and being better able to cope with – a particular practice in the UK too: councils whose political rhetoric is radical, for example, but who crack down on autonomous community organisations which dare to challenge their control (see Martin and McCormack, 1999); or Community Education services, funded by local authorities, which are willing to support radical projects, but only up to a point. In the 1990s, for example, when a Latin American-style popular movement briefly emerged in Scotland (the anti-poll tax campaign), it stood in direct opposition to the local authorities which were responsible for administering the tax. But even Community Education projects which were openly 'Freirian' were unable to work with this movement, directed, as it was, against their own paymasters. Clearly, the issue of state support for popular education and grassroots change is complex. An awareness of the concept of populism, with its dangers and opportunities, is a useful intellectual tool for popular educators wrestling with these issues or engaged in conjunctural analysis. (Confusingly, however, outwith Latin America, especially in development theory, the term 'populism' is sometimes used more favourably (Kitching, 1989; Youngman, 2000)).

Whether within authoritarian, liberal, populist or even revolutionary political climates, the Latin American experience indicates that there are always constraints on how effective popular education might be. The lesson is twofold: firstly, it is important to clarify the constraints (and opportunities) existing at any particular time and consider how these affect the potential for change. Secondly, once identified, the task is then to work hard, and imaginatively, to minimise their effect. While a look at Latin America might inspire creative thinking, at times the constraints in Scotland/the UK may be so different that Latin America has little to offer. The contradiction experienced by radical educators working both 'within and against' the state, for example, has been examined more fully in Europe (Mayo & Thomson, 1995) where Gramsci's notion of civil society as a 'site of struggle' has become a key concept in adult education.

The Practice of Popular Education

By and large, I believe that the methodological questions discussed in chapter three are also relevant to the UK though the 'Conception of a Dialectical Methodology' remains problematic. If activist-organisers connect with the CDM's underlying values, then the distillation of complex philosophy, ethics and social science into a named and recognisable *modus operandi* is of great practical help. As it stands, however, the direct importation of the CDM into the UK would be difficult. In English the language is obtuse and activists would need considerable training before it could be taken seriously: how, when and where this might happen is unclear. Moreover, with the CDM's clear echoes in Marxist dialectical materialism, anyone holding superficial, stereotypical ideas on Marxism would be immediately sceptical, though, ironically, the CDM itself is often invoked against supposedly Marxist vanguards attempting to stifle debate.

Judiciously applied, the various participatory techniques can make a difference to levels of learner participation, the quality of dialogue and, not to be denigrated, the enjoyment of learning. Though I personally refrain from asking Glaswegians to down pens and spontaneously burst into salsa (an extreme example for the purpose of illustration), we should beware stereotyping Latin Americans as fun-loving extroverts and Scots as reticent, dour Calvinists (though I can think of one or two). Gregor (2000) shows that even in Brazil, with Boal's own drama group, many people are at first hesitant to engage with 'unusual' techniques, just as in Scotland. The appropriate methodological approach depends on a number of factors: the context in which the educational work is being undertaken (whether a formal or informal setting), the expectations and open-mindedness of learners and the particular beliefs and personality of the educator. The educator has the crucial responsibility for exploring and negotiating this collective, cultural minefield in which there are few absolute rules. If a particular educator genuinely believes in the value of a ten minute salsa-break and a particular group of learners respects him or her enough to give it a try, it could well work out to the benefit of all (see Kane, 2000c, for a fuller discussion of how particular methods, and the way they are presented, can affect groups differently). Techniques are tools whose success depends to a large extent on the skill of the educator. If progressive educators in the UK are not already familiar with the techniques used in Latin America, they have a treat in store and could make wonderful additions to their repertoire. Learning from problems in Latin America, however, it is also important to guard against either the deliberate co-option of the methodology or the assumption that 'participatory techniques' are, *de facto*, popular education: they can be used by different educators for entirely different purposes.

The organisation and delivery of popular education in Latin America – which, at the middle level (see chapter 1), is based on a network of independent 'support centres' – also provides a useful model for comparison and a stimulus for creative thinking. As it stands, however, it could not be easily reproduced in the UK. Inspired by what they had seen in Nicaragua, for example, activist-educators in Easterhouse, Glasgow, have already attempted to set up such a centre, but to date it is proving a struggle. Few funding bodies are keen to promote up-front projects in radical, grassroots political education (though funding for centres in Latin America is also under threat, as northern NGOs shift priorities elsewhere): clearly, in this new millennium, familiarity with sources of funding and creativity in presenting applications are crucial skills for empowerment. On the other hand, the set-up is not dissimilar to that of Development Education Centres, spread throughout the UK; Oxford DEC, in fact, already employs a 'popular educator' itself. But perhaps as an alternative to setting up new centres from scratch, existing campaigning organisations – which are already 'centres' of a sort – could be encouraged, instead, to develop the specifically educational component of their work: Friends of the Earth (Scotland) provides one example of how this might happen (see Samson & Scandrett, 1999). And here a network serves a useful function: the Popular Education Forum for Scotland has begun to draw campaigning organisations into its ranks and this is likely to increase as the Forum develops. The effect, hopefully, is that popular education will become a more explicit concern in campaigning for change.

The specific support provided by the Latin American centres varies but a key element is the training of activists. The example of IMDEC's 'School of Methodology' – attended by activists from all over the country – is an inspirational model. The Scottish Forum has already offered modest training in this area: if it keeps progressing and procures adequate funding (and there are already signs of success), the establishment of a long-term 'school for activists' is a definite, achievable objective.

A Personal Application of Lessons from Latin America

I conclude with my own personal examples of how popular education in Latin America can relate to practice in the UK and Scotland. In my case this has mostly been within, or in partnership with, the formal education system, not as a generic, community education worker. Though I have run many popular education events for community groups, these have tended to be 'one-offs' rather than sustained pieces of work.

Within campaigning organisations, either as a participant or adviser, I have found popular education particularly relevant to discussions on the educational dimension of leadership. It has been my experience that the culture of campaigning has no innate pre-disposition towards the philosophy and values of popular education. Campaigning involves persuasion, publicity-grabbing, opportunism and the singular pursuit of specific objectives for change: good campaigner-activists are required to be assertive and tenacious. They are already supremely effective 'subjects' of change themselves. Popular education, however, is about helping others become 'subjects' of change and while this partly involves demonstrating what can be done, it also means knowing when to hold back, shun the limelight and encourage others to become the protagonists, even if you could do it better yourself. In some ways, this contradicts the instincts of a good campaigner: how key activists and campaigners handle this (potentially creative) tension is important. Within campaigning organisations, my work often consists of making this dilemma explicit. Campaigners and activists with responsibilities for leadership may not have given thought to their educational role: it is useful to be able to say that from the experience of popular education in Latin America, the key individual is not 'the (professional) educator who works in a centre or a supporting institution. The most important popular educator should be the leader of an organisation' (IMDEC, 1994: 60).

But the areas where I have more experience are Development Education (working with children and schoolteachers), teaching modern languages to adults and the discipline of 'adult education' within the context of higher education. The following discussions on development and higher education, I believe, are relevant to educators working in any area of the social sciences; for those working in areas with no obvious link to popular education, it is hoped that the discussion of modern languages will provide clues as to how such links can be made.

Development Education

Three aspects of popular education, in particular, strengthen or give added creativity to aspects of development education. Firstly, both practices seek to problematise the topic under discussion, encourage critical-political thinking and consider possible courses of action for change: to that extent, all developments in popular education theory and practice are relevant to development education too (and vice versa). Secondly, more specifically, there is the question of methodology: many popular education techniques can be easily adapted to a development education context. As a DE worker I was involved in Boal-type drama activities in which pupils played the role of children from the South. While some of this was straight out of popular education practice, learned through 'osmosis', a familiarity with the work of Boal would have made it more meaningful and effective. Thirdly, the concept of the 'generative issue' is useful for development education too. It encouraged us to capitalise on the enthusiasm for the 1986 Football World Cup in Mexico, for example, running drama workshops in which children took on the role of the inhabitants of Acapulco, re-lived its development into a centre of tourism, worked though the choices confronting inhabitants and learned of the social consequences, the winners and losers. Likewise, to raise awareness about Latin America in 1992, on the 500th anniversary of the 'discovery', we highlighted the (surprisingly numerous) Scottish links with the Caribbean since Scottish, rather than British, issues are significantly more 'generative' in Scotland (challenging, in the process, the common perception that Scotland was a victim of (the English) empire, with no imperialist history of its own (Edward et al, 1994). In adult development education, more specifically, an understanding of the concept of the 'generative issue' would be helpful to activists in any organisation campaigning on global issues (such as the World Development Movement or Cuban Solidarity Groups): rather than imposing an 'outside' agenda on groups, it is better to find out what their 'generative issues' are, start from there are and draw connections between the two sets of concerns.

Teaching Modern Languages

Latin American popular education has also influenced how I teach modern languages to adults. Of all organised adult education classes in the UK, modern languages is probably the subject area in greatest demand: it has become a 'generative' issue in its own right. In the literature on the UK's own tradition of radical adult education, however – and the current debates on how this tradition can be reactivated (Shaw et al, 2000) – there is little on how these issues relate to modern languages. Nowadays, unlike the traditional approach of endless repetitive exercises in grammar, language courses are more practical and functional, aiming to enable learners to speak in real life situations. Typically, course-books focus on how to get by 'at the hotel', 'in the post office' 'travelling by train' and so on. Another common strand are the 'languages for business' courses which aim to help employers and workers better exploit overseas markets. But within the field of language teaching the notion that 'all education is political' is seldom evident. I once wrote an article on popular education and language teaching for a mainstream language-teaching journal: while it was rejected for being 'overtly political'- which was true – the editors refused to see anything political in their regular features on 'languages for business'.

Popular education can contribute to language teaching by challenging teachers to (a) consider the political aspects of their work (intentional or otherwise) (b) encourage learners to think critically about the world and (c) employ an anti banking-education methodology. I think it can do this in three different areas, the first two related to promoting solidarity for popular struggles in the South (though technically this leans more towards 'development' than 'popular' education), the last related to the reality of the learners' own world.

Firstly, in the process of acquiring language skills, students can be acquainted with the world seen from the perspective of those considered 'oppressed' in the areas where the language is spoken. Teaching French, for example, it would be important not to present France simply as a country of white, middle-class, nuclear families (though there is nothing wrong in belonging to any of these categories) but also to bring alive the concerns of the economically poorest in France, whether unemployed or badly-paid workers or ethnic minority groups like Moroccans or Senegalese who are victims of racism.

But many European languages are also spoken in parts of the South. In the UK, research indicates a predominance of negative images of 'third world' people, mainly due to an imperial past and the effect of the media: drought, famine, mud huts, passive victims dependent on 'first world' charity (Meakin, 1996). Even from the beginning, at the stage of introducing different native speakers – saying who they are and where they live, describing their daily routines and so on – a language course can confront these stereotypes and give voice to those who suffer the worst of oppressions. When people from Haiti, Burkina Faso, Brazil or Guatemala are allowed to tell their own stories, they challenge the image of passive victim and provide a very different slant (from 'natural disasters') on the causes of poverty. As cultural background, even a critical examination of why European languages are spoken around the globe in the first place raises important questions about imperialism, slavery, expropriation of wealth and continued 'first world' dominance, to name a few.

Maintaining the focus on the 'third world', as well as allowing the oppressed to speak for themselves it is possible to engage openly in other issues through the medium of the language being studied. The better education materials produced by the progressive wings of development agencies encourage students to explore and discuss the causes of world poverty, especially in relation to first world-third world connections: there is no reason why this cannot be done in a foreign language as well, while students practise their speaking skills, though the particular activity needs to be tailored to the linguistic abilities of the class. But it is possible to do this even at a basic level. The exercise of guessing and analysing who earns what from each stage in the production and distribution of coffee – from peasant cultivators to multinational distributors – would be an example: in a language class, students could do this while practising something as basic as numbers. Development Education has produced a plethora of discussion-based activities – accompanied by relevant, accessible information – many of which can be adapted to a foreign language classroom. These range from ranking exercises and photograph-analysis to role-play and full-blown

---

BOX P: 2
Guy Fawkes the Second

St Peter learns that like his ancestor before him, Guy Fawkes the Second has tried to blow up the British parliament. This time the attempt was successful. Unfortunately, however, Guy Fawkes 2nd kills himself in the process too. St Peter is horrified at such brutality but when Guy Fawkes explains what politicians have done to the most vulnerable in society (in past years, issues highlighted have been the poll tax, the closure of Ravenscraig, attacks on single parents and the disabled) he understands that something is seriously wrong. At the end, in the role of angels, the class decides whether he enters heaven or not.

---

simulation games: they encourage learners to consider who makes decisions and who benefits from change and they cover topics as wide apart as the arms trade, the control of food production and debates over population (see Kane, 1989). A variety of agencies throughout Europe have produced similar resources too, with the added advantage that they are 'authentic', ready-made in the language being studied (Kirby, 1994).

More directly related to popular education, learners can also engage in discussing social issues pertaining to their own society, as well as that of others. Again, this can be done from an early stage and need not be postponed till language skills are highly developed. In their video showing comic sketches for beginners in Spanish, for example, Kane and Morrison (1994) have a section on 'talking politics' though the main linguistic focus is simply regular verbs in the present tense. In a French course at a slightly higher level (Kane, 2000d), in an exercise for introducing past tenses, one fictitious dialogue takes place at the pearly gates between the Christian figure of St Peter and Guy Fawkes 'the Second' who wishes to enter the kingdom of heaven (Box P:2). Tongue-in-cheek, the dialogue attempts to introduce serious issues in an entertaining way and works particularly well when tutors act out the dialogue live in front of the class (Kane, 1995b, explains the methodological approach). Follow-up work challenges students to think about the issues and provides linguistic models to help them express their opinions. Importantly, students also have the option *not* to discuss the issues, a useful approach being to provide, for example, a list of open-ended questions of which students select ten to answer, according to their interests: some questions deal with the serious issues and some do not. The important thing is that issues are raised in the classroom and students are challenged to think. Though education cannot be neutral, equally, any attempt to force-feed a particular viewpoint would be in the worst tradition of 'banking' education: people must reach their own conclusions and dogmatic teaching, even from a progressive viewpoint, is essentially reactionary in treating people as 'objects' rather than 'subjects'.

When students see from example that even at a basic level it is possible to engage with important issues and not simply talk about hotels, directions or the post office – important as these functions are – it opens the door for students themselves to set the agenda and bring up challenging issues which they themselves consider important. I normally divide students into groups of four and ask them to write a short play to be performed in the last class. Every year, without fail, some groups choose to tackle serious issues, albeit with a splash of humour. Once, after only eighteen hours of learning Spanish, one group acted out the life of a South African orange on its journey to Scotland (in the days of apartheid) and finished off by asking students to support the consumer boycott. On another occasion a group delivered a weather forecast which doubled as political satire. Students were able to enjoy themselves, practise what they had learned but be challenged to think – and even take action – at the same time.

And in any discussion of social issues, students can also consider possible action for change. Tutors can introduce the work of international solidarity organisations (Amnesty International or the Central American Committee for Human Rights, for example) or popular organisations indigenous to the countries where the language is spoken, especially if they are keen to forge international links, as in the case of the Zapatistas or the MST. If the issues under discussion are domestic, the same considerations apply.

But it is also important to be realistic and consider the limitations on language teaching's contribution to social change. As regards teachers, the demands are greater than normal: language skills alone are insufficient and while there is no need for a degree in global economics, at least a basic knowledge of development issues is required. We have seen that popular education is most effective when a group is already organised around a particular social issue and then looks for educational support for their struggle: a language class, on the other hand, is a group of different individuals who just happen to have been thrown together. In the most optimistic scenario, discussing issues and the possibilities for action may give birth to an interested, organised group of campaigners. A more realistic outcome is that interested individuals go on to join other campaigning groups which are already established. A typical adult language class is also predominantly middle-class and not instinctively inclined towards radical political perspectives: its 'generative' issues are not those of the 'oppressed'. But the exercise remains worthwhile. It is at least arguable that a better society for the most vulnerable is a better society for all and committed, progressive members of the middle class have always had an important role to play in any movement for social change: the key question, I believe, is not where people come from but whose side they are on.

Higher Education

I teach a course on Latin American popular education as part of an MSc in adult education. Most students are adults already employed in the field. One of the aims of the course is that students should experience – as far as possible – the philosophy and methods of popular education in action, though the context of a higher education course in the UK is clearly a world removed from the struggle of a popular movement in Latin America. While the course content is based around a reality with which students are unfamiliar – and therefore does not start from a 'generative' theme – the course format is consciously influenced by popular education in the following ways:

1. Its political nature is openly declared.
2. Each class focuses on a set of open-ended questions (in the class on Freire, for example, the questions are 'What is Freire all about? What is his basic thesis/philosophy/political stance? How important is it in relation to his methodology? How do you yourself react to Freire? Can you see any problems with his philosophy/method?'). A student starts the discussion with a presentation which addresses these questions; the tutor also makes a presentation and the points raised by both are discussed by all the students. The classes aim to be as 'dialogical' as possible.
3. A full day is spent illustrating some of the methodological techniques in action, from the 'Triple Self-diagnosis' to sociodramas and statues.
4. At the end of each class, students jot down, anonymously (a) their thoughts on the issues discussed that day (b) comments on the way the course is being run. These are collected by the tutor, 'synthesised', typed up and given out to students at the beginning of the next class (Appendix P:2).
5. These comments become the starting point for discussion in the following class (before the next presentation). The intention is to make the implicit explicit, always start from students' perceptions and allow them a say in the running of the course. When collated at the end, they become a form of mini 'systematisation' of the course.
6. Students can negotiate their own essay titles if they develop an interest in a particular area.
7. The limits to doing popular education are 'problematised' in the course itself – one of the essay titles asks '*To what extent do you think the course "Education For A Changing World" was an example of "popular education" in action?*' – and the issue of institutional power is openly addressed. This particularly applies to the allocation of marks. Work should be judged against pre-specified criteria and not, it is emphasised, on compatibility with the views of the marker; students are encouraged to express their own views, backed up by appropriate evidence. However, while this sounds fine in theory,

it is acknowledged that anxious students, understandably, may be sceptical of a marker's ability to remain so dispassionately objective. Thus the element of 'institutionalised power' – the authority to judge and bestow value on students work – may affect the learning experience of students in ways of which tutors are unaware (see also Ellsworth, 1994).

8. Assessed work is handed back with a 'right to reply' form which says: 'Trying to practice some of what popular education preaches, your are invited to comment below on the feedback you have received on your essay, saying whether you agree/disagree, have now seen the light or hotly dispute what has been said. This is to encourage deeper reflection and offer a "right to reply": it would only lead to a change of mark in exceptional circumstances, where the tutor is shown to have clearly missed something important (ie it is not a mechanism for negotiating marks). If you prefer not to comment, that's fine too'. There is no pretence that this does away with power relations but it does give students the last word and challenges the tutor's absolute authority.

The course format – involving students in on-going design and evaluation – allows changes to be made 'on the hoof'. The full-day on methodology was a students' suggestion and the balance of large versus small-group discussion varies yearly, even weekly. It can also lead to some curious developments: I once proposed that in attempting to devolve a degree of institutional power to students, the class-presentations could be 'peer-assessed': it soon became apparent in the weekly written comments that this was a power the students preferred not to have and it was handed back to the tutor.

None of this means that the course is trouble-free. Student differences are sometimes difficult to reconcile. A student once asked that the whole course be teacher-led and lecture-based: what do you do when, in order to avoid 'banking education', you enlist the students' participation to be told that it is 'banking education' they would like? On other occasions, issues have surfaced too late in the course, without appearing in the weekly feedback: so a degree of scepticism is required, for despite consultation and participation there may be other agendas at work of which tutors are oblivious. We might think we know what our students think but how do we know what they think of what we think they think?!

Popular education has also helped me on a course I teach in Dubai. The student intake is multicultural and multinational, from the Middle East and Asia, and I was unhappy with my first attempt at teaching for there were cultural issues I clearly did not understand, particularly relating to gender: as I tried to organise group work it became apparent that some women, though not all, preferred to work on their own.

The next year I began by 'problematising' the issue of culture with the students. I explained my own thoughts on how the course should run (which included mixed-group discussion) but that I knew there may be cultural considerations of which I was unaware. I spoke of my reservations from the previous year and put the responsibility onto students to raise any important issues before the course began. Using the 'post-its' exercise (chapter three) they wrote down any anxieties they had about the course, these were classified into columns and put up on the wall for me and everyone else to see. It was then easy to negotiate the cultural minefield and proceed to the next stage. Most women were happy to work in mixed groups; four preferred to work in a single-sex group and were free to do so. Interestingly enough, as the classes developed they gradually began to integrate into the larger group anyway, culture never being static, always negotiable.

General Comments

Despite the inevitable constraints of working within the mainstream, I find that the principles and practices of popular education constantly influence what I do. It is possible to raise social and political issues in any curriculum. Radical educators occupy an ambivalent position – within and against (though sometimes for) the state – but most have some room for manoeuvre to encourage learners to examine – not have forced upon them – radical ideas. While the concept of 'academic freedom' is still valued, university educators usually have greater flexibility than schoolteachers.

And it is important to argue for popular education principles against the narrow, economistic view of education which is largely dominant in the UK. It is sometimes said, for example, that a university's two 'clients' are students and employers: but it should also have something to offer the 'oppressed' in society. I have seen universities set up student job-fares with the oil company Shell at a time when it stood accused of supporting atrocities in Nigeria: the aim was simply to help students find work. While this is entirely legitimate, there is surely something deficient in an education system which offers up its graduates to multinational companies but never formally asks them to question the purpose and motives of their future employers or examine the balance-sheet of their social contribution (as opposed to their current account)? And what kind of doctors do we produce who may be skilful with their hands but never have to address a question like 'why is life expectancy in suburb A 10 years lower than in suburb B and what can a doctor do to narrow the gap?' In a university context, at least, these types of question can be and sometimes are asked – and be part of assessed work, so that they are seen to be taken seriously – if the educators in place are prepared to argue the case. It has been my experience, from my own practice and from observing others in a variety of different posts, from primary to higher education, that no matter the constraints, an educator motivated by the principles of popular education will find ways of putting them into practice: I hope and believe that it does make a difference.

Conclusion

Throughout the world, educators, activists and grassroots organisations have developed indigenous forms of popular education, appropriate to their own particular time and place. For those interested in making this work more effective, the Latin American experience offers a rich source of inspiration, though the influence of different social and political contexts has to be borne in mind; it is also important not to exaggerate its achievements but to learn too from its limitations. Nevertheless, I believe that radical educators everywhere have much to learn from Latin America both in understanding the relationship between popular education and society and in improving their day-to-day educational practice.

Perhaps the greatest challenge from Latin America is that it forces us to think of popular education in terms of its relationship to a popular movement. The long-term aim of radical, 'popular' education in the UK should be to contribute to the building of just such a movement. This will not easy but the time is right, many seem willing and a number of organisations have already made a start: ¡Adelante!

Appendix P: I
Statement on the Definition and Purpose of the Popular Education Forum for Scotland

Popular Education

Popular education is understood to be popular, as distinct from merely populist, in the sense that:
- it is rooted in the real interests and struggles of ordinary people
- it is overtly political and critical of the status quo
- it is committed to progressive social and political change

Popular education is based on a clear analysis of the nature of inequality, exploitation and oppression and is informed by an equally clear political purpose. This has nothing to do with helping the 'disadvantaged' or the management of poverty; it has everything to do with the struggle for a more just and egalitarian social order.

The process of popular education has the following general characteristics:
- its curriculum comes out of the concrete experience and material interests of people in communities of resistance and struggle
- its pedagogy is collective, focused primarily on group as distinct from individual learning and development
- it attempts, wherever possible, to forge a direct link between education and social action

Linking the Local and the Global

Although the term has come to be associated with relatively recent developments in Latin America, it has strong resonances with both the radical tradition in British adult education and the distinctly Scottish interest in promoting democratic access to the exploration of ideas and to the debate about what counts as worthwhile knowledge.

Popular education seeks to connect the local and the global. In every context it proceeds from specific, localised forms of education and action, but it deliberately sets out to foster international solidarity by making these local struggles part of the wider international struggle for justice and peace.

The Purpose of the Popular Education Forum for Scotland

In the short term the purpose of the Forum is to:
- bring together people in Scotland with an existing interest in and commitment to popular education
- begin to forge active links and solidarity at both national and international levels

In the longer term the Forum seeks to:
- catalyse action by linking local activists, workers and politically committed academics
- produce and provide educational resources for social and political action
- reassert and invigorate adult and community education's role as an integral part of progressive social movements
  (Martin, 1999: 4-5)

Appendix P:2

Selection of Comments from Students after the Session on 'What Is Popular Education?' (1999)

Thoughts on Issues Discussed

1. It would seem that we have to define much more what popular education is *not* rather than what it is. There's still some confusion, perhaps due to our

need for a better understanding of the political context in which popular education takes place.

2. Popular education – definitions a bit clearer.

3. A better understanding of the terminology is needed to be able to distinguish between campaigning and education. I liked the debate about the relevance of popular education here and it made me think about how it could be applied. Raised issues about when this method is used and misused.

4. Raised some good points. Clarified 'popular education'. There is a lot of pseudo-Freire about. How do we challenge it? Handouts very useful. Interesting to make comparisons with our own system and the 'third world'.

5. It highlighted to the group the significance of the different concepts of popular education. I found it very thought-provoking. Enjoyed discussion.

6. Interesting regarding the Spanish translation of 'popular' and how it doesn't mean 'what lots of people supposedly like'. That definition would lead people in a different direction from the Freirian model.

Thoughts on Course Structure

1. Fine

2. Whole-group discussion worked well. Keep the table in the meantime: the change is good.

3. I like the group format. Perhaps more teacher 'intervention' might have been beneficial to tying up loose ends.

4. I didn't like the table being there. The class felt more 'formal' and isolating as a result.

5. I enjoyed the split – part lecture (banking?) and part dialogue and think it was a good balance. We are all aspiring adult educators so I'm sure we are very rigid difficult people who think our own methods are the best/only methods and like to nit-pick how other people conduct their classes

6. We must try and stick to the issues. We have good discussions but we wander and sometimes waste time. Vary the table and the circle.

Addendum: A Checklist for Practitioners

For educators, activists, campaigners, trade union representatives, leaders of organisations, social workers or anyone else working in 'cultural action' for change:-

Here is my own, personal checklist of 'dos' and 'don'ts' in popular education, some easier to implement than others. Condensed, for busy people, into a few hundred words, they are the practical implications of what has been discussed in the preceding chapters. For a less sergeant-majorish approach, an intellectual justification of the particular points selected or a weightier analysis of the issues they raise – read the book!

A Checklist for Practice

The Political Dimension

1. Be aware that ultimately, all education is political.
2. Have a consciously political (as opposed to 'charity-based') commitment to work on the side of the 'oppressed' ('excluded', 'disadvantaged' and so on) for progressive change.
3. Be aware of your own particular political and ideological biases when analysing events.
4. Don't try to hide this bias (though you have to judge when and how to make it known) but don't try to force it on anyone either.

On 'Subjects' of Change

1. Your aim is for ordinary people – as opposed to enlightened or charismatic leaders alone – to become active 'subjects' (or 'actors', 'agents', 'protagonists') of change.
2. Your job is to enable them to examine their social context and consider what they can do to change it.
3. To do so, sometimes you may have to lead by example, where people lack confidence or are unsure how to proceed.
4. But be sure to step back at the earliest possible moment and let others go forward.
5. Be alert to the dangers of doing things *on behalf of* people instead of *with* them.
6. If people make progress, your status as 'leader' or 'educator' will diminish: prepare your ego to cope or you may act, subconsciously, to prevent such progress.
7. Make sure the organisational structure of your group, union, or movement is set up to encourage participation and democracy, not promote the status,

CV or career of its leaders, yourself included (for example, responsibilities should be shared out, key posts rotated).

Knowledge
1. Always remember that learners will know important things which you don't know.
2. But you also know (or should be able to find out) important things which they don't know.
3. Your job is to bring these two areas together in a 'dialogue of knowledges' from which everyone can learn. The starting point is to draw a group's collective perception of the world out into the open.
4. Respect people's knowledge – but not uncritically. We are all exposed to and can absorb reactionary ideas. Don't be a romantic 'grassrootsist'.
5. Remember that people also have thoughts, feelings, hopes, desires, emotions – all of which will affect how and what they think, know and learn.

Methodology
1. Whatever it is that people are really interested in, whatever gets them going – that's the place to start the educational process.
2. Stimulate critical, creative thinking by asking lots of questions, rather than providing ready-made answers.
3. Build up a repertoire of interesting activities and 'participatory techniques' for engaging people in dialogue: try creating new ones of your own.
4. Remember that techniques are only tools: you have to select the right one at the right moment for the right group of people.
5. Don't be obsessed with the need for 'dynamic' activities: there are times when it is entirely appropriate to hear someone give a talk or read a passage from a book, for example (though as a preliminary to further discussion).
6. Be aware that a group is composed of individuals who will learn in different ways and at different speeds.
7. Involve the group in an on-going process of planning, documenting, reflecting on and evaluating the learning process.
8. Ensure there is constant feedback on your own role as educator and learn from your mistakes.

Interpersonal Skills
Don't neglect your basic interpersonal skills (being respectful of others, a good listener, assertive rather than aggressive and so on). Without a basic human relationship between educator and learner, educational theories and techniques are irrelevant.

Useful Websites

Alforja
http://www.alforja.org/indexo.htm
A network of popular education centres covering Central America and Mexico. The site was under reconstruction at the time of writing but gave important links to all the other centres.

CANTERA
http://www.oneworld.org/cantera/education/index.html
An important popular education centre in Managua, Nicaragua, also part of Alforja. It has an excellent website in English referring to events, projects, publications and has some background information on popular education in general. A good starting place.

CEAAL (Consejo de Educación de Adultos de América Latina)
http://www.ceaal.org/
(Spanish only)
The Latin American wide network which brings together some 250 centres involved in popular education throughout the region. The site is informative, good for keeping up to date with events and publications and its list of affiliates is a great place to find out about and make contact with interesting projects in whichever country is of interest.

CIEPAC (Centro de Investigaciones Económicas y Políticas de Acción Comunitaria)
http://www.ciepac.org/bulletins/
CIEPAC has regular updates and analyses on the situation in Chiapas, many of them translated into English. Good maps too.

IMDEC (Instituto Mexicano para el Desarrollo Comunitario)
http://www.alforja.or.cr/centros/imdec/entrada.htm
One of the leading popular education centres in Latin America, at the time of writing IMDEC has an excellent site in Spanish, with details of its 'school of methodology', publications, other activities and links to other 'amigos'. An English site is promised but was not in place at time of publication.

Instituto Paulo Freire
http://www.paulofreire.org/

The Paulo Freire Institute is based in São Paulo, Brazil, and was set up by Freire himself. Its current director is Moacir Gadotti, an important figure in popular education and the author of numerous publications. It is a comprehensive site with information on a wide range of initiatives, plenty of it written in English. It also has links to global networks of people and organisations involved in popular education

Mayalán Cultural Association for Community Development, Guatemala.

http://www.thefoundry.org/~laura/mayalan/index.html

A good website in both Spanish and English with sections on popular education, micro enterprises and loan funds, the women's empowerment programme and the programme in Mayan identity and culture.

MST (Landless Rural Workers' Movement in Brazil)

(English) http://www.mstbrazil.org/index.html

(Portuguese) http://www.mst.org.br/

The MST now has a good website in both English and Portuguese which is kept up to date. It gives good background information on all aspects of the MST, including education, with links to useful articles and international supporters

PULSAR

http://www.pulsar.org.ec/Que_es.htm

(Spanish only)

Pulsar is a wonderful community radio station based in Quito, Ecuador. It provides excellent daily, weekly and monthly news digests from all over Latin America, from a 'popular' perspective. These are sent by email in text and/or audio and subscription is free. The website also gives up to date information and details of how to subscribe.

Rede Mulher de Educação (Women's Education Network)

http://redemulher.org.br/ingles/inicio1.htm

This network is based in Brazil and its homepage announces its involvement in 'almost two decades of feminist popular education, promoting the balance of social relationships between men and women, in harmony with nature.' It is an excellent website in both Portuguese and English covering a wide range of issues related to feminist popular education, with lots of links to other articles, people and organisations.

Glossary of Acronyms and Terminology

English

Christian Base Communities: grassroots organisations set up by the progressive wing of the Catholic Church. Their members are encouraged to engage in a critical, social and political reading of scriptures and become active citizens.

Conception of a Dialectical Methodology: an approach to popular education and campaigning promoted by the Central American network 'Alforja'. It highlights the mutual relationship between action and reflection and encourages people to consider how the political, economic, cultural, religious (etc) aspects of their lives are inter-connected.

Conjunctural Analysis: an exercise to assess the political, economic and social forces in play in a particular society at a particular moment in time: a prelude to deciding what type of action is most appropriate to take.

Development Education: in the UK, a cross-curricular approach to education promoting a critical understanding of global development issues.

Generative Issue: the 'burning' issue in any group or community, the subject 'generating' most discussion.

IMF: the International Monetary Fund.

Neo-Liberalism: free market, laissez-faire economics.

NGO: Non Governmental Organisation.

Populism: a charismatic style of leadership with both left and right-wing traits, ostensibly championing grassroots interests, on the one hand, but authoritarian and conservative, on the other.

Problematise: when educators ask questions and present an issue as a problem, for deeper reflection and analysis, rather than provide answers.

REFLECT: REgenerated Freirian Literacy through Empowering Community Techniques. A global project in literacy and popular education.

'Subjects' (of change): a key notion in popular education. A grammatical analogy, it conveys the idea that instead of having change done to them (and therefore being its 'objects'), ordinary people themselves should become the collective protagonists (and therefore the 'subjects') of change. By extension, it is also used to refer to groups with whom popular educators work: 'the *subjects* in this project are Indigenous people', for example.

Systematisation: often used in the phrase 'the systematisation of experiences', the process of documenting, bringing structure to and trying to make sense of (popular education) experiences which, by nature, tend to develop in unpredictable and sometimes chaotic ways.

Triangular Trade: in colonial times, the shipment of goods from Europe to Africa, slaves from Africa to the Americas and gold, silver, sugar and tobacco from the Americas to Europe.

Spanish/Portuguese/French

Aguascalientes: site of an important convention, in 1914, of the Mexican revolution. Also the name given by the *Zapatistas* to villages designated as cultural centres.

Alforja: a network of popular education centres from Central America and Mexico

Altiplano: a large expanse of flat land high above sea level.

AMNLAE (Asociación de Mujeres Nicaraguenses Luisa Amanda Espinosa): the Louise Amanda Espinosa Association of Nicaraguan Women.

Barrio: neighbourhood.

Basismo: roughly translated as 'grassrootsism', an exaggerated, uncritical respect for grassroots knowledge or culture.

Brigadista: a member of a brigade.

Cacique: a local, political strong-man or boss.

Campesino: 'peasant', but with less a negative connotation than in English.

Caudillismo: strong-man politics or autocratic government.

CEAAL (Consejo de Educación de Adultos de América Latina) the Latin American Council of Adult Education.

Clientelismo: clientelism, system of patronage.

Consulta: an exercise in consultation.

Contras: the counter-revolutionary forces funded by the USA in the 1980s to try and topple the Sandinista government in Nicaragua.

Encuentro – an event where people meet to discuss, debate, exchange views and consider courses of action. A cross between a meeting, conference and encounter, neither term alone is a good translation: the first two are too formal, the last too gladatorial.

EZLN (*Ejército Zapatista para la Liberación Nacional*): the Zapatista National Liberation Army

FMC (Federación de Mujeres Cubanas): Federation of Cuban Women.

IMDEC (Instituto Mexicano de Desarrollo Comunitario) Mexican Institute of Community Development.

Indianismo: the philosophy that indigenous peoples themselves – as opposed to sympathetic others – should lead the struggle for recognition of their own culture, needs and rights.

Indigenismo: beginning in the 1920s, a revaluation and rediscovery of indigenous culture after centuries of racism. Indigenous peoples came to see it as an exercise in paternalistic assimilation and this led, eventually, to its antithesis, *indianismo*.

Indigenista: adjective from *indigenismo*.

Machismo: male chauvinism.

Machista: male chauvinist.

Mestizo: of mixed culture or race.

PRI (*Partido Revolucionario Institucional*): the Institutional Revolutionary Party which ruled Mexico from 1920 to 2000, though its name changed on several occasions.

Refundamentación: the process of rethinking the basics of popular education.

REPEM (Red de Educación Popular entre Mujeres): Women's Popular Education Network.

Sandinismo: in Nicaragua, the political philosophy and practice of the Sandinista government, 1979-1990. It took its name from Augusto César Sandino, the leader of the anti-imperialist struggles of the early 1930s

Tontons Macoutes: 'bogey men', the special police force owned by the Duvalier dictatorships in Haiti

Zapatismo: philosophy of the *Zapatistas*.

Zapatistas: The Zapatista National Liberation Army (EZLN) and followers who rose up on January 1st 1994. Named after the famous indigenous leader of the Mexican revolution, Emiliano Zapata, they struggle for land, autonomy and services for the indigenous peoples of Chiapas. They also engage civil society throughout Mexico in a campaign for participatory democracy.

References

Abers, R (1996) From Ideas to Practice: The Partido dos Trabalhadores and Participatory Governance in Brazil *Latin American Perspectives, Issue 91, Vol 23, No 4,* 35-53

Aguilar, ALT et al (1997) *Movimento de Mujeres en Centroamérica* Managua: Programa Regional La Corriente

Alfaro, RM (1994) ¿Comunicación Popular o Educación Ciudadana? *La Piragua: Revista Latinoamericana de Educación y Política, No 8, 1er Semestre, 14-34*

Allen, T & Eade, J (2000) The new politics of identity, in Allen, T & Thomas, A (eds) *Poverty And Development into The 21ˢᵗ Century, 485-508* Oxford: Oxford University Press

Allman, P (1988) Gramsci, Freire and Illich: Their Contributions to Education for Socialism, in Lovett, T *Radical Approaches to Adult Education: A Reader* London: Routledge

Allman, P & Wallis, J (1995) Challenging the Postmodern Condition: Radical Adult Education for Critical Intelligence, in Mayo, M & Thompson, J (eds) *Adult Learning, Critical Intelligence and Social Change, 18-33* Leicester: NIACE

Allman, P & Wallis, J (1995b) Gramsci's challenge to the politics of the left in 'Our Times' *International Journal of Lifelong Education, Vol 14, No 2, March-April, 120-143*

Allman, P & Wallis, J (1997) Commentary: Paulo Freire and the future of the radical tradition, in *Studies in the Education of Adults Vol 29, No 2 113-120*

Alvarado, E (1989) *Don't Be Afraid Gringo. A Honduran Woman Speaks from the Heart: the Story of Elvia Alvarado* New York: Harper & Row

Álvarez, S (1998) Latin American Feminisms Go Global: Trends of the 1990s and Challenges for the New Millenium, in Álvarez, SE; Dagnino, E & Escóbar, A (eds) *Cultures of Politics, Politics of Cultures: Revisioning Latin American Social Movements, 293-324* Oxford: Westview Press

Álvarez, SE; Dagnino, E & Escóbar, A (1998) Introduction: The Cultural and the Political in Latin American Social Movements, in *Cultures of Politics, Politics of Cultures: Revisioning Latin American Social Movements, 1-29* Oxford: Westview Press

Andreu Abrio, R; Díaz Sánchez, J & Camacho Herrera, A (coordinadores) (1998) *La Educación Popular Ante El Siglo XXI* Sevilla: Librería Andaluza

Antillón, R (1991) *Gramsci y la Educación Popular* Guadalajara, Mexico: IMDEC

Antillón, R (1994) Anexo No 5 ¿Cuáles Son Los Elementos Esenciales de la CMD?, in Jara, OH *Para Sistematizar Experiencias* San José, Costa Rica: Alforja

Antillón, R (1999) Una aproximación metodológica a la investigación del impacto Guadalajara, Mexico: IMDEC

Antillón, R & Orozco O, E (1992) "La Escuela Metodológica" en México: Una experiencia en progreso *La Piragua: Revista Latinoamericana de Educacion y*

Politica, No 5, 55-58

Archer, D (1994) The Changing Roles of Non-Governmental Organisations in the Field of Education (in the Context of Changing Relationships with the State) *International Journal of Educational Development, Vol 14, No 3, pp 223-232*

Archer, D (2000) Discovering new definitions of Reflect: the first Central American meeting *Education Action, Issue 12, 9-11* London: ActionAid

Archer, D & Costello, P (1990) *Literacy and Power: The Latin American Background* Earthscan

Archer, D & Cottingham, S (1996) *The REFLECT Mother Manual: a new approach to adult literacy* London: ACTION AID

Archer, D & Cottingham, S (1996b) *Action Research Report on Reflect. Regenerated Freirian Literacy Through Empowering Community Techniques: The Experiences of Three REFLECT Pilot Projects in Uganda, Bangladesh, EL Salvador Serial No 17* London: Overseas Development Administration

Arnold, R & Burke, B (1983) *A Popular Education Handbook* Ontario: CUSO & OISE

Arnold, R., Barndt, D & Burke, B (1994*) A New Weave: Popular Education in Canada and Central America* Ontario: CUSO & OISE

Arnove, RF (1986) *Education and Revolution in Nicaragua* New York: Praeger

Arnove, RF (1994) *Education as Contested Terrain: Nicaragua, 1979 – 1993* Boulder/ San Francisco/Oxford: Westview Press

Arruda, M (1998) *Interview with author, Rio de Janeiro, March* (Arruda is co-ordinator of PACS, 'Políticas Alternativas para o Cono Sur')

ALER (Asociación Latinoamericana de Escuelas Radiofónicas) (undated) *Educación Popular. Sociodramas: Es Fácil Hacerlos Bien* Quito & Managua: ALER

Austin, R (1999) Popular History and Popular Education: El Consejo de Educación de Adultos de América Latina *Latin American Perspectives, Issue No 7, Vol 26, No 4, July, 39-68*

Barndt, D (1991) *To Change This House: Popular Education Under the Sandinistas* Toronto: Between the Lines

Barnechea, MM., Gonzalez, E & Morgan ML (1994) La Sistematización Como Producción de Conocimientos *La Piragua: Revista Latinoamericana de Educacion y Politica, No 9, 122-128*

Barr, J (2000) *In conversation with author.* Barr is head of the Department of Adult & Continuing Education in the University of Glasgow.

Barrios de Chúngara, D (1978) *Let Me Speak! Testimony of Domitila, a Woman of the Bolivian Mines* New York: Monthly Review Press

Bebbington, A (1996) Debating 'indigenous' agricultural development: Indian organisations in the Central Andes of Mexico, in Collinson, H (ed) *Green Guerrillas: Environmental Conflicts and Initiatives in Latin America and the Caribbean, 51-60* London: Latin America Bureau

Bellé, C (1998) *Interview with Author, São Paulo, May*

Betto, F., Cardenal, F., Fals Borda, O, Osorio, J and Núñez, C (1993) *Vigencia de las Utopias en América Latina: educación popular, pedagogía, fe y política* Guadalajara, Mexico: Instituto Mexicano para el Desarrollo Comunitario (IMDEC)

Betto, F (1997) Sem Terra & Cidadania, in Stédile, JP *A Reforma Agrária E A Luta Do MST, 215 -222* Petrópolis, Brazil: Vozes

Betto, F (2000) Los Desafíos del Movimiento Social Frente al Neoliberalismo, in Agencia Informativa Púlsar *Resumen # 5.110 – jueves 20 abril*

Betuto Fernández, F (1998) Panorama y desafíos de la educación popular en Bolivia, in Andreu Abrio, R et al (coordinadores) *La Educación Popular Ante El Siglo XXI, 75-77* Sevilla: Librería Andaluza

Bickel, A (1999) *Interview with author, San Salvador, August* (Bickel is coordinator of the Salvadorean agency FUNPROCOOP)

Boal, A (1979) *Theatre of the Oppressed* London: Pluto

Boal, A (1992) *Games for Actors and Non-Actors* London & New York: Routledge

Boal, A (1995) *Rainbow of Desire* London: Routledge

Boal, A (1998) *Legislative Theatre* London & New York: Routledge

Bosch, AE (1998) Popular Education, Work Training and the Path to Women's Empowerment in Chile *Comparative Education Review, Vol 42, No 2*

Bottomore, T (ed)., Harris, L., Kiernan, VG & Miliband, R (1988) *A Dictionary of Marxist Thought* Oxford: BlackwellBrandão, CR (1989) *La Educación Popular en América Latina* CEDEP

Brandes, D & Ginnis, P (1986) *A Guide to Student-Centred Learning* Oxford: Blackwell

Broadbent, L (director & producer) (2000) *MACHO* Glasgow: Broadbent Productions (For availability contact 0141 332 2042 or Lucinda@cqm.co.uk)

Broadhead, T (1998) *Bridges of Hope?* Ottawa: The North South Institute

Bruhn, K (1999) Antonio Gramsci and the Palabra Verdadera: The Political discourse of Mexico's Guerrilla Forces *Journal of Interamerican Studies and World Affairs, Vol 41, No 2, 29-55*

Bustillos, G y Vargas, L (1993) *Técnicas Participativas para la Educación Popular Tomo 1&2* Guadalajara: Instituto Mexicano para el Desarrollo Comunitario (IMDEC)

Caldart, RS (1987) *Sem Terra Com Poesia* Petrópolis: Vozes

Caldart, RS (1997) *Educação em Movimento: Formação de Educadores e Educadoras no MST.* Petrópolis, Brazil: Vozes

Caldart, RS (1998) *Interview with author, Porto Alegre, May*

CANTERA (1999) *El Significado de Ser Hombre* Managua: CANTERA

Cardenal, FSJ & Miller, V (1981) Nicaragua 1980: The Battle of the ABCs *Harvard Educational Review, Vol 15, No 1, February, pp 1-26*

Carlsen, L (1999) Autonomía indígena y usos y costumbres: la innovación de la tradición, in Instituto de Investigaciones Económicas UNAM *Chiapas 7, 45-70* Mexico: Ediciones ERA

Carmen, R (1995) Workshop for Enterprise Management vs "British" Enterprise Education: The Difference is in the Context *Convergence Vol 28, No 1, 72-90*

Carnoy, M & Torres, CA (1990) Education and Social Transformation in Nicaragua 1979-1989, in Carnoy, M & Samoff, J *Education and Social Transition in the Third World, pp 315-360* New Jersey: Princeton University Press

Carr, B & Ellner, S (eds) (1993) *The Latin American Left: From the Fall of Allende to Perestroika* Boulder/San Francisco/London: Westview Press/Latin America Bureau

Carr, IC (1990) The Politics of Literacy in Latin America *Convergence, Vol 23, N0 2, 50-68*

Castañeda, JG (1994) *Utopia Unarmed: The Latin American Left After the Cold War* New York: Vintage

Castaño Ferreira, E & J (1997) *Making Sense of the Media: A Handbook of Popular Education Techniques* New York: Monthly Review Press

Castillo, J (1998) Mujeres para el Diálogo, Mexico *La Carta, No 160, 3-4*

Castro, Y (1999) *Interview with author, San Cristóbal de Las Casas, September*

CEAAL (Consejo de Educación de Adultos de América Latina) (1985) *Paulo Freire en Buenos Aires: Acto preparatorio de la III asamblea Mundial de Educación de Adultos.* Buenos Aires: CEAAL

- (1993) *Nuestras Prácticas...Perfil Y Perspectivas de la Formación de Educadores Populares en América Latina* Guadalajara, Mexico: CEAAL & IMDEC

- (1994) Construyendo la Plataforma de la Educación Popular Latinoamericana *La Piragua: Revista Latinoamericana de Educacion y Politica, No 8, 3-13*

- (1995) Conversemos de Nuevo: Temas Para Un Diálogo Entre La Educación Popular Y La Cooperación Internacional *La Piragua: Revista Latinoamericana de Educacion y Politica, No 10, pp134-138*

- (1996) *Nuevos Escenarios y Nuevos Discursos en la Educación Popular – Memoria – Taller Sobre 'Refundamentación De La Educación Popular'* Patzcuaro, Mexico: CEAAL

- (1999) *Plan Global 1998 – 2001* Mexico: CEAAL

- (1999b) *La Piragua: Revista Latinoamericana De Educación Y Política, No 15*

Ceceña, AE (1999) La resistencia como espacio de construcción del nuevo mundo, in Instituto de Investigaciones Económicas UNAM *Chiapas 7, 93-114* Mexico: Ediciones ERA

Celiberti, L (1996) Reflexiones acerca de la perspectiva de género en las experiencias de educación no formal con mujeres, in Buttner, T; Jung, I & King, L (eds) *Hacia una pedagogía de género: Experiencias y conceptos innovativas, 66-80* Bonn: Centro de Educación, Ciencia y Documentación (ZED)

Cendales G, L., Posada f, J & Torres C, A (1996) Refundamentación, Pedagogía Y Política: Un Debate Abierto, in Dimensión Educativa *Educación Popular: Refundamentación, 105-124* Santafé de Bogotá: Dimensión Educativa

Cerioli, RP (1997) *Educação para a Cooperação: A Experiência do Curso Técnico em Administração de Cooperativas do MST* (Unpublished Dissertation). São Leopoldo,

Brazil: UNISINOS

Cernea, M (1992) *The Building Blocks of Participation: Testing Bottom-up Planning. World Bank Discussion Papers, No 166* Washington: World Bank

Chambers, R (1993) *Challenging the Professions: Frontiers for Rural Development* London: IT Publications

Chinchilla, NS (1992) Marxism, Feminism and the Struggle for Democracy in Latin America, in Escobar, A & Alvarez, SE *The Making of Social Movements in Latin America, 37-51* Oxford: Westview Press

Chomsky, N (1999) *Kosovo Peace Accord* http://www.zmag.org/chomsky/articles/z9907-peace-accord.htm

Chossudovsky, M (1996) *Dismantling Former Yugoslavia, Recolonising Bosnia* http://www.communist-party.ca/english/html/yugo_chossud.html

CIAZO (Fundación de Educación Popular) (1997) *Impacto y Fortalecimiento de la Política de Género en Ciazo* San Salvador: CIAZO

CIEPAC (Centro de Investigaciones Centro de Investigaciones Económicas y Políticas de Acción Comunitaria) (1999) *http://www.ciepac.org/bulletins/*

Coben, D (1998) *Radical Heroes: Gramsci, Freire and the Politics of Adult Education* New York & London: Garland Publishing, Inc. Taylor & Francis

Colectivo CEAAL-Bolivia: Movimiento de Educadores Populares de Bolivia (1994) *Educación Popular en Bolivia: Tendencias y Desafíos* La Paz: CEAAL

Collins, JN (2000) A Sense of Possibility: Ecuador's Indigenous Movement Takes Center Stage *NACLA Report on the Americas, Vol XXXIII, No 5, March/April, 40-49*

Collinson, H (ed) (1996) *Green Guerrillas: Environmental Conflicts and Initiatives in Latin America and the Caribbean* London: Latin America Bureau

Costa, M.A.B; Jaccoud, V & Costa, B (1986) *Cadernos de Educação Popular 10. MEB: Uma historia de muitos* Petrópolis: Vozes/NOVA

Costigan, M (1983) 'You Have the Third World Inside You': Conversation by Paulo Freire *Convergence 16:4 32-38*

Council of Europe (1999) *Europe is more than you think* Germany: Publishing and Documentation Service

Costa, B (1987) Para Analisar Uma Prática de Educação Popular *Cadernos de Educação Popular 1* Nova Petrópolis, Brazil: Vozes

Crowther, J (1999) Popular education and the struggle for democracy, in Crowther, J., Martin, I & Shaw, M (1999) *Popular Education and Social Movements in Scotland Today, 29-40* Leicester: NIACE (National Institute of Adult Continuing Education)

Crowther, J., Martin, I & Shaw, M (1999) *Popular Education and Social Movements in Scotland Today* Leicester: NIACE (National Institute of Adult Continuing Education)

Cubitt, T (1995) *Latin American Society* Harlow: Longman

Dalton, R (1985) The Rich, in Simpson, A & Asociación Nacional de Educadores

Salvadoreños Support Group *Learning about El Salvador: A Study Pack for Schools, Trade Unions and Adult Education Groups, p 32* London: ANDES Support Group

D'Angelo, A (1999) *Explorando Nuestros Cambios* Managua: MUSAVIA (Mujer, Salud y Violencia)

Davie, G (1964) *The Democratic Intellect: Scotland and Her Universities in the Nineteenth Century* Edinburgh: Edinburgh University Press

Da Silva, B; Benjamin, M & Mendonça, M (1997) *Benedita da Silva: An Afro-Brazilian Woman's Story of Politics and Love* Oakland USA: Institute for Food and Development Policy

de Brito, PAB (1997) Movimientos Sociales En América Latina Y El Caribe, in Mendoza, R, MdC (coordinación) (1997) *Construyendo Pedagogía Popular: Encuentros de Experiencias Pedagógicas, 77-88* Mexico: SEDEPAC (Servicio, Desarrollo y Paz)

de Hegedus (1995) The concept of evaluation and how it relates to research, *Adult Education and Development, No 44, 61-73*

De La Maza, G (1992) Abrir las Ventanas para Mirar el Futuro: Cinco Reflexiones sobre Alianzas para la Educación Popular *La Piragua: Revista Latinoamericana de Educacion y Politica, No 5, 23-27*

Dellazeri, DT (1998) *Interview with Author, Veranápolis, May*

de Souza, JF (1996) La Educación Popular y La Formación de los Educadores Populares, in Dimensión Educativa *Educación Popular: Refundamentación, 95-104* Santafé de Bogotá: Dimensión Educativa

Development Education Commission (1999) *Essential Learning for Everyone: raising the debate about civil society, world citizenship and the role of education* Birmingham/Ireland: Development Education Centre/ 80:20 Educating and Acting for a Better World

Díaz-Barriga, M (1998) Beyond the Domestic and the Public: Colonas' Participaion in Urban Movements in Mexico City, in lvarez, SE; Dagnino, E & Escóbar, A (eds) *Cultures of Politics, Politics of Cultures: Revisioning Latin American Social Movements, 252-277* Oxford: Westview Press

D'Incao, MC (1997) MST e a verdadeira democracia, in Stédile, JP *A Reforma Agrária E A Luta Do MST, 209-214* Petrópolis, Brazil: Vozes

Demo, P (1994) Investigación Participativa: Discutiendo Exitos Y Amibgüedades *La Piragua: Revista Latinoamericana de Educación y Politica, No 9, 111-114*

Dimensión Educativa (1996) *Educación Popular: Refundamentación* Santafé de Bogotá: Dimensión Educativa

Domínguez, JI & Lowenthal, AF (eds) (1996) *Constructing Democratic Governance: Latin America and the Caribbean in the 1990s – Themes and Issues* Baltimore, Maryland: John Hopkins University Press

Do Vale, AM (1992) *Educação Popular na Escola Pública*. São Paulo, Brazil: Cortez

Duke, C (1990) Grassroots Approaches to Combating Poverty Through Adult Education (Supplement to *Adult Education and Development, No 34*) Bonn:

German Adult Education Association

Eade, D (1997) *Capacity-Building: An Approach to People-Centred Development* Oxford: Oxfam

Eber, CE (1999) Seeking Our Own Food: Indigenous Women's Power and Autonomy in San Pedro Chenalhó, Chiapas (1980-1998) *Latin American Perspectives, Issue 106, Vol 26, May 6-36*

Eccher, C (1995) Educación, Mujeres y Economía Popular: La Necesidad de una Formación Específica La *Piragua: Revista Latinoamericana de Educación y Política, No 10, 99-103*

Ecche, C (1996) in interview with Vera Britto *http://www-personal.umich.edu/-fiatlux/td/eccher/ce-spa.html*

Eccher, C (1998) Red de Educación Popular entre Mujeres de América Latina y el Caribe (Repem) *La Carta, No 160, 5-6*

Edward, M; Kane, A; Kane, L; Kelly, C & McLean, L (1994) *Scotland Slavery Sugar Soap* Glasgow: Strathclyde Regional Council

Ellsworth, E (1994) Why Doesn't This Feel Empowering? Working Through The Repressive Myths Of Critical Pedagogy, in Stone, L (ed) *The Education Feminism Reader, 300-327* London: Routledge

Elster, J (ed) (1989) *Karl Marx: A Reader* Cambridge: Cambridge University Press

Engels, F (1950) *Ludwig Feurbach and the End of Classical German Philosophy* Moscow: Foreign Languages Publishing House

Entwhistle, N., Thomson, S & Tait, H (1992) *Guidelines for Promoting Effective Learning i Higher Education* Edinburgh: Centre for Research on Learning and Instruction

Escobar, A & Alvarez, SE (1992) *The Making of Social Movements in Latin America* Oxford: Westview Press

Esteva, G & Prakesh, MS (1998) *Grassroots Post-Modernism: Remaking the soil of cultures* London/New York: Zed Books

Fals Borda, O (1992) Social Movements and Political Power in Latin America, in Escobar, A & Alvarez, SE *The Making of Social Movements in Latin America, 303-316* Oxford: Westview Press

Fanon, F (1967) *The Wretched of the Earth* London: Pemguin

Faria, H; Muñoz, JV; García, PB; Pontual, P; Haddad, S & Barreto, V *Educação popular em debate* Cadernos de Educação Popular 13 Petrópolis: Vozes/Nova

Fernández, R (elaboración) (1998) *Metodología de Trabajo entre Mujeres. Memoria Tercer Taller, 25 al 28 de Agosto de 1998. Curso Metodológico de Educación Popular entre Mujeres* Managua: CANTERA

Field, J (1988) Workers' Education and the Crisis of British Trade Unionism, in Lovett, T (Ed) *Radical Approaches to Adult Education: A Reader, 224-241* London: Routledge

Findji, MT (1992) From Resistance to Social Movement: The Indigenous Authorities Movement in Colombia, in Escobar, A & Alvarez, SE *The Making of Social*

Movements in Latin America, 112-133 Oxford: Westview Press

Fink, M (1992) Women and Popular Education in Latin America, in Stromquist, NP *Women and Education in Latin America: Knowledge, Power and Change, 171-193* Boulder & London: Lynne Rienner Publishers

Fisher, Jo (1993) Women and Democracy: For Home and Country *NACLA: Report on the Americas, July/Aug, Vol 27, No 1*

Foweraker, J (1995) *Theorizing Social Movements* London: Pluto Press

Franco, J (1998) The Long March of Feminism *NACLA:Report on the Americas, Jan/ Feb, Vol 31, No 4*

Franco, J (1998b) Defrocking the Vatican: Feminism's Secular Project, in Álvarez, SE; Dagnino, E & Escóbar, A (eds) *Cultures of Politics, Politics of Cultures: Revisioning Latin American Social Movements, 278-289* Oxford: Westview Press

Freire, P (1972) *Pedagogy of the Oppressed* Harmondsworth: Penguin Books

Freire, P (1974a) Education as the Practice of Freedom, in *Education for Critical Consciousness 1-84* London: Sheed and Ward

Freire, P (1974b) Extension or Communication, in *Education for Critical Consciousness 85-164* London: Sheed and Ward

Freire, P (1978) *Pedagogy in Process* London: Writers and Readers Publishing Cooperative

Freire, P (1979) *Extensão ou Comunicação* Rio de Janeiro: Paz e Terra

Freire, P (1983) You Have the Third World Inside You: Conversation with Paulo Freire *Convergence Vol 16, No 4, 32-37*

Freire, P (1985) *The Politics of Education: Culture, Power and Liberation* London: Macmillan

Freire, P (1991) *A Educação na Cidade* São Paulo, Brazil: Editora

Freire, P (1993) *Pedagogía de la Esperanza* Mexico: Siglo Veintiuno Editores

Freire, P (1995) *Teachers As Cultural Workers: Letters to those who dare teach* Boulder/ Colorado: Westview Press

Freire, P (1996) *Pedagogía da Autonomía: saberes necesários à prática educativa* São Paulo: Paz e Terra

Freire, P & Faundez, A (1989) *Learning to Question: A Pedagogy of Liberation* Geneva: WCC Publicatins

Freire, P., Pérez, E & Martínez, F (1988) *Pedagogía de la Pregunta* Quito: Corporación Ecuatoriana para el Desarrollo de la Comunicación (CEDEC)

Fukuyama, F (1992) *The End of History and the Last Man* London: Penguin

Gadotti, M (1992) Estado e Educação Popular: Bases para uma Educação Pública Popular, in Gadotti, M & Torres, CA *Estado e Educação Popular na América Latina* São Paulo: Papirus, Série 'Educação Internacional' do Instituto Paulo Freire

Gadotti, M (1994) Escola púbica popular, in Gadotti, M & Torres, CA *Educação Popular: Utopia Latino-Americana 147-164* São Paulo, Brazil: Cortez

Gadotti, M (1994b) *Reading Paulo Freire: His Life and Work* Albany: State University of New York Press

Gadotti, M (1996) (org) *Paulo Freire: Uma Biobibliografía* São Paulo, Brasil: Cortez
Gadotti, M (1996b) *Pedagogy of Praxis: a Dialectical Philosophy of Education* Albany: State University of New York Press
Gadotti, M (1997) *Concepção Dialética da Educção: Um estudo introdutório* 10. ed. São Paulo: Cortez
Gadotti, M & Torres, CA (1992) *Estado e Educação Popular na América Latina* São Paulo: Papirus, Série 'Educação Internacional' do Instituto Paulo Freire
Gadotti, M & Torres, CA (1994) *Educação Popular: Utopia Latino-Americana* São Paulo, Brazil: Cortez
Galeano, E (1973) *Open Veins of Latin America: five centuries of the pillage of a continent* New York: Monthly Review Press
Galeano, E (1991) Encender un fueguito en la memoria o en la imaginación, in IMDEC-CEAAL (Segunda edición) *De Superman a Superbarrio, 61-84* Guadalajara, Mexico: IMDEC-CEAAL
Galloway, V (1997) *In conversation with author.* Galloway is an education worker with the Adult Learning Project.
García, MP (1992) The Venezuelan Ecology Movement: Symbolic Effectiveness, Social Practices and Political Strategies, in Escobar, A & Alvarez, SE *The Making of Social Movements in Latin America: Identity, Strategy and Democracy (150-170)* Oxford: Westview Press
García, PB (1993) *Libertação como plano e sonho de Deus e de homens: Uma experiência de educação popular em área rural* Cadernos de Educação Popular 21 Petrópolis: Vozes/Nova
García A, MdC (1998) Sociedad civil y democracia en Chiapas *El Cotidiano, Revista de la realidad mexicana actual, 87, enero-febrero, 102-110*
García Bravo, W (1993) Elementos Históricos para la Comprensión del Fenómeno Educativo en Zonas Indígenas del Nororiente Caucano *La Piragua: Revista Latinoamericana de Educación y Política, No 6, 73-79*
Genro, T (1999) A importancia de Che Guevara, in Prefeitura Municipal de Gravataí. Secretaria Municipal de Educação e Cultura. *Teoria & Fazeres; caminhos da educação popular, V.5, 17-20* Gravataí: Prefeitura Municipal
George, S (1996) Book Reviews *Development in Practice, Vol 6, No 4, 371-372* Oxford: Oxfam
Ghiso, A (1993) Cuando el saber rompe el silencio... Diálogo De Saberes En Los Procesos De Educación Popular *La Piragua: Revista Latinoamericana de Educación y Política, No 7, 32-36*
Ghiso, A (1997) Unidad y diversidad, continuidad y rupturas, in Dimensión Educativa *La postmodernidad: implicaciones para la educación, 59-72* Santafé de Bogotá: Dimensión Educativa
Gibson, A (1994) Freirian v Enterprise Education: the Difference is in the Business *Convergence, Vol 27, No 1*
Gideon, J (1998) The politics of social service provision through NGOs: A study of

Latin America *Bulletin of Latin American Research, Vol 17, No 3, 303-321*

Giroux, HA (1996) Um livro para os que cruzam fronteiras, in Gadotti, M (1996) (org) *Paulo Freire: Uma Biobibliografía, 569-570* São Paulo, Brasil: Cortez

Giroux, H & McLaren, P (1994) *Between Borders: Pedagogy and the Politics of Cultural Studies* New York/London: Routledge

Godono, P (1998) Tribute to Paulo Freire: His influence on scholars in Africa, *Convergence Vol, 31, Nos 1/2, pp 30-39*

Goldar, MR (1998) Fundación Ecuménica del Cuyo, Mendoza, Argentina *La Carta, No 160, Septiembre, p 4*

Gómez, M & Puiggrós, A (1986) *La Educación Popular en América Latina* Mexico: Secretaría de Educación Pública

Gonzalez, M (1990) *Nicaragua: What Went Wrong?* London: Bookmarks

González A, E (1993) El problema de la calidad en la educación popular: Conceptualización, Sistematización y Monitoreo *La Piragua: Revista Latinoamericana de Educación y Política, No 7, 2do Semestre, 37-42*

González Rodríguez (1998) La Educación Popular: Siembra de futúro, in Andreu Abrio, R et al (coordinadores) *La Educación Popular Ante El Siglo XXI, 91-100* Sevilla: Librería Andaluza

Graciana, MSS (1997) *Pedagogía Social da Rua* São Paulo, Brazil: Instituto Paulo Freire & Cortez Editora

Gramsci, A (1978) *Selections from Political Writings* London: Lawrence & Wishart

Green, D (1996) *Silent revolution: the rise of market economics in Latin America* London: Cassell/Latin America Bureau

Gregor, M (2000) Kites over favelas: stories of hope from Brazil *Concept, Vol 10, 7-10*

Grossi, EP (1993) Ser e aprender em nova sintesis: Construtivismo Pos-piagetiano *La Piragua: Revista Latinoamericana de Educacion y Politica, No7, 2ndo Trimestre, 65-71*

Grueso, L; Rosero, C & Escobar, A (1998) The Process of Black Community Organizing in the Southern Pacific Coast Region of Colombia, in Álvarez, SE; Dagnino, E & Escobar, A (eds) *Cultures of Politics, Politics of Cultures: Revisioning Latin American Social Movements, 196-219* Oxford: Westview Press

Guido, J (1999) *Interview with Author, Mateare, August.*(Guido, who lives and works in Mateare, Managua, is a former participant-organiser in the Nicaraguan Literacy Crusade)

Gutiérrez Pérez, F & Castillo, DP (1994) La Mediación Pedagógica para la Educación Popular San José, Costa Rica: Radio Nederland Training Centre (RNTC)

Guzmán, V (1994) Mujer, desarrollo y educación popular, in Gadotti, M & Torres, CA *Educação Popular: Utopia Latino-Americana 130-146* São Paulo, Brazil: Cortez

Haber, PL (1990) Cárdenas, Salinas, y Los Movimientos Populares Urbanos en

México: El Caso del Comité de Defensa Popular, General Francisco Villa de Durango, in Zermeño, S & Cuevas, A (eds) *Movimientos Sociales en México, 221-252* Mexico, DF: Universidad Nacional Autónoma de Mexico

Halebsky, S & Harris, RL (1995) *Capital, Power, and Inequality in Latin America* Boulder, Colorado: Westview Press

Hall, BL (1998) "Please Don't Bother The Canaries": Paulo Freire and the International Council for Adult Education *Convergence Vol 31, Nos 1&2, 95-103*

Hammond, JL (1998) *Fighting to Learn: Popular Education and Guerrilla War in El Salvador* New Brunswick, New Jersey: Rutgers University Press

Hammond, JL (1999) Popular Education as Community Organizing in El Salvador *Latin American Perspectives, Issue 107, Vol 26, No 4, July, 69-94*

Hannah, J & Fischer, MCB (1998) Learning about globalisation: a comparative study of the role of trade union education in Britain and Brazil *International Journal of Lifelong Education Vol 17, No 2, pp 121-130*

Harris, RL (1992) *Marxism, Socialism, and Democracy in Latin America*, Latin American Perspectives Series, No. 8 Boulder/San Francisco/Oxford: Westview Press

Harris, J (2000) The Second 'Great Transformation'? Capitalism At The End Of The Twentieth Century, in Allen, T & Thomas, A (eds) *Poverty And Development into The 21ˢᵗ Century, 325-342* Oxford: Oxford University Press

Harvey, N (1998) *The Chiapas Rebellion: The Struggle for Land and Democracy* Durham & London: Duke University Press

Hellman, JA (1992) The Study of New Social Movements in Latin America and the Question of Autonomy, in Escobar, A & Alvarez, SE *The Making of Social Movements in Latin America: Identity, Strategy and Democracy (pp52-61)* Oxford: Westview Press

Hellman, JA (1995) The Riddle of New Social Movements: Who They Are and What They Do, in Halebsky, S & Harris, RL *Capital, Power, and Inequality in Latin America, 165-183* Boulder, Colorado: Westview Press

Herman, ES & Chomsky, N (1994) *Manufacturing Consent: the political economy of the mass media* London: Vintage

Hernández, J (1995) El Rosa Y El Azul En Rousseau *La Piragua: Revista Latinoamericana de Educacion y Politica, No 10, 1er Trimestre, 84-90*

Hernández Navarro, I (1999) El laberinto de los equívocos: San Andrés y la lucha indígena, in Instituto de Investigaciones Económicas UNAM *Chiapas 7, 71-92* Mexico: Ediciones ERA

Hernández Pérez, O & Mendoza Rangel, MdC (1999) *Escuela De Liderazgo Y Participación De Las Mujeres Indígenas: Una experiencia de Formación con Mujeres Indígenas* Mexico: SEDEPAC (Servicio Desarrollo y Paz)

Herrera Menchén, M de M (1998) *El Desarrollo de Procesos Acción Socioeducativa Desde La Perspectiva de la Animación Sociocultural* Sevilla: Universidad de Sevilla

Hicks, D (1994) *Educating for the Future: A practical classroom guide* Surrey: World

Wide Fund for Nature (WWF)

Hildebrand, H (1995) Towards acceptance of participatory evaluation *Adult Education and Development, No 44, 7-15*

Hirshon, S with Butler, J (1982) *And Also Teach Them To Read* Westport, CT: Lawrence Hill

Hodkin, RA & Robin, A (1985) *Playing and Exploring: Education through the Discovery of Order* London/New York: Methuen

Holloway, J (1999) Cómo Cambiar el Mundo sin Tomar el Poder, *La Guillotina, No 41, 20-23*

Holst, JD (1999) The affinities of Lenin and Gramsci: implications for radical adult education theory and practice *International Journal of Lifelong Education, Vol 18, No 5, Sept-Oct, 407-421*

hooks, b (1994) *Teaching to Transgress: education as the practice of freedom* New York/ London: Routledge

Hope, A & Timmel, S (1999) (Reprinted Edition) *Training for Transformation: A Handbook for Community Workers. Books 1, 2, 3 & 4* London: Intermediate Technology Publications

Horton, M & Freire, P (1990) *We Make The Road By Walking: Conversations on Education and Social Change* Philadelphia: Temple University Press

Hughes, KP (1998) Liberation? Domestication? Freire and Feminism in the University, *Convergence Vol, 31, Nos 1/2, pp* 137-145

Hussein, K (1997) Participatory ideology and practical development: agency control in a fisheries project, Kariba Lake, in Nelson, N & Wright, S (eds) *Power and Participatory Development: Theory and Practice, 170-180* Exeter: Intermediary Technology Publications

IDS (Institute of Development Studies) (1996) *The Power of Participation: IDS Policy Briefing Issue 7: August* Brighton: IDS, University of Sussex

IMDEC (Instituto Mexicano para el Desarrollo Comunitario) (Undated) *Las Mil Y Una Locuras Que Se Nos Ocurrieron A Partir Del Debate Pedagógico* Guadalajara: unpublished document produced byIMDEC

IMDEC (1991) *Escuela Metodológica Nacional: Partir de La Práctica: Primer Taller* Guadalajara, Mexico: IMDEC

IMDEC (1994) *Ser Dirigente No Es Cosa Fácil: Métodos, Estilos y Valores del Dirigente Popular* Guadalajara, Mexico: IMDEC

INIEP (Instituto Nicaraguense de Investigación y Educación Popular) (1995) *Testimonios de Brigadistas: Cruzada Nacional de Alfabetización* Managua: INIEP

Jara,OH (1989) *Aprender Desde La Práctica: Reflexiones y Experiencias de la Educación Popular en Centroamérica* San José, Costa Rica: Alforja

Jara, OH (1994) El Reto de Teorizar Sobre La Práctica Para Transformarlo, in Gadotti, M & Torres, *CA Educação Popular: Utopia Latino-Americana 89-110 São Paulo, Brazil: Cortez*

Jara, OH (1994b) *Para Sistematizar Experiencias* San José, Costa Rica: Alforja

Jara, OH (1994c) ¿Qué Vigencia Tienen Las Experiencias De Educación Popular? *La Carta, Nove-Dic, Año 17, No 156, p 8*

Jara, OH (1996) Tomando Distancia: La Educación Popular mirada desde otro ángulo, in Dimensión Educativa *Educación Popular: Refundamentación, 83-94* Santafé de Bogotá: Dimensión Educativa

Jara, OH (1998) Educación popular y cooperación al desarrollo ante el siglo XXI, in Andreu Abrio, R et al (coordinadores) *La Educación Popular Ante El Siglo XXI, 27-36* Sevilla: Librería Andaluza

Jáuregui, ML (1993) Hacia una Propuesta de Educación Bilingue Intercultural para la Mujer Indígena *La Piragua: Revista Latinoamericana de Educacion y Politica, No 6, 80-84*

Jelin, E (1997) Emergent Citizenship or Exclusion? Social Movements and Non-Governmental Organisations in the 1990s, in Smith, WC & Korzeniewicz, RP (eds) *Politics, Social Change and Economic Restructuring in Latin America* Miami: North-South Center Press

Kampwirth, K (1998) Peace Talks, But No Peace *NACLA, Vol 31, No 5 15-19*

Kane, A (1996) *Basic Rights Hearing. Witness: Anne Kane, Oxfam* Glasgow: Unpublished Oxfam document

Kane, A (2000) Personal communication with author

Kane, A; Kane, L & Young, S (1985) *Africa and Scotland Video* Glasgow: Oxfam/ Scottish Catholic International Aid Fund

Kane, L (1989) Modern Languages and Development Education *World Studies Journal Vol 7, No 2*

Kane, L (1995) *Personal communication with the staff of the Instituto Mexicano de Desarrollo Comunitário*

Kane, L (1995b) Making a Drama out of a Crisis *Language Learning Journal, March, No 11*

Kane, L (1999) Personal communication

Kane, L (1999b) Learning from popular education in Latin America, in Crowther, J., Martin, I & Shaw, M *Popular Education and Social Movements in Scotland Today, 54-69* Leicester: NIACE (National Institute of Adult Continuing Education)

Kane, L (2000) Language Teaching, Accreditation and the Social Purpose of Adult Education, in Hubner, A; Ibarz, T & Laviosa, S (eds) *Assessment & Accreditation for Languages: The Emerging Consensus?, 11-24* London: CILT (Centre for Information on Language Teaching and Research)

Kane, L (2000b) Review: Popular Education Network of University Educators *Concept, Vol 10, No 1, p 24*

Kane, L (2000c) Letter from Latin America *Concept, Vol 10, 3-6*

Kane, L (2000d) *Lesson plans for Stage Two French course* Unpublished documents

Kane, L (2000e) Popular Education and the Landless People's Movement in Brazil *Studies in the Education of Adults, Vol 32, No 1, April, 36-50*

Kane, L & Morrison, E (1994) *Hablando en Broma: Comic Sketches for Beginners in*

Spanish (video) Glasgow: University of Glasgow Media Services

Kearney, M & Varese, S (1995) Latin America's Indigenous Peoples: Changing Identities and Forms of Resistance, in Halebsky, S & Harris, RL (eds) *Capital, Power and Inequality in Latin America, 207-232* Colorado/Oxford: Westview Press

Killeen, D (1999) Citizenship and Poverty *Concept, Vol 9, No 2, 4-5*

Kirkwood, G & C (1989) *Living Adult Education: Freire in Scotland* Bury St Edmonds: Oxford University Press & SIACE

Kidd, R & Kumar, K (1981) Co-opting Freire: A Critical Analysis of Pseudo-Freirian Education *Economic and Political Weekly, 16, January, 27-36*

Kirby, B (1994) (ed) *Education for Change: Grassroots Development Education in Europe* London: Development Education Association

Kitching, G (1989) *Development and Underdevelopment in Historical Perspective* London: Routledge

Klesing-Rempel, Ú (1999) Perspectivas De La Interculturalidad Y Sociedad Multicultural *La Piragua: Revista Latinoamericana de Educacion y Política, No 15, 41-47*

Knijnik, G (1996) Intellectuals and Social Movements: Examining Power Relations, in Kjaergård, T., Kvamme, A & Lindén, N (eds) *PDME III Proceedings: Numeracy Gender Class Race, 90-113* Landås, Norway: Caspar Publishing Company

Knijnik, G (1997) A contribuição do MST para a educação popular: o novo na luta pela terra, in Stédile, JP *A Reforma Agrária E A Luta Do MST, 263-271* Petrópolis, Brazil: Vozes

Knijnik, G (1998) Exclusion and Resistance in Brazilian Struggles for Land: (Underprivileged) Women and Mathematics Education, in Keitel, C (org). *Social justice and mathematics education: gender, ethnicity, class and the problem of schooling* Berlin: Berlin Universitat Press

Knijnik, G (1999a) Indigenous Knowledge and Ethnomathematics Approach in the Brazilian Landless People Education, in Kincheloe, J *What is Indigenous Knowledge?: Voices from the Academy* New York: Falmer Press

Knijnik, G (1999b) Ethnomathematics and the Brazilian Landless People Education *Zentralblatt für Didaktik der Mathematik n. 31, v. 3, 96-99, junho.*

Knijnik, G (2000) Ethnomathematics and Political Struggles, in Coben, D (ed) et al *Perspectives on Adults Learning Mathematics: research and practice, 119-134* London: Kluwer Academic

Knowles, MS (1980) *The modern practice of adult education: from pedagogy to andragogy* New York: Cambridge Books

Kucinski, B & Branford, S (1995) *Brazil, Carnival of the Oppressed: Lula and the Brazilian Workers' Party* London: Latin America Bureau (LAB)

La Belle, TJ (1986) *Nonformal education in Latin America and the Caribbean. Stability, Reform or Revolution?* New York: Praeger

La Comisiona, Escuela Popular de Oporto (1996) Educación popular y feminismo, in *Cuadernillos Pedagógicos, Abril, No 5, 24-27*

La Cuculmeca (1998) *Educación Popular y Capacitación. Cuaderno de Aprendizaje 1* Jinotega, Nicaragua: La Cuculmeca

La del Barrio, P (1996) *Paquita La del Barrio. Tres Veces Te Engñé Y Todos sus Exitos* Barcelona: BCN Records

Lamas, M (1994) Debate Feminista: a bridge between academia and activism, in Kuppers, G *Compañeras: Voices from the Latin American Women's Movement, 160-162* London: Latin America Bureau

Latin American Perspectives, Issue 81, Vol 21, No 2, Spring 1994

Lane, J (1997) Non-governmental organisations and participatory development: the concept in theory versus the concept in practice, in Nelson, N & Wright, S (eds) *Power and Participatory Development: Theory and Practice, 181-191* Exeter: Intermediary Technology Publications

Leite, S (1997) Assentamentos Rurais No Brasil: Impactos, Dimensões e Significados, in Stédile, JP *A Reforma Agrária E A Luta Do MST, 157-176* Petrópolis, Brazil: Vozes

López Monjardín, & Rebolledo Millán, DM (1999) Los municipios autónomos zapatistas, in Instituto de Investigaciones Económicas UNAM *Chiapas 7, 115-134* Mexico: Ediciones ERA

López Vigil, JI (1995) *Rebel Radio; the Story of El Salvador's Radio Venceremos* London: Curbstone Press/Latin America Bureau

Lovett, T; Clark, C and Kilmurray, A (1983) *Adult Education and Community Action* London: Croom Helm

Lozano, Y (1998) La Participación Política De Las Mujeres Populares: Una Práctica Hacia La Plena Ciudadanía, in Bruch, SA (ed) *Género y Ciudadanía: una construcción necesaria, 51-60* La Paz: REPEM-CIDEM

Maceira Ochoa, LM (1998) *Escuela Metodológica Nacional Ciclo 1998. Cuarto Taller: del 5 al 9 de octubre. Memoria* Guadalajara: IMDEC

Mackie, R (ed) (1981) *Literacy and Revolution – the Pedagogy of Paulo Freire* New York: Continuum

MacLaren, P (1995) *Critical Pedagogy and Predatory Culture: Oppositional Politics in a Postmodern Era* London/New York: Routledge

MacLaren, P (1996) Paulo Freire e o Primeiro Mundo, in Gadotti, M (org) *Paulo Freire: Uma Biobibliografía, 587-589* São Paulo, Brasil: Cortez

MacLaren P & Lankshear C (1994) *Politics of Liberation: Paths from Freire* London: Routledge

Macwhirter, I (2000) How Tyson struck a blow for democracy *Sunday Herald, 28th May, p 13*

Magendzo, SK (1994) La Sistematización Como Acto Comunicativo y Su Relación Con El Constructivismo *La Piragua: Revista Latinoamericana de Educación y Politica, No 9, 136-140*

Malamah-Thomas, DH (1987) Community Theatre with and by the People: the Sierra Leone Experience *Convergence Vol 20, No 1 pp 59-68*

Mariño, G (1993) Constuctivismo y Educación Popular *La Piragua: Revista Latinoamericana de Educacion y Politica, No 7, 2ndo Trimestre, 62-64*

Martin, I (1999) Introductory essay: popular education and social movements in Scotland today, in Crowther, J., Martin, I & Shaw, M *Popular Education and Social Movements in Scotland Today pp 7-25* Leicester: NIACE

Martin, I (2000) Talking With Dinosaurs *Adults Learning, Vol 11, No 5, 26-27*

Martin, I & Shaw, M (2000) Community Work, Citizenship and Democracy: Remaking the Connections *Community Development Journal, Vol 35, No 4, October*

Martin, H & McCormack, C (1999) Making connections: learning through struggle, in Crowther, J, Martin, I & Shaw, M (1999) *Popular Education and Social Movements in Scotland Today, 253-262* Leicester: NIACE (National Institute of Adult Continuing Education)

Martinic, S (1994) Saber Popular e Identidad, in Gadotti, M & Torres, CA *Educação Popular: Utopia Latino-Americana, 69-88* Sao Paulo, Brazil: Cortez

Martinic, S (1995) *Cultura y política en educación popular: principios, pragmatismo y negociación, Introducción* CESO Paperback No 22

Martinic, S (1996) La Construcción Dialógica de Saberes En Contextos de Educación Popular, in Dimensión Educativa *Educación Popular: Refundamentación, 65-82* Santafé de Bogotá: Dimensión Educativa

Martins, J de S (1997) A Questão Agrária Brasileira e o Papel do MST, in Stédile, JP *A Reforma Agrária E A Luta Do MST, pp 11-77* Petrópolis, Brazil: Vozes

Marx, K & Engels, F (1996) *The Communist Manifesto* London: Phoenix

Mata García, B (1994) *Un Modelo Participativo y Autogestivo de Educación Campesina* Mexico: Universidad Autónoma Chapingo

Mavrocordatos, A & Martin, P (1997) Theatre for development: listening to the community, in Nelson, N & Wright, S (eds) *Power and Participatory Development: Theory and Practice, 61-71* Exeter: Intermediary Technology Publications

Mayalán (1999) http://www.thefoundry.org/~laura/mayalan/index.html

Mayo, M & Thompson, J (Eds) (1995) *Adult Learning, Critical Intelligence and Social Change* Leicester: National Institute of Adult and Continuing Education (NIACE)

Mayo, P (1993) When Does it Work? Freire's Pedagogy in Context *Studies in the Education of Adults Vol 25, No 1, pp 11-30*

Mazo, L, CI (1996) Investigación acción participativa en la perspectiva de género: una metodología, in Buttner, T; Jung, I & King, L (eds) *Hacia una pedagogía de género: Experiencias y conceptos innovativas, 66-80* Bonn: Centro de Educación, Ciencia y Documentación (ZED)

McDonald, S (1998) Popular Legal Education in Downtown Santiago *Convergence Vol 31, Nos 1 & 2, 147-155*

McGrath, M (1999) Workers as citizens: trade union education in the new Scotland, in Crowther, J, Martin, I & Shaw, M (1999) *Popular Education and Social Movements in Scotland Today, 216-225* Leicester: NIACE (National Institute of

Adult Continuing Education)

Meakin, CB (1996) *Guidelines for Global Issues in Technology* London: Intermediate Technology

Mejía, MR (1988) *Itinerario temático de la educación popular* Santiago: CEAAL

Mejía, MR (1990) *Educación Popular. Historia – Actualidad – Proyecciones* Santa Cruz de la Sierra, Bolivia: UNICRUZ, AIPE, CEAAL

Mejía, MR (1993) Educación y Política: Fundamentos para una Nueva Agenda Latinoamericana. *La Piragua: Revista Latinoamericana de Educacion y Politica, No 7, 7-21*

Mejía, MR (1995) *Transformação Social* São Paulo, Brazil: Cortez

Mejía, RM (2000) Uneasy Allies: The Far Right Comes to Power *NACLA Report on the Americas, Vol XXXIII, No 5, 11-12*

Melrose, D (1985) *Nicaragua: the Threat of a Good Example* Oxford: Oxfam

Menchú, R (1991) *I Rigoberta Menchú* London: Verso

Mendoza, R, MdC (coordinación) (1997) *Construyendo Pedagogía Popular: Encuentros de Experiencias Pedagógicas* Mexico: SEDEPAC (Servicio, Desarrollo y Paz)

Merkx, A (1993) La Cuestión Bilinguística Intercultural en la Agenda Educativa de América Latina *La Piragua: Revista Latinoamericana de Educación y Politica, No 6, 53-56*

Meyer, M & Singh, N (1997) Two approaches to evaluating the outcomes of development projects *Development in Practice, Vol, 7, No 1, 59-64*

Miller, V (1985) The Nicaraguan Literacy Crusade: Education for Transformation, in Duke, C *Combating Poverty Through Adult Education: National Development Strategies, pp 103-130* London: Crook Helm

Montenegro, S (1994) The future from a female point of view, in Kuppers, G (ed) *Compañeras: Voices from the Latin American Women's Movement, 173-177* London: Latin America Bureau

Montenegro, S (1997) Interview given in *Voices on the Left: 16 Activists Reflect on the Current Political Moment, NACLA Report on the Americas, Vol 31, No 1, 44-46*

Morrow, F (1974) *Revolution and Counter Revolution in Spain* New York: Pathfinder Press

MST Setor de Educação (1994) *Caderno No 3: Alfabetização de Jovens e Adultos.* Porto Alegre, Brazil: Evangraf

MST Setor de Educação (1996) *Princípios da Educação no MST.* São Paulo: MST

MST (1998) *Dados básicos da situação da terra no Brasil* URL: Núñez, C (1992) *Educar Para Transformar, Transformar Para Educar* Guadalajara, Mexico: Instituto Mexicano para el Desarrollo Comunitario (IMDEC)

Mughan, T (1999) Intercultural competence for languages students in higher education *Language Learning Journal, December, Number 20, 59-65*

Mulusa, T (1995) Evaluation of NGO adult education and development programmes *Adult Education and Development, No 44, 17-24*

Navarro, Z (1997) Sete teses equivocadas sobre as lutas no campo, o MST e a reforma agrária, in Stédile, JP *A Reforma Agrária E A Luta Do MST, 111-132* Petrópolis, Brazil: Vozes

Nelson, N & Wright, S (1997) Participation and Power, in Nelson, N & Wright, S (eds) *Power and Participatory Development: Theory and Practice, 1-18* Exeter: Intermediary Technology Publications

Núñez, C (1990) '*Más Sabe El Pueblo ...Anécdotas y testimonios de educadores populares latinoamericanos*' Guadalajara, Mexico: Instituto Mexicano de Desarollo Comunitário

Núñez, C (1992) *Educar Para Transformar, Transformar Para Educar* Guadalajara, Mexico: Instituto Mexicano para el Desarrollo Comunitario (IMDEC)

Núñez, CH (1993) Permiso Para Pensar...Educación Popular: Propuesta Y Debate *América Libre, No 2, Abril-Mayo, 46-61* Buenos Aires: Liberarte

Núñez H, C (1998) La educación popular en el proceso de desarrollo y fortalecimiento de la sociedad civil en México, in Andreu Abrio, R et al (coordinadores) *La Educación Popular Ante El Siglo XXI, 37-47* Sevilla: Librería Andaluza

Núñez, C; Caruso, A; de Souza, JF; Osorio, J; Fals Borda, O & Roseo, R (1992) *Desde Adentro: La Educación Popular Vista Por Sus Practicantes* (2nd edition) Mexico: CEAAL & IMDEC

Ochoa, A (1979) La Maldición de Malinche, in *El Cancionero Popular: Amparo Ochoa* (audio-cassette) Mexico: Discos Pueblo

O'Hara, M (1996) Paulo Freire e Carl Rogers, in Gadotti, M (org) *Paulo Freire: Uma Biobibliografia, 593-595* São Paulo, Brasil: Cortez

Orellano, L (1999) *Interview with Author, San Salvador, August* (Orellano is co-ordinator of the Salvadorean popular education centre, CIAZO)

Orwell, G (1989) *Homage to Catalonia* London: Penguin

Osorio V, J (1996) Hacia Un Balance De La Refundamentación De La Educación Popular, in Dimensión Educativa *Educación Popular: Refundamentación, 9-18* Santafé de Bogotá: Dimensión Educativa

Otto, W & Stallard, C (1976) One Hundred Essential Sight Words *Visible Language, 10(3), 247-252*

Pagano, A; Turner, L & Ghiso, A (1998) Comentando la Declaración de Hamburgo *La Piragua, Revista Latinoamericana de Educación y Política, No 14, 2ndo Cuatrimestre, 9-17*

Palma, D (1992) *La Sistematización Como Estrategia de Conocimiento en la Educación Popular* Santiago, Chile: CEAAL

Pape, J (1997) Khanya College Johannesburg: ten years of 'education for liberation': an assessment *International Journal of Lifelong education Vol 16, No 4, pp 290-307*

Patterson, L (1999) Social movements and the politics of educational change, in Crowther, J., Martin, I & Shaw, M *Popular Education and Social Movements in Scotland Today, 41-53* Leicester: NIACE (National Institute of Adult Continuing

Education)

Patterson, L (2000) *Citizenship in Scotland* Edinburgh: Moray House Institute of Education, University of Edinburgh

Pearce, J (1986) *The Promised Land* London: Latin America Bureau

Peresson, M., Narmo, G & Cendales, L (1983) *Educación Popular y Alfabetización en América Latina* Bogotá: Dimensión Educativa (Quoted in Gutiérrez & Castillo.1994)

Pérez, E (1993) 'Educación Popular, Partir De Lo Que Sí Tenemos' *América Libre, No 3, 42-48* Buenos Aires: Liberarte

Petras, J (1997) Os Camponeses: Uma Nova Força Revolucionária Na América Latina, in Stédile, JP *A Reforma Agrária E A Luta Do MST, 271-277* Petrópolis, Brazil: Vozes

Petras, J (1999) ONGs y movimientos socio-políticos *PROCESO: El Salvador, Año 19, número 848, marzo 24, 6-7*

Petras, J & Morley, M (1990) *US Hegemony Under Siege: Class, Politics and Development in Latin America* London/New York: Verso

Petras, J & Morley, M (1992) *Latin America in the Time of Cholera: Electoral Politics, Market Economics and Permanent Crisis* New York/London: Routledge

Petras, J & Vieux, S (1994) Latin America The Brazilian Presidential Elections A defeat for the PT, but not a victory for Cardoso *http://zmag.org/ZMag/articles/ dec94petras.htm*

Phelps, C (1995) Lenin, Gramsci, and Marzani *Monthly Review, November, 53-54*

Phnuyal, B; Archer, A & Cottingham, S (1998) Participation, Literacy and Empowerment: Reflections on REFLECT *PLA Notes (participatory learning and action) 32, June* London: IIED (Internatinal Institute for Environment and Development)

Ponce, D (1999) *Interview with author, San Salvador, August* (Ponce is an educational consultant working for IMDEC and Alforja)

Pretty, JN & Scoones, I (1997) Institutionalizing adaptive planning and local-level concerns: Looking to the future, in Nelson, N & Wright, S (eds) *Power and Participatory Development: Theory and Practice, 157-169* Exeter: Intermediary Technology Publications

Puiggrós, A (1994a) Historia y Prospectiva de la Educación Popular Latinoamericana, in Gadotti, M & Torres, CA *Educação Popular: Utopia Latino-Americana 13-22* Sao Paulo: Cortez

Puiggrós, A (1994b) Politics Praxis and the Personal: An Argentine Assessment, in McLaren, P & Lankshear, C *Politics of Liberation:Paths from Freire* London: Routledge

Quintanilla, A, M (ed) (1998) *Los Desafíos Ético-Políticos De La Educación Popular En La Transición Al Siglo XXI : Un Encuentro con Giulio Girardi, Educador Popular y Teólogo de la Liberación* La Paz: CENPROTAC & PRODIS YANAPAKUNA

Quiroz Martín, T (1997) Women, Poverty and Adult Education in Chile, in Walters,

S (ed) *Globalisation, Adult Education and Training: Impacts and Issues* London: Zed Books

Radcliffe, S (1999) Civil Society, Social Difference and Politics: Issues of Identity and Representation, in Gwynne, RN & Kay, C (eds) *Latin America Transformed: Globalisation and Modernity* London: Arnold

Rebellato, JL (1998) Desafíos éticos y políticos desde la globalización al pensamiento crítico latinoamericano, in Andreu Abrio, R et al (coordinadores) *La Educación Popular Ante El Siglo XXI, 57-66* Sevilla: Librería Andaluza

Rees, J (1998) *The Algebra of Revolution: The Dialectic and the Classical Marxist Tradition* London/New York: Routledge

Regino Montes, A (1999) Los pueblos indígenas: diversidad negada, in Instituto de Investigaciones Económicas UNAM *Chiapas 7, 21-44* Mexico: Ediciones ERA

REPEM (Red de Educación Popular entre Mujeres) (1994) Taller Género y Ciudadanía *La Carta, Mayo-Junio, No 155*

REPEM (Red de Educación Popular entre Mujeres) (1998) Así se hace, extracts quoted in *Adult Education and Development, No 52, 9-70*

Reyes Ruiz, J (1999) La Sustentabilidad Y Su Interpelación A La Educación Popular *La Piragua: Revista Latinoamericana de Educacion y Politica, No 15, 27-33*

Rigal, L (1994) Educación Popular y Escuela Pública: A Propósito de una Investigación en Marcha *La Piragua: Revista Latinoamericana de educación y Política, No 9, 2do Semestre, 141-148*

Rivero, JH (1993) *Educación de Adultos en América Latina: Desafíos de la Equidad y la Modernización* Lima: Tarea

Roche, C (1999) *Ipact Assessment for Development Agencies: Learning to Value Change* Oxford: Oxfam

Rockwell, E (1998) Democratización de la educación y autonomía: dimensiones históricas y debates actuales *El Cotidiano, Revista de la realidad mexicana actual, 87, enero-febrero, 38-47*

Rogers, A (1992) *Adults Learning for Development* London: Cassell

Rowlands, J (1997) *Questioning Empowerment: Working with Women in Honduras* Oxford: Oxfam

Rowntree Foundation (Income and Wealth Inquiry Group) (1995) *Inquiry into Income and Wealth* York: Joseph Rowntree Foundation

Ruiz Abascal, A (1998) Desarrollo local e interculturalidad en el trabajo con gitanos/as, in Andreu Abrio, R et al (coordinadores) *La Educación Popular Ante El Siglo XXI* Sevilla: Librería Andaluza

Sáenz López, SR (2000) *Interview with author, Glasgow, April* (Sáenz is co-ordinator of the Movimiento Comunal Nicaraguense in Matagalpa)

Samson, S & Scandrett, E (1999) Environmental Citizenship and Environmental Justice: Friends of the Earth Scotland's Catalyst Project *Concept, Vol 9, No 2, 26-27*

Sandiford, P., Lankshear, C., Montenegro, MM., Sánchez, G & Cassel, J (1994) The

Nicaraguan Literacy Crusade – how lasting were its benefits? *Development in Practice, Vol 4, No 1, February*

Schild, V (1998) New Subjects of Rights? Women's Movements and the Construction of Citizenship in the "New Democracies", in Álvarez, SE; Dagnino, E & Escóbar, A (eds) *Cultures of Politics, Politics of Cultures: Revisioning Latin American Social Movements, 93-117* Oxford: Westview Press

Schugurensky, D (1998) The Legacy Of Paulo Freire: A critical review of his contributions *Convergence, Vol 31, Nos 1 & 2, 17-29*

Sérgio, F & Stédile, JP (1993) *A Luta Pela Terra No Brasil* São Paulo: Scritta Editorial

Sérgio, FG (1997) Religiosidade E Fé Na Luta Pela Terra, in Stédile, JP *A Reforma Agrária E A Luta Do MST, 279-292* Petrópolis, Brazil: Vozes

Sérgio, FAG (1999) *Histórico Do Movimento Dos Trabalhadores Rurais Sem Terra (MST)*MST correspondance

Shah, P (1997) Farmers as analysts, facilitators and decision-makers, in Nelson, N & Wright, S (eds) *Power and Participatory Development: Theory and Practice, 83-94* Exeter: Intermediary Technology Publications

Shaw, M; Thompson, J & Bane, L (2000) Reclaiming Common Purpose *Adults Learning/Concept/The Adult Learner 2000: Special Millenium Issue, Summer*

Sinclair, JM (General Consultant) (1992) *Collins Softback English Dictionary* Aylesbury: Harper-Collins

Slater, D (1985) (ed) *New Social Movements and the State in Latin America* USA: Foris

Smith, S (1994) Mistaken identity – or can identity politics liberate the oppressed? *International Socialism, No 62, Spring, 3-50*

Soethe, JR (1994) Educación Popular: Concepciones Históricas, Construcción de Paradigmas y Teoría-Práctica *La Piragua: Revista Latinoamericana de Educacion y Politica, No 9, 152-159*

Sonpal, D & Acharya, B (1995) Challenges in Identifying Indicators *Adult Education and Development, No 44, 53-60*

Stahler-Sholk, R (1999) Central America: A Few Steps Backwards, a Few Steps Forward *Latin American Perspectives, Issue 105, Vol 26, No 2, March, 3-12*

Stédile, M (1998) *Personal communication*

Stédile, M (1999) *Personal communication*

Stédile, JP (1997) *A Reforma Agrária E A Luta Do MST* Petrópolis, Brazil: Vozes

Steele, T (1999) With 'real feeling and just sense': rehistoricising popular education, in Crowther, J., Martin, I & Shaw, M *Popular Education and Social Movements in Scotland Today, 95-105* Leicester: NIACE (National Institute of Adult Continuing Education)

Stephen, L (1997) *Women and Social Movements in Latin America: Power from Below*, Austin, USA: University of Texas Press

Sternbach, NS; Navarro-Anguren, M; Chuchryk, P & Alvarez, SE (1992) Feminisms in Latin America: From Bogotá to San Bernardo, in Escobar, A & Alvarez, SE

The Making of Social Movements in Latin America, 207-239 Oxford: Westview Press

Strathclyde Regional Council (1993) *The Social Strategy for the Nineties* Glasgow: Strathclyde Regional council

Subirats, J (1993) El Enfoque Conceptual y Metodológico de la Educación Popular Intercultural y Bilingue *La Piragua: Revista Latinoamericana de Educacion y Politica, No 6, 66-67*

Tandon, R (1995) Participatory evaluation in adult education *Adult Education and Development, No 44, 25-32*

Taylor, PV (1993) *Texts of Paulo Freire* Buckingham: Oxford University Press (OUP)

Tennant, M (1997) *Psychology & Adult Learning* (second edition) London/New York: Routledge

Torres, A (1997) La Constitución del Sujeto Social, in Mendoza, R, MdC (coordinación) *Construyendo Pedagogía Popular: Encuentros de Experiencias Pedagógicas, 71-76* Mexico: SEDEPAC (Servicio, Desarrollo y Paz)

Torres, AC (1994) La Investigación En La Educación Popular: el estado de la cuestión en Colombia *La Piragua: Revista Latinoamericana de Educacion y Politica, No 9, 117-121*

Torres, CA (1990) Adult Education and Popular Education in Latin America: Implications for a Radical Approach to Comparative Education *International Journal of Lifelong Education, Vol 9, No 4, 271-287*

Torres, CA (1990b) *The Politics of Non-Formal Education in Latin America* New York: Praeger

Torres, CA (1996) A voz do biógrafo latino-americano: uma biografía intelectual, in Gadotti, M (org) *Paulo Freire: Uma Biobibliografía* São Paulo, 117-148, Brasil: Cortez

Torres, RM (1988a) *Educación Popular: Un Encuentro Con Paulo Freire* Lima: TAREA

Torres, RM (1988b) *Discurso y práctica de la Educación Popular* Quito: Centro de Investigaciones

TVE International (1997) *March for Land* London: The Television Trust for the Environment

United Nations (1997) *United Nations Human Development Report*

Urzúa, GC & Taulis, DT (1994) *EZLN: El Ejército Que Salió de la Selva. La historia del EZLN contada por ellos mismos* Mexico: Grupo Editorial Planeta

Valenzuela, M (1999) A propósito del género como eje transversal de la educación. Una conversación con Malu Valenzuela *La Piragua: Revista Latinoamericana de Educacion y Politica, No 15, 34-40*

Vargas, V (1994) El Movimiento De Mujeres En América Latina Y Las Paradojas De La Democracia *La Carta, Nov-Dic, No 156, p 5*

Vários (1994) Educación Popular en América Latina: La Teoría en la Práctica, in Gadotti, M & Torres, CA *Educação Popular: Utopia Latino-Americana 281-294*

São Paulo, Brazil: Cortez

Vásquez, N (1996) La mujer salvadoreña y la teoría eminista en la educación popular, in Buttner, T; Jung, I & King, L (eds) *Hacia una pedagogía de género: Experiencias y conceptos innovativas, 118-123* Bonn: Centro de Educación, Ciencia y Documentación (ZED)

Vega, M (1999) *Interview with author, San Salvador, August* (Vega is an educator with the Salvadorean agency PRODECOSAL)

Veltmeyer, H; Petras, J & Vieux, S (1997*) Neoliberalism and class conflict in Latin America: A Comparative Perspective on the Political Economy of Structural Adjustment* London/New York: Macmillan/St Martin's Press Inc

Viezzer, ML & Moreira, TA (1995) Mujeres En Acción De Ciudadanía Contra El Hambre, La Miseria y Por La Vida *La Piragua: Revista Latinoamericana de Educacion y Politica, No 10, 104-112*

Villanueva, A (1998) Organizaciones Femeninas Populares: Una Trayectoría de Ciudadanía Y Participación Política, in Bruch, SA (ed) *Género y Ciudadanía: una construcción necesaria, 71-88* La Paz: REPEM-CIDEM

Villavicencio, M (1994) The feminist movement and the social movement: willing partners?, in Kuppers, G *Compañeras: Voices from the Latin American Women's Movement, 59-70* London: Latin America Bureau

Vio Grossi, F (1994) La Investigación Participativa: Contexto Político Y Organización Popular, in Gadotti, M & Torres, CA *Educação Popular: Utopia Latino-Americana p111-121* São Paulo: Cortez

Wallace, T (2000) Introductory essay. Development management and the aid chain: the case of NGOs, in Wallace et al *Development and Management* Oxford: Oxfam/Open University

Walters, S & Manicom, L (eds) (1996) *Gender in Popular Education: Methods For Empowerment* London/New Jersey: Zed Books

Wanderley, LE (1994) Formas E Orientacões Da Educação Popular Na América Latina, in Gadotti, M & Torres, CA *Educação Popular: Utopia Latino-Americana 50-68* São Paulo: Cortez

Warren, KM (1998) Indigenous Movements as a Challenge to the Unified Social Movement Paradigm for Guatemala, in Álvarez, SE; Dagnino, E & Escobar, A (eds) *Cultures of Politics, Politics of Cultures: Revisioning Latin American Social Movements, 165-195* Oxford: Westview Press

Wearne, P (1996) *Return of the Indian: Conquest and Revival in the Americas* London: Cassell/Latin America Bureau

Weiler, K (1996) Freire and a feminist pedagogy of difference, in *Boundaries of Adult Learning, 128-151* London & New York: Routledge

Welsh, P (co-ord) (1996) *Comunicación y Masculinidad. Memoria Primer Taller Temático. Curso Metodológico de Masculinidad y Educación Popular* Managua: CANTERA

Welsh, P (co-ord) (1997) *"Hacia Una Nueva Masculinidad": Impacto de los cursos*

Metodológicos de Masculinidad y Educación Popular "CANTERA" 1994-1997 Managua: CANTERA

Westwood, S (1992) When Class Became Community: Radicalism in Adult Education, in Rattansi, A & Reeder, D *Rethinking Radical Education: Essays in Honour of Brian Simon* London: Lawrence & Wishart

Winn, P (2000) Lagos Defeats the Right – By a Thread *NACLA Report on the Americas, Vol XXXIII, No 5, 6-10*

Wong, PL (1995) Constructing a Public Popular Education in São Paulo, Brazil *Comparative Education Review, vol 39, no 1, 120-141*

Yashar, DJ (1996) Indigenous Protest and Democracy in Latin America, in Domínguez, JI & Lowenthal, AF (eds) *Constructing Democratic Governance: Latin America and the Caribbean in the 1990s – Themes and Issues, 87-106* Baltimore, Maryland: John Hopkins University Press

Youngman, F (1986) *Adult Education and Socialist Pedagogy* Kent: Routledge

Youngman, F (2000) *The Political Economy of Adult Education and Development* Leicester: NIACE

Yúdice, G (1998) The Globalisation of Culture and the New Civil Society, in Álvarez, SE; Dagnino, E & Escóbar, A (eds) *Cultures of Politics, Politics of Cultures: Revisioning Latin American Social Movements, 325-352* Oxford: Westview Press

Zarco Mera, CA (1998) Educar para la autonomía: Hamburgo y la educación popular en América Latina *La Piragua: Revista Latinoamericana de educación y política, No 14, Segundo Cuatrimestre, 18-24*

Zermeño, S (1997) State, Society and Dependent Neoliberalism in Mexico: The Case of the Chiapas Uprising, in Smith, WC & Korzeniewicz, RP (eds) *Politics, Social Change and Economic Restruct*

Index

Books from the Latin America Bureau

The Latin America Bureau is an independent publishing organisation. It works to broaden public understanding of issues of human rights and social and economic justice in Latin America and the Caribbean.

LAB provides in-depth material for campaigners:

Deeper than Debt: Economic globalisation and the poor
George Ann Potter
Debt is the defining development campaign of the turn of the millennium. It has mobilised more people than any other North-South issue since the end of the Cold War. But understanding debt is only the beginning of getting to grips with the global inequality built into neo-liberal market economics. **Deeper than Debt** does just what the title suggests: it goes beyond an analysis of how debt cripples poor countries and examines how debt allows rich countries to dictate trade terms and economic blueprints.
£8.99/162 pages/ISBN 1 899365 46 X

Direct testimonies from the region's most vulnerable:

Hidden Lives: Voices of Children in Latin America and the Caribbean
Duncan Green
Child labourers, street children and shantytown kids are portrayed in the West as helpless victims. But if you talk to the children, a different picture emerges. **Hidden Lives** explores the lives of these children through their own eyes and voices.
Duncan Green travelled to Brazil, Jamaica, Peru, Colombia, Honduras and Nicaragua to interview children and the adults involved in improving their lives.
£10.99/ISBN 0 304 33688 2

Authoritative country profiles:

The Brazil Reader: History, Culture, Politics
Robert M. Levine and John J. Crocetti (eds)
An unparalleled introduction to Brazil, through extracts of essays, history, poetry, literature and contemporary comment.
'What gives **The Brazil Reader** its special cachet is freshness, sensitivity and empathy in its diversity of perspectives on Brazil, from the top down, from the bottom up, and from somewhere in the middle.'
Stanley J. Stein, Princeton University
£16.99/527 pages/ISBN 1 899365 39 7

304

Topical social analysis:

We Will Not Dance on Our Grandparents' Tombs
Kintto Lucas
Translated by Dinah Livingstone

In January 2000, the indigenous people of Ecuador walked into the capital Quito where they demanded - and got - the resignation of President Jamil Mahuad.

'Levantamientos indigenas' (Indian uprisings) have taken place for 500 years. The contemporary indigenous movement in Latin America was signaled by the recent mobilisations in Ecuador, the first in 1990, as resistance to celebrations of the 500th anniversary of Columbus' 'discovery' of the Americas. Their slogan then was: 'We will not dance on our grandparents' tombs.' In 1999 indigenous people ruled Ecuador, if only for a few hours. Kintto's book brings together topical articles covering the levantamientos of 1999 and 2000 with interviews with indigenous leaders to provide a unique insight into one of the strongest movements in Latin America. The selection of essays and background information on the problems facing indigenous people today make this a fascinating introduction to Ecuador.

The book covers environmental issues, health and education, political representation, the effect of genetically-modified foods, the patenting of indigenous seeds and the taking of blood samples of indigenous people without their consent. The book includes a background and history of indigenous people and B/W photographs.
Kintto Lucas is a Uruguayan journalist who lives and works in Ecuador.
£8.95/138 pages/ISBN 1 899365 49 4

Pinochet: The Politics of Torture
Hugh O'Shaughnessy
'Essential background from one of the most authoritative commentators on South American politics. A timely and fascinating book.'
Pick of the Week in the Guardian:
'A vivid picture of Pinochet's rise to power and its aftermath.'
Financial Times
'A fast-moving and revealing account....that presents new damning evidence linking the Chilean military with drug running and illicit arms trading.'
Times Higher Education Supplement
£8.99/182 pages/ISBN 1 899365 41 9

To order these books, please send your order with payment by cheque or credit card details to:
Latin America Bureau, 1 Amwell St, London EC1R 1UK
Tel: 020 7278 2829 Fax: 020 7278 0165 email books@lab.org.uk

For orders within Europe add 20% for post and packing.
For the rest of the world, add 20% for surface post and packing, 50% for airmail.
Please make cheques out to the Latin America Bureau.